A Daily Devotional for Women by Women

In God's Garden

Ardis Dick Stenbakken, Editor
Dorothy Eaton Watts, Associate Editor

REVIEW AND HERALD® PUBLISHING ASSOCIATION
HAGERSTOWN, MD 21740

The authors assume full responsibility for the accuracy of all facts and
quotations as cited in this book.

This book was
Edited by Jeannette R. Johnson
Copyedited by Delma Miller and James Cavil
Designed by Patricia S. Wegh
Cover design by Genesis Design/Bryan Gray
Electronic make-up by Shirley M. Bolivar
Cover illustration by Lynn Gertenbach
Typeset: Minion 11/13.5

PRINTED IN U.S.A.

03 02 01 00 99   10 9 8 7 6 5 4 3 2 1

R&H Cataloging Service
Stenbakken, Ardis Dick
    In God's garden, edited by Ardis Dick Stenbakken.

    1. Devotional calendars—SDA.   2. Devotional calendars—women.
3. Women—religious life.   4. Devotional literature—SDA.   I. Title.

                    242.643

ISBN 0-8280-1434-5

"A special thanks to my assistant, Iris Stovall, who does an enormous amount of work to keep the devotional project runnning."—Ardis Stenbakken

The Women's Devotional Series

The Listening Heart
A Gift of Love
A Moment of Peace
Close to Home
From the Heart
This Quiet Place
In God's Garden

Visit us at **www.rhpa.org** for more information on Review and Herald products.

The Moon Is Falling

And there will be signs in the sun, in the moon, and in the stars; and on the earth distress of nations, with perplexity. Luke 21:25, NKJV.

I stood on the beach of my hotel on the beautiful tropical island of Martinique, surrounded by warm sand and the mysterious shapes of mountains and hills in the dark. The only sound was the gentle waves washing against the beach. Dark clouds racing across the full moon's face made it seem as if it were hurtling at a tremendous pace toward earth. Would this be our next environmental disaster? Where would it hit? And would it break up into chunks of cheese? How would we survive without a moon?

I thought of a teacher with whom I had taken a class called Current Events at the Rush Hour. For an hour each week we discussed everyday happenings, national and international. He was a brilliant man, and we were eagerly caught up in his ideas.

"There's only a 50 percent chance that we will survive the nineties," he said at the first class period, and promised to tell us what he meant at the last class period. We left the class somewhat disturbed over this statement.

Finally, it was time for the last class. He didn't mention this topic we had been harboring all these weeks, but it was still on our minds. After class we stopped by his desk and asked for his explanation.

"Well," he said, "there are two possibilities: one is for a developing country to have nuclear weapons and to use them irresponsibly, and the other is to have a major environmental disaster."

I stood silent for a moment, then quietly said, "I worship a God who is in charge of all these events."

He looked up at me sadly and said, "I don't believe in God."

I know the moon is not falling, because I believe in a God who holds it in place. I believe in a God who commands the events of the new millennium, and all will work to His timetable. He is watching over and caring for us.

DESSA WEISZ HARDIN

Where Do You Shop?

When someone becomes a Christian he becomes a brand new person inside. He is not the same any more. A new life has begun! 2 Cor. 5:17, TLB.

Life was wonderful. I was 13 and in junior high. I had fit easily into my niche in the chaos of adolescent society, and it was especially important to me—this was the ninth school I had attended. And now that my parents had finally settled into a place that they liked, I felt secure and comfortable enough to pursue new friends and enjoy what this new school had to offer.

Ours was a big family. I was the oldest of eight children, and the ninth was due at Christmas. My dad worked in a machine shop for a large aircraft company, and my mom maintained our comfortable home and cooked great meals.

Then, without warning, everything changed. My dad had an accident at work that injured his back, leaving him unable to move and unable to work. As the weeks passed and funds dwindled, my mother found creative ways to economize.

Shopping at the local thrift shop was one of them. Every Wednesday evening we piled into the old Ford and invaded the AMVETS thrift shop. Wednesday was the day they put out the "new" stuff. Wednesday was also yellow-tag day—everything half off. My mom would spend hours finding just the right bargains to clothe my brothers and sisters. I hated it at first— the smell, the idea of wearing other people's castoffs, and the frustration of not being able to comply with the standard of junior high fashion. However, I grew very capable of creating looks that were unique and stylish. Shorten here, lengthen there, a change of buttons, different sleeves—any one of these could change a garment entirely, giving it a whole new look. Many times my friends wanted to know where I shopped. After a while, because I understood my family's situation, I wasn't embarrassed to tell them.

God's love is very much like this. Where we view others or ourselves as useless and outdated, God sees possibility and usefulness. And with His creativity, He shortens our anger, lengthens our understanding, adding humor here and wisdom there, thus transforming us into the unique individuals He intended us to be. The transformation will be obvious. Others will want to know "Where do you shop?" It will be our ministry to tell them.

TERRI CASEY

Angels in St. Petersburg

I am going to send an angel in front of you, to guard you on the way and to bring you to the place that I have prepared. Ex. 23:20, NRSV.

"Hurry this way; the plane is leaving! Hurry!" The young Russian rushed my friends up the dimly lit stairway in the direction of an Aeroflot plane that would take them from Moscow to St. Petersburg—without me. "We could purchase only seven tickets," he said.

Suddenly he came running back and hurried me up the stairway, having been able to purchase one more ticket. I stepped out onto the tarmac, where I could see six planes. I started for the plane where the most people were still loading. "St. Petersburg?" I asked. A few heads nodded.

When no one was in St. Petersburg to meet me, I paced the dimly lit terminal all night. At 4:00 a.m. the airport manager offered me the use of the VIP room. Thinking no one would find me there, I declined. At 6:00 a.m. another manager came on duty and suggested I take a taxi to a nearby hotel.

"My friends will never find me if I leave," I said. I waited for the morning flight from Moscow. No one.

At 3:30 p.m. the manager again urged me to take a taxi to a hotel. "This man, he is a good man. Don't worry. He will take you to a hotel," she said.

I agreed, and we drove to a hotel miles across the city on the Baltic Sea. *Who would ever know if I died?* I thought. Not having many options, I paid $45 for one night (more than a month's local salary) and forfeited my passport at the counter. The taxi driver insisted on carrying my one bag up to my room. He warned me to keep my door locked and said he would call at 7:00 a.m. to see if I needed a ride to the airport. Then he was gone, and I slept.

The phone rang at 7:00. Was it evening or morning?

"Helen, we're so sorry!" My friends had gone to the airport looking for me and had happened to meet the airport manager. She happened to remember which hotel I was taken to.

Angels in St. Petersburg? I know of at least two.

HELEN STILES

Words

Death and life are in the power of the tongue. Prov. 18:21, NKJV.

She holds up a gift at her party, eyes shining, cheeks blushing, lips smiling. I think, *What a beautiful girl she is. She seems to be so happy, as though she doesn't have a care in the world.*

I know better. She grew up in a place where cruel tongues worked. They called her unkind names—pinhead, potbelly, bird legs, slouch. Her gifts and talents were minimized, while her imperfections and weaknesses were displayed for all to see. She always felt inadequate and unacceptable, even to God, because she couldn't be perfect. She always struggled with her self-image and wound up alone and in pain.

How I wish I could go back in time and find that girl. I would say to her, "You're precious in God's sight, His princess, the apple of His eye. Even when people are cruel and hurtful, Jesus always loves you, and He's there to comfort you and weep with you when you're hurting." I wish I could go back and teach her how to find the shadow of His wings. I wish I could go back and call her pretty names and encourage her that God wants only the best for her, His precious little daughter. I wish I could say, "No matter what other people say, you are beautiful, for God sees the beauty in your heart. Even though you are imperfect in some ways, God is making you into a masterpiece, and He'll never give up on you. You'll never be alone, because God is your Friend and your Father." I wish I could go back all those years and speak words of life to her instead of words of death.

But I can't.

I know that this girl is now a woman, and she enjoys a close relationship with Jesus Christ. She has found the shadow of His wings, and she has learned how to receive His love, comfort, and healing. She has learned that the only person she can ever really trust is Jesus. Even though she's far from perfect, she continues to let the Lord use her and work with her in any way He sees fit. Even though she still sometimes experiences sadness and pain, God has put a song of joy in her heart.

You see, I was at the party when that picture was taken so many years ago. That blushing girl with the beautiful smile was me.

Lord, help me today to say a kind word for You. Please help me to listen to Your voice assuring me.   LYNDA MAE RICHARDSON

The $100 Piano

I will mention the lovingkindnesses of the Lord . . . , according to all that the Lord has bestowed on us, . . . according to His mercies. Isa. 63:7, NKJV.

For several weeks I had been scanning the classified ads for a piano to surprise our daughter and her three children. The advertised prices for used pianos were $395 and up. "Lord, help me to find a good piano for $100," I prayed. The days slipped into weeks, and still no piano.

One Monday afternoon when the newspaper came, I was impressed to read the classified ads. There it was; the last ad at the bottom: "Piano, with antique finish, in excellent condition—$100."

While dialing the number, I kept praising the Lord. An appointment was made to see the piano at 1:00 the next day.

When the elderly lady invited me inside, I saw the piano in an alcove just off the living room. She urged me to try the piano. After playing several songs, I gave her the $100.

Then she placed another piece of music on the piano and asked, "Do you know this song?" She asked that I play it while she sang.

"Before you leave, I would like to tell you something," she said. "Yesterday, a lady was here, and she almost got the piano. I asked her to play the same piece that you just played, and she fumbled and blamed her mistakes on the piano and said the piano was no good. I got angry and wouldn't sell it to her. I believe it was meant for you to have this piano."

"God saved the piano for me," I said. Then I explained the circumstances that had led to the purchase. She agreed that God wanted my daughter and her three children to have this piano.

Sometimes God alters circumstances so our prayers can be answered. He still performs miracles, even if it's helping me to find a $100 piano.

MABEL ROLLINS NORMAN

Plenty of Room in Heaven

Two men will be in the field: one will be taken and the other left.
Two women will be grinding at the mill: one will be taken
and the other left. Matt. 24:40, 41, NKJV.

It was my privilege to attend a large church concert. It was inspiring to see people who came from 208 different countries. That day it was estimated that there were about 45,000 attendees, although the main auditorium could hold only 22,000.

That's where I saw the queue of hungry people who wanted to get a hot lunch. One of those people was my husband, who said he would get food for both of us. After an hour of waiting, I thought about following him. Unfortunately, I couldn't locate him. When I went back to the meeting hall, a friend said that food wasn't to be taken outside the cafeteria. So off I went back to look for my husband again.

It was about 1:30 when I spotted him with the trays of food. Since large crowds were milling around the entrance of the main auditorium, I suggested that we just eat at the cafeteria. As soon as we finished, we headed to the auditorium. I asked my husband to go on ahead, and I'd catch up to him later.

When I reached the doors, I was stopped by the security guards. "There are no seats," they said. "Nobody else is allowed inside." I felt like one of those five foolish virgins in Matthew 25. The guards were sending people to another room where they could watch the program through closed-circuit TV.

But I wouldn't give up. I went through another entrance, hoping to get into the main hall. Once again the guards wouldn't let me past the door. There was no room and no seats inside. I was disappointed, and I thought of my husband, who was "in" while I was "outside." Matthew 24:40 and 41 flashed through my mind: "Two men will be in the field: one will be taken and the other left. Two women will be grinding at the mill: one will be taken and the other left." Oh, what a sobering thought! What a scary event!

As I watched the program on the TV I thought to myself, *My husband is inside, but I am left outside. Is this what will happen to me when the Lord Jesus comes to claim those who will inherit the new earth?*

I am thankful that heaven won't have only 22,000 seats. There is going to be room, plenty of room, for everyone. Everybody is invited and will have a place, if she accepts God's gracious invitation.   OFELIA AQUINO PANGAN

Where Are You, God?

O my God, I cry in the daytime, but thou hearest not;
and in the night season, and am not silent. Ps. 22:2.

"Where are You, God?" I prayed. "When our little kitten was dying we prayed, and You healed him. When I lost my billfold we prayed, and You watched over it all winter on top of the store building until we found it. But now I *really* need You, and You don't answer. Do You just care about kittens and billfolds?"

For six months I had existed on practically no sleep. It seemed that my husband, who had Alzheimer's disease, never slept. So neither could I. Many days I had gone to work without sleep. Finally, I retired and moved closer to our children.

We had to live in a small apartment, literally locked in by a dead bolt. The first day in our new location I put my husband's name on a waiting list for the Alzheimer's unit in a local nursing home.

My children stopped by almost every day, but it was the nights that were so hard. I'd follow him around, trying to settle him down, but in my own frenzy I only made things worse. I took all breakables to my bedroom; I removed the mattress from my bed and pushed it against the door so he couldn't open it. It was the only way I could get a little sleep.

Upon awakening, I'd find the whole apartment trashed—the bookcase, TV, and couch tipped over in the middle of the living room; his bedding and mattress off his bed. Smiling, he'd announce, "My, I had a good day's work!" In his confused mind, he had just packed up another missionary family and sent them overseas, just as he used to do years earlier.

But the Lord was there. He did care. He gave me strength and helped to work things out. At first I had to settle for a nursing home with a very poor reputation, but I spent many hours with my husband each day and was able to make friends and offer encouragement to the employees, residents, and their families. Finally, I was able to move him to a first-rate facility.

God does work everything out in His time. He does care about people—not just kittens and billfolds.

IVADEL PETERSON

Despite Failure

I have no greater joy than to hear that my children walk in truth. 3 John 4.

The final stages of labor began about 11:00 p.m., and by 4:00 a.m. Shawn had arrived. As I looked down at his small, wrinkled, red face, I vowed I would do my best as a Christian mother.

Weeks and months passed. Shawn's greatest asset was his smile; he smiled at everyone. But I found there were times that smile could be a real liability. When he disobeyed, Shawn smiled, and his smile made being consistent difficult.

Being calm was even harder. All day I found myself yelling, "Shawn, don't! Shawn, don't!" I grew desperate. I didn't want my son to remember only "Shawn, don't" about me. Reaching the ideal was going to be very hard.

Teaching order was even harder. One night after he went to bed, I looked around. Under the chair was his toy telephone; a sock peeked out from under the couch; and his fuzzy black-and-white dog sat under the table. I burst into tears. *I just can't do it right, God. I'm a failure as a mother.*

Each week we went to church. Shawn progressed from cradle roll to kindergarten to primary. He liked to sing the Sabbath school songs he was learning at home as he played. Jesus became his friend.

There were times I still raised my voice, and sometimes toys were left lying around. My home was not the perfect home I envisioned the day I became a mother. Thoughts of *If I were a better mother, if I studied more, if I tried harder* still plagued me.

One Friday evening during a meeting, the minister gave a call to those who had never been baptized. Shawn's firm young hand pulled my head down so he could whisper in my ear. "Mommy, I love Jesus and want to be baptized. Come with me."

I looked down at the serious face of my 8-year-old. Tears dimmed my eyes. "Are you sure?"

"Yes, Mom. I want to be baptized."

I nodded. Together we walked toward the front.

God was real to my son. *Thank You, God,* I whispered, *for working—in spite of my failures.*   CONNIE WELLS NOWLAN

Turn to the Right

*For the ways of the Lord are right, and the righteous
will walk in them. Hosea 14:9, NASB.*

When we returned from our vacation in late February, we discovered
that our favorite religious television station was no longer on its
usual satellite channel. We checked their monthly newsletter, which stated
that the new location was Galaxy 23. *No problem,* I thought, noting that the
Satellite Guide confirmed that it was indeed on Galaxy 23. Grabbing the remote, I confidently turned to Galaxy 23, only to find a movie in progress.
Strange, I thought.

During the next two weeks, between my busy activities, I tried to find
the station. Periodically, I checked Galaxy 23, hoping that somehow 3ABN
would magically appear, but each time I found only an ever-present movie.

After more than two weeks, I called the satellite store where we had
bought our set. After listening to my plight, the technician directed me to
turn to Galaxy 23. Following his phone directions, I pushed two buttons on
the remote and was in "program installation" mode.

"Now," the technician advised, "push your 'right' button to the right
until the picture changes."

I pushed "right" three or four times, and the movie gave way to my religious station! "It's a little fuzzy," I remarked.

"Push right again until it comes in clear," he instructed.

Two more right pushes, and the picture was perfect. Out there on the
airwaves, so close that it took less than two minutes to find it, was the blessing I had been seeking. All it took was the right direction.

Is this the way our lives are sometimes? We know we have a problem,
and we struggle to solve it by repeating behavior that doesn't work, or we
complain or indulge in negative thinking. In the back of our minds we may
know where to find a solution, but we are too busy or too involved in other
things to seek the help we need.

Finally, giving up on our failed solutions, we turn to God, and He directs us. Because His way is right, I want always to be in tune with my
Father in heaven and allow Him to direct me always. How about you?

MARILYN KING

O Ye of Little Faith

And he said, Come. And when Peter was come out of the ship,
he walked on the water, to go to Jesus. Matt. 14:29.

Growing up on a tropical island, I had never skied. The whole idea of skiing scared yet fascinated me. My big chance came when Dan, my fiancé, said that he would teach me to ski. Imagine my horror when Dan calmly announced that we would begin on the intermediate hill. He said that the intermediate hill was longer, but had the same degree of steepness as the bunny hill.

After what seemed like mere minutes of instruction, he announced that I was ready to go down The Hill. Unfortunately, because of my sulking about not going to the bunny hill, I hadn't been listening carefully to the instructions he had been giving me. Muttering under my breath, I pushed off and started downhill. Suddenly I was veering wildly to the left. Then my legs went out from under me, and I was rolling over. This happened three times. With each struggle to right myself, I was becoming more and more frustrated, angry, and just about ready to hit Dan with my ski poles. Finally, I yelled out, "I'm not learning anything here! Why can't I just go to the bunny hill? You're—you're trying to kill me!"

Dan looked at me in resignation and said, "You're not trying. You're giving up. Why don't you trust me? I know you can do it; just don't give up before you even try."

I collected myself and went to the bunny hill. Alone. On the bunny hill they told me to do exactly the same things that Dan had instructed me to do. And yes, I fell over again and again before finally learning to ski in an upright position.

Later Dan told me he felt hurt when I didn't trust him and that I thought he would put me in a situation in which I would harm myself and get badly hurt. He loved me and wanted the best for me.

Can you even imagine how hurt God is when we don't put our trust in Him? I thought about Peter and what happened when he tried to walk on water. When Peter let go of trusting, sustaining faith, he sank. The Lord reached out and grasped Peter's hand, thus saving him from drowning. The Lord bids us, "Come! Just trust Me and experience what I will do for you today."

LYNNETTA SIAGIAN HAMSTRA

The 'Ard

*If you have faith as small as a mustard seed, you can say to
this mountain, "Move from here to there" and it will move.
Nothing will be impossible for you. Matt. 17:20, NIV.*

Mama, can we have a san'box like Michael's?" 3-year-old David asked. I
had just picked him and his 10-month-old brother up from playtime
with a friend, and their favorite pastime was playing in Michael's sandbox.

"Honey, I'm afraid we can't have a sandbox in an apartment," I explained. "You need a yard for a sandbox."

"Then can we have a 'ard?" he asked.

"David, Dad and I have tried to find a house with a yard, but we
haven't found one we can afford," I said.

"Jesus will help us find one!" David answered. "I know He will. I'll
ask Him!"

That night at bedtime we had our usual prayer. I was about to turn off
the light when David jumped out of bed. "Mama, we forgot to pray for a
'ard!" He dropped to his knees, folded his chubby hands, and pinched his
eyes tight. "Dear Jesus," he said. "Please send us a 'ard so me and Scotty can
have a san'box. Amen!"

Several minutes later the telephone rang. It was a friend who asked,
"You don't know of anyone who would like to rent a house, do you?"

"Well, yes," I answered. "Why?"

He described a nearby house he had rented but now would not be able
to move into. It had three bedrooms and a large yard with shade trees.

Early the next morning we went to see the house. On the way I prayed,
*Lord, I can't afford carpet or drapes, or rent much higher than we're paying
now.* As we walked into the house my eyes fell on the carpet—and the
drapes. It wasn't a luxurious house, but it seemed right. Then I looked out
the kitchen door and spotted a flat place that was just perfect for a sandbox.

We moved into that house, and before the furniture was in place or the
dishes unpacked, I heard pounding in the yard. David and his dad were
piecing together some wood to make a sandbox.

CHARLOTTE ISHKANIAN

God Loves You

I have loved you with an everlasting love. Jer. 31:3, NRSV.

It was purely because of a higher salary that I quit a job I loved, working with people whom I adored, and took a job an hour's drive away. I hate to drive in freeway traffic, and my new boss proved to be impossible—just as I had perceived during my initial interview. But I thought that since I was working to supplement the family income I had an obligation to make as much money as I could, so I kept on working.

After six months of battling traffic to get to the detested job, I became ill and missed two weeks of work. One morning shortly after returning to work, I found myself in another traffic tangle. Hoping to gain a bit of composure, I turned on the radio and tuned into a religious program.

Then from a ramp on my right, a car began merging into my lane. I thought it was coming right into my car. My stomach tightened and my knuckles turned white as I grasped the steering wheel. I don't know who went where, but as soon as the merge was safely negotiated, I pulled over to the side of the road. By then my head was throbbing, and I didn't see how I could get up enough courage to reenter the traffic. Just then the announcer said, "Remember, God loves you."

Yes, I thought, *God does love me, and He has given me a mind to think. I don't need to be put on a guilt trip when I veto other people's requests and opinions. I can say "No." It's smart to listen to my own feelings and to know my own limitations, because God does love me and He created me the way I am. I am important to God.*

That day was truly the first day of the rest of my life. I not only made a new commitment to God and thanked Him for His protection, but I made a new commitment to myself. I soon gave notice to take a part-time job—close to home.

I still get apprehensive when traffic starts merging from my right, but I need that stress occasionally to remind me of the day I learned that God really does love me.

BARBARA HUFF

A Letter to My Father

*I will be a Father to you, and you will be my
sons and daughters. 2 Cor. 6:18, NIV.*

Dear Father,
Before I begin my day I just want to thank You for keeping in touch with me concerning all the problems I've shared with You. You always seem to have the right answers. Your wise counsel yesterday solved my entire dilemma, and so quickly!

Please tell my Elder Brother that I am overwhelmed by His offer to be my attorney, and at such a sacrifice to Himself, especially when He knows I am totally unable to pay the tremendous price involved. The effort He has taken to show me how to plead my case and execute my affairs is invaluable.

I also want to thank You with all my heart for the wonderful Gift You have given me. He seems to respond whenever I invite Him, and what a Comforter He has been! I am eagerly awaiting the full measure of His presence You have promised to send as soon as I am ready to receive it.

Please convey to the rest of my family how eager I am to see them. They are absolute angels—especially the one who has protected me so very often. I can hardly wait to hear all the details concerning their involvement in my life.

And Father, I do appreciate all Your letters to me; I read and reread them so often. I even share them with my friends, and some of them would like to meet You. I've told them I'm adopted, and a few of them have asked if there is any way they could be adopted also. Could You show them how to go about this?

By the way, I understand that the house being built for me is beautiful! I haven't sent You enough toward it even to begin to make a significant difference. I don't mind if it isn't very large, but I would like it to be located near You so I can see You and my dear Brother often.

Thank You for all the ways You have shown Your care. I don't think I can ever make this up to You except to tell everyone I know how wonderful You really are.

With all my love,
Your Lonely Child

PS: When is my Elder Brother coming back to get me? I'm so homesick! I hope it won't be long.
LORRAINE HUDGINS

Memories . . . Memories . . .

Praise the Lord, O my soul, and forget not all his benefits. Ps. 103:2, NIV.

I work in a rehabilitation center for people who have suffered a head injury. One of the most interesting areas of my work is helping people who have severe memory problems. For some of them a sentence is forgotten as soon as it is said, and we have to devise all kinds of ingenious ways to help them live their lives as normally as possible without the memory we all depend on.

Sam felt that nothing nice ever happened to him. His family was always taking him to places and making life fun for him, but the minute the experience had ended, it was as if it had never happened. We made him a scrapbook for menus, entrance tickets, photos, and details about things he had done with his family. The family made videos of Sam having some great times, and he could watch the videos and relive the experiences as often as he wished.

Then there was Anna. She too had severe memory problems. We introduced her to a couple diary books she could use with her teenage children. Parenting is challenging enough, but if you can't remember the important issues in your child's life, then it becomes very difficult to parent effectively. The children used the diary books to write to their mom so she could read and reread what they wrote whenever she wanted to. Then she would write back to them. That way, the children could still have a close relationship with her, even though she couldn't even remember how old they were.

The biggest difference between Anna and Sam was that Anna was rarely ever sad. She was full of fun and good humor, joking about her memory difficulties. When I commented on this one day, she said, "Well, the great thing is that now I can't remember what I'm supposed to be worrying about. So I just enjoy being happy!"

These two people reminded me how important it is to remember the good things that happen to us—and how important it is to forget our worries, giving them all to Jesus. Then we too can simply enjoy being happy in His love for us.

KAREN HOLFORD

Flat Tire

Call upon me in the day of trouble;
I will deliver you, and you will honor me. Ps. 50:15, NIV.

I was 22 years old and the proud, new owner of my very first car. One evening, after spending the weekend with my parents, I got ready to drive back to school. Just before I took off I joked about getting a flat tire and my lack of knowledge about car care.

"I'll teach you how to change a tire the next time you come home," my dad promised.

When I left my parents' house the sun was about to set, and it soon became pitch-dark around me. An uncomfortable feeling grew inside of me as I drove down the road, a lake on one side and a forest on the other. There were no houses along the road, and very few cars passed by. As I was entering the most desolate part of the road, one of the tires went flat. What was I to do? A few trucks passed at high speed, but I decided I wouldn't even attempt to stop them. I was paralyzed with fear, imagining what could happen on a lonely road like this.

"Please, dear Lord, help me!" I cried. Those were the only words I could pray, over and over, while my heart pounded faster and faster.

Suddenly a small vehicle pulled in beside my car. A middle-aged man stepped out and approached me, asking, "Do you have a problem with your car?"

"My tire is flat," I said, "and I haven't any idea about how to change it."

"Do you have a spare tire?" he asked. I nodded. I opened the trunk and handed him the tire and the tools. A few minutes later the job was done. Before the man left, he said, "Drive carefully!"

Back on the road again, I thought about how swiftly God had answered my prayer. *I asked for help, Lord, and You sent it. I called, You answered, and I do feel honored. May my life also honor You today.*　　HEIDI LILLIAN KAMAL

Trucker Angels

It shall come to pass that before they call, I will answer;
and while they are still speaking, I will hear. Isa. 65:24, NKJV.

It was 6:45 that snowy morning, and I was on my way to school on the Vermont state highway when the snowplow crossed in front of me just as I was ready to turn onto the exit. The snow from the plow was blowing so hard that I couldn't see where I was going. He kept on going, not realizing the trouble he was causing me. I said a quick prayer and steered straight ahead but couldn't tell if the plow was still in front of me or where the exit was.

When I emerged from the blowing snow I was wedged in a snowbank, and no amount of reversing could get me out. While my small car did very well on straight going, it wasn't designed to cope with snowbanks. I needed help, and I needed it soon.

Now, what do I do, Lord? I asked silently.

Immediately I noticed a truck stopping. Two men came toward my car. "Can we help you, ma'am?" they asked.

"Yes," I nodded, handing them the snow shovel I always carried with me in winter.

They set to work and had me back on the road in 15 minutes. They would take no pay, but I certainly heaped volumes of vocal gratitude on them for their help.

These men may not have been angels from heaven, but they were still "angels of the Lord" to me. To receive help at that time of the morning on a little-used highway was a miracle. There wasn't much traffic on that road even in the middle of the day. I firmly believe the Lord knew there was no way I could have gotten out without help, and He impressed those men to provide it.

We are so slow to ask You for help, and You are always so ready to help when we need it. My prayer for today is that I will remember to be in constant touch with You, increasing in faith as You bless. LORAINE SWEETLAND

Kissing the Owies

Come to me, all you who are weary and burdened,
and I will give you rest. Matt. 11:28, NIV.

I picture myself, a 5-year-old girl, bouncing around the playground, trying out everything—the swings, the slide, the merry-go-round. I climb up the jungle gym, hang by my knees for a few seconds, then drop to the ground.

While still on my hands and knees where I landed in the sawdust, I notice someone sitting nearby watching me. I run over for a closer look, and stare for a few seconds—I think I've seen Him somewhere before . . . Maybe in a picture. He looks so kind.

"I know; You're Jesus!" I blurt out.

He smiles and nods. Then, patting His knee, He invites, "Would you like to sit here?"

I let Him lift me up. Impulsively I lift my knee to show Him a bruise, saying, "I banged it and it hurts. Can You kiss it?" He does, and it doesn't hurt anymore. So I show Him a skinned elbow. "This hurts, too." He kisses it, and the scrape disappears.

Eventually the squirmies take over, and I slide off His knee, declaring, "I'm gonna go play now; 'bye."

Before I'm able to slip away He says, "I'd like to kiss the owies on the inside, too."

I just look at Him without moving, watching His face. What does He mean? He looks so kind.

I nod. Somehow I'm not frightened, even though I don't know what's going to happen.

He gently picks me up and sets me on His lap. He pats His chest and says, "Lay your head here." Silently I obey. Wrapping His arms around me, He cuddles me close to Himself. In the most soothing voice He tells me, "I love you so much. You are My special girl." Running His finger through my hair, He kisses my forehead and begins to rock me as He softly sings, "Jesus loves me, this I know . . . " I relax, listening to His heart beat, and start breathing in rhythm with His breathing. Soon my eyes droop, and I drift off to sleep in the most secure, safe place I've ever known.

Lord, today when I experience some of life's hurts, help me to come to You to let You kiss the owies on the inside. JOYCE WERTZ HARRINGTON

All Life Should Be So Easy

*You will tread our sins underfoot and hurl all
our iniquities into the depths of the sea. Micah 7:19, NIV.*

This past year I have become quite proficient in word processing. A secretary by trade, I've been typing for years, but word processing uses an entirely different sphere of the brain. It's like driving a moped for years, then switching to a Cadillac—the same rules of the road apply, but it's a whole new driving experience.

A handy function of my word processor is spell check. You click a button, and the computer catches any misspelled words and offers alternatives. It even works with those pesky i-before-e words, such as receive and relieve. So you can type as fast as your little fingers can fly and go back and fix the spelling later. All life should be so easy.

My favorite icon is the "undo" button. You just click on it, and whatever you've just done gets undone. *Zap!* It's gone—just like that. Just like it had never been there.

Wouldn't it be nice if real life had an undo button? We make a mistake; we press our undo button, and *zap!* It's gone! We made a decision we wish we hadn't, press undo—it's undone. Hurt someone you love? Do something stupid or illegal? No problem! Press undo—it's undone. No reputation to live down, no bad habits to break, no lost trust to win back. Wouldn't that be wonderful?

Our human equivalent, I suppose, is saying "I'm sorry." Yes, it helps, but it doesn't undo it. Saying "I'm sorry" is really more like liquid paper covering up a typo than the zapping of the undo button. With liquid paper, there is always evidence that something was there at one time. The undo button leaves no trace.

There is no earthly "undo" icon, but there is a heavenly one. Jesus came to earth to die in our place, so that we might live eternally. Isaiah 1:18 says, "Though your sins are like scarlet, they shall be as white as snow" (NIV). In 1 John 1:9 we're promised, "He is faithful and just and will forgive our sins and purify us from all unrighteousness" (NIV). So we just have to pray, confess our sins, and believe that God's love will "delete" all our sins and "undo" our unrighteousness. All life should be so easy! NANCY HADAWAY

God's Guiding Concern

I will guide thee with mine eye. Ps. 32:8.

I hurried to get ready for the meeting I was to attend in a different city. While reaching for a set of electric curlers, I remembered a long-distance call I needed to make. The conversation delayed me. *Now it's too late for breakfast,* I thought. Then the telephone rang. Another interruption. "We're to leave at 7:30," a friend reminded me.

"Yes, I know. But it's only 7:20, and I'm on my way right now!" I closed the door and hurried to the elevator. On the way down I took out my keys, ready to dash to my car. Outside, the fresh, crisp air felt good, but halfway to my car I stopped.

"Oh," I moaned. "The curlers! But I didn't plug them in—I changed my mind." I again started toward the car, then stopped again, afraid the curlers were indeed plugged in. I stood there as if frozen. Finally, in desperation, I prayed, *Lord, if I should go back, please make me go back!*

Suddenly I ran back into the building. *This is ridiculous,* I chided myself as the elevator moved upward. *But if I don't, I'll be worried all day about whether or not the curlers are plugged in.*

Reaching my apartment, I unlocked the door, rushed to the bedroom, and ran around the side of the bed to where the curlers lay. They were in their case, on top of a magazine I had been reading the night before. My heart pounded.

"What?" I exclaimed. "I can't believe it! The set is connected!" I quickly unplugged the curlers.

O God, I cried, *thank You so much for making me come back! Suppose I had not; suppose I had not!*

The curlers would not have automatically turned off. The metal poles on which they rested would have continued to heat, finally igniting the paper, the bed covers, and possibly burning the apartment. And I would not have known until my return at nightfall—to nothing! I shuddered at the thought. My tiredness was suddenly gone, and how I thanked God! I hurried now to join the others who would be driving to the meeting.

Oh, thank You, dear Jesus, I silently prayed, *for the Holy Spirit. And thank You, Father, for laboring with me until I listened.*   AUDRE B. TAYLOR

My Worry Basket

Peace is my parting gift to you, my own peace, such as the world cannot give.
Set your troubled hearts at rest, and banish your fears. John 14:27, NEB.

I had no peace because I wasn't accepting the people I couldn't change. Nor was I changing the only one I could—myself. In my weakened condition following breast cancer surgery, depressing thoughts clouded my vision. I needed to look up, but couldn't seem to do it until my son interrupted.

He knelt by the bed, speaking softly. "What is bothering you most, Mom? Picture that problem right now—feel the weight of it. Be aware of your feelings about it. Now imagine placing it in a box. Take time to wrap it up well; tie the string and put it in this huge basket. Keep packing up everything that worries, hurts, or angers you. Put them all in the basket."

It took time to look inward, to bring out and pack up attitudes, issues, problems, pain, guilt, and fear that had been depressing me. Finally all my packages were in the big basket.

"Mom, you're fascinated by hot-air balloons. Well, the basket you just filled is attached to a red-and-yellow one. Look! The ropes are getting tight; the wind is tugging at the balloon and lifting it off the ground. It's a heavy load, but the balloon is climbing toward heaven. Up and away it goes, ascending until it's only a speck against the cloudless sky. You've just let go of all your troubles and sent them up to Jesus. Now get some rest; enjoy your freedom." He slipped from the room.

I was feeling light and free; this imagery was too good to stop. I wanted to picture what would happen when the hot-air balloon got to heaven. I pictured Jesus strolling among empty mansions, lonely for His children. The hot-air balloon settled on the velvet grass like a giant mushroom at His feet.

I imagined His nail-scarred hands reaching into my basket, taking out my box of guilt. "You are forgiven," He whispered. He smiled when He opened up my resentments. "I'm glad she's finally giving these to Me." He unpacked a concern, handed it to an angel, and said, "Take care of this for My child."

I visualized Jesus dealing with every problem until the balloon basket was empty. Sensing the Saviour's presence, I drifted happily into a serene sleep.

LILA LANE GEORGE

More Songs in the Night

Where is God my maker, who giveth songs in the night? Job 35:10.

The night was dark and heavy on my shoulders. I couldn't sleep. I don't remember what the problem was, or the solution that eluded my thinking. I don't remember any feeling except aloneness, and some despair. I felt forsaken—especially by God.

I had been a Christian all my life. God was my friend. I remember as a child taking my Bible and my collie dog and spreading a blanket under our large mulberry tree. I'd read my Bible and talk about my life with God, my friend. Now even He wasn't understanding. Finally, in the darkness I cried "God, are You there?"

I tossed and turned. *Well, since I can't sleep, I might as well listen to some music and read,* I thought as I turned on the light. I had lots of cassettes on a stand by the bed, but this time I reached far back into the nightstand drawer and found a tape, one that I hadn't heard for a long time—and even then hadn't played it all the way through. I didn't even look at the titles; I just slipped it into the tape deck and turned out the light.

The first words I heard of the song were "He is there." It was amazing that I should pick the tape that answered my question from the hundreds I owned. I listened to the song several times that night, and found comfort. My Friend was still there, caring about me.

Once when I was feeling sad over the death of a loved one, I heard a song that I had never heard before: "When There Are No Answers, There Is Jesus." I stopped asking, "Why?" And again a song in the night brought new hope.

Another time I was losing hope because of a back injury and was afraid that I'd never walk again. One night I limped to my tape cabinet to rummage through the cassettes until I found the one that said, "He will open up the doorway you never knew was there." And looking back, walking again with a strong back, God has opened up many doorways I never knew were there—doorways of friendship, of service, of creativity, of more songs in the night.

Edna Maye Gallington

Gentle Reminder of God's Love

For he will command his angels concerning
you to guard you in all your ways. Ps. 91:11, NIV.

Lord, I prayed as I bent over the steering wheel, *the road is long, the car is unfamiliar, and the body is tired. Please get me to Massachusetts safely, and send Your angels with me.*

I was leaving my home in Maryland to drive a friend's car to my parents' home, where my dad would become its new owner. The car was a larger member of the Chevy family than my own, and I felt uncomfortable in it. At least an eight-hour drive lay ahead of me, and I was both physically and mentally fatigued. I needed the assurance that those angels would be with me.

Midway up the New Jersey Turnpike, when a sign announced a service area in one mile, I prepared to pull off for gas and some exercise. But then, seeing another sign that said "Next service area 22 miles," and noticing that the gas gauge wasn't near "empty" yet, I decided to drive on.

Impulsively, as the exit to the nearer service area approached, I changed my mind again, pulling off the highway and up to the gas pump. When the station attendant asked to check under the hood, I hesitated before assenting. I'd heard more than my share of stories about men who take advantage of women drivers!

"Ma'am, would you please come take a look?" the attendant asked after lifting the hood and poking around for a minute. He pointed to a radiator hose. "If you plan to drive much farther, you'd better get it replaced. It could burst and drain all the water out of the radiator and leave you stranded on the highway."

Still skeptical, I agreed to the replacement. After seeing the worn-out hose with its large bulge, I knew my 10 minutes and $21.40 had been well spent.

As it turned out, the service area 22 miles up the turnpike was closed. Had it been an angel who whispered in my ear to pull off the highway when I did, knowing the car wouldn't make it to the next service area? To a weary woman whose spirits were lower than usual that Friday morning the thought that it might have been was a comfort, a gentle reminder of God's care.

JOCELYN FAY

My Identity

Nor is there salvation in any other, for there is no other name under heaven given among men by which we must be saved. Acts 4:12, NKJV.

It was a balmy Georgia morning, buzzing with activity. Famous faces, Secret Service persons, and waiting news media people in a crowd of 20,000 created an atmosphere of excitement and expectancy.

My contact person had thoroughly briefed me for the assignment—a once-in-a-lifetime opportunity. I was to be the sign language interpreter for former president Jimmy Carter, Mikhail Gorbachev, and other dignitaries. As the other platform guests took their seats, I timed my approach to reach the front of the platform to coincide with President Carter's opening remarks.

Just then I noticed a six-foot-five-inch Secret Service man standing directly in front of me, blocking my passage. "Excuse me," he said firmly as we stood face-to-face.

"Yes, I am the interpreter," I confidently responded.

"Who is your contact?" he questioned. I had spent the morning focusing on the technical aspects of the assignment—the correct spelling of "glasnost" and "perestroika"—not the contact person's name! My stress level rose dramatically. I decided to remain calm. If I could remember my contact person's name, she would verify my place on the platform.

Miraculously, I remembered the woman's name, and with my identity intact I could accomplish the service I had been sent to perform. Her name was my salvation that day. Her name was my ticket to the program. Her name gave me my identity.

When I am fully aware of "whose" I am, my identity is rock solid. Isaiah 43:1 confirms it: "I have called you by your name; you are Mine" (NKJV). I can go anywhere and accomplish anything, just by knowing whom I belong to. My life depends on knowing His name. There is "no other name under heaven" that offers us such complete access to a knowledge of our worth in Him.

His name is our salvation. His name is our ticket to heaven. His name gives us our identity.   LYNN MARIE DAVIS

Expiration Dates

*Just before Jesus comes probation will close. Then those who
are unjust will continue to be unjust, and those who are filthy
will remain filthy. The righteous will continue to be righteous,
and the holy will remain holy. Rev. 22:11, Clear Word.*

One of my New Year's resolutions was to clean cupboards and throw away all expired medicines and stale food. I looked through my cabinets and searched for the dates on the packages. To my surprise, I found I had kept some things far beyond their expiration date, and I had even carried them along when I had moved more than two years earlier!

Now I knew why the Alka-Seltzer wouldn't fizz anymore and why the aspirin hardly fazed my headache. Expired! All my saving instincts had done no good. I was forced to believe the truth. The dates stamped on the packages really did mean that the contents became useless after that deadline. My trash bin began to fill up as I tossed in item after item of expired products. Time had run out on them.

God has put an expiration date on me and our world too. I need to redeem the time I have and prepare for His coming before it is too late. I know—and have received—the admonitions and warnings. I have no excuse to procrastinate.

Even though I do not know the exact expiration date of my life on this earth, I do know the time is near. I see the signs of Jesus' coming fulfilling all around me. Jesus said, "Watch therefore, for you do not know on what day your Lord is coming" (Matt. 24:42, RSV).

Too bad I wasn't watching those expiration dates on my medicines or I would have replaced them and been ready for the unexpected illness that occurred! I'd also like to throw away some other things I've had too long, such as old hurts and grudges. I need to replace them with love and forgiveness.

*I want to be ready for the final expiration date of this old world, Lord.
Even though those old medicines had no immortality, I can have it because it's
a promise You've given to me!* BESSIE SIEMENS LOBSIEN

My Big Brother

*Jesus understands every weakness of ours, because he was
tempted in every way that we are. But he did not sin! Heb. 4:15, CEV.*

The climb to Yosemite Falls seemed unending. Ahead of me, my older
sister, Debbie, and my brother-in-law slowly but surely were making
their way up. Then way ahead of them, at the front of the line, was my big
brother. Each step he took seemed easy; he made this treacherous hike look
like a stroll in the park. Pulling myself over the next rock took all my extra
energy, and I collapsed on the boulder, tears of frustration filling my eyes as
I watched the other three climbing, never seeming to tire.

I'll never make it! I screamed inwardly, my breath coming in short
gasps. I closed my eyes and rested my head on my hands. I was ready to
give up. Suddenly I heard footsteps. I opened my eyes, and there was my
big brother! He sat down beside me, put his arm around my shoulders, and
squeezed me tight.

"Ter, I understand just how you feel. Sometimes when I'm playing
sports, and my team is losing, I feel like crying too. I'm so tired and feel bad
about losing, and I can't breathe 'cause I'm trying not to cry. Yet I can't
stop; I've got to finish the rest of the game. Believe me, I know exactly how
you feel."

Burying my head in his side, I cried. How could he know exactly what I
was thinking at that very moment? Looking up, I smiled.

He pulled me to my feet. "Come on, Ter; we still have a long way to go.
But if you want, I'll carry you up."

Grinning with embarrassment, I declined. Laughing, he gave me a
shove in the upward direction, and we continued up the trail. We finally
did reach the top, and believe me, it was worth the effort.

I have another Big Brother. His name is Jesus. Sometimes as we're
climbing the narrow path of life, we feel so tired. Just as we're about to
throw in the towel and give up, here comes our Big Brother, ready to give
us a boost. He's always there to sit down and tell us that He knows exactly
what we're going through.

He says to us, "Come on; we still have a long way to go, but I'll carry
you there."

TERRI WEBB

Split Pea Soup for My Heart

He did not leave you without evidence of himself in the good things he does for you: he sends you rain from heaven, he makes your crops grow when they should, he gives you food and makes you happy. Acts 14:17, Jerusalem.

She is the epitome of a successful, independent woman, this friend of mine. She is articulate, resourceful, multilingual, poised, and beautiful. I am awed by her and feel privileged to be listed as her friend. When she told me that she was having outpatient surgery the following week, we prayed together on the spot. For the next few days I prayed for her every morning, and twice on the day of the operation. But that was it. What more could I do?

She called me from the recovery room that day. "Praise God!" she almost shouted. "I am alive!" I had no idea that she had struggled with that fear. Then she asked, "How long will it take to make me a pot of your split pea soup?"

Grateful that she needed something I could do, I hurried through the motions of making her supper. It was only a pot of soup—split peas, carrots, onion, sweet potatoes, blended with my signature seasonings and simmered on the stove.

Serving it to her later that evening, I sat with her as she savored it slowly. Returning the bowl, she murmured through her bandages, "Thank you for sharing your gift with me." It took me awhile to understand what she meant: she had tasted God's blessing in the soup.

This dish now represents more than mere sustenance. Often it is a Friday night tradition; at other times it means the warmth of fellowship for hungry students on chilly, wintry evenings. Sometimes my friend and I use it instead of a get-well card for recuperating shut-ins.

I am no gourmet chef, but this soup is special. Not just because of its flavor or its texture, but because of what it has come to symbolize to us—a simple, God-blessed gift from the heart.

Thank You, God, for showing us that there are traces of You in the simplest things. Thank You for opening our eyes to the fact that little becomes much if Your blessing is there. Thank You for using me. GLENDA-MAE GREENE

Perspective Is Everything

Eye hath not seen, nor ear heard, neither have entered into the heart of man, the things which God hath prepared for them that love him. 1 Cor. 2:9.

Being severely deformed and in a wheelchair has not been easy. The stares and the hardships of many surgeries have had their toll on me. In my early 20s, I, like Job, had learned through Bible studies that there is meaning to the war on Planet Earth.

My dad was a World War II hero who always stated, "There are no atheists in the foxholes!" When you're under fire, quick wits, fast movements, and agility, along with strong belief systems, come into play. I've come to the conclusion that in the battle between good and evil in my life every day my perspective is my greatest strength!

I chose to become a reading teacher shortly after I was baptized, because I saw a world suppressed by illiteracy and ignorance. I thought that if you can read, you can learn, and "the truth will set you free" (John 8:32, Amplified). Coping becomes easier when you know why the war is going on.

My freedom has come through my awareness of the goodness of life to develop me through my new perspective. Has it been painful? Yes. Has it been easy? No. Like Job, do I see meaning in my suffering? Yes! As Helen Keller said, "I use my will, choose life and reject its opposite nothingness!" She also said, "Life is nothing if not a daring adventure!" As a youngster reading her book, she was a woman of strong faith who always gave me hope. She too was severely challenged, but was a woman of strong faith. Do you ever get depressed?

Do you ever feel you're all alone in a senseless world, unloved and unlovable? Leslie Kay, a writer I enjoy, posed these questions and concluded "that on the cross Christ bore away my squalid birthright of alienation and depression. He died the equivalent of my second, eternal death!"

I praise our infinite Father for those individuals who have made a difference in my pained, yet glorious life of awareness—those heroes and heroines, individuals who have made a difference in the foxholes of life for me. "For since the beginning of the world men have not heard, . . . neither hath the eye seen, O God, . . . what he hath prepared for [her] that waiteth for Him" (Isa. 64:4).

So as we love and wait, study and grow, we are reconciled by Christ's death and have before us an incredible future—heaven's eternal adventures await us. Let's go!

CHRISTINA CURTIS

My Best Friend

A soft answer turneth away wrath: but grievous words stir up anger. Prov. 15:1.

Judy, Billy, and our daughter, Karen, were having such a good time playing outside our duplex on the swing set in our tiny backyard. The three, all about the age of 3 or 4, were fast friends, playing together whenever possible, especially in my cozy, protected backyard where both Judy's mother and I could keep a watchful eye and ear.

This particular morning, with Karen happily occupied, I busied myself with the multitude of household tasks a homemaker finds herself responsible for every day. Before too long childish voices were raised in an argument. The peace was broken when Billy asserted, "My best friend is Judy."

"No, she isn't," insisted Karen. "Judy is my best friend." Back and forth they went until, in a sweet little voice, Judy began to sing a song they had all learned in their Bible class:

"'My best Friend is Jesus, Jesus, Jesus.
My best Friend is Jesus, Jesus, Jesus.'"

When Billy and Karen heard this, they calmed right down and joined in Judy's song. Soon they were peacefully swinging again, laughing and having a good time, with all the argumentative spirit gone, replaced by the Holy Spirit.

No wonder the Bible says that we should be like little children, putting aside our differences and quickly allowing the Holy Spirit to change our thinking and actions and lead us in a better course.

What a blessing Bible-based songs and lessons can be for children and for those who work with them. We benefit from their songs, prayers, memory verses, Bible stories, and faith in what our heavenly Father can and will do for us, not only in church, but also in our homes.

Like Judy, Billy, and Karen, let us make Jesus our best friend, allowing Him full control of our lives.   MAE E. WALLENKAMPF

Friends Are for Sharing

You are my friends if you do what I command. John 15:14, NIV.

I pressed my nose against the window, trying to see as much as I could of the blue-green waters below. Some places were so clear that I couldn't tell where the water ended and the sand began unless a gentle wave carried some bubbly foam on its curling crest. I tried to imprint the picture on my brain so I'd be able to share it when I got home. Seeing the picture was only half the thrill—the other would be sharing it with loved ones.

This was not the first time this had happened. I recalled standing above Peyto Lake in Banff National Park. Incredible color! And there had been another time . . .

Scenic vistas are not the only thing I have only partially enjoyed because there was no one to share with. There have been concerts, funny stories, cute things the kids said, powerful sermons, or just incredibly smooth ice cream on a hot summer evening.

I am not usually alone. My husband is generally nearby and enjoys these things as much as I do. But life being what it is, there are times when something very special happens that would be so much better if there were just someone with whom to share it.

Don't you suppose that is the way it is with God? Heaven was as good as it could be, but He wanted someone who could share it with Him—someone who would enjoy sharing a quiet spot, just basking in each other's presence. And there was that entire universe all planned, with endless variety, color, movement, light, growth, and change. How wonderful to meet with a friend in the cool of the evening, to share insights and new discoveries! So He made us. Man and woman. In His image. To share. To enjoy together. To feel complete in the common joy of sharing.

You know what happened. Sin. Estrangement. Separation. But there is a plan. The separation will not last forever. He made us because He wanted to be with us, and He died to bring us back again as special friends. Alleluia! I can hardly wait!

Lord, forgive me the sin that separates. I so look forward to being with You and sharing our mutual joys. Thank You for the plan of salvation that will unite us soon. ARDIS DICK STENBAKKEN

Ten Extra Days

Now unto him that is able to do exceeding abundantly above all that we ask or think. Eph. 3:20.

For the seventeenth time we had boxes stacked in every room. They filled the garage and lined the hallways. We were moving again. This time I was happy, because it would bring us nearer our children and grandchild who had, until now, been 3,000 miles away. Nevertheless, I felt stressed and under pressure.

"I've tentatively booked the moving van for the eighteenth," Ron said as he left for the office.

A quick calculation told me we could not be in our new home in Maryland until the twenty-fifth. I would be tired after nearly a week of travel across the country. Then I would have only one day to arrange my house, find my seminar materials, and travel 250 miles to speak at a women's retreat on the twenty-seventh.

Lord, I can't do it! I complained. *I will be too tired from the move to do my best at the retreat. Could You please somehow give me two or three extra days? It would make a big difference!*

An hour later Ron called with news. "The British Columbia van can't take us until next month. I'm going to check other conferences to see if something can be arranged sooner."

My heart lifted. "Yes! Lord, here is Your chance! Can we get an earlier date? Please?"

A few moments later Ron called back. "The Washington Conference van is going empty to the East Coast. They will be glad to move us, provided we can be ready by Sunday morning, the eighth, at 9:00. Can we do it in three days?"

"Yes!" I spoke without hesitation. "We'll be ready!"

I looked at the calendar. The Lord had given me not just two or three days, as I had requested. He had just handed me the gift of 10 extra days! "Incredible answer to prayer," I wrote in my journal.

As a result of our early move, I was able to get my house in order with plenty of time to rest and prepare for the retreat weekend. It was a great gathering, intense, but I was rested and able to cope. God had once again shown His lavish love, doing abundantly above all that I had asked or thought.

DOROTHY EATON WATTS

Together

*And let us consider how we may spur one another on toward love
and good deeds. . . . Let us encourage one another—and all the more
as you see the Day approaching. Heb. 10:24, 25, NIV.*

Puah glanced behind her. She saw no one. "Shiphrah," she whispered,
"what shall we do?"

"What do you mean?" Shiphrah spat. "Pharaoh didn't suggest we kill
Hebrew boy babies. He *commanded* it."

"Yes, I know." Puah gazed across the Nile River as if longing to disappear into some faraway land. "Pharaoh gives orders. Subjects obey orders."

Shiphrah and Puah plodded together toward Goshen, one heavy foot-
fall after another. They were midwives, and the fate of the boy babies of
their people was in their hands. Would they, at the risk of their own lives,
hand a wailing baby boy to his mother? Or would they snuff out the infant's life, as Pharaoh had ordered?

Scripture doesn't tell us the details of Shiphrah and Puah's decision, but it
does tell us the results: "But the midwives feared God, and did not as the king
of Egypt commanded them, but saved the men children alive" (Ex. 1:17).
Shiphrah and Puah respected God more than they feared any earthly king. But
how did they corral the courage to act contrary to Pharaoh's command?

Would it be safe to assume that Shiphrah and Puah enjoyed godly
friendship? Did they encourage each other? Were they stronger in their association together than either of them would have been by herself?

While they waited for the next delivery, did Shiphrah and Puah recount
the stories of God's leading in Joseph's life, and Jacob's, and Abraham's,
and Sarah's? Did they note how God blessed the Hebrew people, even then,
in spite of cruel oppression? Did they recount God's counsel? Did each
plead with God for strength for each other?

Shiphrah and Puah's courage inspires me. Their example reveals an opportunity that is mine also—to encourage and strengthen a friend.
Together Shiphrah and Puah stood courageously for God. If you had been
Shiphrah and I had been Puah, would we have encouraged each other to
stand for principle? What if they were you and me, and it were today?

HELEN LINGSCHEIT HEAVIRLAND

Comforted by the Snow

Even though I walk through the valley of the shadow of death,
I will fear no evil, for you are with me; your rod
and your staff, they comfort me. Ps. 23:4, NIV.

After having traveled halfway around the world, we at last arrived in the United States for our son's funeral. My faithful sister met us. I fell on her shoulder and wept. It was cold, so she wrapped us with overcoats. We had come to the U.S. before, but never during winter. I wondered why God had brought us to this country at the time of the snow.

God had impressed me to write a letter to my son about three days before he passed away. In it I urged him to change his way of life. Not wanting to offend him, I wrote that letter in the form of a parable. I pictured him as a child playing on the railway tracks with the speeding train on its way. Because I could almost hear the whistling of the train, I cried out to God to pull our son to safety.

I planned to mail the letter the next day, but instead we learned the sad news in the morning. Unknown to us, our son passed away the very same time I cried to God to save him. We learned later that Psalm 51, containing David's prayer of repentance, was our son's favorite text. I am convinced that our son prayed the same prayer. We believed this because of the prayer he had written and kept in his Bible before he passed away. He wrote his name as one who praised God for having not rejected him or withheld His love from him. We treasure this legacy.

We woke up early in the morning the day before the funeral to the whole neighborhood covered with snow. The scene was like a dreamland to us who were seeing snow for the first time. I reached out for the snowflakes, still falling quietly and gently, covering the ugly ground with a beautiful white blanket. I believe our son's desire to be washed and be made whiter than snow (Ps. 51:7) seemed assured; God had done just that for him. I pictured the blanket of white snow over our son's resting place as Christ's beautiful white robe of righteousness (Isa. 61:10) for every sinner. Indeed, the snow has comforted me.

BIRDIE PODDAR

Wrong Place

When he, the Spirit of truth, is come,
he will guide you into all truth. John 16:13.

Nine of us planned to hold a religious service for 250 women in a state prison. Since we were coming from different directions, we agreed to meet at the waiting station of the women's facility, where we would also secure our passes at 9:30 a.m. so that the service could start at 10:00 sharp. This would give us time to make our second appointment at 1:00.

My husband and I arrived at exactly 9:30. Because we thought we were the very first to arrive, we proceeded to the waiting station. My husband asked the guards if any of our companions had already come, but the answer was no.

As time passed by, we kept on looking at our watches, at the entry, but to our disappointment not one of our group came. Finally, at 10:00 a chaplain came to us and asked, "Are you sure this is the place where your service will be conducted? Another group is coming today, but I won't mind if you come some other time."

My husband and I looked at each other. "Is there another facility for women?" he asked.

"Yes, just go back where you entered. Turn left; across the street is the second facility for women," responded the chaplain.

By the time we had driven to the second prison, our companions were already stretching their necks, wondering whether we were coming or not. Someone was already preparing to preach, in case we didn't appear.

What a lesson for us! I couldn't believe we made that mistake, waiting at the wrong place. We were there, we thought, at the right time and at the exact place. But we were wrong. Could it be that as we await our Lord's return we would be waiting at the wrong place?

I do want to be ready when You come, Lord. I don't want to be found in the wrong place. Please send Your Spirit today to guide me into all truth, to the place I should be when You return.   OFELIA AQUINO PANGAN

Wafted Wings

For thy Maker is thine husband; the Lord of hosts is his name. . . . For the Lord hath called thee as a woman forsaken and grieved in spirit. Isa. 54:5, 6.

It was 7:15 a.m. when the phone rang. Jane, my friend, sounded desperate. "Can we meet for breakfast? I'm afraid I just can't handle today alone. I'm due in court at 10:00."

I made mental adjustments to my plans, put my family on their own to get out the door that morning, and headed for Jimmy's 24-hour restaurant. Zipping through traffic, I thought about what Jane was up against—a bitter divorce and a dispute over who would raise the four children. Today was the final custody settlement.

We sat in a corner booth, our heads bent together, tuning out the noisy world of people beginning their day. Jane's tears kept spilling onto her plate.

"I'm so terrified that the court won't let me keep the kids. They'd have more material things with their father, but they won't have a Christian environment," she confided. "I prayed all night, but it seems like the cloud won't lift. I can't get any peace of mind at all," she said.

I took her face in my hands. "Dear friend, I'm so sorry about your pain. Don't give up because you feel shut in and alone. God has some wonderful comfort particularly for you. I want to share something from a favorite author of mine."

Jane took my book and read: "Angels of God had charge over His people, and as the poisonous atmosphere of evil angels was pressed around these anxious ones, the heavenly angels were continually wafting their wings over them to scatter the thick darkness" (*Early Writings*, pp. 269, 270).

We felt God's presence in that corner booth as we asked God to send angels to waft their wings over Jane's darkness.

Supper was on that evening when Jane burst into the kitchen, looking 10 years younger. "It's a miracle! The judge and attorneys agreed to give me more than I had dreamed. The children stay with me, and I will have enough money to run the house and keep the kids in church school." She hugged me and raised her arms above her head. "Talk about wafted wings!"

MARILYN J. APPLEGATE

An Audible Answer

He will be very gracious unto thee at the voice of thy cry. Isa. 30:19.

I was offered a supervisory position in the Department of Education, where I had been employed for several years. Such an opportunity did not present itself often, yet I somehow felt hesitant about accepting it. "I'll let you know in a couple days," I said. To help me reach a right decision, I sat down with paper and pen and started listing the pros and cons.

The next morning I knelt and prayed a prayer I had never prayed before—I asked the Lord for an audible answer! I arrived at work a little early that morning and picked up materials on my desk to deliver to the associate superintendent's office.

To my surprise, when I entered his office a gentleman was sitting on the sofa, reading the Bible. "Well, how are you this morning?" he asked in a cheery voice.

"I've been chosen for a promotion to a higher supervisory position," I told him, "but I can't make up my mind."

"Congratulations!" he said, smiling. Then he asked, "Where will you be working?"

When I told him, his smile vanished, and he looked very serious. "I'd rather take a cut in pay than work there!" He continued, "Maybe the verse I read this morning will be of help to you. 'Take a low position and the Lord will exalt thee.'"

A good friend of mine was then chosen. At first, all seemed to go very well for her. I was tempted to wonder if I had made the wrong decision. However, things were not to remain that way for long. Changes took place within the organization. Later she confided to me that if she had known all the frustrations that were ahead of her, she would never have accepted the position. It had been so bad she was taking medicine for stress.

Over the years I have had similar experiences of prayer answered almost immediately. Oftentimes, however, God's answer is delayed for months—or even years. Perhaps He is testing my faith, or perhaps His answer is "No." Of one thing I am certain: God does hear our prayers when we cry out to Him.

Lord, I thank You for answering my prayer and for people who are ready and willing to be used by You too. May I be such a person today.

GRETCHEN ARMSTRONG

Broken, Faded, and Worn

And God said, "Let the water teem with living creatures." . . .
Then God said, "Let us make man in our image." . . . *God saw all
that he had made, and it was very good. Genesis 1:20, 26, 31, NIV.*

I thought I was walking on the beach all alone, enjoying the presunrise
moments when a large dog nuzzled my hand from behind. Before I could
pull my hand away from his cold nose, slobber dripped from my hand. YUK!

"You're lucky. My dog doesn't make up to strangers easily," said a soft
voice. I didn't feel lucky; I felt dirty.

Turning, I faced a very plain, not attractive, weathered woman with hair
blown from the ocean breeze. She held a plastic bag well filled with shells.

I hadn't seen any worth picking up, so I asked, "How did you find so
many shells . . . ?"

Before I could finish my sentence she said, "I pick up broken ones and
those which are brownish and gray. They are all really very pretty."

"See?" she said as she displayed several from her bag. The broken ones
did look all right when I imagined what the missing parts could have
added. "This one isn't a very attractive color but look how it glistens." She
smiled. Surprisingly, I was admiring her collection. The shells truly did have
nice shapes and graceful lines. Then she offered, "God made them all."

The sun was fully up and I needed to leave, but not before I picked up
some beautiful shells of varying kinds, colors, and growth stages. And yes,
some were chipped and broken.

My life has some chipped and broken parts, but God made me. I am
not now perfect, but God made me and by His grace He remade me too.

Into my pockets were tucked several shells; they now reside on the floor
of my shower. Each time I use my shower to wash away the soil of the day,
I am reminded that "God made them all." The broken ones; those of different colors; ones with faded colors and worn edges. God made them all.

Frequently my shower becomes a *Thank You, God,* experience. I thank
God for the woman with the dog sent to help me understand the beauty in
the broken and faded, the aged and imperfect individuals I encounter daily,
myself included.

God, help me as I strive to love everyone. Every condition. Every day. Amen.

ELIZABETH STERNDALE

Communion Peace

The Lord will bless his people with peace. Ps. 29:11.

My mother was in a nursing home many miles and states away from me. I knew she couldn't get out to church, so on one of my visits I asked, "Mother, how long has it been since you were able to participate in Communion?"

"Oh, I don't know," she said. "It has been years. A chaplain did come not long ago to hold Communion in the chapel. I wanted to go, but I had a cough. I didn't want to disturb the others."

"We'll have Communion this very night," I promised her. "I've brought along some unleavened bread."

Immediately I began searching for the items we would need. In her room I found a metal tray, some medicine glasses, and a plastic pan. At supper, instead of the usual grape juice, all they had was cranberry juice. We saved some and set up everything we had gathered for our Communion service in her room. When I looked for the unleavened bread, it had somehow gotten lost in the cleaning of her room, so we used graham crackers instead.

Since Mother was unable to kneel, I asked, "Do you prefer to wash hands or wash feet?"

"I prefer to wash feet," she said.

It was easy enough for me to wash hers. When it was time for her to wash my feet, I put the pan of water on a footstool in front of her. As we progressed through the service with Scripture and prayers at each step, she began to eagerly participate. I could tell she was enjoying the experience.

She told me afterward, "I didn't realize how much I missed by not being able to participate in Communion for so long."

How meaningful the Communion service can be, even if we have to improvise and make it simple! Our souls need this bit of peace and quiet communion to restore us and make us whole again in Jesus.

When the world is falling apart, Lord, thank You for this example of the peaceful communion You share with us so willingly. The Communion service brings us a sense of Your presence and Your peace today as I commune with You.

PEGGY HARRIS

Search and Find

*Look for it as for silver and search for it as for hidden treasure,
then you will understand the fear of the Lord and
find the knowledge of God. Prov. 2:4, 5, NIV.*

Y ou'll find Isaiah to be a wonderful book," my husband, an avid Bible
reader, told me. I had read Isaiah several times, but with his enthusiastic remark I determined to read it again.

My husband was right—Isaiah is a wonderful book! I was thrilled by the
picture of God's throne, surrounded by adoring seraphs. I heard God's quest
for someone to go for Him and Isaiah's quick and willing response. I read the
scriptures regarding Himself that Jesus quoted during His life on earth. I
sensed again His suffering to assure salvation for me. I read some of Isaiah's
messages mentioned by the disciples and by Paul and reinforced in Revelation.

As I neared the end of the book, two lifelong friends passed away rather
suddenly. I was deeply grieved. True, they were elderly, but they had meant
so much to me and to our whole community. We had lost so much. Why?

Then I arrived at Isaiah 57. There was my answer: "Devout men are
taken away, and no one understands that the righteous are taken away to be
spared from evil. Those who walk uprightly enter into peace; they find rest
as they lie down in death" (Isa. 57:1, 2, NIV).

Just when I needed it, Isaiah provided solace and understanding. And it
is not only in sorrowful situations that Isaiah brings consolation. There is
so much in his book (and in all Scripture, for that matter) that provides
fresh insights into a happy, joyful life.

As I study it more diligently, I find the whole Bible is like a mine filled
with precious ore. At surprising times and in amazing ways it reveals great
veins of spiritual wealth. It enhances my understanding of God. It answers
my questions. It gives direction to my life. And it brings me hope and peace
and security. Best of all, it enriches my inmost soul.

*Lord, You have already answered all my questions and needs. In the busy-
ness of my life, help me to remember to take time to search Your Word.*

LOIS E. JOHANNES

Send Me

Also I heard the voice of the Lord, saying:
"Whom shall I send, and who will go for Us?" Isa. 6:8, NKJV.

We had finished our noon meal, and a free afternoon waited for us. I thought of Katie, who had buried her husband two weeks before. I thought of how difficult it must be for her to be alone with her 8-year-old son and 6-year-old daughter. They had been such a close family, and now the husband and father was gone.

I spoke about it to my husband. "Let's go see if Katie is at home. Maybe she would enjoy some company."

"OK," my husband agreed. "Let's go!"

"We want to come too!" our two girls chimed in. "We want to play with Katie's children."

So we all climbed in the car and headed for Katie's house. In a few moments we rang the bell. She came to the door and exclaimed, "Oh, God, thank You for answering my prayer!"

"We answered your prayer?" I asked. "What do you mean?"

Katie explained how lonely she had been feeling since the funeral. "Today I paced the floor in the living room. I saw so many things that reminded me of him—a chair he had fixed, a door he had painted, his favorite picture in the frame he had selected, and the sofa where he used to rest every evening. I felt so alone. The tears ran down my cheeks. I cried out to God in my pain, 'Please, please God, send someone to visit us. I can't stand this loneliness any longer.'"

Her smile was radiant. "And then you came!" she said. "God sent you in answer to my prayer!"

We felt thankful that God had been able to use us to answer Katie's prayer. We know that sometimes God can (and does) send His heavenly angels to care for the needs of His children. But more often He needs a human face and human words and deeds to supply the longings of another person's heart. So He speaks to us and lets us be His messengers of love.

Lord, make me ready today to be Your messenger of love. Show me what You want me to do. Here I am, Lord. Send me. MILDRED C. WILLIAMS

An Awesome God

"Because he loves me," says the Lord, "I will rescue him;
I will protect him, for he acknowledges my name." Ps. 91:14, NIV.

As I got into my car one February morning, I asked the Lord to be with me on the road. Weather forecasts warned travelers of treacherous black-ice road conditions, especially during the early morning hours. I checked my rearview mirror often for traffic. Even though I had been driving slower than the posted speed limit, I had a feeling I needed to slow down even more. I continued watching my mirror as I approached the cloverleaf off-ramp and was relieved to see I was still alone on the road. Halfway through the single-lane exit I found myself in an uncontrollable spin. I called out, "Lord, save me!"

In the next few seconds I made a complete 180-degree turn and found myself facing in the opposite direction. As I came to a complete stop in the middle of the exit ramp, my immediate concern was my car and what damage I had sustained. With rubbery legs, a painful fingernail, and shaking like a leaf, I extracted myself from the car to survey the anticipated damage. I checked the front of the car first, and then the back. To my absolute amazement, I saw no dents or scratches, and realized that I had not heard any crashes but only felt the terrifying spin. Thankfully, I realized that my car was intact, and that I had had no contact with the three-foot-high cement guardrail along the overpass exit ramp.

In the next few seconds, as I was still standing by my car, I noticed a police car with its lights flashing. The officer approached me, and with a gentle voice asked me if I was all right. He asked if I could continue driving, or should he help me. I said I thought I was all right and would be able to drive. He then informed me that I would have to back up for the remainder of the exit ramp. I followed his hand signals, and at the end of the ramp I was able to back my car into an oncoming adjacent lane. Now facing the right direction, once again I was on my way.

I know the Lord heard my cry for help and saved me that day. We serve an awesome God! ERIKA OLFERT

Even Address Books

I will instruct thee and teach thee in the way
which thou shalt go: I will guide thee with mine eye. Ps. 32:8.

I was heading toward Santa Rosa with mixed emotions. I have a propensity for getting lost in Santa Rosa, yet I enjoy the shopping malls and like to visit a cousin and his wife who live in Oakmont, across the city.

I decided to go by way of Mark West Springs Road, with easy access to the Coddingtown Mall. I dreaded finding my way across the city. I finished my shopping quicker than I had expected, and there was no excuse for not going to visit my cousins. I got out my address book and phoned my cousin. His wife answered, assuring me they would be glad to see me.

Because the route I had expected to take across the city had barriers, one-way streets, and freeway cloverleafs, I was soon thoroughly lost. After asking directions at least twice, I took an hour getting to Oakmont. While visiting with my cousin I mentioned an acquaintance and reached for my address book to verify the name. There was no address book in my purse. I visualized it lying in the Coddingtown phone booth.

"Well, I'll go home by way of Coddingtown and look for that address book."

"You won't find it." My cousin was emphatic.

"I have to try," I insisted.

They briefed me on the quickest route to Coddingtown, and the trip back was quicker and easier. I reached the mall and walked to the booth. No address book. After stopping at the two nearest stores with the same result, I headed back toward the parking lot. Coming toward me was a security officer. Without much hope, I went to meet him.

"Officer, about two hours ago I left an address book in a phone booth . . ."

He smiled. "Yes, it was turned in to me. I took it to the manager's office in the main entrance."

Thanking him, I hurried to claim it at the office.

Amazed that I would encounter this one officer, I returned to the car, thankful for a God who takes care of even address books.

BARBARA H. PHIPPS

Following Directions

In all thy ways acknowledge him, and he shall direct thy paths. Prov. 3:6.

"Chelcie, I need to ask a favor of you," my office manager said. "I'll be traveling tomorrow, so I won't be coming in to the office. However, there are some important documents at home that are needed here. Would you mind following me home to pick them up?"

"I'd be glad to," I agreed. I knew her well and had been by her house before.

As we pulled out of the car park, she stuck her head out her window and called, "Be sure to follow me, Chelcie."

I did follow her—most of the way. Then we reached a double road, and the traffic began to build up in the left lane. Impatient, I pulled into the right lane and passed her. After all, I knew the way to her house, and I hate sitting in traffic jams. I expected her to pull out and follow me, but she didn't.

I reached her house and pulled into the driveway. I waited and waited. There was no sign of her. I felt relieved when I finally saw her car come down the road and pull into the driveway. I got out of my car, smiling at her, feeling proud of the fact that I had avoided all that traffic and had arrived first.

"I don't live here anymore, Chelcie," she said. "That's why I asked you to follow me."

I was embarrassed. We had lost precious minutes because I thought I knew the way.

The Christian life is sometimes like that. Recently a group of young people came to my house. As we sat around talking, most of them seemed concerned with the problem of knowing what God wanted them to do. They were impatient because God did not act as quickly as they expected Him to act. It's easy to feel that way.

Today I want to be more willing to trust You, God, and to acknowledge You in all my ways so that You can direct my paths. I wonder how many times I have run ahead of You, and You have had to come searching for me. I want to be more patient, willing to follow where You lead.

CHELCIE STERLING-ANIM

Our Father Cares

*Call upon Me in the day of trouble; I will
deliver you, and you shall glorify Me. Ps. 50:15, NKJV.*

I sat outside the intensive-care unit of a hospital in Madras, India, pleading with the Lord as my husband lay in bed, recuperating from a heart attack.

James and I had come to Madras to plan for an evangelistic meeting with the local pastor. We were getting ready to leave for an appointment when my husband's face contorted with pain. He complained of a pulling pain in both his arms and a heaviness in his chest. He didn't look normal. I helped him lie down on the bed, then contacted the local pastor.

It was a Sunday, and no doctor was available. James said he was feeling better and slept for some time. The next day the pastor and I took him to a doctor, who told us that my husband had had a mild heart attack and needed medical attention immediately.

I didn't know anybody except the pastor and a few church members, and knew of no hospital. So I placed my trust in the few people I knew and let them help us. The doctor recommended a cardiologist and with a prayer sent us to the hospital. I felt all alone, darkness creeping around me, but I clung to the Lord.

As I sat outside the ICU, I searched my mind for God's promises to comfort me. Two verses from the Psalms kept ringing in my head: "Yea, though I walk through the valley of the shadow of death I will fear no evil; for You are with me; Your rod and Your staff, they comfort me" (Ps. 23:4, NKJV). "God is our refuge and strength, a very present help in trouble. Therefore we will not fear, even though the earth be removed" (Ps 46:1, 2, NKJV).

After a three-day stay in the ICU, I had the joy of thanking the Lord with my husband for sparing his life and granting us more time to continue serving Him together.

Our Father cares when we go through times of trouble. He is actually right by our side, holding us in His loving arms even before we ask Him. *Help me to keep my trust in You today too, when things are going well. Keep me close, Lord.*   JULIA JAMES

The Rainbow of His Love

*I do set my bow in the cloud, and it shall be
for a token of a covenant between me and the earth. Gen. 9:13.*

As I turned the car onto the freeway, I saw a most beautiful rainbow arched across the sky. I drove to the side, turned off the motor, and sat feasting on the beauty—the rainbow of His love, the rainbow of His promise.

It had been a tiring and seemingly wasted Sunday afternoon. As a representative of a religious television program, I was trying to contact people who had requested a visit or literature from the program. I chose Sunday afternoon to visit those who hadn't been available during the week. *Surely,* I thought, *if they're not home during the week, they'll be at home on a Sunday afternoon.* My discouragement at not finding anyone at home seemed to be reflected in the weather, which was a contrast of drizzling rain and intermittent sunshine.

That's when I saw the delicate colors of the rainbow across the sky. *Like the rainbow, Christ's love encircles the earth, reaching to the highest heavens, connecting men and women with God, and linking earth with heaven,* I thought. The peace and assurance of His love erased all discouragement as I continued gazing until the colors gradually faded from the sky.

Was precious time wasted that afternoon? Was I alone in my search? No, the Lord was also searching. And behind one of those doors on which I had knocked, Mamie and Homer were also seeking God. Mamie's response to the card left in their door that afternoon resulted in an appointment to study the Bible with them. Several months later they yielded their hearts to the Lord in baptism. Their dedicated service to the Lord is the fulfillment of His promise, the rainbow of His love.

This rainbow experience with Mamie and Homer seemed to be a foretaste in miniature of the great gathering around the rainbow encircling the throne of God in heaven. God's rainbow of love is more than a pledge of His faithfulness: it is a pledge of His love and desire for all people on earth to know Him.

Lord, today set Your rainbow of love in my heart. And may I be a rainbow of promise to each person I meet, reflecting Your faithfulness and Your love.

BEATRICE HARRIS

Best Friends

Beloved, let us love one another; for love is of God, and he who loves is born of God and knows God. 1 John 4:7, RSV.

Joann and I have been best friends since we were teenagers. We've always had that special something that bonded us together. As kids we shared secrets and giggled, dreamed dreams together and comforted each other. We grew up depending on each other and developing a trust that the years only strengthened.

The day Joann married, she and her fiancé, along with another friend, arrived at my house to pick me up, and we drove three hours to the home of a favorite minister. After a sweet ceremony, the four of us drove the three hours back home, rejoicing in "our" victory.

Several years later at my own wedding, Joann stood as my matron of honor. For months we had planned my special day. Joann had skillfully sewed my wedding dress, coordinated my bridal shower, and attended to every detail. As we hugged and giggled before beginning the wedding march down the aisle of our small church, I knew that God had blessed me in a special way by giving me a friend closer than a sister.

During the years that followed, we spent endless hours at each other's homes, shared church responsibilities, and delighted in her two lovely daughters.

When Joann moved to another state three years ago, we both wondered how we would deal with the separation. We knew our friendship would last forever, but we missed having each other close by.

Last week we spent an hour talking on the phone. It was one of those times when trouble had come our way. As we've done so many times over the past 20 years, we talked and cried and prayed until God began to give us the answer. As I hung up the phone, I felt engulfed in the love of my friend.

In John 15:15 Jesus says, "I have called you friends." Not only does He give us the priceless gift of human friendship in this life, but He offers Himself as a best friend, too.

I love Joann. She's my dearest earthly friend. But the Author of friendship holds the supreme place in my heart. How about you? Is He your best friend too?

JOAN BOVA

My Prince of Peace

And he will be called Wonderful Counselor,
Mighty God, Everlasting Father, Prince of Peace. Isa. 9:6, NIV.

In 1992 I received a familiar postcard in the mail, reminding me of my annual mammogram. That was one appointment I could easily put off, but common sense always took over. At 51, I knew it was necessary.

This time something suspicious showed up, and the radiologist said I needed a biopsy. The questionable area was so tiny I felt confident all would be well.

Not so. In that one-eighth-inch spot I had ductal and lobular cancer. Since it was confined, the surgeon said I could take my time to study treatment options.

When I met with a radiologist, I asked, "How much radiation can a person have in a lifetime?" I was concerned because I had been treated with it for Hodgkin's disease 24 years earlier. "You can't have any," he replied. "Most likely your cancer is a secondary cancer caused by that radiation. I'm recommending to your surgeon that you have both breasts removed."

His words burned a hole in my soul, and I left his office dazed. *How could he be so blunt!* I thought as I headed for the stairs where my angry tears wouldn't be seen.

I was determined to prove drastic surgery wasn't necessary. I began going to the hospital medical library to research other cases like mine. I became desperate for a cure short of losing a breast.

In time all my research came to nothing and a surgery date was set. My church family gave me hope and promises of prayer in my behalf. I was even anointed. With all this encouragement I resigned myself to the inevitable. *Lord,* I prayed, *it's in Your hands. Help me accept this loss.*

The morning before surgery, I wanted to finish a project. I was on my hands and knees in the bathroom laying self-stick tiles when my husband came by and said, "Why are you so happy?" When I asked him what he meant, he said that I was humming.

It was then I realized I was in a state of perfect peace. The Lord had miraculously answered my prayer, and He has continued to carry my loss to this day. He is my Prince of Peace. DONNA MEYER VOTH

The Dress

And why take ye thought for raiment? Consider the lilies of the field, how they grow; they toil not, neither do they spin. Matt. 6:28.

The long-awaited letter finally arrived. I'd been chosen as a vocalist for a Christian convention. What a privilege! What a joy! And oh, what a scare! Had I lost my mind and finally gone over the deep end? Me, singing in front of all those people? What made me think I was good enough? One thought after another tumbled through my mind in rapid succession. Then another thought burst in—what would I wear?

I had one good dress, but I had worn it many times. What would I do? That's the question I asked my heavenly Father. *My Father, I thank You for the privilege You have given me; I know You will help me sing to Your honor and glory. But what will I do for a dress? I have no money, and the family cannot help at this time. Please give me a nice dress. In Jesus' name, amen.*

Several weeks later when some money came from an unexpected source, I was sure God had answered my prayers. I found a lovely pink dress on sale. One week before the convention a member of my church knocked on the door of my mother's house and asked for me. She came in bearing one of those dress bags that you know come from the costliest dress shops.

"Here. Put this on," she said, taking a beautiful frost-green sheath dress out of the bag.

I took one look at it and decided it wouldn't fit. No one could go out and buy a dress for me without my trying it on, especially a dress of this style.

"Try it on," my mother insisted.

The dress slid over my head and settled comfortably over my hips. It was perfect—a dress ordered for me by my Father!

Not only did You bless, but You blessed twice. Help me today to be continually aware of all the big and little things You do for me. I love You!

JUNELL VANCE

Fallen-Cake Christians

*Now unto him that is able to keep you from falling,
and to present you faultless before the presence of
his glory with exceeding joy, to . . . God our Saviour. Jude 24, 25.*

When our son was turning 4, he watched me bake a cake. "What kind is it?" he asked.

"Chocolate marble," I replied.

"What's it for?"

"Your birthday."

"Oh, boy!" He jumped for joy. The minute his feet hit the floor, I looked through the Visibake window and saw the cake fall.

"Oh, no!" I groaned. "It's ruined."

"You could bake another one," Ricky suggested.

"There's not enough time," I explained.

"You could put lots of icing on the low end." Ricky was trying to be helpful.

"I don't think so. Whoever ate that part would get sick from so much sugar."

"Maybe you could saw some off the high side and put it on the low part," he mused.

"You know, that just might work!" I told him. So I took a saw-toothed bread knife and did some cutting and rearranging, using some of the icing as glue. Once it was frosted, it looked quite presentable. I thought about the Bible verse about Ephraim being a cake unturned (Hosea 7:8). Could that be how the term "half-baked Christian" originated? And could there be such a thing as "fallen-cake Christians"?

As new Christians we may make a wonderful beginning, then may have spiritual problems to such a degree that we fall from grace. And instead of being rising Christians, our Christian experience goes flat.

When this happens, should we give up? Never! God may need to do some spiritual surgery on us—even better than the onetime fix-it job I did on the cake. God can help us daily to put our lives together again in such a way that someday Jesus will be able to present us faultless before God as His children.

We may, at times, be fallen-cake Christians. But, thank God, we don't have to stay that way!

BONNIE MOYERS

From Junk to a Treasure

Two vessels of fine copper, precious as gold. Ezra 8:27.

My mother was a great saver of letters, lunch paper wrappers, and bits of wool. The list was endless. She always said, "One day you might need it!" Her little house became more and more cluttered up.

I would feel quite depressed when visiting her to find junk stacking up all over the place. My brother and I offered to help her sort out and throw away, but she wouldn't let us.

When she died, we had to sort out and throw away. What a monstrous task! Bagloads of materials, books, magazines, letters, cards, photos, pots and pans—you name it, it was there.

Out of the "junk" I salvaged a folder containing some crochet shawl patterns, yellow and brittle with age, that had belonged to my grandmother. Next I discovered two large copper trays, one rectangular and one octagonal.

"Do you want to keep these?" my husband asked. "Do you think they are of any value?"

I picked them up and looked at them. They were pitch-black and filthy with dirt. Then I remembered the history of the octagonal tray. This tray had been given to my mother by her cousin, Josanna. It had belonged to Josanna's mother, Priscilla, and might have been one of her wedding presents. That would make it nearly 100 years old.

I took this antique tray home and polished it until I could see the reflection of my face in it. Now it is *my* treasure, as precious as gold, ready to be used at any time needed.

I thought of what Jesus has done for me. He found me in the pit of despair. He cleansed the dirt from my soul. He shone me so I can resemble His grace. Yes, He saw some use for me, so I can serve my neighbors and be precious like gold in His sight.

PRISCILLA ADONIS

God's Timing

Behold, I send an Angel before thee, to keep thee in the way,
and to bring thee into the place which I have prepared. Ex. 23:20.

Our plane had landed in Tobago. We were about to take off for
Trinidad when a voice on the intercom said, "All passengers deplane.
We're having a problem."

Twenty-five minutes later we were called back and were soon airborne.
Lord, are You traveling with me? I whispered. Somewhere in the dark waters
below, my father had been lost when I was a child. Would I also perish there?

While I was breathing my timid prayer, four missionaries were waiting
in the airport in Trinidad for my arrival. An animated conversation was
going on among these hospital employees. The laboratory technician made
a remark, and one of the others laughingly retorted, "How would you
know? You're only a poor missionary."

Suddenly the banter was interrupted as a troubled voice asked, "Are
you really missionaries?"

When the answer was in the affirmative, the stranger continued, "May I
tell you our troubles? We too are missionaries. My husband had surgery in
one of the local hospitals. His abdomen is filled with an abscess, and we are
waiting for a plane to take him to New York."

The nurses realized there would be no more air traffic departing from
Trinidad until the next day. As they explained the situation to the distraught couple, they suggested that they come to the mission hospital right
there in Port of Spain. "We have an excellent surgeon," they added.

Their new friends grasped the opportunity. The chaplain and others had
prayer for them. Three days later the patient was walking down the hallway
of the hospital. Someone remarked, "Quite a coincidence you came here."

"No, it was a miracle" was the grateful reply.

Then I knew why my flight had been delayed—to save the life of one of
God's children.

Lord, I believe You have a plan for my life and a plan for my day. Help me
not to fuss when my plans are interrupted. Keep me aware of Your guidance in
the affairs of this day.   MYRTLE A. POHLE

Following

I have no greater joy than to hear that my children walk in truth. 3 John 4.

One of our family traditions is a singing blessing while we all hold hands, including any guests who might be present. This particular evening our daughter, Janice, and her fiancé came home after we had eaten. They sat down to their evening meal together without us. They looked at each other, and everything was perfectly still for a few moments. Then they smiled at each other and began our traditional singing blessing. It was almost more than I could do to keep from crying with joy—Janice and Terry had learned to love our singing blessing too. They were following after us.

Being a flower lover, I have had a habit of putting throughout the house vases filled with roses or dahlias or something colorful from outdoors. This summer there had not been a great abundance of flowers, and I had made very few arrangements. One day I found in my bathroom a vase filled with ferns, one rose, and two sunflowers. It was almost more than I could do to keep from jumping for joy—Janice had learned to love flowers too. She was following after me.

Our new granddaughter was about 2 months old when our Peter called. "We're going to have Susan's dedication in a few weeks. Her other grandparents are coming. Would there be any chance you could come too?" It was almost more than I could do to keep from crying with joy—Peter and his precious wife would train that dear little one in the faith. They were following after us.

As I remembered these incidents, I thought of my relationship with God. Do I follow after my heavenly Father's training, example, and teaching? Am I copying Him in the way I choose to live my life? Do I follow after Him in the way I treat others? Do I show the same traits of compassion, patience, self-control, and sacrifice? Can He look at me with tears in His eyes and say, "She is following after Me"?

Lord, today I would like to bring You joy! Help me to be careful to walk in Your footsteps, to be like You, to bring You the joy I have felt with my children!

RUTH WATSON

Caught in the Crossfire

In my distress I cried unto the Lord, and he heard me. Ps. 120:1.

One night in 1978 my husband and our 9-year-old daughter left me and our three other children at home in Kolasib, India. He was to conduct a cottage meeting in a house about a third of a mile away. That night about 8:00 the soldiers who were fighting for independence entered the town and fought with the government troops very close to our house.

As we heard the sound of gunfire, my children clung to me in terror. I dared not venture out because of danger from bullets whizzing over our house. So I did two things that night. One was to pray. In my distress I cried to the Lord, believing He would hear me. The other was to take all of our trunks and other things and line them around the walls. We then crawled into our makeshift bunker.

After a short time my husband and my daughter returned and joined us in our bunker. We huddled together, making ourselves as small as possible. My husband told me that the people at the meeting were in a panic when they heard the sound of guns. He asked them to be calm and offered a prayer for protection.

He decided to take the risk and come to us to where the fighting was taking place. Carrying the lighted kerosene lantern, he walked ahead of our daughter along the now deserted road. At intervals they heard shooting and never knew when they might walk into the direct line of fire. Though it was only a third of a mile, my husband felt that it was one of the longest roads he had ever traveled. Incessantly he called on God to overshadow them and to help them reach home.

Then in the darkness, in our makeshift bunker, we thanked God for His protection over our family. We felt at peace in the midst of the battle, for we knew God was with us.

Be near me today, Father, for I also am caught in battle—the battle between Christ and Satan. My only safety is staying close to You, moment by moment, where I am safe from Satan's attacks.

C. KHAMLIANI HMINGLIANA

Unseen Help

The angel of the Lord encampeth round about them
that fear him, and delivereth them. Ps. 34:7.

We left Atlanta shortly after midnight, heading south to Florida for a funeral. Our trip was uneventful until 5:30 the next morning, when I started to drive so that my husband could sleep. Shortly after we passed Gainesville, Florida, I saw what appeared to be a bridge looming before us. I couldn't stop, nor could I swerve to avoid it.

"We've hit something!" I screamed.

Glass splattered all over us, and the glove compartment door popped open, cutting my husband on his right hand.

We heard the voice of a man asking, "Is anyone hurt? O God, please let them be alive!"

An 18-wheel tractor-trailer had hit a van from behind and jackknifed across both lanes of the highway. All lights on the truck were out, and it had no reflector on it. Our car had gone under the truck.

The van, which had two young men in it, had been knocked about 250 feet off the highway. One of the young men had serious head injuries. Our car was crushed up to the windshield and roof. We had to crawl out on the passenger's side, since the door on the driver's side couldn't be opened. By the time we emerged from the car, some people in a camping vehicle stopped to assist us. They had a CB radio that they used to call for emergency assistance.

When the ambulance arrived, the paramedics examined us. The only injury was the small cut on my husband's hand. We were able to get another rental car and continue to Miami. The rescue and ambulance crews told us how amazed they were we had escaped with so few injuries. We believe that God sent His angels to protect us that morning.

Lord , today I thank You for the angels who, though unseen, are my companions wherever I go. Remind me often of their presence in my life, guiding, protecting, and encouraging me.   CAROLYN T. HINSON

He Is Coming—Are You Ready?

You too, be patient and stand firm,
because the Lord's coming is near. James 5:8, NIV.

Myatt Drive traffic was backed up for more than a mile, all four lanes bumper to bumper, barely inching along. This was not a busy thoroughfare, and it was past rush hour, so I thought there must have been an accident. The neighborhood was mostly residential, other than a large truck manufacturing company up ahead. As I approached the trucking company, I noticed police cars lined up on either side of the road, plus two large media vans parked near the entrance.

That's when I noticed large banners, lettered in bright red and blue across the white background, flying high above the front entrance gates. The bold message proclaimed, "He Is Coming—We Are Ready." Security guards posted at the gates allowed no one to enter. Traffic was now at a complete standstill.

The voices of the guards echoed back and forth over speakers. "When is he expected?"

"I don't know, but it must be soon."

"Is everything in order?"

"Yes, everything has been inspected, and we are ready."

"Has everyone received their authorization to see him?"

"Yes, their credentials have all been approved."

"I wonder why he has been delayed?"

"I don't know, but we have been eagerly waiting his coming for a long time."

Finally the traffic began to move forward. As I rounded the corner I observed another large banner under the American flag: "Welcome, President Clinton."

Perhaps we need to hang the banners out. "He Is Coming—Are You Ready?" I wonder how many of us are moving through life in slow traffic, totally oblivious to the spectacular coming event. If such preparations are made in anticipation of seeing our president, how much more should we have everything in readiness to meet our Lord. If we were given the date of His coming, would traffic flow on as usual? Would we not put first emphasis on having our house in order and making sure our credentials are all approved? Do we not wonder why He has been delayed? Just maybe we aren't ready.

BARBARA SMITH MORRIS

If Only I Had Prayed!

Forgetting those things which are behind, and reaching forth
unto those things which are before, I press toward the mark
for the prize of the high calling of God in Christ Jesus. Phil. 3:13, 14.

I was busily checking doctors' orders on patients' charts and giving instructions to my workers when the Holy Spirit spoke to my heart. "Kay, you need to go pray with Mr. Johnson."

As the evening nurse in charge on the orthopedic ward, I had talked with Mr. Johnson earlier in the day as I made the rounds of all my patients. He had been in a work accident and nearly severed three fingers. He seemed to be recovering nicely; however, his spirits were down. He and his wife had been arguing.

The gentle voice of the Holy Spirit was drowned out in my busyness. As the orders on the charts were completed, I forgot all about the Spirit's impression. The evening shift ended at 11:00, and I gave the night shift a report and went home.

The next day I learned that Mr. Johnson had experienced a fatal heart attack and died during the night. Remorsefully, I asked Jesus to forgive me for not listening to and heeding the gentle appeal to pray with this patient.

Could my prayers have made a difference in Mr. Johnson's life? What if I had taken the time to visit with him about his concerns? What if I had shared Jesus with him?

If I had interceded for him, the angels could have surrounded him with an atmosphere of peace instead of strife. He might have lived to discover a meaningful relationship with Jesus and with his family.

However, there is no profit in thinking about what might have been, for the past cannot be recalled. What I can do is accept Christ's forgiveness and claim His power for a fresh start. I cannot live in the past; I must live in the present. But I certainly did learn a lesson that I hope stays with me.

Today, compassionate God, help us to choose to listen to the gentle appeals of Your Spirit. Today, make us quick to respond. Today, make us available to be channels of Your love and compassion. KAY COLLINS

Roots

*And I pray that you, being rooted and established in love,
may have power, together with all the saints, to grasp how wide
and long and high and deep is the love of Christ. Eph. 3:17, 18, NIV.*

The very year I landscaped my yard *would* be the year one of southern California's worst freezes came along. I was out of town when it arrived, and returned home to find that half or more of the flowers and trees I'd been nurturing for eight months had shriveled up and turned brown.

The garden section of our local paper cautioned us not to prune the dead foliage prematurely. Leave it, the paper said, to protect whatever remained of the plants from further damage. And be patient!

Regular inspection tours proved the newspaper right. One by one, the plants began reviving. In the end, only two didn't recover—kalanchoes I'd planted just a few weeks before the frost.

Saddest-looking, at first, was a small jade plant that once had been glossy green. While the larger jades discarded their dead leaves and renewed themselves almost immediately, this one just sat there, a withered skeleton. Finally I gave up on it. But as I reached down to uproot it, I noticed tiny, yellowish-green leaves growing from several of its lower joints. Wonderful! It too was going to make it.

"Plants do that," said a more experienced gardener friend when I told her about it on the phone. "It's a miracle."

The miracle, as I've thought about it since then, has to do with roots. Transplanted into the soil but not yet firmly grounded, the newly planted kalanchoes didn't have a chance. With eight months' head start, the jade plants' root systems sustained them through one of California's coldest winters.

Life has winters too. Winters of loneliness, of grief, of profound pain. Are you firmly rooted and grounded in God's love, sufficiently prepared to make a comeback after winter's worst? Am I? By God's grace, I hope so!

Help me, Lord, to put my roots deep in Your love today so that I may withstand life's hard winters when they come.   JOCELYN FAY

Divine Deliverance

Being confident of this very thing, that he which hath begun a good work in you will perform it until the day of Jesus Christ. Phil. 1:6.

Daddy had a wonderful habit of giving our marvelous mom Sunday mornings off by piling us children into his bright red MG convertible and taking us on a long drive through the mountains above Fresno. We always loved our special time with Dad, and he was a topnotch driver.

One Sunday morning when I was 8 years old, we were enjoying our usual wonderful ride along a mountain road. On one side the mountain reached straight up, and the other side dropped straight down for several hundred feet. A great view, but that first step would be a long one if one decided to exit the road!

None of us sensed the impending danger, but suddenly, as we rounded a curve, our tires caught gravel, and we began to roll down the road toward the cliff—no guardrail, just imminent death for all of us.

Only later did I discover what had happened in a matter of seconds: Daddy had his hands firmly fixed on the steering wheel as the car repeatedly rolled over and over, but try as he might, he could not control that car. He was silently praying, *Lord, help!* when he felt a pair of huge, invisible angel hands covering his on the steering wheel, turning the car in a flash toward the mountainside so that it would stop just short of careening us hundreds of feet down into an instant grave.

Although we hadn't seen another car on that remote road for what seemed like ages, soon after the accident several cars arrived, each having a physician who was willing to give us the help we needed to get to a hospital.

Why did God spare our lives that day? Perhaps our mission for God was not yet finished. Perhaps He had some work yet to do to prepare us for His coming.

I know, Sovereign God of my life, You have begun a good work in me and will perform it till the day Jesus Christ comes in the clouds of glory. Lead me in service to You this day.   JUDY COULSTON

Always by Our Side

I will never leave thee, nor forsake thee. Heb. 13:5.

My family had never experienced war before we were caught up in the bitter Liberian rebellion in 1990. Closer and closer, the rebels of the National Patriotic Front of Liberia approached the city of Monrovia.

Rice, Liberia's staple food, was scarce and had become as precious as diamonds. You could be shot on sight for possessing any quantity of rice. Soon our rice was all gone. There was no hope of getting more. Realizing that we were starving, we decided to escape to the countryside, with the intention of reaching my homeland, Sierra Leone.

There we met Buluma, a man who decided to take us in, even though he knew nothing of our background. We then realized God was close by our side. We ate cassava. No more rice. Ellen, the youngest of my three daughters, protested, "Daddy, Mommy, I don't want foo-foo." My husband and I had to plead with the children to eat the food available. What should we do? No rice and no alternative. *Lord, help us* was the common prayer on our lips.

When we heard that the troops of the Economic Community of West African States were about to enter the area where we were staying, we were sure that the Lord was going to rescue us through them. But the forces came and went, leaving us behind. *God, are we going to stay in this strange land?* I asked myself in tears.

An escape through the bush proved a difficult journey that ended up separating me from my husband and three children. *God, where are You?* I cried. I just gave up and felt that whatever happened was best. At one point I stepped on a thorn about three inches long, but I did not feel it. With the thorn in my foot, I saw a cobra coming in front of me, but with courage I would not normally have had, I kept walking in front of it until it finally ran away from me. The thought of meeting my family had gone, and I felt I was going to be killed by the rebels pursuing me from behind. But God was not far from us. We were reunited and rescued.

After the whole episode, we managed to travel back to Sierra Leone. God is always by our side. I experienced His promise "I will never leave thee, nor forsake thee" (Heb. 13:5). CATHERINE F. KAMBO

A Bargain?

Your word is truth. John 17:17, NIV.

Everyone loves a bargain! So when our group of three families was returning from a vacation in the mountains and saw our favorite variety of mangoes at a bargain, we were delighted.

This trip home was a pleasant one, including a two-and-a-half-day steamer ride down the river. Periodically, the steamer docked at small towns. At one of these stops we disembarked and visited the marketplace. And that's where we found it—a wonderful bargain: scarce but very popular and expensive cherished mangoes. Or so we thought. And 100 of them could be purchased for only $2. We were certain that nowhere else could they be secured at this ridiculously low price. One family selected two baskets. We purchased one. The third family was experimenting with a canning process, so they bought 15 baskets.

The weather was warm, and the mangoes ripened rapidly. To slow the ripening and prevent spoilage, we spread the fruit out on tables on the boat beneath an overhead fan operating at full speed. Nursing our overripe fruit, but still exuberant over our bargain, we arrived home two days later.

And there they were—the very same choice mangoes in our local market! They were firm, fresh, luscious, and available at the same low price—$2 for 100 mangoes. Sometimes a bargain just isn't a bargain!

I've stumbled upon some other unprofitable bargains in life too. In my efforts to find truth and establish my own relationship with God, the fanciful explanation of some ancient formula for life can seem stimulating and fascinating. Briefly fascinating, that is, until I realize it is totally inadequate for the pursuit of the relationship I covet.

Then I discover that the formula that will lead me to my goal lies between the covers of my Bible. The biblical formula "I am the way and the truth and the life" (John 14:6, NIV) has been demonstrated and verified.

It guarantees the desired eternal relationship. And besides that, the price has already been paid! Now, *that* is a bargain!   Lois E. Johannes

One Day at a Time

Preserve me, O God: for in thee do I put my trust. Ps. 16:1.

One of the things I do to get exercise in summer is to mow the lawn with an old-fashioned push mower. As I begin I look at the size of the yard and I think, *I'll never get through.*

But when I focus on the backyard only, it doesn't seem like such a big task. *I can handle this,* I tell myself.

Then I tackle the side yard. No problem. Section by section, I push the mower, and soon I am finished with the task. There are, however, some sections of the yard that are difficult—edges near flower beds or rock borders. But my husband takes his power edger and does these parts, and soon we are done.

In winter I exercise on my treadmill and Cardioglide. As I begin I find time crawls slowly if I glance at the clock. "Five minutes! Ten minutes!" I groan inwardly. But when I put on my headphones and listen to tapes of my favorite hymns, I forget to watch the clock and concentrate instead on the beautiful words. "How Great Thou Art," "What a Friend We Have in Jesus," "The Old Rugged Cross"—time passes quickly, and before I realize it my exercise routine is completed.

So it is with daily life. I may feel burdened with pain, cares, sorrows, heartaches, and think I can't possibly handle it all. "How long?" I groan. The burden of life sometimes overpowers, me and I think I cannot bear it.

Then I realize I must take life one day at a time, one burden at a time, and not look at the whole span ahead of me. And when I fill my thoughts with prayer and praise of a wonderful God, meditating on His Word, I can get through whatever turmoil exists. And what I can't handle—the really tough parts—God will be there, like my husband with the power edger, doing the hard parts for me. Praise the Lord!

Lord, when I focus on my cares and burdens and all of the work I have to do in the next few days and weeks, I wonder how I will ever survive. Help me to live one day at a time with You, trusting You to do the hard parts for me.

PAM CARUSO

Everyone Needs a Hug

Love covers over all wrongs. Prov. 10:12, NIV.

This morning I drove my 5-year-old granddaughter to school. It was evident when I picked her up that she was not having a good day. Halfway to her school she complained of a tummy ache. When none of my solutions was acceptable, she came up with her own solution.

"Go back, Grandma," she begged. "I need a hug from my daddy."

"It's too late," I replied. "But when we get to school I'll give you two hugs, one for Daddy and one for Grandma."

A few minutes later I knelt beside her in the school parking lot and gave her five hugs, one each for her daddy, mommy, grandma, grandpa, and our dog, Matt.

"One from my sister," Rachel implored.

So I gave her four more hugs: one each for her sister, Bethany, her brother, Calvin, and her other two grandparents. I figured that made her quota for the day.

"OK," she said with a little smile. "I'm ready for school."

If we grown-ups were as honest as Rachel, we would all admit we need a few hugs at times to make everything all right so we can get through our day. On the 15-minute drive from her school to my work I thought of some of the times a hug from a friend had seen me through a difficult day.

I thought of how often I am in a position to provide hugs, both actual hugs and symbolic hugs, to hurting women in my churches and community. I have seen a profusion of bumper stickers admonishing such things as "Have you hugged your child today?" or "Have you hugged your horse today?" Children and animals need love and appreciation, but so do adults. So do church leaders, both male and female.

We can give hugs through many means: a smile, a handclasp, a telephone call, a word of affirmation, a note of thanks, a small gift, a postcard, a fax, or an E-mail message. It takes only a moment to tell someone "I appreciate you." It takes little effort to say "I am praying for you." It doesn't take long to write a note: "I like what you did." How easy it is to say "You are a blessing to me." Then why do we do it so seldom?

DOROTHY EATON WATTS

Reunited!

*No more shall there be in it [New Jerusalem]
an infant that lives but a few days. Isa. 65:20, RSV.*

About once a year Mother would open the trunk in which she kept Donald's baby clothes and take each piece out, fingering them and then replacing them, as she would pack away her dreams.

In the spring of 1923 my parents had welcomed their first child, a beautiful baby boy, into their home. Joy filled their hearts as they tenderly cared for him. He seemed so healthy and robust that they were puzzled and distressed when he became ill at the age of 3½ months.

It quickly became apparent that he could not live. The nearest hospital was 50 miles away, and to a struggling young farm couple it might as well have been 500. In those days surgeons rarely could operate successfully on an infant, so it seemed of no use to pursue such a remote hope. And so after a few days of intense suffering, their little darling died. Their grief must have overwhelmed them, replacing the great joy they had known.

Feeling that their lives might have meaning again with another child, my mother conceived within days, and in due time I arrived.

Often in my childhood I dimly perceived that I was somehow a replacement for the baby they lost. I knew that I was dearly loved, but I also knew that in no way could I take the place of "little Donald," and neither would my younger brother, who delighted my parents by his arrival 13 years later.

At some point in my slow spiritual growth it occurred to me that had he lived, I would not have been born. So in fact I owe my physical life to his death.

I look forward to the day when Jesus calls the sleeping saints from their graves, and my mother and dad will be reunited with their firstborn. Joyful smiles will light their faces as they look upon this precious baby and realize they will have the privilege of watching him grow up in heaven. And my brother and I too will at last get to know this child we've never known but always loved.

MARJORIE KINCAID

Dolly's Weak Spot

Man looks at the outward appearance,
but the Lord looks at the heart. 1 Sam. 16:7, NIV.

Dolly, the German shepherd, had come to spend some time with us while her owners were on vacation. She was a regal animal, and I was pleased to care for her. Schultz, our dachshund, was happy for the company.

Our yard had been prepared especially for Schultz. My husband had fenced the entire backyard, then within the yard he had constructed low fences around the garden areas. He had also poured cement under the gate so Schultz couldn't dig out.

One afternoon it began to sprinkle, and I decided to hurry out to my garden and cut some lettuce for supper. The splotches of rain on my head didn't bother me, nor did they seem to bother the dogs, who, of course, had followed me outside. After entering the vegetable garden, I carefully hooked the little gate behind me, because I didn't want eight extra feet in the garden where mud was beginning to form. As I snipped lettuce, a horrific crack of thunder, accompanied by an electrifying flash of lightning, disrupted our peaceful garden reverie.

Dolly cleared the fence with a mighty jump. Trembling, she hovered near me. She wasn't as brave as she appeared! More celestial fireworks made me wonder if it were safe for me to be outside. Evidently Dolly wondered about both of us, for she plopped right down in front of me in the middle of my lettuce bed. There she sat, glued to the lettuce. All the while, Schultz looked dolefully at us through the fence.

Back in the house Dolly didn't leave my side. She stood close to me as I washed the lettuce. Any security she may have ever had was gone until the storm stopped and the sun came out.

I had found the weak spot in her armor and was choosing to ignore it and not discuss it with her. She needed love and assurance, not scolding and censure. She certainly wasn't always the brave, strong-hearted animal that she appeared to be.

Don't be fooled by outward appearances. Maybe there's someone with a weak spot in her armor who needs your love today. Put your arm around her, ignore her weaknesses, and accept her as she is. Share God's love.

BARBARA HUFF

Playing With Idols

If anyone secretly entices you—even if it is your brother, your father's son or your mother's son, or your own son or daughter, or the wife you embrace, or your most intimate friend—saying, "Let us go worship other gods"... you must not yield to or heed any such persons. Deut. 13:6-8, NRSV.

A Christian teacher was teaching her little first graders about idolatry. Holding up a ceramic cat, she asked, "Can this be an idol?" Every head shook a vigorous no-o-o—except for one little girl. She raised her hand and said, "Well, it can be if I pray to it."

What a wise little girl! A modern idol may not look like an idol or be where one would expect to find an idol, because modern idols can be what we make of them and where we find them. They may look like common, everyday items, but if we let them become the object of our devotion, they are idols. I may not pray to it, but if it becomes more important than my God, is it not my idol?

The teacher challenged the little minds again. She held up a toy and asked, "Can this be an idol?" Once again every little head shook back and forth, and they all chorused, "No-o-o!"

The same little girl raised her hand once more and said, "Well, it can be if I stay home from church to play with it."

I would never dream of bowing down to an idol—and I'm certain you wouldn't either. But how often have we stayed home from church or other religious meetings so we could play with our idols? What have we allowed to become more important than the worship of our living God? For some of us, it might be our work; we're too exhausted to get up for church. Or it might be the television or a new book. Or our car or boat. It could be our home at the beach or in the mountains. Perhaps a talent on which we depend for status, support, or esteem. It could even be a friend or relative, someone who "secretly entices" us to miss worship or who lessens our enthusiasm for Bible study and devotional time.

Little children have their toys, and so do grown-ups. I have no idea what your idols may be, but I have a pretty good idea of what mine are, and I think it's time I do a little housecleaning to sweep them out and return God to His proper place in my life.

ARDIS DICK STENBAKKEN

The Lock Was in My Hands

Where is the flock that was given thee, thy beautiful flock? Jer. 13:20.

I looked at the blood in disbelief. How could this have happened to the happy family under my care? The father always sang, but I was never sure if it was about blessings or burdens, because he sang in another tongue. Had the family tried to warn me about this impending tragedy?

Instinctively I knew the enemy. I had seen him a few months earlier, an evil look in his eye and an attitude of blatant disregard for law and order. Now the whole family was gone.

I fell into the easy chair to watch my friends. I hadn't long to wait. The weasel paraded into plain sight with an air of determination to eliminate another family of canaries. I ran to get my 18-year-old son, who quickly dispatched the enemy.

I sat grieving for some time, twisting the one remaining feather in my hands, trying to gain a lesson from the experience. The fresh spring morning with its promise of new life failed to lift my spirits.

I found myself asking God where He was when the enemy attacked. After all, hadn't I dedicated my flock to Him, tithing my income faithfully and giving a goodly sum to worthwhile projects?

My eyes repeatedly returned to the empty cage with its little lock dangling from the open door. Then these words struck home to my heart: "The lock was in your hands."

Had I forgotten to lock the cage? Had I taken their safety for granted? I generally thought of the lock as a way of keeping the birds inside their cage; now I realized how necessary it was to protect them from the enemies without.

I wondered if Satan was weaseling himself into my own living room while I read promises about clean hands and pure hearts. Am I faithful in reading God's words of counsel to my flock morning and evening that I might secure the lock of their heart against the enemy of souls?

It didn't take much imagination that morning in my bird room to envision myself empty-handed at the great bar of God when He asks, "Where is the flock that was given thee, thy beautiful flock?" Now is the time to lock the door against Satan.

LINDA FRANKLIN

Hallelujah, I'm Alive

Thus will I bless thee while I live:
I will lift up my hands in thy name. Ps. 63:4.

I awoke early to the singing of the birds and immediately remembered it would be another day of packing. I wanted to turn over and go back to sleep, but work needed to be done. I crept silently through the house to pick up the Boston *Globe* from the front porch. As usual, I turned to the quotation of the day: "How I long for a little ordinary enthusiasm, just enthusiasm—that's all. I want to hear a warm thrilling voice cry out, 'Hallelujah, Hallelujah, I'm alive.'"

Later that day we decided to drive the 70 miles up to our new house in Kennebunk, Maine, to do some business. It had rained in Kennebunk, and the world shone and glimmered in the sunlight. After we stopped at the bank to open an account, my husband drove to the realtors and I walked to the library. Soon I set out to walk back downtown to meet him.

I crossed the main street at the pedestrian crosswalk. The car on my right stopped and motioned for me to cross. I looked to the left and saw the other cars far down the street. Just as I was almost across, a car drove past me, fast, hitting my hand and causing me to drop my bag. For a moment I couldn't believe what had happened. I realized that my finger hurt and that the car was slowing down. A woman looked back, so I indicated that I was all right.

Others, however, were upset. The policeman across the street was concerned about me.

"I'm OK," I assured him. "I am new in town and am not sure what happened."

He said, "You were in the right, as you were in the crosswalk." After further reassurances from me he left to find the blue car.

As I stood there alone on the sidewalk my first thoughts were *Hallelujah, Hallelujah, I'm alive!* Just so little time and space had been there between me and a terrible accident. Each day our song and prayer should be "Hallelujah, Hallelujah, I'm alive." Life is a wonderful gift that God has given us. Let us celebrate His goodness today. Hallelujah!

DESSA WEISZ HARDIN

The Touch of His Love

*The angel of the Lord encampeth round about
them that fear him, and delivereth them. Ps. 34:7.*

My foot jammed on the brake as I glanced down at the speedometer—almost 60 miles per hour. I looked again at the pickup that had just pulled out from the stop sign and was now blocking the road straight ahead of me. Thoughts flashed through my mind. *If I broadside the pickup, I will kill its driver. And what will happen to us?* My father was in the front seat of the car, and my mother was on the passenger side in the back. We were only four to six car lengths from impact!

The sound of the tires leaving rubber on the pavement froze the driver of the pickup, who also slammed on the brakes. I couldn't maneuver the car around either end of the pickup. My father's words, when I was learning to drive, flashed into my mind: "Don't ever hit a car head-on; take the ditch."

I veered to the right, and the nose of the car dropped into the ditch. The next thing I knew we were at a dead stop, and the car was pointed up the bank to the right. Dad was unfastening his seat belt. Mother was alive and stirring.

The pickup started to drive away, then stopped and came back to the scene. I called 911 on the cellular phone; people started to arrive to help. It was only then that I realized what had happened. The ditch was so deep that the front end of the car hit the bottom as it dropped in, which buckled the frame. The car then spun around 90 degrees and started up the other side before it stopped.

Dad had to have several weeks of therapy for his back, and Mother had a large knot on her head and one on her leg, both of which healed in time. I had neck and lower back pain. When I went home that evening, I asked our loving heavenly Father to please heal me so I could help Mother and Dad in recovering from this accident. The next morning I was fine—no aches, no soreness, no pain!

Looking back on the accident, I know who steered the car into the ditch and then on to safety. An unseen hand had taken control! Oh, what a caring heavenly Father we have, who looks out for our every need. We again had experienced the touch of His love.   CONNIE HODSON WHITE

Resting Secure

Let the beloved of the Lord rest secure in him,
for he shields him all day long. Deut. 33:12, NIV.

The trip home took me along 100 miles of Texas interstate highway and through a small town. As I left the interstate, I was singing; I was glad to be going home for the weekend, pleased with our new Toyota and with my new dress. It was silky soft and fell from the shoulders into the flouncy fullness of a deep frill bordering the skirt.

A dangerous 90-degree bend lay just ahead. Suddenly a car sped toward me around the bend. Its back wheels left the road, skidding along the soft shoulder, coming out of the curve sideways. The driver pressed hard on the accelerator, trying to regain control. His back wheels now gripped the road surface, and he shot across the road, slamming into my driver's side door. As my car and I went sailing through the air, twirling over and over, I saw the car interior spinning around me.

The next thing I knew I was lying motionless on my back inside the up-turned car, both legs up in the air, knees slightly bent, feet together against the back of a seat. There was a good view of the sky through a large hole ripped out of the floor. The sides and roof of my car were all mashed inward. Only shallow breaths were possible because of a pain in my side, but I could feel and move everything, including my head.

Legs appeared at the window spaces, followed by the drunken faces of the youths from the speeding car. Soon paramedics arrived. They had me inch my way, slowly, on my back, out through a window space and onto a waiting gurney.

Eyeing the state of my crumpled car, a paramedic exclaimed, "Boy, the angels were sure with you, lady!" The insurance adjuster later told my husband, "The driver of this car obviously did not survive the crash."

In the ambulance I realized that my body and clothes had defied the laws of gravity. I had landed with my legs safely in the only available space—knees, feet, high heels, and hose all intact. Furthermore, it was as though an unseen hand had pulled my voluminous skirt with its heavy frill up into the air and modestly over my knees.   BRENDA SIMNETT-PRATT

Can They Tell Who You Are?

Thus you will know them by their fruits. Matt. 7:20, RSV.

Every day Joanne cheerfully goes to the post office, a 15-minute walk from our Nicosia office, to get the mail in her red-checked wheel bag. One day I asked if I could come along. We walked fast, appreciating the things we saw, and saying hello to people we met. There were mailboxes full of mail. Joanne carefully put all the mail in her red-checked wheel bag.

"We've come to the climax of the journey," Joanne said, showing me the way to a small tea shop at the back of the post office. As we sat under the shade of the tree, three malnourished cats edged toward Joanne. She opened the pocket of her red-checked bag and got out a plastic bag.

"What's that, Joanne?" I asked.

"This is cat food for my friends," she said as she distributed the food to her friends and patted each of them.

When it was time for midyear meetings, Joanne had to go to Lebanon to record committee minutes. I was left to collect the mail. Like Joanne, I got the red-checked wheel bag and headed to the post office. As I approached the gate of the building, I saw Joanne's three cat friends. They now looked better than the first time I saw them. They came running toward me as if to say, "Here's Joanne!" They patiently waited until I got the mail from the boxes.

"Now what do you want me to do, Joanne's friends?" I asked. I could see in their eyes the longing for something. Following Joanne's example, I proceeded to the tea shop, opened the pocket of the red-checked bag, and poured out some of the cat food.

The next day and the days after that the three faithful cats were there waiting. How did they know it was me or Joanne? The red-checked bag was their identifying factor. They knew that in that bag was something for them.

How will the world identify us as God's children? How will they know we have something for them? Do we carry the red-checked wheel bag of Jesus' love? There are many malnourished souls waiting for someone to share with them the food of the Word. JEMIMA D. ORILLOSA

A Revelation

*For as in the days that were before the flood they were eating
and drinking, marrying and giving in marriage, until the day
that Noe entered into the ark, and knew not until the flood came,
and took them all away; so shall also the coming
of the Son of man be. Matt. 24:38, 39.*

Nine days before my mother's eighty-second birthday I found myself going with her to the emergency room. We left 12 sleepless hours later. Incessant praying sustained me through the experience. Doctors had repeatedly conferred with each other and ordered test after test. Nurses' busyness implied having more assignments to complete than time allowed.

I ordinarily appreciate the services of the hospital security guards, but this time they seemed to be an obstacle to my staying by my mother's side, especially when they would ask me to leave the area. Finally I obtained permission from a doctor to remain by her bedside. Prayer works!

As I was experiencing this critical event I reflected on God's blessings in my relationship with my mother. From childhood through adulthood one of my prayers has been to be able to help my mother. My prayer had been answered: I was able to talk with her daily, able to purchase material needs for her, able to handle her business and take her to preventive medical care checkups. We were able to attend church together as part of a three-generation extended family unit.

It was in the emergency room that I realized how easy it is to be focused on tasks rather than people. There was much busyness around me, but they didn't care about my mother as I did. That's when I had a clear mental vision of the fulfillment of Matthew 24:38, 39. I understand how people can miss the coming of the Son of man.

Lord, please help me to keep my eyes and attention on You. I don't want the busyness of this day to get between me and my relationship with You—and may I always be ready to meet You personally. AVIS H. W. BROWN

A Lesson Well Learned

Because of your faith it will happen. Matt. 9:29, TLB.

When my niece, Jocelyn, was 12, she spent the weekend with me. On Sunday we planned to make several stops before I took her home. One of them included a mini-shopping spree at the mall, which she antici-pated with glee.

Following a quick breakfast, we jumped in the car to begin our day's excursion. However, when I turned the key, nothing happened. After sev-eral tries I looked to see what I had left on overnight that had drained the battery. The dome light! All of our plans were ruined.

I told my niece we would have to call AAA and wait for them to come. That could take an hour or more. She was visibly disappointed. She was looking forward to the new clothes, school supplies, and games that were on her shopping list. Again I tried to start the car, primarily so that when I called AAA I would be able to describe the sound the engine was making.

After a time my niece said, "Let's pray."

I really didn't want her to pray in vain and lose her confidence in prayer, so I slowly said, "It won't help. Jesus can't fix dead batteries. We'll have to call AAA."

As I tried starting the car one last time I said to my niece, "Get your books and pocketbook, and let's start upstairs."

I just happened to look over at her and saw that she was praying. *Oh, no!* I thought. *How will I explain to her when nothing happens?* But the en-gine sounded like it was going to catch. I tried again. The engine started, and we were on our way.

I am encouraged each time I recall that experience. I too now believe that Jesus *can* fix a dead battery. With Him all things are indeed possible!

When there seems to be no logical way out, the innocent faith of a child in God's promises can be a great blessing and bring immeasurable rewards.

Lord, give me the faith of a small child today. Help me to remember that with You all things are possible.						LORNA JONES MCKINNON

Foolish and Blind

Hear now this, O foolish people, and without understanding;
which have eyes, and see not; which have ears, and hear not. Jer. 5:21.

My husband kept urging me to find the hummingbird hidden in the picture. At first I couldn't see it. He could see it, but no matter how hard I tried, I could not find it. I felt very foolish.

A group of office workers were standing around the newest, three-dimensional, computer-generated picture. If you looked at it just right you were supposed to be able to see into the depths of the picture to find a hidden picture within a picture. When someone was able to see the extra dimension, you could always tell. Their eyes would widen with delight, and they would beam with joy and satisfaction or even shout for joy. There were several besides me who wore a blank look. I felt foolish and blind. Jokingly I told the others that I was too much of this world to be able to grasp things of a higher and nobler nature.

Later we went to visit our nephew. In his home I saw a book of these 3-D pictures. I decided that I should try once more to test my ability. I sat alone, determined to master the secret of the magic eye. Suddenly my eyes opened up, and I was able to see into the depths! And not just into one picture, but into every picture in the whole book. With delight I exclaimed, "It was worth spending my train fare coming here!" My nephew laughed; he knew, of course, that our coming had been for another reason. To me, it was a great accomplishment to find out I was not so foolish and blind after all.

Many times we are also too blind to see the depth of meaning and great beauty in the Holy Scriptures. We see only the surface. We need to dig deep into the Scriptures, as for hidden treasures (Prov. 2:1, 4, 5).

We cannot afford to remain foolish and blind when the Scriptures hold treasures of wisdom, knowledge, comfort, and peace. Above all, we must avail ourselves of the gift of eternal life found within our reach.

Lord, open my eyes. May I see the depths of the truths You have for me. May I spend time in the joy of discovery. Open my understanding to Your great treasures today.
                                                              BIRDIE PODDAR

My Plan

*Don't be afraid. . . . You intended to harm me, but God intended
it for good to accomplish what is now being done. Gen. 50:19, 20, NIV.*

Daily exercise, medication to swallow three times a day, weekly trips to the hospital, afternoons in bed, and days battling with the frustration of constant pain are definitely not what I had envisioned for myself.

I had figured that by the time my two daughters started full-time schooling I would start full-time ministry, assisting my pastor-husband. Instead, I have a full-time job endeavoring to prevent my degenerative illness from developing too quickly.

On those days when I wonder if God is really in control of my life, the experience of Joseph gives comfort. Everything seemed so wrong for Joseph. I'm sure his life was not the way he had planned it. He experienced the stresses of a dysfunctional home and struggled with the rebukes of his brothers for his famous dreams.

His life took a dramatic downward plunge when his hate-filled brothers sold him into slavery. Even his good looks led him to imprisonment for a crime he did not commit. When the possibility of release arose, he was forgotten.

God, however, constantly blessed Joseph, not by releasing him from trials, but in other ways. At the end of his topsy-turvy life Joseph was able to say to his brothers, "You intended to harm me, but God intended it for good."

Satan seeks to harm us by breaking our lives into fragments of despair, confusion, and anxiety, but God intends those experiences for good. Since the diagnosis of my illness four years ago I have become increasingly aware of the good that God intended for me. I have seen a God who at every obstacle of my illness provides for my needs. I have seen a God who has opened up ways of ministry that I find exciting and challenging. I have seen a God who is truly loving, truly powerful, truly forgiving, and completely faithful to His promises.

No, the life I live is not the one I planned for myself. Spiritually it is better than I ever imagined!

MARY BARRETT

Why?

For now we see in a mirror, dimly, but then face to face. Now I know in part, but then I shall know just as I also am known. 1 Cor. 13:12, NKJV.

As I was cleaning our son's room, a piece of paper fluttered off the top of his desk. He was only 7 or 8 years old, but already he showed artistic ability and signs that he was a deep thinker.

I bent over to pick up the paper to put it back on top of his desk. As I looked at it, I saw that it was a three-part drawing. Part one showed a tombstone with some flowers lovingly placed in front of it. Part two showed what was either partial remains of a bombed city or one that had been leveled by some natural disaster. Part three was the silhouette of a one-legged person with a crutch. The caption at the top of the page was one small word: "Why?"

Why indeed? Yes, we know that things are not right in our world because of sin. Some things aren't hard to understand, such as troubles we bring on ourselves. It's not too surprising if someone who smokes heavily develops lung cancer or that an alcoholic gets cirrhosis of the liver. But why do careful, health-conscious people fall prey to cancer and other dreaded diseases?

And why are drunk drivers permitted to cause the death of so many innocent people? Is it fair that peace-loving civilians get caught in the crossfire of war or that natural disasters destroy untold numbers of human lives and inflict incalculable amounts of property damage on our planet?

If we have trouble understanding these things, but are faithful Christians in spite of it, we'll someday see God face-to-face in heaven. He will answer our questions as to why specific things happened. And our new, improved minds will be able to comprehend what He tells us about life's "whys," and we will know that He does all things well. And He'll wipe all our tears away (Isa. 25:8).

Lord, I too often wonder why there is so much suffering. I long for the day when You will make all things plain, when You will wipe away all our tears. May that day come soon!

BONNIE MOYERS

Words Aptly Spoken

A word aptly spoken is like
apples of gold in settings of silver. Prov. 25:11, NIV.

My mother-in-law definitely was not typical. Not if typical meant being dour, unbending, stern, sullen, gloomy, or other disagreeable adjectives frequently attributed to mothers-in-law.

In reality my mother-in-law was unobtrusively helpful, unaffectedly affable, and agreeable. She welcomed us in-laws. She delighted in each grandchild's arrival and their subsequent antics.

Then came news that my mother-in-law was ill. It could be a light stroke. It could be a brain tumor. Nothing was absolutely definite. Some days speech and mobility were better than other days.

Our family took a long weekend to drive across the state to visit her. While we were there the family transferred her by ambulance to a large city hospital. As we were about to leave the hospital to return to our home, we gathered around her bed to tell her goodbye. We were sure she would be well soon.

The goodbyes said, we turned to leave, but I unexpectedly turned back. I took my mother-in-law's hand and without planning ahead said simply, "Thank you, Mother, for always being such a wonderful mother to me. I love you."

With difficulty she responded, "Anything I may have done was done with the greatest of pleasure. I love you too."

The anticipated recovery was not to be. Within a few days she quietly passed away. As I have pondered my relationship with my mother-in-law I have recalled that last conversation and have been a bit surprised and gratified that although I am a rather reserved individual, I had expressed my sincere feelings so spontaneously.

Lord, help me to look for opportunities to express appreciation to the people in my life. May I find that person today to whom I can speak words of love. Help my words to be like apples of gold in settings of silver. LOIS E. JOHANNES

Putting Off Repairs

Therefore you also be ready, for the Son of Man
is coming at an hour you do not expect. Matt. 24:44, NKJV.

Car trouble! Don't you just hate it? And I had it.
There I sat, first car in line, waiting for a train to go by. Things such as trains always happen when you're in a hurry, right? But this was really bad timing.

My car was having its own problems. Things weren't looking too good as I watched smoke coming out from under the hood. I turned off the key. Immediately I had second thoughts. *Oh, no! Why did I do that? What if I can't start it again?*

By now there was quite a line of cars behind me, and probably most of them were more eager than I was to get somewhere. If I could see past the truck beside me and tell when the end of the train was coming, then, hopefully, I could start the car and be ready to take off when the last train car went by. But I couldn't see past the truck, and I couldn't tell when to start my car. *I'll probably sit here and hold up all this traffic. How did I ever get myself into this mess?*

I really shouldn't have found myself in that situation. Although I knew there was a problem, the car was still running, so I just hadn't taken time to take it in. Besides, I needed to go somewhere.

That led me to thinking of Christ's second coming. We know the end is coming. We know that we should be ready so that when He arrives we are prepared. Nothing should keep us from being ready.

But things keep going wrong, and we are so busy we put off asking God to help us repair the problems in our lives that keep us from running smoothly. Perhaps our doing this keeps others from getting to the point where they need to be too.

Thank You, Father, for helping my car to start when the train finally passed. I know You are coming soon. Please help me with the repairs that need to be made so I am ready.

DONNA SHERRILL

That Stubborn Lock

Cast all your anxiety on him because he cares for you. 1 Peter 5:7, NIV.

It had been a long day, and I was eager to get to my hotel room to go over my presentations for the next day. The thought of getting a little extra sleep was most welcome as well.

I whipped out my key to insert it in the lock—but it wouldn't go in. *This is strange,* I thought. *It worked a couple hours ago when I checked in.* I tried fitting it in the deadlock. Wrong shape. I tried the door keyhole again.

It was then that I noticed a little pin protruding next to the keyhole. I had a feeling the pin had something to do with the key not fitting, but I had no idea what. So I trudged back downstairs to the desk. The desk clerk said I must have set the deadlock. I didn't remember locking the deadlock, but he gave me a second key for it, and back up I went to Room 234.

Nothing fit. Back down to the desk. This was really getting upsetting. The poor desk clerk was by himself and very busy, so I waited. I tried desperately to think. *What lesson should I be learning from this?* I could think of nothing positive. If I was supposed to be learning patience, it was only partially working. I did, however, think of the sermon I had heard earlier in the evening: God cares, even if things are not going well. He may not be getting me out of my aggravating situation, but He cares. I was not in a life-threatening situation, and eventually something would surely work out.

The clerk called the maintenance man, who told us what to do. Back up to the room I went. That deadlock would not release. Back to the now slightly less crowded lobby. The clerk went to give the lock another try. He had no luck again.

It was now 10:30, and I was getting more and more tired but kept reminding myself that God cares. The maintenance man arrived and got the door open after about 10 minutes but could not explain why the lock had been so difficult.

My presentation material went together quickly and easily, and I was soon in bed, thanking the Lord not only that I was in my room, but that He had been with me all the day. In all the happenings of my day (or your day), He cares.

ARDIS DICK STENBAKKEN

Disappointment Turned to Joy

Weeping may endure for a night, but joy cometh in the morning. Ps. 30:5.
Your sorrow shall be turned into joy. John 16:20.

It was almost time for my husband to go on a tour of the Holy Land. It should have been an exciting time for all of us, but because his ticket arrived only the day before his departure, there had been many hassles and frustrations. He didn't leave in a very pleasant frame of mind. In fact, he didn't even say goodbye to me. This upset me after all I had done to try to help him. It had not turned out the way I had hoped at all.

Now I had to make a decision. I could continue to lick my wounds and feel sorry for myself, or I could get up and find something to cheer me. I decided to try the latter. I got out a sermon, written especially for women, about joy. It helped. Then I read a beautiful story about Eleanor Roosevelt and her trials and troubles. This was just the right thing for me.

I phoned my children and received comfort and support. They even came to see me, even though it was raining and an ice-cold wind was howling. We enjoyed a few hours together.

My daughters said, "We're sorry, Mom; we brought nothing nice for you, and you have given us so much." I told them they gave *me* so much. Their sacrifice to come visit me under those wintry conditions meant a great deal to me. Their love and care was shown to me when I needed it most. They even followed up with calls on a regular basis to find out how I was. Because of my decision, I really was doing much better.

My sorrow turned to joy, Lord. Weeping may endure for a night, but joy really does come in the morning. Thank You for that today. May I always search for the good instead of focusing on the bad. Be with me, Lord, that this too will be a good day, filled with joy. And Father, thank You, too, for each member of my family.

PRISCILLA ADONIS

The Dream-Come-True Miracle!

Every good and perfect gift is from above, coming down
from the Father of the heavenly lights. James 1:17, NIV.

As soon as I saw the price of the wonderful sewing machine that could embroider beautiful flowers, butterflies, hearts, and patterns, I knew it could be only a dream. I could never justify the expense. On top of the machine price, I would have to buy the design disks, the thread, and other expensive accessories. I put all thoughts of owning such a machine out of my mind.

I've always loved sewing. I love creating beautiful things for my home, presents for friends, and banners for church. So my parents gave me a sewing machine for my eighteenth birthday. It went everywhere with me as I mended, made drapes, clothes, bridesmaid dresses for my wedding, and then baby dresses for my daughter. I used to joke about my machine having sewn hundreds of miles of seams!

But at last my old machine choked and spluttered to a halt. Its motor had burned out and was irreparable. I didn't know what to do. We were short of money, and I resigned myself to getting a cheap, secondhand model.

Then the miracle happened. Bernie, my husband, was visiting an elderly woman named Hilda. During his visit he mentioned my problem with the sewing machine. Hilda said, "Oh, she can have mine! I'm diabetic and can't see to use it anymore."

Bernie imagined an old Singer treadle machine as he followed her into her back room. She opened a cupboard and there, under a cloth, was my dream machine, complete with every accessory, plus the embroidery disk and four boxes of silken embroidery thread in every color under the sun! It even had a walking foot for machine quilting.

I could hardly believe this wonderful machine was to be mine! I called Hilda and told her she was the source of a miracle. She said she believed God had inspired her to buy the machine so that one day she could give it to me. I couldn't help thinking of my amazing, loving Father, who supplies all my needs—and even my wants! KAREN HOLFORD

Through Wind and Rain

For He says to the snow, "Fall on the earth"; likewise to the gentle rain and the heavy rain of His strength. Job 37:6, 7, NKJV.

I can still remember the large drops of rain that fell that Friday evening as day turned to night. It was the kind of night that you'd want to be home, to meditate quietly and calmly. But instead we were making an emergency trip.

We had packed quickly. My husband reluctantly accepted the responsibility of driving on such a rainy night. We gathered our children and prayed diligently for God's traveling mercies, as we had done so many times in the past. We rather dreaded the long ride from Pensacola to Houston and were physically exhausted after the long day. We just wanted a good night's rest.

It was not unusual to have heavy rain in March. After all, it was nearly springtime! But there was no way we could have known that God had planned much more than rain. Within four hours the rain turned to snow, falling in such a swift, quiet manner it seemed God Himself was speaking to us. As my husband drove and I held on to my seat, our children slept. Hearing our chatter and the excitement in our voices, they awakened to witness the quiet, soft flakes that blanketed our surroundings.

We were Floridians! Snow was the kind of weather that we only heard about over the television and wished for. And now, in the midst of our journey, we were blessed with more snow than we'd ever seen before in one place!

For many miles we could not stop or turn back, but could only go forward very slowly. The night was black on either side, and the heavy winds shook our Ford Bronco many times. But we knew God's presence was near and that He allowed angels to watch over us and guide us safely through to our destination.

Thank You, Lord, that in the storms of my life You are with me. I depend completely on You for safety, comfort, and rest. You are my provider, my sustainer, and my protector.

ALETHEA HENDRIETH

The Father of Single Parents

As a father has compassion for his children, so the Lord tenderly sympathizes with those who revere Him. For He knows what we are made of; He keeps in mind that we are dust. . . . The Lord's faithful love rests eternally upon those who revere Him and His righteousness on the children's children. Ps. 103:13-17, MLB.

Most of the time I enjoy life as a single parent. There have been days I've wished for some flesh-and-blood person I could always count on. And once in a while it scares me—like the evening I realized my daughter had been lying about her homework. For several weeks she'd been telling me she didn't have homework, that she was getting it done at school. The phone call from the teacher set the record straight.

I was angry at first. She had deliberately lied. The atmosphere in our home was stormy as restrictions were laid down and plans made for the catch-up work. Later that night, after we had talked quietly and she was in bed, I was frightened.

I remembered the nights I had been too tired to listen as she tried to tell me about her day at school. Often I was preoccupied with worries about bills and unfinished projects at work. My own growing-up years had not allowed me to be a child, and many times I had to remember children are not small adults. Perhaps I expected too much responsibility from her and hadn't watched enough.

I felt overwhelmed as I knelt to pray. I had not grown up in a Christian home, and was raising my daughter by a completely different value system than I had had. I frequently questioned what I was doing and wondered if there might be a better way. I faced the questions again that evening, feeling very small and alone. I cried out to God, pleading for whatever guidance He thought I needed.

As I wait before You in silence, I sense Your arms of love stretched out to me and my daughter. I feel Your concern for us. I know I have nothing to fear. I know I am not really alone. Your faithful love is here with me, and I treasure its warmth.

DOTTI TREMONT

Miracles Do Happen!

Commit your way to the Lord; trust also
in Him, and He will do it. Ps. 37:5, NASB.

I had not dated for more than 35 years, and dating in your 60s is quite a different experience from the good old days. After my husband died, I promised myself that I would not remarry. One long, stressful, terminal illness was enough for me. But I have always been a very social person, so after a while I got out into the community just so that I could be around people.

I had really enjoyed being married. So after nine years of being single, I decided I really didn't want to live out the remainder of my life alone. Then my youngest daughter told me about a woman who had written out the qualities she wanted in a husband and had put the list in her Bible. This sounded like a very good idea to me, in view of my past experiences with doing things on my own. So I made out my list.

First of all, I wanted someone who loved the Lord, someone interested in religion. I wanted him to have a sense of humor and enjoy music. I wanted someone who enjoyed spending time with me and was affectionate. I wanted him to be willing to talk out problems. I wanted someone who was interested in healthful living. And last of all, I wanted someone who enjoyed photography, one of my favorite hobbies.

I put the list in my Bible, tucking it firmly in place, and said to the Lord, *OK Lord, it's up to You now. I've told You what I want; now I am going to let go of this and leave things up to You.* It was going to be a big adventure for me to see what, if anything, came from this.

About four months later I was attending a function at our local senior center. I started to chat with a gentleman I thought I had seen there a few times before. It was only a brief meeting, but as I was about to move on, I gave him a big smile. That did the trick for him, and he asked to see me.

As we became better acquainted, the items on my list of qualities in a mate began to check out all the way down the line. After three months of courtship, we were married. We both are convinced that the Lord brought us together. What a wonderful lesson in trust I have gained from this experience!

SHEILA SANDERS DELANEY

Salvation Is for Everybody

*This is good, and pleases God our Savior, who wants all men
to be saved and to come to a knowledge of the truth. 1 Tim. 2:3, 4, NIV.*

We heard a knock at the kitchen door. It was a couple we knew, coworkers just passing by. So we started visiting at the door. We were enjoying ourselves very much. The wife started talking about her husband's boss, who felt he could criticize her husband's work in a harsh way. This situation irritated her husband and made him very unhappy. He always shared this with his wife, who then became very tired and upset.

That day she talked and talked, giving us examples to demonstrate that the boss was really a mean person. I agreed with her; I could understand her feelings, because I had also suffered several similar situations. The troubles for them had continued so long that the wife was suffering with pain in the upper back, and other symptoms that showed she was passing through a very stressful time. She was seeing a doctor.

The conversation lasted for a while. Suddenly the husband said to her in a thoughtful way, "Honey, I want to tell you something. God loves and wants to save this man too."

That statement astonished us—and her. She stopped talking. Suddenly I saw that her husband had a very valid point. I realized that this rude colleague was also under God's eyes. God cared for him, talked to his conscience, called matters to his attention, gave him lessons and opportunities to change, just as He worked with the rest of us.

That experience helped me understand more about God's patience. He works with us and waits patiently for us to react and accept what He is doing in our favor. He wants us to change. He wants to give us a new heart. But He does not force us to accept His offers. He is there, always trying. He does not condemn us when we are facing a disagreeable situation. I am glad our God is long-suffering, aren't you?

Please, Lord, help me to be more loving, patient, and understanding today. May I be slow to judge and quick to love all those around me.

ELLEN E. MAYR

Gloomy Days

The Lord is close to the brokenhearted and saves those who are crushed in spirit. Ps. 34:18, NIV.

Perhaps you too have sometimes felt crushed in spirit. No doubt you have become the victim of unkind words or deeds, as I have. Perhaps sleep would not come as you thought about the situation. How encouraging it is to know that the Lord is close when we are downhearted.

I had had a rather unsettling experience. I felt hurt, and the clouds of gloom and despair seemed to hover for too long. Talking my problems over with my close friends helped a bit, but my feelings were not imaginary—they were real.

One morning as I sought to arrange my cluttered thoughts I cried out to God. *Lord, help me. Speak to me. I need to hear from You. How do I handle this situation? Give me wisdom.* I lay on my bed, waiting for an answer. I knew from experience that the Lord would save me out of all my troubles, and I was willing to wait. I had no intention of getting out of bed before I got an answer.

I turned on my radio. The announcer was giving the weather forecast for the day. Two minutes later the following words of a song caught my attention: "Why should I feel discouraged? Why should the shadows fall?"

The words spoke to my gloomy, discouraged heart. I sensed the presence of my heavenly Friend as the song continued: "His eye is on the sparrow, and I know He watches me."

I closed my eyes. *Thank You, Lord, for hearing me. Thank You for giving me the assurance that I am not alone. I can feel You just wrap Your great big arms around me and tell me that I am special.*

He loved me. He was going to help me get through the situation. The lyrics were the most appropriate for the situation.

God has many different ways to speak to us. I got out of bed, and throughout the day the lyrics and the tune reverberated in my mind.

Lord, thank You for reminding me today of Your love. As I go through this day, help me to remember that You hear and answer every cry from a broken heart and a crushed spirit.

ANDREA A. BUSSUE

Songs in the Night

*Yet the Lord will command his lovingkindness
in the daytime, and in the night his song shall be
with me, and my prayer unto the God of my life. Ps. 42:8.*

It was 1:00 or 2:00 in the morning when screams coming from nearby reached my consciousness. I struggled awake, only to find myself in the nightmare instead of escaping it. A girlfriend in the next room was screaming that she couldn't feel her legs. My first thought was that she must have slept on them wrong and they had gone to sleep, but her voice held notes of terror I had never heard before. She continued screaming that someone was choking her, that she couldn't breathe, and suddenly I sensed the very real presence of evil spirits.

Through my fear-numbed mind came the thought, as if it were a command, that I needed to sing! At the same instant, the beautiful contralto voice of my roommate began "Jesus loves me, this I know." All I could do was mouth the words as tears rolled down my cheeks, and my heart cried out to God for deliverance.

I had taken a year out of college to teach at a mission school on a small island in the Pacific. Having grown up in Indonesia, I was familiar with cockroaches, the need to boil all drinking water, and the challenges of sporadic electricity. I hadn't anticipated any culture shock during the year and really hadn't experienced much. However, nothing in all my experience and 20 years as a pastor's daughter had prepared me for this.

Even though my body was still rigid with fear, I found a whisper, and then I was singing, "They are weak, but He is strong." The noises from the next room began to lessen, and soon the girl and her roommate were crawling into our room. They were shaking and crying, but we all could feel a strong peace begin to take over. My roommate started singing "Amazing Grace," and after a few more songs together, we were able to gather in a circle and pray.

The mission school had experienced many difficulties. The devil had used this opportunity to torment and to try to discourage us, but it was the beginning of my realization that there is never a night so dark that Jesus cannot light it with His presence. There is never a fear so strong that God cannot break it with His power. DENISE HANCOCK BENNER

The Appointment

Are any among you suffering? They should pray. . . . The prayer
of the righteous is powerful and effective. James 5:13-16, NRSV.

W hat time can I see you?" Tracy asked. "I know that I am not one of
your students, but the vice principal told me that you are an elder
and that I should talk to you."

I told Tracy my free time, and we promised to meet in my classroom.
She arrived almost precisely at the specified time. The smile came easily before the many tears. She spoke about her family's chaotic conditions. "I
hate living there without my father," she said quickly. "My mother's job is
taking her away from the family so much that we are not a family anymore.
I do not talk to her, and she only fusses when she talks to me. My only
source of help is my boyfriend," she explained through sobs.

Recognizing her inability to go on, I quickly said a silent prayer. "Is
there a male family member you can confide in?" I asked. "What about an
uncle, godfather, or even your pastor?"

"My uncle lives far away, my godfather is in jail, and I can't stand
my mother's pastor," she responded quickly. My silent prayers became
more intense.

"I want you to make me a promise," I told her.

She nodded.

"Schedule a time—and stick to it—when you will pray for your mother
especially and the other siblings of your family. Do it daily," I counseled.

"I do this already!" she almost yelled as the tears continued.

I quietly repeated my advice and stressed the word "daily."

"All right," she said, calming.

We prayed, hugged, and cried together. She promised to return in
about a week. She never did, but her big smile and wave when we met on
campus told the story.

Lord, so often we become overwhelmed. We need Your advice and Your
help in our times of trouble. You always listen. Thank You for helping Tracy.
May we always remember to come to You with our needs.

MARGARET B. LAWRENCE

A Good and Faithful Servant

Remember how short my time is. Ps. 89:47.

M r. Kelly was indefatigable in his work for the underprivileged in the community, as well as working tirelessly in almost every department within the church. I had been wanting to do a "This Is Your Life" program to honor him, but had put it off. When I heard he was almost 80, I knew I must do it immediately. The fact that he had just received the Commander of the British Empire award from the queen added impetus to the project. His trip to Buckingham Palace to accept his award from the queen occurred a week after he had celebrated his eightieth birthday.

Plans were well under way when, to my horror, I found that my degree finals commenced not two months after the planned program, but two weeks afterward! Mr. Kelly's daughter kindly suggested a postponement, but I declined the tempting offer. Two weeks before the program, Mr. Kelly was taken to the hospital. Cancer was diagnosed a few days later.

The doctors urged us to continue with our plans, and although very ill, Mr. Kelly rallied his considerable willpower to leave the hospital for a day, as he thought, for a program about a charity close to his heart. His surprise when he found the packed church was for him was moving to behold. That night we honored his lifelong work and honored his inspiration to so many who were now following in his footsteps.

Three days later the doctors operated. A week later Mr. Kelly's great and generous heart stopped. The night before his operation he and I talked about his program. Typically, Mr. Kelly spoke not of the honor or the plaudits, but of his delight that so many had heard about the Saviour he loved. He knew that he faced death, but he did so with the calm assurance that whatever the outcome of the operation, Christ's coming is near and he would soon see his Saviour. Mr. Kelly passed away a few days later.

What if I had delayed!

I am so thankful I followed the promptings of Your Holy Spirit. The experience also reminds me of how dangerous it is to put off the important things—especially honoring You with my life. Today, Lord, I give You my life, for I remember how short my time is. AUDREY BALDERSTONE

Strangers or Friends

A merry heart maketh a cheerful countenance:
but by sorrow of the heart the spirit is broken. Prov. 15:13.

Talking and eating seemed to be the main occupation, day after day, as we spent our vacation with our son, Steve, and friends in California. Then one Friday morning my husband woke up with numbness on his right side. He and Steve, both physicians, diagnosed it as a stroke. He was admitted to the hospital.

At last he was stabilized and admitted to a comfortable room. A friend drove me back to Steve's apartment for a couple hours. I needed to do a washing. I had keys to the laundry room at the far end of Steve's apartment complex, so I trudged over with my load of clothes. I was still worrying about my husband's illness.

A pleasant, elderly woman was there to do her wash as well. I courteously asked questions about the machines. "You must be new here. Have you just moved in?"

I told her my story of visiting my son and my husband becoming ill.

Without hesitation she looked at me and said, "Now listen. If you need a ride to the hospital to visit your husband, just let me know. I can take you anytime. Well, don't call after 9:00 p.m., as I am usually in bed then." She thought a moment and quickly added, "But if it is an emergency, I can get up. Please call me anytime. I am retired, and I am right here." Because of her openness and friendliness, Doris became my friend that day, right when I needed one.

It was a difficult time, but the many people around me helped so much. They did not seem like strangers. They took me in as a friend and made my days so much brighter. God was good to us.

Lord, please help me to remember who are my neighbors, who are my sisters and brothers day by day. May I keep my heart merry as I reach out to them is my prayer. May I help them to have a merry heart.

DESSA WEISZ HARDIN

Why Goodbye?

*And God will wipe away every tear from their eyes; there shall be
no more death, nor sorrow, nor crying. There shall be no
more pain, for the former things have passed away. Rev. 21:4, NKJV.*

It was 9:30 p.m., and we were at the entrance of the university campus to tell the American students goodbye. Friends, teachers, and deans wanted to share this moment.

Nine months had gone by, months that had witnessed many new things, hard and easy times, but best of all, unique, life-transforming experiences. But now it was time for the Americans to go back home. It was time to say goodbye.

This intercultural experience had given the Americans a new language, the perception of another culture, a closer relationship with God, and friends they could never forget. Now it was over.

And I would never forget them. We had shared many cultural trips, long hours of talking, and classes. We had learned from one another; we had laughed and cried together. Now it was ending.

The van that would take them to Buenos Aires arrived. I was looking at my friends as they hugged other friends, wrote down last-minute addresses, and took a last look at the campus. And then I saw Tanya coming toward me. She hugged me and started to cry. Finally she managed to say, "Why? Tell me, why do we have to say goodbye?"

That night I found it hard to sleep thinking of those words: Why goodbye? And I could not do anything but give my heartfelt thanks to God because I know a better time is coming, a time when we do not have to say goodbye ever again.

Thanks for the wonderful hope that we will meet each other again very soon. I can see myself hugging You and Tanya in heaven. We will be crying, but our tears will be tears of eternal joy. I will hug every one of my friends, and we will have lunch together the second Sabbath in heaven, and we will never say goodbye again!   LORENA FINIS

Identity Found

We are the children of God. Rom. 8:16.

Our daughter, Jennifer, had been asked to sing for the Hauula church service. Leaving home very early on the appointed morning, we drove to the church. It was a beautiful Hawaiian day, the deep-blue sky reflected in the depths of the tranquil Pacific Ocean. Tall palms swayed in rhythm to the cool, crisp Hawaiian breezes. The sun seemed to be trying to outdo itself as it shone on every blade of leaf and grass, bringing out the most vivid shades of green among the trees and shrubbery lining the sides of the Koolau Mountains. Every bend in the road was a glorious kaleidoscope of God's majestic creation.

"How should I introduce myself?" Jenny asked suddenly.

"Perhaps it would be nice to inform the congregation that you are a junior attending Hawaiian Mission Academy," I suggested.

My answer seemed to satisfy her, but then she turned to me and asked, "Mom, what would you say if you were in my shoes?"

I was stumped for an answer. Indeed, what would I say? I have been known as "Norma," "Joe's wife," and "Joey's mom" or "Jennifer's mom." On the phone I always introduce myself as "Norma, from the church office." Was there more to my identity than that?

Sensing the turmoil going on within me, my husband gave my hand a squeeze and then quickly turned his attention to negotiate a bend in the road. There before us lay another dazzling display of God's magnificent creation. In a gentle but excited tone my husband quietly voiced the answer to the question that had so eluded me. "There," he said. "Aren't you glad you are a child of the heavenly Father?"

A child of the heavenly Father indeed! An heir to the heavenly kingdom, a daughter of the King of kings! What better identity could any of us possibly ask for?

As I go about my daily tasks, help me to remember who I am. May I represent You in the best possible way this day. NORMA C. GALIZA

Our Father Cares

Answer me when I call to you, O my righteous God. Ps. 4:1, NIV.

G od, I whimpered, *You know where it is. You help little kids find stuff.*
Why aren't You helping me? Again and again I complained to my patient heavenly Father. It was bad enough that nearly three feet of snow had
buried my car—and now this! I was in real trouble.

Reality had struck when I stepped off the commuter plane into the dark
of the north Michigan winter after a joyous class reunion in sunny
California. The little airport terminal was empty—all personnel were plane-
side. *This could be grim,* I thought as I opened one door after another in
search of a shovel. Successful at last, I trudged back out to the empty parking lot to begin digging.

That is when the lens popped out of my glasses. Frustration mounted
as I crawled about, half blind, brushing about mounds of fluffy snow with
my bare hands, searching, searching in the dim light of the parking lot for
that all but invisible object.

"Finding the proverbial needle in a haystack would be a piece of cake
compared to this," I muttered.

Finally, in shivering despair, I trudged back to the airport, still whining
inwardly. There behind the desk was a person, a real, live, bundled-up girl.
"Could I borrow a flashlight?" I asked.

"Sure," she grinned and strode off beside me to the parking lot as she
listened to my predicament. She scanned the snow I'd been sifting through.

"Here it is!" she casually announced as she picked up my lens. Then
without a word she proceeded to shovel out my car.

"Are you an angel?" I whispered.

She thought I was joking. But I wasn't, really. How could she know that
God had sent her to reassure His doubting, fussing child that He really did
care for her?

Lord, this is so like You, to come to me in this little crisis. Forgive my unbelief.

ALICE FAHRBACH

Burden Bearers

Carry each other's burdens, and in this way
you will fulfill the law of Christ. Gal. 6:2, NIV.

It was a bittersweet time in my life. My youngest daughter was expecting her first child just about the time that my mother was scheduled for cataract surgery. Since they lived 500 miles from each other, I would have to make a choice. I couldn't be in both places. I knew my mother had many supportive friends close by, so I was helping my daughter when the phone call came. My mother wouldn't be having the scheduled cataract surgery after all because she was ill with hepatitis.

Although 80 years old, she had been her usual active self only weeks before when I had been with her. Church activities, crocheting afghans, visiting shut-ins, letter writing, and her many friends kept her busy and happy.

As soon as I was able I went to care for my mother. Now that I was there to see that she had nourishing meals, I was certain she would soon be up and around again. However, instead of improving, her physical condition was going rapidly downhill. It seemed she had lost her will to live. When the doctor told me that Mother could be expected to live only a month or two, I decided to stay with her so that she could spend her last days in her own apartment where she had been so happy.

It wasn't easy to be on duty around the clock. But for an hour or two each day, friends of my mother came by just to give me a little respite. Someone even came in so I could attend church and stayed long enough for me to have a relaxing meal with friends afterward. In times of crisis there was always someone I could call who would come quickly to help. Just little things perhaps, but they meant so much in my time of need. I felt surrounded and supported by the love and warmth of my mother's friends.

Indeed these friends were following Paul's admonition to "bear each other's burdens," something that even the poorest of us can do. It may be helping a weary mother by running errands or caring for her children now and then. Perhaps we can invite a lonely single to lunch or to go on a shopping trip. There are so many opportunities to help others with their burdens if we only look. And the blessing is for the doer as well as for the receiver.

BETTY J. ADAMS

No U-turn

Narrow is the way, which leadeth unto life. Matt. 7:14.

One dark night I found myself driving on a steep, narrow highway with no shoulder on the road. Suddenly my headlights caught the sign with the international emblem for "No U-turn!" With no shoulder on the road I could instantly imagine how hazardous it would be to try to make a U-turn on that windy, narrow grade.

My next thought was of a popular bumper sticker that reads "If you're headed in the wrong direction, God allows U-turns." This was in direct contrast to the No U-turn sign I had just encountered. What was the difference? In silent darkness I drove on in deepest thought.

The difference was apparent. Yes, if we're headed in the wrong direction, God indeed not only allows U-turns, but very much encourages such action. In fact, God is continually seeking ways to woo us back to the right road, much the way I imagine an ardent suitor courts the one he desires to marry. But God is far more loving, attentive, creative, and persistent in the way He goes about winning us to Himself.

Furthermore, God has given us a good road map in both the living and the written Word so we can know we are on the right road. With heaven as our goal, once we are on the right road there is no reason to make a dangerous U-turn.

Once we're secure on His vantage ground, headed toward heaven, I picture God fervently encouraging us to make no U-turns, but to keep going along that narrow, steep, upward grade with all the power and protection He's eager to give us.

After seeing the No U-turn sign that night on the narrow highway, I've made a commitment to make no spiritual U-turns on my way to heaven. We're just too close to the end of earth's history to turn back now.

Won't you join me in a firm resolve to stay on the path that leads to eternal life?

Lord, I'm on my way. I don't want to make any U-turns or turn back today. Guide, guard, and bless my path that I may arrive at my heavenly destination.

JUDY COULSTON

He's Coming

For yet in a very little while, He who is coming
will come, and will not delay. Heb. 10:37, NASB.

My husband's work requires him to travel for days—and sometimes for weeks—at a time. These times of separation are difficult for both of us. We keep in touch with frequent letters and phone calls, but these are not the same as having him here.

I've learned to cope during these times by doing a special project to surprise him, something I know will especially please him. All the while I am planning toward the day of his return. The night before he returns, I am up late, making sure the house is spick-and-span, that his favorite food is prepared, that there are flowers on the table, the nightstand, the dresser, everywhere!

When I pick him up at the airport the children are clean and tidy, and I am dressed and groomed in the way he likes best. All this effort is never wasted. He always admires the clean house, comments on my appearance, and appreciates any special things I have done for him while he is away. My chief consolation during the times of absence is knowing that the homecoming will be so tender, so special, so exquisite.

While I am making all these preparations, my heavenly Bridegroom reminds me of another homecoming that He is preparing for me. He is eager that I should be delighted with His preparations. He is planning a mansion for me, decorating it expressly for my personality. He is filling it inside and out with flowers that will never die. He tells me that the feast that He is preparing for me will satisfy my keenest tastes and keep me young forever. He daily tells me that He longs for us to be together, face-to-face, and He promises that the homecoming, the marriage, will be so tender, so exquisite, as if I were the only one.

Just as I plan for my husband's return, we must work and plan so we are ready when Jesus comes. There are character traits and habits to train, parts of lives to clean and reorganize so that when He comes He too will be able to delight in us. The amazing thing is that He even helps us get ready.

Does your heart fill with longing to see Him? Oh, mine does!

SARAH L. BURT

Fifteen on the Windowsill

*Either what woman having ten pieces of silver, if she lose
one piece, doth not light a candle, and sweep the house,
and seek diligently till she find it? Luke 15:8.*

The blizzard of 1996 had come to Washington, D.C., and the entire city
became a winter wonderland with approximately 30 inches of beautiful, white snow. The driveway and the walkway to my house and the street
in front were impassable. We had definitely been snowed in.

It was exciting at first, but after three days passed and no snowplow had
come through our neighborhood, it became a bit frustrating. My husband
and I were trying to figure out what to do when suddenly the doorbell rang.
A young man with a shovel in hand asked if we wanted our snow shoveled.
He did a good job cleaning the walk and driveway and shoveled a pathway
so the car could drive onto the street to the main thoroughfare. Our problem was solved.

We decided to go to the post office, but when we were ready to go my
husband asked, "Where are my keys?" We looked on his desk where he
usually put them, but they weren't there.

I had a duplicate key for the cars, but there were other keys we had
to find—keys to open the doors of the church and doors to various
church departments. I searched everywhere, upstairs and downstairs,
praying as I searched.

At that point I could see that my husband had begun to weaken from
the stress. I was sure God knew my husband's physical condition, and in
His time He would lead us to those keys. I took another look on the desk
and in the desk drawers.

Suddenly the words "Look outside" came to my mind. Immediately I
went to the door, opened it, and looked outside. Because it was very cold, I
just stuck my head out. And there on the windowsill by the door lay the 15
missing keys. My husband had laid them there while cleaning the snow
from his boots.

*When the lady in the Bible found her coin, she called her friends to rejoice
with her. So now I rejoice in You for helping me find the keys. You strengthen
my faith.*   ANNIE B. BEST

Labor Pains

I hear a cry of a woman in labor, a groan as
of one bearing her first child. Jer. 4:31, NIV.

Cheryl is my neighbor. When I talked to her Sunday she was very pregnant and very uncomfortable, as the baby was due the next day. But no word came Monday or Tuesday. I saw her at a restaurant Wednesday night. Nothing was happening. Thursday passed. Friday morning her husband told me they had been in the hospital overnight but had been sent home. She had been so uncomfortable and had had pains severe enough that she had not slept in almost 36 hours. She had a doctor's appointment that afternoon. I saw her afterward, walking around the block, stopping from time to time because of the pain. Friday evening Dave reported that the pains were severe enough that Cheryl was in tears.

I took a loaf of fresh bread over to them a couple hours later. Cheryl said the pains were coming about every five minutes. Her previous delivery had been by Cesarean, so she was not sure what to expect and was so tired and so uncomfortable she was dreading what lay ahead. I was concerned and worried, as she was almost worn out and real labor had not even started. I began praying for her in earnest.

I also started thinking about a Bible survey I had done earlier in the book of Jeremiah. Perhaps you remember that God had told Jeremiah not to marry. So it is interesting that he writes about the trouble women face. Nine times he likens real trouble and anguish to that of a woman in labor. I am convinced that if we women did not forget the pain of labor, none of us would ever have more than one child. Somehow, through inspiration, Jeremiah understood the pain of women.

Jeremiah identified with the disenfranchised, those whose pain was ignored by the world. But Jeremiah also brings us the promise that God will always be with us if we turn to Him. He says in Jeremiah 31:13: "I will turn their mourning into gladness; I will give them comfort and joy instead of sorrow" (NIV).

Thank You, Lord, for understanding what we are going through at all times. God bless little Anne Marie, born Friday night. Be with us today, giving us gladness, comfort, and joy.   ARDIS DICK STENBAKKEN

The Last Straw

Cast all your anxiety on him because he cares for you. 1 Peter 5:7, NIV.

We had just returned from our first family vacation in six years. I felt fit and well and ready to tackle anything. The very next day the blow fell! My brother, Roy, had terminal cancer. No longer did I feel ready to tackle anything. Every fiber of my being screamed inside that I couldn't, wouldn't, didn't want to face yet another death. It wasn't fair. I couldn't cope with it.

For the next few days I went through the familiar motions—escorting my brother to his examinations and scans, talking with the doctors, the oncologist, the nurses, and putting on a cheerful face when I went into my brother's room, and then letting the cloud descend again as I left the hospital.

I felt really rebellious. As far as I was concerned, God had sent just a bit too much. My brother was too young to die. Mutinous thoughts rolled around, sapping my energy and making me really unhappy. I realized I couldn't go on like this. It was something that I just had to cope with; I knew I was deliberately denying myself the strength I needed. God was already giving me the strength to deal with Roy; now I needed the strength to deal with myself.

As soon as I turned to Him, He was there. The dark cloud lifted, and although the sadness was still inside, I was no longer wasting precious energy on fruitless mutterings. I was able to bring my brother home. My cheerfulness was no longer an act. It was a privilege to care for Roy and to make him comfortable, and we were able to share precious hours together.

There is no greater privilege than to care for someone in the last hours of life and to be with them when they close their eyes in their last sleep. One is very aware at that time of the fragility of life. God did not create us to die. He did not send sickness and sorrow into this world. It grieves Him as much as it does us to witness pain and distress. He longs to put His loving arms around us. He longs more than we do for the day when sickness, sadness, and death will be banished. Until then, He offers His strength to help us deal with whatever comes our way. If you feel that you just can't take any more, turn to Him. You will find you can.

AUDREY BALDERSTONE

Palacio Real

He carefully watches over all those who love Him, but He will not save the wicked from the consequences of their sins. Ps. 145:20, Clear Word.

We were being true tourists in Europe. After spending most of the early part of the day shopping for souvenirs, my husband, sister, and I attempted to visit a palace, only to find that it was closed for the day. We were all disappointed, but each of us seemed to want to do something different next. It was not too late in the afternoon, so I wanted to continue to shop. My husband was ready to try another Spanish meal, and my sister had had enough of both and was ready to head back to our hotel to rest. So we decided to each go our own way.

My sister felt she could catch a taxi back to the hotel alone, but somehow my husband felt he and I should at least see her to a taxi, as we were on the way to continue shopping and to eat.

It was broad daylight as we approached the nearest intersection; my husband was walking a few paces ahead and my sister was walking by my side. We noticed a group of three young men standing on the sidewalk watching us. Just after we passed them, we met two older couples walking toward the young men. Within seconds we heard a loud scream and turned around to see one of the men attacking one of the women with a knife. He knocked the woman down in the middle of the street, trying to get her belongings. Her scream attracted so much attention that the attackers ran across the street into an alley. We stayed long enough to make sure the woman was all right, then decided to return to the hotel together.

So much could have gone wrong. The woman could have been killed. We could have been robbed and hurt too. We were especially glad we had not left my sister alone.

Sometimes we feel everything is going just fine, but in a blink of an eye the devil will come along with devious plans of his own. Once we got back to our hotel, we prayed a prayer of thanks to the Lord for His loving care.

MARLA HINSON FORDHAM

Getting Lost

For thy name's sake lead me, and guide me. Ps. 31:3.

My family was new in Cyprus. After our first church service there we went home to get something before heading out for our lunch appointment. It was only a few miles from the church to our home, but there were several turns and streets involved. The road signs in Cyprus are so small that one can hardly see them—or there's no sign at all. But we drove on, feeling confident that we knew how to get to our new home.

Unfortunately, we turned too soon. We drove around and around but couldn't find our way home. Everything seemed so different; we had turned so many times that we didn't even know how to get back to where we'd started.

After an hour of this our youngest daughter woke up from her nap in the back seat and asked, "Mommy, are we lost?"

"Yes, sweetheart," I admitted. "I think we are lost."

Finally, after driving around aimlessly for what seemed an eternity, we found our way back to the church. Then my daughter piped up, "Mommy, you know I just prayed right now, and Jesus answered my prayer!" (I wished I'd thought of that earlier!)

We tried to find our home once again, taking the same route, but this time we found the right street that connected to our road. We laughed when we realized that we had been driving around in circles. We were so close to the right street.

In my Christian experience it is easy to lose my way too, especially when I take a detour. When life seems too harsh, do I stop right where I am? When it seems nobody cares, do I give up? Or do I continue the journey and find the right way with Jesus?

And most of all, do I pray for guidance? Sometimes I too wander around too long before seeking guidance from the true Source of wisdom. Oh, for childlike faith that prays "right now."

Lord, You are the way, the truth, and the life. When it seems I'm going around in circles, help me to find my way to You. Lead me; guide me. Show me the way. JEMIMA D. ORILLOSA

What Good Are You?

For the Son of man came to save the lost. Matt. 18:11, margin, TEV.

During one of my mother's visits with us she bought me a pot scrubber. When she handed it to me she said, "It is a nice one. Try to keep it in good condition." I was baffled by her comment, because I knew that I could not use the scrubber without getting it messy. Sure enough, a few visits later she noticed the scrubber sitting in the pull-out shelf under the kitchen sink and wondered why I still had not used it.

A few years later one of my Christmas gifts from my parents was a pair of very nice leather gardening gloves. Again my mother cautioned me, "Be careful not to get them dirty." This time I voiced my frustration and teasingly reminded her of the pot scrubber. After all, the very nature and function of pot scrubbers and gardening gloves includes getting dirty. Although I had some fun teasing her about it, I undoubtedly have inherited that same senseless tendency. People harass me because I cover up the mats in my car to keep them clean.

Fortunately, not everyone is quite as quirky as my mother and I are. Most people can enjoy using things for their actual purpose. Unfortunately, there are many people who view their personal function as Christians the way I protect the mats in my car. They socialize only with other Christians. They volunteer their time to work only for those who are already Christians. They minister only to the people already in their church. They are like nice, clean pot scrubbers sitting on the shelf. What good are they?

I am so grateful that Jesus not only died for us but also lived His life as an example for us. He did not come to earth and live a good but passive life until He eventually died. He realized His mission. He saved the lost. And He put His hands in and proactively got dirty in order to save us!

You and I each have a mission too. Is our Christianity sitting on a shelf because we want to keep it covered up, protected, or "clean"? It's time to realize the mission God gave us and begin fulfilling it today.

As I think about my plans for today and this week, Father, help me to serve those around me who are in need. Help me get my hands dirty serving You. Help me to fulfill Your purpose in putting me here.

LAURA PASCUAL DANCEK

I Shall Supply All Your Needs

*For your heavenly Father knows your needs
before you even ask. Matt. 6:8, Clear Word.*

I had decided to stay home with our daughter for at least her first two years. This decision put us under quite a financial strain, but we felt it was in the best interest of our family.

One day we awoke with just enough food for breakfast and a light lunch—there was nothing beyond that. During family devotion we especially thanked God for His provision and care extended to our small family.

About midday my husband was impressed to walk to the post office, a mile or two from our home. He decided to walk in order to save the limited amount of fuel he would need for the scheduled evangelistic meeting in the evening. Shortly after he left, an elderly church sister arrived at the door. With a timid smile she handed me a basket. It contained freshly baked bammies (a bread made from cassava), fish, fruits, vegetables, and yams. I stood at the door holding the basket, not knowing what to say. Finally she broke the silence. "While I was working in the garden, I was impressed to take this basket to you. I felt that I had to come now and not later."

I thanked her, and as soon as she left I put the basket down and headed to my room to praise God for His special care of my family.

Before I could get up off my knees my husband came in with bags of groceries in his arms. "You will never believe this," he said. "Mother sent us a letter with some money. She just wanted to know that her first granddaughter was fine, but she did not want to send an empty letter." Because of the exchange rate where we lived, when converted into our currency the money lasted to the end of the month. There was even enough to put away in our little savings account.

God's storehouse is never empty. While we were praying, He was providing for our needs. He is just waiting to meet your needs today and always too.

GLORIA GREGORY

Disappointment to Joy

*Now glory be to God who by his mighty power at work within us is able
to do far more than we would ever dare to ask or even dream of—infinitely
beyond our highest prayers, desires, thoughts, or hopes. Eph. 3:20, TLB.*

B ecause of a change in assignment, I recently had to drive from Norfolk,
Virginia, to Scott Air Force Base in southern Illinois. Just before sunset
I decided to stop for the night at a little town in the mountains. Once settled in my room, I looked at my map to see where the next fairly large town
was so I could find a worship service to attend in the morning. I got up
early and dressed for church.

I arrived about 10:30 at the town in the West Virginia mountains that I
had decided on. I found two churches and called the first one and spoke to
someone about directions. Because I was unfamiliar with the town I had a
hard time explaining to him where I was, but he thought he knew and gave
me very explicit directions. I began driving in the direction I thought I was
supposed to go and ended up on a back road that seemed to be winding
higher and higher into the mountains. I was becoming more and more
frustrated; the directions seemed all wrong. On the verge of tears, I prayed.
*Maybe he thought I was on the other side of the freeway, and I should go in the
opposite direction.* I tried that, and the directions were perfect.

Soon I was at the church. I slipped in the door just as the pastor finished
his sermon, so I quietly went back out the door before anyone saw me. I was
so disappointed that I had missed the service, but I did want to let the gentleman I had spoken to on the phone know I had made it OK. I asked a man
to let him know I was all right. However, the man insisted that I come in
and join them for lunch. I was still upset about missing the service, but I
finally agreed, and was very glad I did. Everyone was so friendly—it was a
wonderful time of fellowship. If we put our trust in God, what He has
planned is infinitely better than all that we can think or imagine.

*Life doesn't always turn out as we hope, but You always care for us. I may
never get back to West Virginia, Lord, but I look forward to seeing You and
those dear people in heaven.*　　　　　　　　　　　　　　　NANETTE BURKES

Friends

A friend loveth at all times, and a brother is born for adversity. Prov. 17:17.

We had just finished the church service when someone touched me on the shoulder and said, "I am Angelica." That's when I remembered we had agreed, by phone, that we would talk. So we went to a small room. When I saw her the first time, I thought she was very young, and couldn't imagine she might be married and have three adolescent children. She was dressed inappropriately for church. Her hands shook constantly and her eyes were red, the result of a sleepless night full of weeping. She told me that she was taking 28 pills a day.

She also told me she had been baptized as an adolescent, and that she normally attended the church meetings. I had never seen her. I listened carefully, and we agreed to meet again. After prayer I asked if I could give her a hug. I wanted to let her know as much love as possible and that I understood her tragedy, that she could depend on me. She began to cry uncontrollably. As we were leaving she said, "I am 49 years old and cannot remember that anybody has ever given me such a loving embrace."

Many years have passed. Angelica is my friend today. I learned to love her and accept her as she is. She no longer dresses as she did, and she helps those in greatest need. I have never been able to forget what she said after that prayer. Constantly I think of the many people around me who need a friendly hug, a smile, acknowledgment, or a simple act of empathy. From the contacts that I have with so many, my conclusion is that behind almost every face there is a tragedy. Even for those who are always smiling. Many times these are the ones who suffer the most. How very important it is to have a friendly hug and an attentive ear during the difficult moments of life.

Lord, You have given us an opportunity. More than opportunity, it is a privilege. In helping others we forget ourselves with the small or large problems we may have. Let us place ourselves in Your service, God, to be instruments in Your hands today and always.   CRISTINA FERNANDEZ

One Step Forward, Two Steps Back

I have loved you with an everlasting love;
I have drawn you with loving-kindness. Jer. 31:3, NIV.

Wearily I climbed the stairs to our apartment. It had been a long, stress-filled day. I was tired. But stepping through the front door, I was greeted by a wide, toothless smile from my 7-month-old daughter, Kelsi-Anne. Her expression of utter joy at seeing me made me feel special and loved. Fatigue slipped away in that moment.

Instead of picking her up right away, I sat on the floor across the room from her and called, "Kelsi-Anne, come to Mommie. Come on."

With an unwavering smile and her eyes fixed on my face, she pushed, pulled, kicked, and rolled herself in my direction. It didn't matter to her that for every inch of progress, she seemed to slip back two inches. Her determination to reach me was heartwarming. I could have picked her up and carried her, but I knew she needed to perfect her crawl.

After a few minutes she did make progress, however. When she reached me, her squeals of delight showed her ecstasy at reaching her goal. I held her close, my own heart pounding with love for her. I had never known such love until I became a mother. Now I began to understand a little better God's sacrifice when He sent His only Son to die for us.

Dropping to my knees that night, I prayed to be like a child in my faith journey. And like Kelsi-Anne, to keep my eyes fixed on my goal and on my Maker. Despite the challenges, I am determined to pull, push, and roll my way to Him with joy in my heart and heaven in my vision. He has called me and has promised to be waiting for me.

Thank You, heavenly Parent, for showing me, through my baby, that if I keep my eyes on You, what I regard as one step forward and two steps backward is progress in Your eyes. Thank You for staying with me in my spiritual crawl to perfection. Thank You for the insightful gift of a mother's love.

APPY NIYO BENGGON

Through the Fire

When thou passest through the waters, I will be with thee; and through the rivers, they shall not overflow thee: when thou walkest through the fire, thou shalt not be burned; neither shall the flame kindle upon thee. Isa. 43:2.

Our daughter Lisa came to visit me while my husband was away on business.

Shortly after 5:00 a.m. I heard a loud noise like an explosion or a brick being thrown through a window. Thinking it was the latter, I jumped out of bed and rushed down the hallway. Simultaneously, Lisa had gotten off the couch and started up the stairs to meet me, exclaiming, "Mama, the house is on fire! We've got to get out of here!"

I saw flames leaping toward the ceiling in the TV area. The TV had exploded from the heat of the fire.

Lisa dialed 911, and we rushed out of the house. Within five minutes all emergency vehicles arrived. The firefighters fought the fire for about three and a half hours as we stood with most of our neighbors in shock and amazement. It was an electrical fire that had spread rapidly through the entire house. We had lived there for more than 20 years, and everything we owned was destroyed by flames, smoke, or water.

Friends shared their home with us for two months. Then we moved to another house. Our friends, relatives, church members, coworkers, neighbors, and even strangers who had heard about our plight helped support us in the time of difficulty.

About seven months later our house was repaired enough that we could move back in, although we still did not have furniture. For a few weeks we slept on the newly carpeted floors.

Through the experience we learned to trust in Jesus for everything in life. We know He was with us that night of the fire, protecting us, and He was with us in the months that followed. Indeed our God is so good!

CAROLYN T. HINSON

Our Unwanted Enemy

And it is he who will supply all your needs from his riches in glory,
because of what Christ Jesus has done for us. Phil. 4:19, TLB.

Loneliness gate-crashes into the lives of women at unexpected times. It either blunders into our world, leaving us visibly barren and bereaved, or quietly leaks into our lives as rapidly as blotting paper absorbs fallen ink.

Loneliness takes hold of our hearts when we realize there is no one to share our deepest desires, our darling dreams, and our dreadful doubts. It clutches at our minds when we stand in a crowded room and watch our spouse share a hearty joke with a fellow worker or watch our children share silly, giggly secrets with their friends. We then know that we are utterly alone.

The feelings of aloneness and isolation are often a part of womanhood. To live with it, without fear, is the challenge. Even those of us with the most loving marriages, the most successful careers, the most rewarding mother-hoods, sometimes have to wrestle with our unwanted enemy—loneliness.

Yet we are never alone. When we invite God to peek into our hearts, to understand our fears, to encourage our dreams, to securely hold our hand, we have a companion who touches our innermost needs. We have a friend who leads us to other friends.

For the times in my life when I have been wrapped in the clutches of loneliness, God has always, without fail, answered my prayers. In all our years of ministry and moving our home, God has frequently led me to a special friend, either in the church or in the ministry or in the neighbor-hood. He has led me to Sally, who shares my love of badminton. He has given me the gift of Amelia and Marci, who cause tears to dance down my cheeks as we laugh together. He has introduced me to Karie, who under-stands and encourages me in my yearning to share God. He has guided me to Janet and Dolly and Cathy and Eve, whose quiet, gentle conversations soothe my sometimes stressed-out spirit.

If loneliness is your companion at the moment, try not to be depressed or discouraged by it. Instead, express your desire for friends to God. Then with excitement and expectancy, watch as God meets your need.

MARY BARRETT

Take It to the Lord

So if the Son sets you free, you will be free indeed. John 8:36, NIV.

Less than two weeks after I was baptized I really messed up. But I was lucky. No one was hurt. No one found out. And I'm not going to tell you what I did. I will tell you that my first thought was to wonder what lie I could tell if I needed to protect myself. The whole picture came into focus, and the enormity of it all became clear.

I couldn't believe I'd done it, and was distressed over my first reaction. I didn't think God liked me much right then. I know I didn't like myself at all. God seemed gone, gone, gone. This was all new territory to me. Had this happened a year earlier, I wouldn't have even given God a thought.

"What do you do when you really mess up?" I asked a friend on the phone a few days later.

"Honey, you'll just have to take it to the Lord" was her recommendation.

Ouch! Even if I could find the Lord, I didn't want to tell Him about it. The next day I asked a friend at work the same question. Her answer was close to the first one: "Take it to God."

I rather expected at least an admonition not to do it anymore or something, but God didn't say anything, and neither did I. It seemed that He was waiting patiently. I was just waiting. I remember thinking, *Here I am; now it is Your move. You know I am so sorry.* Maybe He was waiting for me to look at Him, but try as I might I felt I could not raise my head. I couldn't lift it up. I was sure I couldn't do it. I couldn't face Him.

Then the hand that was holding me by the shoulder gently drew me to His side. He wrapped His arms of love around me. I was fine.

Of all the possible things I had imagined or expected, this was not one of them. How great You are over all the earth, and how great You are to me. Your forgiveness and acceptance are beyond my comprehension. Praise the Lord.

ALICE HEATH PRIVE

A Friend in Jesus

Casting all your care upon him; for he careth for you. 1 Peter 5:7.

When the worship leader announced the opening song, it took effort to keep the groan to myself. Of all the songs in the hymnal, why did it have to be "What a Friend We Have in Jesus"? I first learned that song in our local language 30 years ago. We sang it in English in high school and in college. Translated into Amharic, it was a favorite in Ethiopia. Now here it was again in French. *Why that old song again? I am not going to sing it again!*

As the song progressed, however, I couldn't keep my eyes off one participant on the platform. I couldn't hear her voice, but her face glowed and her eyes shone as she sang.

" 'We should never be discouraged' "—she shook her head slightly, almost imperceptibly. " 'Can we find a friend so faithful?' " Her look showed a challenge. By now I was humming. By the third stanza I was singing as loudly as the sister next to me. " 'Precious Saviour, still our refuge.' " The words burst alive with meaning. Hadn't He been our refuge just the night before?

We were going to Lusaka, Zambia, from Lubumbashi, Zaire, when my husband found the headlights of an oncoming truck too bright. We moved to the edge of the road, off the asphalt. The truck roared by. That was close! We stopped to check the tires. From the way our son Paul's voice sounded, I knew it wasn't just a flat tire. The sharp edge of the asphalt road had cut into both left tires. "Lord, if it were one tire, we could solve the problem. But two tires, at this time and in this place . . . This is Your problem, for we can't solve it," I whispered.

We tried to stop many vehicles for help, but only one stopped. His tires didn't match ours, but he said he had a friend just a few miles ahead who could help. He drove my husband there and back and helped us get back on the road. At almost midnight we reached our destination.

"Is there trouble anywhere?" Yes, there is. But there is nothing we can't take to the Lord in prayer, no trouble that He has not made provision for. What a Friend! When pressures and trials abound, I now sing or hum this song.

BIENVISA LADION-NEBRES

What Selma Taught Me

*God is our refuge and strength,
an ever-present help in trouble. Ps. 46:1, NIV.*

Selma came from Sarajevo and into our lives. She was only 11 when she
fled with her Christian Croatian mother on the last train out to "freedom." Before the train left the station, she hugged her Muslim father. Tears
were in his eyes. They had lost their home, he had lost his business, and
now it seemed that they might lose each other.

"Don't worry," said Selma. "I'll see you in 10 days." It would be four
years before they were reunited.

She then moved from place to place, always trying to stay one step
ahead of the war. They lived one summer on strawberries and cottage
cheese because that was the only local food available. They bathed in water
left out in the sun to warm because there was no electricity.

I met her when aid workers brought her to England for a summer of
freedom. The incredible suffering that Selma had been through did not
seem to have damaged her zest for life. She had learned some deep lessons,
and she shared these with us.

She said, "God has always been there for me, even though many of my
friends have turned away from Him. Some of my classmates have died; they
are like little buds of life that will never blossom. But whenever I say goodbye to a friend, I always say I will see you in 10 days, because this life on
earth is only for 10 days compared to heaven.

"I have learned that all I can own is what I can carry in two bags, comfortably, because each time we have to run, that is all I can take from one
place to the next. It has helped me to see what is really important in life."

Selma laughed and played, and even picked strawberries with us. When
she finally had to return home, she wrote a card to our children. "Thank you,"
it said, "for giving me back some of the childhood I had lost in the war."

Thank you, Selma, for all you shared with us, and for all we learned
from you.

*Lord, thank You for reminding me this morning that what really matters
in life is love, hope, friendship, and trust in You!* KAREN HOLFORD

Thoughts on a Dying Easter Lily

When the perishable puts on the imperishable, and the mortal puts on immortality, then shall come to pass the saying that is written: "Death is swallowed up in victory. O death, where is thy victory? O death, where is thy sting?" 1 Cor. 15:54, 55, RSV.

This morning when I walked into my kitchen I was appalled. My beautiful Easter lily stood forlorn in the window. Two of its blossoms were drooping; another was already shriveled. Only two weeks ago it had been vibrantly green with seven perfect buds. Once a symbol of resurrection, it was now well on its way to death.

To make things worse, beyond the glass, where there should have been a carpet of green, white snow blanketed the lawn. And more was falling. *This is no time for winter,* I thought. *It is spring!*

The contradiction of Easter lily and dead blooms, resurrection and death, is all too obvious in our world. Yes, Christ has conquered death. Even so, plants, animals, and people die. Things just are not right. Death comes all too regularly to interrupt life. Decay overtakes my prettiest blooms.

The dismay I felt this morning over death, in spite of the resurrection, Paul called "groaning in travail," having labor pains (Rom. 8:22, RSV). I remember those! My husband still teases me about squeezing his hand until it hurt!

I know there will not be many more snowfalls this spring. I know that if I plant the lily bulb I will have buds and blooms next year. Likewise, I know that death and winter will not last forever. The day will come when the "trumpet will sound, and the dead will be raised imperishable, and we shall be changed" (1 Cor. 15:52, RSV).

Then there will be no more dead Easter lilies or snowstorms when the daffodils are trying to bloom. Mortality will give way to immortality. We shall sing, "Death is swallowed up in victory. O death, where is thy victory? O death, where is thy sting?"

But until then, Lord of the resurrection, give me Your divine patience to hope and wait. Let me also share the warmth of Your love with others while we all hope and wait for the day when Easter lilies will last forever.

NANCY JEAN VYHMEISTER

The Impossible Is Easy

For nothing is impossible with God. Luke 1:37, NIV.

I'm sorry. The next 24 hours are crucial. Your son either will begin to get well or will die in that time."

Alex was 6 years old and in the first grade when his head started to ache and he began to experience serious stomach upset. He had always been such a strong, intelligent little boy that it seemed impossible to believe the doctor's crushing words. And yet there they were, stark and plain.

We had taken Alex to a doctor right away, because it was obvious his condition was serious. He had no explanation or diagnosis for Alex's condition. A second doctor examined him but had no diagnosis either. Finally, the third doctor suspected meningitis. He ordered a test of the spinal fluid. My husband and I clung to each other, crying as Alex cried. The result: meningitis. The doctor gave no hope—he could do nothing more. The next six hours would tell the story.

That night Alex's condition worsened. His face was extremely pale; his stomach would keep nothing down, not even water; the sedatives were giving him no release from his pain or fever.

The doctors ordered another spinal fluid exam. The virus was multiplying fast. We looked down at a little boy who was going to die and turned to the only source of help—to God in prayer.

That was 10 years ago. Alex is a strong young man now. He has never had a relapse. The impossible had not only happened, but looked easy. Science and medicine had not been able to offer help or hope. Only God had been able to make a difference.

Father God, today we face new challenges. Sometimes the situations seem impossible to us. But if it is Your will, You can do the impossible and even make it look easy. Today I depend on You and Your will for my life.

IVANI ISABEL MELO DE ANA

Easter Miracle

*The Lord will sustain him on his sickbed and
restore him from his bed of illness. Ps. 41:3, NIV.*

It was Good Friday, a warm, sunny day. Down at the end of the hospital corridor, near the special care unit, I saw my friend Karen sitting in her wheelchair, staring out the window. Her father was in the intensive-care unit on a respirator. She and the family were being encouraged by doctors and nurses to remove the life supports.

Karen was distraught. "How can I tell the doctor to remove the life supports?" she agonized.

Earlier that day, using a spelling board, her dad had spelled out the words "I love you, and I want to see you in heaven." My friend talked to me about her father, her special friend, and what a blessing he had been to her. "He was always there when I needed him," she said. "He knew the right things to say and to do to make me feel better. He's been a special help to others, too. How can I possibly decide that it is time for him to go?"

Good Friday. The perfect reminder of the resurrection. Still she didn't feel she could decide to turn off her father's life supports. We talked for a while, then prayed about it. "Please, Lord, take this decision out of Karen's hands," I asked. "We want to leave this matter in Your hands, to let You decide."

On Easter Sunday Karen's father was doing better, so they removed most of the life supports. They kept him on oxygen, and by Wednesday they moved him to a regular room and took him off the oxygen completely. The Lord had given him more time to live. Karen and I knew it was a direct answer to prayer. No longer did she have to make a painful decision. God had made it for her in a very positive way.

Thank You, Lord, for this Easter miracle. We don't always see such direct answers to our prayers. Perhaps it is because many times we don't trust You enough to ask and believe. Help me today to not only give You my problems, but to trust You with them.

DARLENE YTREDAL BURGESON

But It Looked So Good!

The Lord seeth not as man seeth; for man looketh on the outward appearance, but the Lord looketh on the heart. 1 Sam. 16:7.

I had grown very attached to my tooth, but it was becoming expensive, both in money and pain. It had been oversensitive for five years; now I was unable to sleep for the throbbing. It had been filled and refilled, drilled and redrilled, tested and retested. The dentists were inferring that the pain was in my head! That tooth looked good on the surface—the enamel was clean and strong, the filling was perfect. But the pain drove me to concede that extraction was the only way I would be able to eat and sleep again.

Actually, the extraction was not as traumatic as I had anticipated. Afterward, the dentist asked if he could dissect my molar. We discovered that it was cracked in quarters and had a hole in the center that led out the side of a root, directly into my bloodstream and sensitive nerves. He marveled that I had not suffered infection along with the pain, or that I could have waited so long to have it fixed.

I began to wonder how many things in my life I might consider comforting but which the Lord looks upon as an indulgence, eroding the very foundations of my Christianity—even though on the surface they may not look too bad, and may even be socially acceptable.

I thought about how I judge a sister for her obviously harmful, and perhaps socially unacceptable, habits when I cannot see the pain in her heart. Do I pray and wait for an opportunity to listen to her pain and help her bring it to the Lord, or do I pass a judgment along the ever-swaying wire of Christian gossip?

I must seek to understand and comfort, never condemn. Do I assume that because someone looks good on the outside they have no troubles on the inside?

As I seek to understand others, the Lord seems to send comfort to my own heart.

Thank You, Lord, for looking into my own heart and seeing my needs.

LINDA FRANKLIN

Cobwebs and Snow

*Thou wilt keep him in perfect peace, whose mind
is stayed on thee: because he trusteth in thee. Isa. 26:3.*

The windows that look out into the woods and bird feeders nestled there constantly call to me. Getting my work done never seems important when I look out to see the birds beginning to change into their brilliant spring and summer wardrobe of yellows, purples, oranges, and iridescent blues and browns.

The deer wander through the yard to sample the luscious new grass. It must taste better than that in the meadows where they live, because they visit often throughout the day. They are changing their dark winter coats for a brighter tan-orange for summer. Some of their flanks are swelling with the new spring feed and the promise of new life in May.

What is this? Large flakes of fluffy white snow! The last days of April! A strong north wind swirls the flakes into multiple small white tornadoes. "How beautiful!" I exclaim as I sink into my grandmother's rocking chair to watch. The view consumes me now as I turn my weary mind to my Lord. He always knows what will relax and calm me.

Fluffy snow fills the spiderwebs in the crooks of the huckleberry bushes, and the floor of the woods looks like a cotton patch. Snow piles up on the tops of the feeders, contrasting brilliantly with the flashing colors of the birds as they come and go to eat.

With my eyes filled with the beauty around me, my mind whirls with thoughts of sin and white snow and forgiveness. Then His perfect peace caresses my soul as promised, and I thank my Lord for filling the cobwebs of my life with the fluffy white snow of His forgiveness. "Though your sins be as scarlet, they shall be as white as snow" (Isa. 1:18).

You are an awesome God. Please fill my life today with the gentle peace that comes from You. Cover my sins, leaving my heart with a new, clean landscape of Your purity.
MARJORY BUTTON BODI

Emergency Room Vigil

*God is our refuge and strength,
an ever-present help in trouble. Ps. 46:1, Clear Word.*

The phone call came just as I was leaving to attend a committee meeting. The nurse in the emergency room told me that our son had been in a terrible car accident and wasn't expected to live. She said my husband and I should get to the hospital as soon as possible.

We called the pastor and asked him to pray for our son, Jack, and have the committee pray as well.

When we arrived in the emergency room, we were directed into a side room. The doctor came in and told us Jack had a serious head injury and other complications. Our son might not survive the night.

Since we were not allowed to see him for a little while, my husband and I prayed. It was the most difficult prayer we ever prayed. We were not only asking for our son's healing, we were asking that the Lord's will be done. If He saw that healing Jack was not His will, we would accept this answer to our prayers.

The following five days were critical. The neurologist couldn't assure us that our son would ever recognize us or be able to function as a normal person. Many prayers were prayed for our son. Many family members and friends came to visit him in the hospital.

The evening of the fifth day one of his best friends was trying to converse with Jack when all of a sudden our son started talking sense and knew who was visiting him.

His friend came running out of the critical-care unit, laughing and shouting, "He knows me!" A week later Jack left the hospital.

Jack still had a ways to go to full recovery, but he was able to graduate that spring with his high school class. The Lord is good.

Lord, it strengthens my faith to know You still heal people today. I know that You always do what You know is best. Give me faith that keeps trusting You even if You choose not to heal someone I love.

PATRICIA MULRANEY KOVALSKI

Life's Lavender

It is a good thing to give thanks unto the Lord. Ps. 92:1.

My husband and I were worshiping with Christian believers in the Crimea, a short drive from the Black Sea. We had stayed at the church in Simferopol to greet members before coming to the pastor's house for a home-cooked meal.

Now, after several courses of wonderful Ukrainian dishes, we pushed back from the table to try to catch our breath. I was always overwhelmed by the effort that my Soviet sisters put into a meal. Nothing was easy, and I knew it! I'd noticed the well in front of the house, where the family drew their water to cook meals, to bathe, and to do the family wash.

I remembered the rough dirt road leading up to the house, and even now I watched as their oldest son sat quietly in the background. He was home for the weekend from a sanitarium, where he was being treated for tuberculosis. The room was alive with the generous spirit of this family, but the hardships of their daily lives lurked in the shadows. Then there was the pain of this bright young son with a crippling disease. It was clear to me that their life was not a "bed of roses" by any stretch of the imagination.

On either end of the food-laden table, rose-colored drapes fluttered in the breeze. "What is that I smell?" I asked.

"Lavender," my host replied.

"It's wonderful!" I responded, and in a flash the pastor's young daughter was up and out of the back door. Moments later, she returned with a handful of the sweetest-smelling lavender I'd ever encountered. Again and again I held the blossoms up to drink in nature's perfume, while across the table from me the pastor's wife sat beaming. She was obviously pleased that they had produced something that I was so enthusiastic about.

"Yes," she said with a broad smile, "we're so fortunate to live in a field of lavender!"

How her words touched my heart! This spiritual sister of mine had modeled Christ, and I remembered her convincing smile long after I left the warmth of her home. I vowed that in the future, even when circumstances were less than perfect, I too would choose to praise God for the "lavender" in life!

ROSE OTIS

A Miracle!

*Many believed in his name, when they
saw the miracles which he did. John 2:23.*

In the summer of 1994 my husband, Wayne, discovered a lump behind
his right ear. Naturally he became quite alarmed, and consulted our
physician immediately. The lump refused to respond to conservative treatment. Our physician then referred Wayne to a skilled oncologist who, after
completing a number of tests, decided to operate.

As soon as our friends and relatives became aware of the situation, they
offered remedies, prayers, and assurance. Meanwhile Wayne was experiencing fluctuations in his faith. I encouraged him to trust God and believe in
His power to take care of this troublesome lump.

On the day scheduled for the operation, we arrived at the hospital
much earlier than necessary. Just after Wayne was prepared for the operating room, we prayed once more that God would cause the lump to disappear, if it was within His will. After the prayer a blanket of peace
enshrouded us. Then the orderly wheeled Wayne out of the room.

A half hour passed. I started to doze, but was soon awakened by sound.
I looked up and there was Wayne, returning on a stretcher steered by an
orderly and a nurse. Still sedated from the anesthetic, he explained, with
some help from the nurse, that after the anesthesia was given, the team was
ready and the surgeon scrubbed. The doctor checked one last time for the
lump. It was not there! A miracle! There was no need for surgery. God had
tested our faith. He had given us a demonstration of His power at the
eleventh hour.

A sense of our awesome God surrounded us, and right there we offered
a prayer of praise and thanksgiving. In a short while we were on our way
home, still awestruck by the love of God.

Sometimes God answers yes and sometimes no. Although we might
never know the reason why, we can still trust Him to do what is best for us
because He is God. And He alone knows what the future holds.

MARIA G. MCCLEAN

Deep Roots

It was majestic in beauty, with its spreading boughs,
for its roots went down to abundant waters. Eze. 31:7, NIV.

The maple tree stands straight and tall, the tips of its branches reaching the top roofline of the house, protecting the deck from the westward evening sun.

Five years ago there was a violent electrical storm. After a night of heavy rain and howling winds, we awoke to find our large maple tree on the ground. Its strong trunk was split down the middle as if it had been attacked by a giant saw. It had taken 14 years for it to shade the porch from the late-evening sun. My husband took the chain saw and made a smooth cut close to the ground.

Late in the summer we observed a small shoot in the yard where the tree had stood. It fell prey to the lawn mower. Another shoot appeared, this time with a single maple leaf on it. I went out one day to discover our young grandson had broken it off to play with. We explained to him that it was a little tree trying to grow and that he should leave it alone.

The following spring a small, straight shoot appeared where the tree had once stood. It seemed to actually grow before our eyes. By the beginning of winter it stood nearly five feet tall. We feared for its life that hard winter, but it again leafed out with a small plumage of maple leaves. That year it doubled in height.

Early the next spring a severe ice storm covered all the trees and shrubs with a thin coat of ice right at the time of budding. Our young tree was bent halfway to the ground with the weight of the ice, its largest branch broken off. But once again it slowly began to straighten up, and new branches began to appear.

Now after only five years here stood a miracle of nature, as tall and stately as it had been before. But I remember that deep down below the ground are the old roots, the life of the tree, still strong and vital, providing life to the new tree above.

Like the tree, we are buffeted by the storms of life. But if we have deep roots, grounded in faith, we can rise up, defeat our adversaries, and become strong with each new trial. Like the tree, the unseen strength from within will restore us with vitality and new growth. All we have to do is establish our roots in the love of Jesus Christ.   BARBARA SMITH MORRIS

Getting Away

*And he [Jesus] said unto them, Come ye yourselves
apart into a desert place, and rest a while. Mark 6:31.*

Because Monday, April 28, was a new South African holiday called
Freedom Day, I decided to do all the cooking and laundry the day before so we could spend time out and not have to rush home. We visited the
Kirstenbosch National Botanical Gardens. People came from far and near
to visit this beautiful garden full of trees, shrubs, and plants from many
countries. Each is marked with its scientific name, common name, family
name, and place of origin.

The garden also has an herb section where blind folk can smell the fragrances of the different plants. A river runs through the garden that reminds me of the Garden of Eden. Guinea fowl roam freely. We saw one
family with a new chick, who was trying to keep pace with the parent fowls.

We have a special bench we like to sit on to reminisce. It was in this
garden that we spent many hours during our courting days. It was in this
garden that we had our wedding pictures taken. It was in this garden that
we admired the various species of the South African national flower, the
protea, and named our eldest daughter, Heidi. These memories are so precious to us.

It was on this last occasion at Kirstenbosch that we saw the most beautiful bird of birds—the sunbird. I had seen only pictures of them before,
but now I saw them for real—the breast of bright red, and bright metallic
green on head and back. There it was in all its beauty, flying from flower to
flower and on the highest branches of the tree.

It is so good to get away once in a while, having a chance to rest and
think about the blessings God has given in the past and to appreciate the
variety of God's goodness around us. I really enjoyed Kirstenbosch.

*Thank You for the invitation to leave my cares behind and to spend some
time with You, my Creator. It makes me want to plan to be with You in heaven!*

PRISCILLA ADONIS

Wanderwegs

You have made known to me the path of life; you will
fill me with joy in your presence. Ps. 16:11, NIV.

I caught bus 19 near the train station in Bern, Switzerland, and rode it to the end of the line. I followed the sidewalk around the circle to a signpost that read "Wanderweg." I had encountered this word before in various parks around Bern. Each time it identified a well-kept path for walking, jogging, or cycling. Each one had been an adventure. This one led through Elfenau Park.

The path led to a maze of interlocking wanderwegs, each one inviting me to explore the beauties of the countryside. I followed one along a knee-high field of corn. I sat for a while, watching swifts fly above a small, red-roofed village. I followed another path that looked down on the river, and spotted gray herons fishing from a log.

I took another wanderweg that led to the backwaters of the river, where I saw a pair of mute swans leading seven cygnets. Another path took me by a wall covered with wild roses and bushes laden with sweet-smelling white blossoms. I stopped beside a field of new-mown hay and breathed deeply of its earthy fragrance.

For two hours I wandered, paying little attention to direction. Finally my tired legs told me it was time to head home. I headed to the right and up a hill. At a crossing of paths, I found signs labeled with the destination at the end of each trail. I chose one that said "Elfanau Bus."

I'd had a good time alone, but I wished my husband could have been with me. That would have made it better still!

My life is like a wanderweg adventure, I mused. *There are many paths that make up the maze of my experience. A lot depends on which path I choose to follow. Sometimes my life's path goes up, and sometimes it goes down. Sometimes it is light with sunshine, but other times dark with shadows. Wherever my wandering takes me, I do not walk alone. The Saviour walks with me and shows me the way home again.* DOROTHY EATON WATTS

Rested Eyes

Come unto me, all ye that labour and are
heavy laden, and I will give you rest. Matt. 11:28.

Spring is my favorite time of the year. After a long, gray winter the earth seems to burst forth again, alive with hopes of better days to come. Almost suddenly the gray is replaced with vivid shades of greens, from the palest yellow green of the weeping willow to the deepest forest evergreen.

The redbuds are magnificent. The dogwoods dress in crisp, starched white. The flox paint the ground pale lavender. The golden tulips are brilliant. Stalwart irises pop their heads upward, smiling at the sun. Sweet fragrances of spring fill the air. The Master artist has a beautiful eye in designing the color scheme for each birth of spring.

The mountains of eastern Kentucky have been especially splendid this spring. The rugged terrain of the hills and valleys is becoming a hidden mystery again, shadowed by the newly budding leaves. I view God's handiwork each day as I make the 50-mile journey to work and home again. Although the colors of fall are absolutely breathtaking, I believe early spring is even more spectacular. What blessings I have received as I motor along, oohing and aahing over the panorama! What an inspirational way to begin and end each workday!

Working in the health-care setting, I see many people who are struggling. They fight against infirmities, heartaches, pain, despair, and heartbreak. It seems they don't have eyes to see nor energy to marvel over God's beautiful creation.

To all whose vision is clouded by pain and care, He invites, "Come, let Me give rest to your heart and mind. Let Me re-create your life; let Me give you new eyes, eyes with 20/20 vision to see the beauty of My love for you."

What a wonderful Saviour! The birth of this new spring coincides with the springing forth of new life in my heart. Although the way may not always be clearly defined, I can rest knowing that my loving Father is leading me by the hand. I can rejoice over the new creation He's making in me!

Lord, today give me rest as I put my hand in Yours. Give me new eyes that see Your love in all the beauty around me. CAROLYN BRACKETT KASSINGER

The Talkin' Bird

We know and rely on the love God has for us. God is love. 1 John 4:16, NIV.

When I moved to Alaska several years ago, I left behind family, friends, and a familiar lifestyle to begin a new way of living. My new husband's cousin told me something that has been a source of inspiration ever since. One day as we were walking down the path from our church in a bush village, she remarked, "Do you hear the little golden-crowned sparrow singing its three-note song? It's singing 'God Loves Me.'"

I listened carefully, and it really did sound like that was the song. Many times during the summers since then I have awakened in the early morning to hear "God loves me," a message I really needed.

Recently the little bird that lives in a tree outside my window sang only two notes: "God Loves." It sang this message several times before finally singing "God Loves Me." I wondered why it was giving me this message until later in the day when the opportunity came to share with a hurting daughter. I was able to tell her that "God loves" not only me, but all His children. That was what the bird was telling me when it sang "God loves."

One evening at worship I shared these thoughts. Then I asked a 3-year-old girl, who had been listening carefully, "What does the birdie say?"

"I don't know, Beverly," she replied. "I've never seen no talkin' bird."

Her response made me wonder if I am open to all His messages of love. I pray that I am, even hearing it from a "talkin' bird."

Not only does He tell us in the Scriptures that He loves us, but "it is written upon every opening bud, upon every spire of springing grass. The lovely birds making the air vocal with their happy songs, the delicately tinted flowers . . . , the lofty trees of the forest . . . , all testify to the tender, fatherly care of our God and to His desire to make His children happy" (*Steps to Christ*, p. 10).

Lord, today I want to hear Your voice, however You may choose to speak to me. Help me to assist others that they too may hear the message of Your love, even from "a talkin' bird"! BEVERLY MOODY

Life's Illumination

Your word is a lamp to my feet and a light for my path. Ps. 119:105, NIV.

It was just what we had hoped for—a path to the top of the falls! We had followed the shallow stream, at times walking on the stones in the streambed itself, to reach the foot of the falls. Now there was a clearly defined path that would take us to the top of the falls in only 45 minutes. Or so we thought.

We started out, reasoning that we would be back to the cars easily by 5:00 or 5:30. But after 45 minutes of brisk walking the falls did not appear. In reality it took us an hour and a half to reach the top. Could we possibly be out of the forest before dark? We hurried. Twilight doesn't last long in a forest full of huge trees and dense undergrowth.

Too soon it became completely dark. We knew the general direction to go because we could hear the noise of a generator close to where we had parked the cars. Infrequently we caught a glimmer of light from that generator.

How could a night be so dark? Progress was slow and hazardous among the fallen branches and stones. We decided to walk single file, holding hands. It reassured me to know someone had taken the step just ahead of me safely and that strong hands would steady me if I stumbled. And that occasional brief glimmer of light from the generator heartened us.

David's life seems to have been something like our return from the falls after dark—uncertain, perplexing. But his description of the illumination provided for his life was not a glimmer. He described it as a lamp and a light. "Your word," he wrote, "is a lamp to my feet and a light for my path."

I must have no concern for the uncertainties of life when Jesus has taken the steps before me. It encourages me to know it is He who holds my hand, steadies me, and keeps me from falling. And He provides a light, not just a glimmer, to guide me safely home.   LOIS E. JOHANNES

Rainbows Won't Wait

Life is more than food, and the body than clothing. . . . Be dressed in readiness, and keep your lamps alight. . . . Blessed are those . . . whom the master shall find on the alert. . . . You too, be ready. Luke 12:23-40, NASB.

Every so often there is an opportunity for a golden moment to be added to my treasure store. One such occasion occurred as I rushed between home and work on Highway 101, responding to an emergency page to go to the hospital.

Suddenly I spotted the most beautiful rainbow I had ever seen, highlighted by the yellow disk of the sun peeking out of the rain-washed hills. The colors arched from high in the distant hills on one side of the highway, down to a few feet above the ground on the other side of the road. As I looked at the brilliant colors of the rainbow, my spirits rose. I was in a hurry, but something inside me said, "Stop. Savor the moment." So I did.

A few minutes later in the emergency room, I remarked, "I just saw the most beautiful rainbow. I don't think I've ever seen one so brilliant!"

A doctor paused and asked, "Did you notice that it was a double rainbow? Come outside; I'll show you."

He showed me another arch, parallel to the first, that seemed to envelop the world in joyful color. A golden moment was deposited in my memory bank. A couple minutes to pause for ecstasy and celebration in the midst of hurry was the day's highlight.

Patricia Clafford strikes a resonant note in my heart when she exclaims, "The work will wait while you show the child the rainbow, but the rainbow won't wait while you do the work."

Hurrying through life, how close I come to missing its most meaningful moments, golden moments that nourish the soul.

At this moment I am savoring the delight of Your presence. Help me pause often today to savor Your love and the delights that You give me. Open my eyes to the many colors of Your care. Help me to take time to share with others the wonders of Your creation, because rainbows really don't wait.

SHARI CHAMBERLAIN

My Eyes Are for God

Cast thy burden upon the Lord, and he shall sustain thee: he shall never suffer the righteous to be moved. Ps. 55:22.

When I visited her in the penitentiary I could not imagine how this victim of an unhappy and disastrous love affair could choose a direction for her life so different from what we desired for her. She had been such a sweet girl with such tender and delicate eyes. We had given her such a special name, meaning my eyes are for God. However, she turned her eyes away from Him and set them on the enemy.

She had studied in the best parochial schools, attended church, and many times used her voice and musical talents in church programs. What causes a young girl with so many possibilities and opportunities to choose friends and paths that are so different? I could not stand to see the life of unhappiness my daughter was living with a man who was a drug addict.

"Where did I fail?" I cried until there were no more tears to cry. Not only did I feel a personal failure, I was afraid to speak of God and His goodness to others because I had been unable to convince my own daughter.

One day, in my depression and sorrow, I was touched by these words: "Rise up! Each one is responsible before God for their own guilt. No one has the right to take away the happiness of your salvation."

From that moment on, my usual happiness returned, and I decided not to allow anything or anyone to steal my peace or to affect my relationship with Christ. Now I knew God was on my side and cared about my daughter. Now I was confident and full of hope that God could solve everything in His own time.

And when least expected, it happened. My daughter has recovered and is very happy as she finishes her college course and works.

Many Christian parents are in anguish because of children who are unbelievers. In their pain they lay down and lose the happiness of living for Christ. But our Father desires that they rise up and entrust the care of their children to Him. His hand is always extended with love and power to save.

MARIA DE JESUS VALE MENEZES

City Birds

And having food and raiment let us be therewith content. 1 Tim. 6:8.

While waiting at a drive-through window to place a fast-food order, my 13-year-old daughter, Julie, and I watched some birds flock around a nearby dumpster. We heard the flutter of wings as a sparrow emerged with a french fry in its beak.

"Wonder how well its babies like french fries," Julie mused.

"Probably some of the best 'worms' they've ever tasted," I replied, chuckling.

"Wouldn't that spoil their appetite for plain, everyday worms?" Julie wondered.

"Having never tried worms, I'm not sure," I laughed. "Maybe they just eat the French fries as an occasional treat."

Another sparrow flew by with a bit of chicken in its beak.

"Look!" we both exclaimed in unison.

We watched as a robin pulled on a worm from the middle of a grassy island. Nearby a nuthatch scurried up a tree trunk, scavenging insects that lived under the bark.

"H'mmm . . ." I was thinking out loud. "Wonder if city birds ever have cholesterol problems or fall over dead from heart attacks. These birds seem peppy enough. In spite of their sometimes questionable diet, one thing we can admire is their ability to adjust to their situation and environment." The birds sang and seemed just as happy as any country birds we had ever seen.

"People could learn some real lessons from these birds," I told Julie. "Things such as making the best of less-than-ideal situations and being content with what they have. Somehow they seem to know that their heavenly Father feeds them."

"City birds are neat!" Julie agreed.

Our order came, was paid for, and we left. But the lesson of the city birds stayed with me.

Lord, help me to be content today with what I have. Help me to make the best of whatever this day brings, even when things are not what I would like them to be.

BONNIE MOYERS

In Memory Of . . .

*Now this is eternal life: that they may know you, the only true God,
and Jesus Christ, whom you have sent. John 17:3, NIV.*

Genealogy, reportedly the fastest-growing hobby in the world, is one of my interests. Family history research can be frustrating, time-consuming, and expensive. But when an elusive ancestor or hidden fact comes to light, I feel a thrill of excitement. Contact with distant living relatives engaged in the same activity has brought new friends.

Even apart from "digging up" ancestors, I enjoy wandering around old churchyards. There are so many hidden stories behind the words on the tombstones. "In loving memory of . . ." is a standard inscription. But in how many homes did death bring relief from tyranny? "Widow of the above" may reveal that a woman had been left without a husband while she still had a young family to raise. The nameless "child who died in infancy" speaks of life's hazards in the days of inadequate medical care. In the same grave may be "beloved wife of . . ," followed by a date showing that she died within days of the nameless child, another statistic in the tables of maternal mortality.

Some stones are inscribed with verses of warning to readers, advising them to prepare their lives for the day of judgment. Other stones tell nothing, because the words of "loving memory" once inscribed on them have weathered away.

Then there are unmarked graves. Perhaps the family did not have enough money to pay for a memorial, or it had fallen down and been removed.

I have thought, *What if I am buried in an unmarked grave? What if no one records my virtues on a stone memorial? What if years or centuries pass, and I just become a remote name in the records of the family genealogist?*

But I have no worries about being forgotten. I am the dearly beloved daughter of an eternal Father. Further, I am comforted by Bible promises. First Corinthians 15 offers me absolute surety for the future: "We will not all sleep, but we will all be changed. . . . The trumpet will sound, the dead will be raised. . . . Death has been swallowed up in victory. . . . Thanks be to God!" (verses 51-57, NIV). JAN CLARKE

Acceptance

The wisdom that comes from heaven is first of all pure; then peace-loving, considerate, submissive, full of mercy and good fruit, impartial and sincere. James 3:17, NIV.

I sat in the surf, building a sand castle with Bunky and thinking that life couldn't get any better than this. We were newly engaged, and this was my first visit to meet his family. Everything to make me feel loved and welcomed had been done.

That evening there was a watermelon feast church social in honor of our engagement. I enjoyed meeting the church family, and I ate an enormous amount of watermelon. That night the guest bed felt wonderful as I snuggled down to sleep.

The next thing I knew I seemed to be sitting on the wet sand with the surf swirling around me. And then I awakened—wet, cold, and horrified! I leaped from the sopping-wet guest bed and burst into tears!

The next morning, when Bunky called me to breakfast, I knew how a condemned person feels. Trembling and mortified, I made an entrance into the kitchen. Bunky noted my stricken face.

"What's wrong?" he asked, alarmed.

"Are you ill?" Bunky's mother wanted to know.

Bunky's father put down his morning paper and studied my face. "What's the problem, girl?" he asked.

"I wet the bed!" I blurted, my face heating up.

Bunky and his mother began to laugh. Bunky's father grinned and said, "Son, once she's housebroken I think she'll make a fine wife!"

In spite of this embarrassing, colossal goof, I was made to feel loved, secure, and fully accepted into the family. I realized that because Bunky loved me, they loved me too—no matter what.

I often remember this incident when I meet new Christians. These new believers do not know us very well, but they long to become loved, secure, and fully accepted into the church family. Will we wait for them to "fit in" with our culture and our patterns of behavior before accepting them into our fellowship? Or will we overlook their embarrassing goofs because we know how much Jesus loves them? And because He loves them, will we also love them, no matter what? ELLIE GREEN

Remember the Saucer

My cup overflows. Surely goodness and love
will follow me all the days of my life. Ps. 23:5, 6, NIV.

In my mother-in-law's china cupboard sat her collection of bone china teacups, each of a different design. Some were short and round. Others were tall and sleek. Their handles varied from plain to those with filigree designs and other ornate configurations. Some were decorated with gold leaf and bands of silver. Their beautiful colors covered the spectrum of the rainbow. With each cup was a matching saucer.

Cups originally were without saucers. When filled to overflowing, the liquid would run onto the table or drip onto a person's clothes. Any drips would run down the cup and stain the tablecloth. Then someone fashioned a saucer with a little ridge to hold the cup in place and catch any overflow.

Every woman is like a cup. We are each diverse and have needs and wants that vary. We need to be filled with a variety of "beverages." Filling your cup with laughter requires a saucer. Listen in your mind to the gentle ripples of light laughter; then hear it grow to a hearty belly laugh, filling your cup. Get the saucer out quickly, because it is sure to spill over, and you don't want to lose a bit of the joy. The rim is needed to hold the cup stable as your giggles make your hand unsteady.

Fill your cups with love—love of family, friends, neighbors. Joy, peace, and contentment quickly follow when cups of life are filled with love. Remember your saucer to catch the overflow. Share your love until it makes other women's cups overflow, and they will have to remember their saucers as well.

Saucers were also designed for drips. The drips are like little irritations in life. Recently I looked out my window, and there on my front lawn were the neighbor's cattle. A real drip! I needed the protection of my saucer.

Think happy thoughts and fill your cup and let that overflow onto your saucer. The Lord is delighted when we remember to use our saucers.

EVELYN GLASS

Please Control My Imagination!

Let him have all your worries and cares, for he is always thinking about you and watching everything that concerns you. 1 Peter 5:7, TLB.

There was a note on the table: *Gone kayaking. Meet us at the Yarra Bridge at 5:00.*

Diamond Creek, usually much too shallow to kayak, was in flood, and two adventurous teenagers had gone to challenge it. Twice that day I had crossed Diamond Creek and the Yarra River into which it feeds, so I had noticed how high the water was running. Now I realized there were two kayaks out there somewhere.

As I drove toward the bridge, thunder pealed and rain pelted down. The windshield wipers swished frantically, but could not cope. I pulled to the side of the road and waited until the cloudburst was over.

The river was higher than ever, brown and bubbling with rafts of foam and debris. I pulled into the muddy parking area and switched off the engine. The rumble of traffic over the bridge and the rushing and crashing of the water were the only sounds.

Five o'clock. They were late. The river was full of fallen trees hidden by the water, undercut banks, flood-borne logs, and unexpected currents. But more dangerous than the rushing river was my overactive imagination. I pictured capsized kayaks, struggling teenagers, and our frantic searching for their bodies. By the time 15 minutes had passed, I was imagining burials instead of baptisms that were planned for the following week.

Then two small kayaks shot around the corner. The paddlers missed the usual landing place but tangled in some scrub farther down and pulled themselves toward the bank.

All that wasted worry! As two muddy teenagers recounted their adventure, I counted the cost of an overactive imagination. I was far more exhausted than they were!

Lord, my imagination is a mixed blessing. Please take charge of it and remind me that You want to take all my worries and cares (even the imaginary ones). You are always thinking about me and watching everything that concerns me.

GWEN PASCOE

Almost on Empty

*Fools enjoy doing wrong, but anyone with
good sense enjoys acting wisely. Prov. 10:23, CEV.*

I looked at the gas gauge. Less than a quarter tank of gas was left. I didn't want to brave the cold, 25-degree weather to stop at a filling station. Besides, I was making good time and wanted to get to my mom's. Only 25 miles to go. I could make it. I continued driving, passing several gas stations along the way. *I'll fill up when I get home*, I thought.

Fifteen minutes later the gas gauge needle pointed to "E." I knew I hadn't acted wisely or responsibly, and wished I had opted to refuel when opportunity had presented itself. I was worried that the car would run out of gas and I'd be stranded. Would a gas station be open on New Year's Day in this small town? Expecting to see the red flashing light indicating my fuel was just about gone, my eyes remained transfixed on the little square on the dashboard. *How much time will you lose now?* I scolded myself as I drove down the interstate, slower now, trying to conserve my gas.

"Whew." I breathed a sigh of relief as I saw my exit. I drove into the main thoroughfare. Everything seemed to be closed. Where, oh where, was a gas station that was open?

Then I saw it. A little corner service station! *Just for me*, I mused. I drove in, stepped from the car, and asked for a fill-up. *Close call, lady*, I reprimanded myself. *Don't ever do that again!*

After paying the bill, I traveled the remaining half mile more relaxed. I could drive around and visit my friends now. My tank was full. I was ready.

I pulled onto my mother's street and parked the car. God had spared me the anguish of being stranded, even though I had not acted wisely. I was truly thankful.

Lord, I admit I'm almost on empty spiritually much of the time, and the warning light is flashing. I know I'm in danger of being stranded in Satan's territory. Thank You for promising me sufficient fuel to meet every need. May I never again pass Your filling station without getting a full tank of Your goodness, mercy, and love.

IRIS L. STOVALL

Peaceful Harbor

Wine is a mocker, strong drink is raging:
and whoever is deceived thereby is not wise. Prov. 20:1.

About 10 years ago I discovered a wonderful town called Rockport, Massachusetts. Friends had told us it had beautiful bed-and-breakfast places and quaint little art and souvenir shops. The restaurants serving delicious homemade foods are right on the water so you can see the ocean and the boats.

My husband and I went to Rockport for our thirtieth anniversary. It was all that our friends had told us. I was most impressed by the Hannah Jumper Restaurant. The story of Rockport 100 years ago was told there.

According to the story, all the fishermen were alcoholics. The women were disgusted and unhappy because of the abuse they and their children suffered. They met to discuss the situation, but were afraid there was nothing they could do.

Then one brave woman, Hannah Jumper, spoke up. "Look, ladies, the only thing to do is take axes, go where all the kegs of liquor are stored, and break them open!"

Some ladies were frightened, but Hannah encouraged them. They gathered some axes and went to the building where the kegs were and used the axes on them. As the kegs broke open, all the liquor flowed in the streets.

Meanwhile their husbands came in from fishing and heard all the noise. When they saw what their wives had done, they were very upset. But when they saw how strong their wives were, especially Hannah Jumper, they agreed that there would be no more drinking in Rockport! They went to the town hall and made a law: there would be no liquor sold or bought in Rockport. That law is still in force today.

I'm so grateful there are women who can make a difference. There are so many evils, such as alcohol, in the world about which You have warned us, Lord. Today I want to take You at Your word. I long to make a difference where I live. Then I won't mind living here until You return!

LENA CRESSOTTI

A Sense of Touch

If I only touch his cloak, I will be healed. Matt. 9:21, NIV.

Working as a caregiver at a hospice has made me realize how important is the sense of touch. Our most effective means of communicating our feelings to our patients is by holding their hands, hugging them, gently massaging their aching arms, legs, and backs. They enjoy every moment of this and literally "purr" with pleasure. The warmth of human touch makes them feel special. They appreciate the fact that we treat them as living rather than dying people.

Satisfaction is, however, not only for the recipient, for in touching others we convey our love and compassion in a tangible way that words somehow fail to do. By touching empathetically, we are also blessed.

The woman with the issue of blood wanted to touch the hem of Jesus' garment as an act of faith in His divine power. She did not feel the need to be touched as much as to touch. She was well aware of the fact that her uncleanness made her untouchable. No one would want to risk being made ceremonially unclean by touching her, so she had long since become used to being shunned by society.

In spite of the frustration, self-pity, and disappointment of the past 12 years she did not despair. Her hope rested in touching the hem of His garment. So strong was her faith that she believed she would be healed if she could just touch Him.

Can you imagine her joy and gratitude when she was, in fact, healed and when she heard the precious words "Take heart, daughter, . . . your faith has healed you" (Matt. 9:22, NIV)?

I need to touch Jesus just as the woman did. I too am sick from sin and the cares of this life. I must touch Him when I am in need of comfort, when I need to be forgiven, when I need to be healed—physically and spiritually. I also must touch Him when I need to share my joy and gratitude.

And I know that when I reach out to touch Him, He will reach out His arms of love to touch me. His touch will make me whole.   FRANCES CHARLES

One Day on Mount Hope

*For the Lord himself, with a cry of command, with the archangel's
call and with the sound of God's trumpet, will descend from heaven,
and the dead in Christ will rise first. Then we who are alive, who are left,
will be caught up in the clouds together with them to meet the Lord in
the air; and so we will be with the Lord forever. 1 Thess. 4:16, 17, NRSV.*

It was a hot summer day. The sun forced its way past the lacy leaves of the
locust trees whose best effort could produce only a light shade. In Mount
Hope Cemetery, Kate Roberts' children cried as they buried their mother.

Pastor Chamber said, "A mother in Israel has fallen," and all nine of
her grieving offspring knew it.

Tears wet my cheeks, too. As a daughter-in-law, I knew Mom Roberts was
a woman of integrity, who had done her best as she raised nine children alone.

When I remember that day in Mount Hope Cemetery, I feel the heat
and hear the droning bees and chirping crickets. The breeze gradually dried
the tears from our faces till the only moisture was from perspiration
brought on by the fiery sun.

As we left the cemetery and drove down the hill, my husband, Rich,
said, "Barb, do you know what I want?" Rich seldom talks about what he
wants, so when he expresses a desire I listen. "I know where I want to be
when Jesus comes," he said. "I want to be right here on Mount Hope.
There are so many dear saints resting in this place, and I want to see them
come out of their graves when Jesus calls them."

That day on Mount Hope, Rich and I assumed Jesus would come during our lifetime. But the years have gone by, and it won't be too many more
until we will join those who have laid down their burdens. We still don't
know what it is like to see someone we love raised from the dead.

But Jairus knew. The widow of Nain knew. Mary and Martha knew.
And our God knows. He was there when Jesus came from the tomb.
Someday we will know too. Instead of funerals, there will be a party that
day, a magnificent celebration in Jesus' house and joyful singing on the
streets of the New Jerusalem.

BARBARA ROBERTS

First Mother's Day

In my Father's house are many rooms; if it were not so, would I have told you that I go to prepare a place for you? John 14:2, RSV.

I have been looking forward to this Mother's Day for many, many years because it will be my first celebration as a mother. At first I hoped to be given some pampering and perhaps get out of some of my usual responsibilities. My gifts would be given by my daughter via my husband, since she is still very young. I envisioned it as my day off for the year when my husband could walk in my shoes. And in the coming years it would be a day when my children would lavish me with gifts and the royal treatment.

As the day grows closer, I realize that those dreams are not what I really want. A Mother's Day alone to do my own thing will only be empty. Visions of being waited on and pampered have faded—I want to celebrate being a mother, not get out of being one! I am excited to think about spending quality time with my daughter and husband. I want to relive the development of our family. I feel privileged to be Chelsea's mother, and I am eager to spend the day conveying that to her. I want to hug her for as long as she will let me.

This seems so odd to me now. It is in such opposition to my previous concept of the holiday. Instead of a time to show appreciation for the mother, I truly feel like celebrating my opportunity for motherhood. It has made me wonder if that is how God feels about us coming home. We are His daughters. When we accompany Jesus to heaven, He will be providing the party, even though He is the one to whom we owe our all. When we should be demonstrating our gratitude to Him, He will be celebrating us.

I am one among countless mothers who had a difficult time becoming a mom. As with most things in life, the harder you have to try for something, the more you appreciate it when you have it. Maybe God, in His love and eagerness to have us with Him, wants to celebrate by recounting the development of our relationship with Him, by laughing with us, or by making us a feast at His table. Maybe He just wants to envelop us in His arms and tell us again and again how much He loves us.

LAURA PASCUAL DANCEK

I Don't Want to Be Left Behind

Therefore you must be ready; for the Son of man is coming at an hour you do not expect. Matt. 24:44, RSV.

A trip to the airport to meet my husband or children is always one to which I look forward. These are happy moments—lots of talking, squeezing of hands, eye contact, and a lot of "Oh, how I missed you!"

Driving home alone after taking loved ones to the airport is something else, however. It's not an easy trip; it's a lonely, quiet, and heartbreaking trip. Now I was at the airport again, a trip I dreaded the most.

The girls were flying back to school, so I waited until the plane lifted off. It was lonely and hot where I was standing. As I watched the plane ascend, I waved my hand with a wish and a prayer: "Wish I could fly with you. God be with you. I love you!"

Driving home that day was one of the most lonely trips I had ever made from the airport. I was crying, feeling lonely and left-behind. Suddenly I began to think about flying away home with Jesus. I am eager to go but know I still have some things I need to have changed in my character first. *Please, help me, Lord.*

I started feeling excited when I thought of my forthcoming trip with my Lord. It will be only a fun-filled trip with the Lord. I thought of the endless conversation we will have. I will have fun talking with Him, holding His hands, and feeling the scars that my sin has caused.

The excitement of my upcoming trip was so great that I didn't realize I was already home. I got out of the car, went upstairs, and thanked my Lord for the wonderful time driving and talking with Him. I told Him I look forward to the final trip with Him!

Lord, are You eagerly waiting for me to come home? When I take family to the airport I realize how important family really is and how I want to be part of Your family. I also want to be sure that my family is all there with You too. Guide and bless us, Lord, and do hasten that day. Send Your Holy Spirit to help me be ready.

JEMIMA D. ORILLOSA

Prayer Changes Things

Ask, and it shall be given you; seek, and ye shall find. Matt. 7:7.

After 14 years of living happily in the same apartment, Mother was being forced to move because of circumstances beyond her control. My sisters and I welcomed the idea of having Mother come live with us. Each one of us offered her a home. She flatly rejected our invitations.

On Wednesdays, my day off, I'd pick her up and take her to fill out applications at nearby senior citizen apartment buildings. We drove, we walked, we rode until we were tired. We went for interviews. Almost everywhere we went we were informed that there was at least a two- to three-year waiting period. The conditions that were forcing her to move were becoming unbearable. Her situation burdened me tremendously.

When I reached home after a short visit with her one Sabbath afternoon, I remember praying, *Father, You know where every vacant apartment is located in the city and state. Please prepare one of them for my mother, one where she'll be near us, one where we will feel she'll be safe.*

As I got up off my knees I felt as if the weight of the world had been lifted off my shoulders. I knew my prayers were already answered.

Two weeks after I prayed this prayer, Mother received a phone call. The caller made an appointment to talk to her about an application that she had previously submitted to a housing development agency.

Two weeks later she was asked to look at several apartments that were being renovated and to choose one for herself.

Mother moved about a month later. The development lies within a five-mile radius of our homes. Each of us can reach her in five to seven minutes by car. Security guards are stationed in every section of the development at all times.

Thank You, Father, for answered prayer. I praise You with my whole heart, for all good things come from You. I will praise You today and every day for Your many blessings.   CORA A. WALKER

The Rainbow

There before me was a throne in heaven with someone sitting on it.
And the one who sat there had the appearance of jasper and carnelian.
A rainbow, resembling an emerald, encircled the throne. Rev. 4:2, 3, NIV.

The magnificent towers of the Mackinac Bridge loomed on the horizon. The first 50 miles of our trip had been in steady rain. But now, as we approached the five-mile-long span that connects Michigan's two peninsulas, the sun in all its splendor burst through the rain-laden clouds. Slowly, slowly, the raindrops ceased.

As we entered the bridge approach we saw one of God's special handiworks—a rainbow of such brilliant hues it seemed to vibrate. It appeared to be resting on the highway, near the first bridge tower.

As our car neared the rainbow, I slowed it almost to a crawl—I didn't want the moment to pass too quickly. I could hardly believe what would soon happen—we would actually drive through the rainbow! The children's excitement rose to a fever pitch as they also realized what was about to take place.

Words cannot adequately describe my feelings as we literally drove through the colors of the rainbow. I thought, *What a beautiful expression of God's love to mankind and the promise of heaven.* I felt warmth and coolness, joy and peace. There were bubbles inside me; my skin tingled and had goose bumps!

I remember thinking, *I feel as though God has just kissed me!* My heart was so full I thought my skin would burst and expose it. I did not want to leave the warmth and the love I felt. When I am a very old grandmother I will remember the experience as vividly as I do this very day.

I want to thank You someday, my heavenly Father, in person for giving me such a precious moment in time. But for today I will thank You for raindrops, sunbeams, prisms, rainbows, warmth, love, and kisses. I will think of the rainbow that always surrounds You—how I long to see that sight! I love You, God.

BETTY R. BURNETT

The Surprise Party

*Trust in the Lord with all your heart and never
depend on your own understanding. Prov. 3:5, Clear Word.*

During my second week of teaching at Tucson Junior Academy, Ruth asked me to go with her to a women's meeting. Ruth's husband was the school principal, so I went.

As we walked into the church basement I felt strange. The room was dark. *What a spooky place!* I thought. *So quiet and forlorn!* I followed closely behind Ruth.

Just as I passed the entrance of the meeting room I heard a chorus of ladies shout "Surprise!" The lights came on, and I saw many big smiles and heard the burst of laughter from the ladies who came to meet me.

The most common surprises are birthday parties. Many children arrange surprise wedding anniversary parties for their parents. Some friends plan surprises too, and Pauline and Ruth had done this for me. They were well aware that I had come to Tucson with almost nothing. So Pauline arranged the surprise welcome shower, and Ruth was responsible for getting me there.

The surprise party brought untold blessings—appliances; linen for bedrooms, kitchens, and bathrooms; beautifully wrapped brooms; a dustpan; wastebaskets; kitchen utensils; and much more to completely furnish my home. Every item was something I needed.

Tears flowed down my cheeks. I was so stunned! My heart was full of emotion. I could not utter any other word but "Thanks!" I couldn't believe what was happening! That basement room was full of things that my family and I used every day for many years.

Someday there will be another surprise party for all who are waiting for Jesus to come. May we be ready to meet Christ, even if He surprises us with His coming, "As a thief in the night."

Lord, I can't wait until I can experience Your surprise party for me in heaven! I can't even imagine all of the wonderful gifts You'll have for me there.

Esperanza Aquino Mopera

This Battle Is Not Yours

Faith is the substance of things hoped for,
the evidence of things not seen. Heb. 11:1.

Three months after graduation from college I was still looking for a job with no hope in sight. Finally, I was offered an assignment as a receptionist through a temporary agency, but it was not what I really wanted.

I prayed, fasted, and asked the Lord specifically for the kind of job, salary, and coworkers I wanted. But I was still worried. *Why doesn't God answer my prayers?* I wondered.

The next assignment was another receptionist job, and I hated answering telephones. This company, however, had the latest software packages on the market, so this was my opportunity to learn all that I could.

One day I felt impressed to walk around the office complex. I found a temporary agency that I had planned on registering with but never had, so I registered with them during my lunch hour. The next day I was laid off my job unexpectedly. Less than a week later the temporary agency I had just registered with called me for a two-week assignment.

Although I didn't want a short-term assignment, I decided to take the position anyway. Everything went well; it seemed like the perfect position, just what I had been praying for. I decided to interview for the position permanently, so I submitted a résumé.

Still worrying and doubting, I started reading about prayer and fasting. I found I was missing one important thing: faith. I did not have faith in what I was asking the Lord for. I wanted His help—I kept worrying. Finally I could see that God had been taking me through meaningful jobs, helping me to grow professionally.

The two weeks turned into a month, and I interviewed for the position, but I no longer doubted or worried. I had decided to let go and let God. I had faith that He would do what was best for me in His time.

Two days later they offered the position to me. That was a glorious day, but what was even more glorious was that for the first time I could honestly say I had faith in God. I could see that He knew what was best for me. Whatever you ask for when you pray, believe it, and it will be yours!

TABITHA MERSHELL THOMPSON

Anxious Thoughts

When my anxious thoughts multiply within me, thy consolations delight my soul. . . . The Lord has been my stronghold, and my God the rock of my refuge. Ps. 94:19-22, NASB.

Our family planned a week of camping and boating with my parents at a mountain lake about 30 minutes from our home. We had a lovely four days of fellowship, sleeping out under the stars, and singing while my husband and son played their guitars. My mother wrote poems, I caught up on some reading, the children perfected their waterskiing techniques, and all seemed idyllic.

Then my husband had a waterskiing accident. We made a rushed trip down the mountain to the doctor. X-rays revealed two fractured ribs. We were suddenly torn away from our children during our family vacation. My husband was in a lot of pain, and suddenly life was no longer wonderful.

While I was waiting at the hospital, unable to concentrate on the hospital TV or the well-worn magazine in my hands, God brought Psalm 94:19 to my mind: "When my anxious thoughts multiply within me, thy consolations delight my soul."

During that first sleepless night spent away from our children I asked myself, *Lord, what are Your consolations in this situation?* And then, slowly, my prayer became, *Please show me Your will in this situation.* In my wondering and questioning, doubting and fears, God consoled my soul. Texts such as "All things work together for good"; "They that wait upon the Lord," and many others flowed through my mind. As I drifted off to sleep I thought, *God has never failed our family in the past. He will work this situation out too.*

Five days later my thoughts weren't quite as troubled. We were all back home together, and with the children's help our camping gear was stored away. My day was filled to overflowing. One child had the flu, mountains of laundry awaited me, a writing deadline was fast approaching. This was to have been our "official" first day of home school. To top it all, I had a temporarily disabled husband recovering upstairs.

Lord, even with a busy day ahead, I remember how You have proved to be my stronghold in the past. I trust You for today and for the rest of my life.

JUDY MUSGRAVE SHEWMAKE

Our Tree of Life

Hope deferred makes the heart sick, but a longing fulfilled is a tree of life.
Prov. 13:12, NIV.

No, the baby is not up for adoption!"
That was a surprise and a disappointment. I wanted that baby! His mother had died when he was born, and he already had eight brothers and sisters.

My husband and I had been pastoring and teaching the little church school in beautiful Salmon, Idaho. We had taught together for six years. Now I wanted to be a mother. Several mothers-to-be met to sew for their expected babies one afternoon. I felt left out and almost in tears. Later, when I mentioned my longing to my host, she encouraged me by saying that if I stayed around there, probably I'd also be fortunate!

Dear Lord, if You'll give me a baby I'll dedicate him to You, I prayed often.

After some medical help, soon I was pregnant too, but I didn't breathe it to a soul. However, on the Fourth of July I was so sick our picnic group guessed!

I didn't want to teach, so we resigned from our pastor-teaching job. Because all suitable teaching positions for my husband had already been filled, we decided we would need to go live with my parents until he found a job.

Usually he was the one to cheer me. But this time I said, "No, something will show up."

One evening he asked me to read for worship. We were reading through Proverbs and were ready for chapter 13. I read verse 12: "'Hope deferred makes the heart sick, but a longing fulfilled is a tree of life.'" I felt it was a message for us. The very next day was the first regular school day, but nothing had shown up for us yet.

We went to bed. At 10:00 there was a loud knock on the door. "That's our tree of life!" I almost shouted. Sure enough, we were informed that my husband was needed at a boarding school to teach one of the Bible classes and to keep the books in the business office.

Praise the Lord! We got the job and had our son, too! God, You are so good!

PHYLLIS THOMPSON MACLAFFERTY

The Master of the Winds and the Waves

Who is this? Even the wind and the waves obey him! Mark 4:41, NIV.

The northeastern Montana weather was warmer than usual for December on the day of my mother-in-law's funeral. Instead of a blinding blizzard and frigid temperatures, the elements delivered driving rain with temperatures in the low 40s with 45-mile winds.

As we prepared to leave for the service, my husband remarked that the weather would not make it easy to have a meaningful graveside service. A canopy with protective sides was a luxury the little country cemetery near the family farm did not provide.

Shortly before dusk that afternoon, the funeral procession turned off the main highway and slowly wound its way 30 miles down a muddy, gravel road. The wind drove the rain in sheets against the windshield of our car, and the wipers struggled to maintain visibility for us. We finally rounded the last bend. I wondered whether anyone but the immediate family would venture out of their cars.

As we pulled in behind the hearse to wait for the rest of the procession, the rain slowed to a drizzle—and stopped altogether. Stepping out of our cars, we noticed that the fierce wind had also died away. Then, just as the pastor started to speak, the dark clouds parted and the peaceful cemetery was bathed in the soft, warm glow of the setting sun. Few times in my life have I felt the presence of God in such a powerful way. Even the funeral director, obviously moved by the miraculous change in the weather, had tears in his eyes.

The miraculous interlude did not last long. Ten minutes later, as we walked from the car to the little country church where the women of that close-knit farming community were lovingly preparing a meal, I had to grab my husband's arm to support me against the strong wind and driving rain. But how grateful we all were that the Master of the wind and the waves had enfolded our grieving family in His arms and touched us with the assurance of His love, comfort, and peace.   CINDY WALIKONIS

Clutching at a Straw

Love the Lord your God, listen to his voice, and hold fast to him. Deut. 30:20, NIV.

Three-year-old Nathan loved watching his kite bob about in the summer breeze. One morning he wanted to hold the string all by himself for a few minutes. I needed to change Joel's diaper, so I agreed that Nathan could hold the string, as long as he didn't let go.

While Nathan was standing there, looking up at the colors dancing against the white, fluffy clouds, his older friend, Martin, came along to play. "Can I hold your kite, please, Nathan?"

As Nathan handed over the kite, the inevitable happened. Somewhere between Nathan and Martin, the string slipped out of their hands, up and away. The kite, free at last, sailed toward the cliffs and the sparkling ocean. Nathan sobbed as his kite disappeared.

We went inside again, sad at our loss. A while later I glanced out the window. Amazingly, I could still see the kite. As I watched I realized that it was not flying away! It was bobbing about, but not becoming smaller as I expected. I left the children with a friend and went to explore. I soon figured out that the kite string was caught on something in the field next to ours, populated by cows and thistles. The fine, nylon string of the kite was virtually invisible. I scoured the field, watching the movements of the kite in an effort to locate where the string may have been caught. It was a long search. At any time I expected that kite to break loose and disappear.

Finally I located one tiny loop of string, right near the handle, that had twisted itself around one single blade of grass. That tiny plant was clinging to the wayward kite with all its strength, though battered and bent. The kite was saved. As I brought it home I knew it was the answer to a little boy's prayer.

I also discovered the importance of hanging on tightly, even when there seems to be little hope. The kite had clung to something tiny and apparently fragile, but there was strength in the little plant. If a kite can be saved by clutching at a straw, how much more can we learn to love God, to listen to Him and hold fast, never letting go, no matter what blows us around.

KAREN HOLFORD

Firstborn

Lo, I am with you alway, even unto the end of the world. Matt. 28:20.

My first child did not arrive easily. I was young, apprehensive, and far from my parents' home. Five months into my pregnancy, I fell and broke my tailbone. In the weeks after that I was in and out of the hospital with hemorrhaging.

Once I went to the hospital thinking the baby was coming early and spent the whole night there. A young nun, who was taking care of me, seemed to float in and out of my consciousness. She looked like an angel with her white headdress, big blue eyes, and radiant smile. By morning nothing had happened, and I was sent home to wait in bed.

In my eighth month I was in trouble again. The year was 1941, just three weeks after Pearl Harbor. I wondered if we would have to flee to the mountains and have our first child born there. More hemorrhaging sent me back to the hospital. After several hours on the X-ray table, two doctors decided our baby had to be taken by cesarean section. I was glad it was going to be over soon and finally felt fairly confident.

As they prepared me for surgery, I joked like a little child whistling in the dark. They placed a mask over my face and told me to count. When I breathed in, it seemed as if my whole head became a large, black void. Suddenly I had a terrible thought: *I may not wake up till the resurrection.* I prayed, *Jesus, please, go with me and take care of me.* At that moment the black void of my mind became radiant with the single word "Jesus" as I slipped into unconsciousness.

My next conscious moment someone was telling me, "You have a fine, healthy baby boy."

I have always treasured that answer to a young woman's prayer. In that one word was all the assurance I needed. Jesus. He meets our every need.

I'm waiting to see that name emblazoned again across the darkened sky in the not too distant future. Even so, come, Lord Jesus. You are all we need.

FAITH KEENEY

Help in Trouble

God is our refuge and strength, a very present help in trouble. Ps. 46:1.

It was an overcast, rainy morning. The streets were drenched from a recent downpour. My daughter and I had driven this route many times before, but this morning was destined to be different.

She was employed north of the location where I worked. Because we shared one car and she had an earlier schedule, we drove to her place of employment first. As I complacently drove that morning I discussed the miserable traffic. It seemed worse than usual because of the rain.

Suddenly, without warning, a car stopped in front of us. I knew the speed of our car would not allow me to stop quickly enough to avoid an accident. I applied the brakes quickly and firmly anyway, forgetting that I'd been told never to apply regular brakes firmly and quickly on a wet pavement.

Our car spun wildly. It appeared that the traffic before and behind us stood still.

"Mother, what's happening?" my daughter shouted.

"Pray!" I yelled back. Then I added in a low whisper, "O God, save us!"

The wheels on the car spun onto the grassy median. With a deflated tire, the car stopped spinning immediately. A service station manager from a nearby service plaza later told us that everyone who had witnessed our spinning car had said a prayer for our safety. They were surprised to see that no harm had come to us.

We were safe and unharmed because God answers instant prayer. When His children are in trouble and call, there is an answer.

Lord, how reassuring it is to remember that You, our prayer-answering God, are a very present help in trouble. And an instant help, too. Again, thank You. May I be aware of Your presence with me all day, in all I do, but especially when I'm in trouble.

H. ELIZABETH TYNES

Thoughts in the Emergency Room

O Lord, you are a God of compassion. You are gracious and kind,
slow to anger, abounding in love and faithfulness. Ps. 86:15, Clear Word.

During the past five years I have spent many hours in the hospital emergency room with family members who have been sick or injured. While waiting there, I have seen people who apparently had been waiting for a long time. Some didn't appear to have illnesses that were emergencies, but others were obviously seriously ill, and there was no doubt they needed urgent medical care. The treatment rooms were full most of the times as doctors and nurses attended the sick. Ambulances continuously rolled in with more patients to be treated.

As I looked over the crowd on one particular visit, several things crossed my mind. First, I breathed a silent prayer of thanksgiving that I was in good health and sound mind. Second, I pictured in my mind the crowd that followed Jesus. The lame, blind, paralytic, demon-possessed, and the woman with the abnormal issue of blood. The dirty, the poor, the sane, the insane, the young, and the old. Some even disguised their identity. Some had followed Jesus from place to place for several years. Regardless of their circumstances and culture, they all longed for the same thing: the look of compassion in Jesus' eyes, the healing in His hands. Just a touch of His robe and the forgiveness of sins that only He could give was theirs.

And then it hit home. During the times I spent waiting in the emergency room, did I speak words of encouragement to anyone? Did I give a friendly smile? Did I offer to get a drink of water? Did I whisper a prayer on anyone's behalf? Did I share the love of Jesus and tell how He died to save all and that He is coming back again soon?

O Lord, You are a God of compassion. You are gracious and kind, slow to anger, abounding in love and faithfulness. Please forgive my negligence in showing Your love. Give me the courage to do what I can whenever I can for others so they will be drawn to You for complete physical and spiritual healing.

MARIE H. SEARD

God Shows His Love

I love the Lord, because he hath heard
my voice and my supplications. Ps. 116:1.

It seemed that everything was going wrong in my life, and the problems were accumulating.

I live in a country home. A small stream passes through our property and often overflows, causing flooding. When the waters go down, the soil doesn't dry completely. This provides the perfect spot for the breeding of thousands of mosquitoes that pester humans and animals 24 hours a day.

It was one of those days, and I was depressed. I had so many problems, then on top of everything else were the mosquitoes. While I was taking care of our animals on the patio, I looked up to the heavens and said, "Lord, from Genesis through Revelation it is written that You are good, but at times it is difficult to believe. Please help me!"

A little later I looked up again to the heavens and repeated my little prayer. It seemed so difficult to believe, and I had no idea how God could get rid of the mosquitoes, but I knew that the only solution lay in His power.

That very evening a strong wind came. The trees and the plants bowed against the force of this wind. It was so strong that some of them even broke and fell. This was unusual, and I was surprised at such a strong wind. Afterward, when everything had returned to normal, my son and I went out to access the damage. We had to remove a tree from the road because neither people nor automobiles could get past.

The following day I was surprised to discover that all the mosquitoes had disappeared. What a blessing! Yes, God answered my prayers. What an experience to feel His love and marvelous blessing.

Lord, today I want to give my life completely to You. I want to trust You more, especially during those times when everything seems to go wrong. Help me to remember that You are indeed good, a God who hears me when I pray.

SIEGRID ODETTE LÜTZ

Armies of Heaven

*O Lord God of the armies of heaven, don't let me be
a stumbling block to those who trust in you. Ps. 69:6, TLB.*

Just the other day I went to a special graduation at the Air Force Base. The first group of graduates were military personnel who had been going to college classes. Four colleges and universities provide classes at the base for military personnel and others who also take classes there.

The proceedings were carefully planned, and all the protocols carried out in the proper order and with dignity. When the military personnel were presented their diplomas by the college deans, they were also congratulated by the general. And those new graduates did salute very smartly!

After the Air Force college group received their diplomas, the other college deans presented the diplomas to civilian graduates in caps and gowns. The military personnel saluted the general when he congratulated them, and the nonmilitary graduates shook his hand.

One young woman was so engrossed with her new master's degree hood that had just been placed over her head that she walked right by the general without a look in his direction. He glanced after her with an amused look, and many of us noticed her omission.

This little vignette is a reflection of my own omissions, I thought. *In God's army there is also a commander in chief, the General, whom we respect. Most know His power and are sincere in their salutes. However, some are so absorbed in their own concerns that they don't even notice the General's presence, walking on by without proper reverence or respect.*

Like the young woman who bypassed the general, I too sometimes bypass God. When I do that I am missing His blessing. He also misses my responses of love and appreciation.

Lord God, General of my life, help me today to keep my thoughts on You. Help me give You the respect You are due. I look forward to that final graduation day!   JULIA L. PEARCE

My Passport

And ye now therefore have sorrow: but I will see you again, and your heart shall rejoice, and your joy no man taketh from you. John 16:22.

Passports and tickets in hand, we joined the long line of travelers at the airport check-in counter, happy and expectant. We were headed home to the land we loved!

Ahead of us, a young man was clearly in some kind of difficulty, although at first we couldn't imagine what his problem was. He searched through his pockets and battered briefcase and then, as light dawned, slapped his forehead in despair. "My passport!" he groaned. "I must have left it in the desk drawer at the hotel! Please, don't go without me. I'll be back."

He had forgotten his passport; he couldn't go anywhere. Not even the ticket agent, with all his authority, could allow him to travel without that all-important documentation. He hurried off to get it. We took his place at the counter, where we handed over our passports and tickets and were soon on our way home. We never saw the young man again. The plane left without him.

An acquaintance of mine, who had recently spent several weeks in a country where conditions were less than desirable, told of her homesickness while there. She made certain that every day found her prepared for the time when she could board an airplane for home. Mentally and physically, she was packed, ready to go at a moment's notice.

"Do you know what I did every morning as soon as I woke up?" she confided. "I kissed my passport." Her passport represented hope and a means of entering a country she loved.

Jesus and all He stands for is our passport to the kingdom. Without Him we have no chance of entering heaven. With Him we are assured of entry. Do we make sure that connections with Him are always fresh and living? Are we certain that nothing has been forgotten that might bar our entry into that better land to live with Him forever? Is our heavenly home so precious that nothing else compares with it? Do we "kiss our passport" every morning?

EDNA MAY OLSEN

Department Store Miracle

I will recount the gracious deeds of the Lord, the praiseworthy acts
of the Lord, because of all that the Lord has done for us. Isa. 63:7, NRSV.

The Harris department store flyer caught my eye. They were having a sale! Flipping through the pages of the brochure, I spotted something that would be perfect for my granddaughter's birthday. Calling my sister, who lives two houses down, we arranged for a shopping expedition. We would visit the store that afternoon.

Not wanting to be unduly tempted to make purchases I could ill afford, I left both credit card and checkbook at home. I carried only cash in a navy-blue pocket folder.

At the clothing department I could not find the specific item I wanted. I pulled out the sales brochure and got the attention of a clerk who pointed me in the right direction. Finally, purchase in hand, I went to the counter to make the payment. I reached for the pocket folder and blanched. It was not there! I had no idea what had happened to my money.

My sister came to my rescue and wrote a check, but my mind was in a quandary. Did I leave the money at home? We went back to see but had to make two stops before we could get home. Three and a half hours later we searched the house. Still no money.

At that very moment I heard an inner voice urging me to go back to the store. Driving back, I begged God in a brief sentence to keep my money safe and all but ran to the clerk to inquire if anything had been turned in. Nothing had. Then she told me how a short time before some lady had left her bag in the dressing room. In a split second, it was gone.

"I'm sorry," the clerk commiserated. "You might as well bid that money farewell.

I didn't want to hear that. Dejected, I took a dozen steps away from her. And then I saw it! There, in plain view, was my navy-blue pocket folder with every precious dollar enclosed.

God is still in the miracle-working business! VALDA A. NEMBHARD

Praise God in Everything

*The Lord gave me everything I had, and they were his
to take away. Blessed be the name of the Lord. Job 1:21, TLB.*

I was newly married, had a comfortable home, and a job I enjoyed. I had grown up in a wonderful family with my needs and desires looked after and had not experienced any great losses.

Several years later my husband and I decided it was time to bring children into our family, and shortly thereafter I got pregnant. Things didn't go right from the start—lots of bleeding and pain. Then early one morning, when I was only five weeks pregnant, my husband took me to the emergency room, where the doctor told us that I was probably miscarrying and would have to be monitored.

All through the day I prayed the shepherd's psalm, and I kept begging the Lord to let this baby live. *Why should this be happening to me?* I wondered. I didn't believe God wouldn't answer my prayer and save our baby. When they told me I had miscarried and would have to have surgery, I was distraught. How could God have let this happen? We wanted this baby!

Two weeks later I was again in the emergency room with severe pain and more bleeding. I had not miscarried, as the doctors had thought. I had an ectopic pregnancy and would have to have surgery again before my fallopian tube ruptured.

During the next few months and years I had many emotional ups and downs as we struggled to get pregnant again. I fought with God over the "fairness" of life when I saw other women pregnant or with new babies. Finally, we came to realize that it was likely we would never have our own biological child. It was then that I knew what it meant to have something precious taken away without knowing the answers, but still trusting in God to take you through the life He has given you.

The story could end there, but it doesn't. Three years after the first two surgeries and after many visits to infertility specialists, I discovered I was pregnant. The Lord had heard us and gave us a beautiful daughter to love. I don't know why He answered our prayers and not those of some of my friends who are still childless, but I do know that He has many ways to fulfill His plans in our lives. He will teach us to praise Him in all situations if we don't give up on Him.

LORENA LYN LENNOX

Family Reunions

They will see his face, and his name will be on their foreheads. Rev. 22:4, NIV.

I was a teenager before I met my only living grandparent. Being from a fragmented family, I know little of my heritage. As a child of divorce I never knew the fun of family reunions. When childhood friends talked about family reunions, I could only imagine the "niceness" of it. One friend complained about her aunt Margaret always saying the same thing to her at every family gathering: "Look how tall Bonnie has grown. Bet they can't keep her in skirts." I secretly thought her aunt Margaret must be wonderful.

Reuniting with family can serve as a foretaste of the heavenly reunion. The generational get-togethers could be a small, just-a-few-people affair or they could be a more than 2,000-person gathering, such as the descendants of African slaves and White slave owners experienced when they converged at Sommerset Plantation in Creswell, North Carolina, a couple years ago.

My friend Ruth Calkins evaluates family reunions this way: "Family reunions provide something that says 'I belong.'" She's right. Reunions update us. They add strength to the family, recharging us.

Ruth tells me about her mother, Anna Finck, who came to the United States from Czechoslovakia. Her father came to make money, then planned to return home. Instead, he found the Lord and stayed.

Reunions bond. For Christians it's an opportunity to give something for our children to pass on. These days as a wife, mother, and grandmother, I know the joy of reunions. I no longer live vicariously through others' experiences. I'm probably a lot like my childhood friend's aunt Margaret.

However, because I'm a part of God's family, the heavenly reunion is the one that excites me the most. I claim the promise Jesus gave: "And if I go and prepare a place for you, I will come back and take you to be with me that you also may be where I am" (John 14:3, NIV).

That will be some family reunion!

BETTY KOSSICK

Comfortable Angels

If any of you lack wisdom, let him ask of God. James 1:5.

A ngels like organization, and your angel would be very uncomfortable in your room right now!" My frustration overflowed as I looked at my teenager's room.

"But Mom, my angel goes with me and isn't here to see it, so why worry?"

With the addition of "teen" to his age came cockiness. I had trouble because Shawn's wings of independence had sprouted in uncomfortable angles. My friend Bonita had raised three boys. She listened and smiled as I poured out my troubles. She understood. "I refused to clean my boys' rooms," she said.

"But I don't want my son to be a slob!" I replied.

"Me either. I wouldn't dare drop my coat on one of their chairs or leave a pencil on their desks now." I knew her boys were now through college, so I waited. How had she done it?

"How did you change them?" Her success made me more than interested.

"I shut their doors and wouldn't let the mess stray into the rest of the house."

"You didn't make them clean?"

"No! And I had three times the mess you do."

"Does it take forever?" I pictured the room I had just left.

Five years later I walked into Shawn's dorm room. His books were all standing from shortest to tallest, his pencils were sharpened carefully and placed by size. His bed had no wrinkles, and his clothes were hung carefully in the closet.

Shawn was trying on his graduation gown with a yellow tassel for scholarship. He looked at me and smiled. "Mom, are you proud?"

"Of course. Why, shouldn't I be?"

"By the way, how do you like my room?"

"I can live with it," I smiled.

"Think my angel would be comfortable today?" Together we laughed.

"He'll be going down the aisle with you anyway. Come on; it's time to go. He wouldn't want to miss your graduation any more than I do."

CONNIE WELLS NOWLAN

Lessons From a Rose

There is a time for everything. . . . A time to cry and a time to laugh.
. . . A time to be quiet and a time to speak up. Eccl. 3:1-7, NLT.

She came into my office for her weekly session. The usual smile was on her lips, but her cheeks were tear-smudged. I could see pain. I asked no questions, but waited for her to share.

Eventually she said, "My daughter Kayla is having a problem at school. The substitute teacher accused her of cheating because she had gotten a perfect score on her math test. Kayla loves math; she is good at it. But she walked out of the classroom in despair. She came home so broken, so discouraged, so—" Words failed, and tears threatened.

I made a mental note to see if there was something I could do. But two days passed, and I still had not acted. I didn't know what to do.

At the end of the week the mother was back. There was a glow in her eyes, and the spring was back in her step. "I had the most marvelous experience yesterday!" She almost sang the words. And she proceeded to tell me about the all-night prayer session she had had with God. "Then He gave me an idea," she said.

Going to the nearest flower shop, she had purchased a pale-pink rose that had just started to open. She took it to the school that noon and offered the flower to the teacher. "You see this rose? This is my daughter," she said. "I think she is special. But like this rose, she is fragile. We have to treat roses with great care."

She was about to develop the analogy further, but the teacher got the point immediately. Misty-eyed, she told the mother that she too had worried about the effects of her words. Right after lunch she apologized to Kayla, and then to the entire class.

Smiling, Kayla bounced through the door that evening, sharing with her mother the joys of the school day. Then she settled down to do her math assignment. All of this happened because of the prayer-filled gift of a single rose.

I learned a lesson that day. There are some things that only God can fix. I needed to learn to stand back and let Him work.

Lord, help me to remember that there is a time to speak and a time to remain silent and let You work.   GLENDA-MAE GREENE

A Place of Refuge

God is our refuge and strength, a very present help in trouble. Ps. 46:1.

I was preparing the lessons for a new week for my students in the one-room elementary school where I taught. I flipped open the teacher's manual for grades 1 to 4 Bible class. Aha! A new memory verse! I scanned the words, thinking how I would present it so the children would really understand. No use having them learn words like a parrot!

"God is our refuge and strength, a very present help in trouble." They would understand "strength" and "help" and "trouble." No problem there. I made a mental note to explain that "very present" would mean "always here with us." They knew "present" meant the opposite of "absent." God is really "present" with us.

Now, what about "refuge"? I could tell about the Old Testament cities of refuge where people who had been accused of a crime could flee to be safe until their case could be heard. That might catch their interest. Probably they hadn't even heard about that. I also could talk about a wildlife refuge, where animals could be safe from hunters. I thought most of them would know about those.

The next day I started the older students on their work, then called grades 1 to 4 up to the class table. "New memory verse," I said cheerfully, and read it to them. " 'Refuge' means a place of safety," I explained as I began the class. "Can anyone give me an example of what refuge means?" I thought one of them might come up with one of the examples I had. It would be better if they thought it out themselves.

But second grader Johnny had his own idea. "I know, Teacher," he explained enthusiastically. "It's like home base in a ball game!"

O Lord, help me to remember that when troubles pursue me, there is always a safe place to which I can run. It's a place where I can rest, catch my breath, get my priorities straightened out, find forgiveness and peace—and be safe! Help me to remember, in this game of life, to head back to "home base," where You will always be waiting.   SYLVIA M. ELLIS

Gone, but Not Forgotten

Give freely without begrudging it, and the Lord your God will bless you in everything you do. Deut. 15:10, NLT.

My grandma had disabilities from childhood. She was born in 1909, and when she passed away at the age of 87, she was deaf and nearly blind. For many years she relied on her ability to read lips and write notes to communicate with others. In many ways she was locked in a prison because of her disabilities.

Grandma loved to go places and to have company. When I was a girl, the Dorcas women would come to Grandma's house to make quilts. She faithfully wrote to family and friends and always remembered our birthdays. She eagerly waited for our letters.

My home is blessed, but it has also become a kind of private prison for my husband and me because we have a severely mentally retarded son, Sonny. Our closets, cupboards, interior and exterior doors must be locked to protect him. Sonny must be watched every minute. Although all three of us are doing the best we can, he constantly tests us. Writing letters and receiving letters, phone calls, and visits have helped me endure. Grandma faithfully wrote to encourage me while she lived.

Recently, while visiting my family, I entered Grandma's room. She was anointed in this room, and this is where she passed away. I stopped to look at some things on my grandma's dresser. "Those were things of Grandma's that didn't sell in the yard sale," my aunt explained.

Among the things was a plaque that caught my attention. I knew it was meant for me to find it just then. I'm calling it a belated birthday gift from Grandma:

Count your garden by the flowers,
Never by the leaves that fall.
Count your days by golden hours,
Don't remember clouds at all.
Count your nights by stars, not shadows.
Count your years with smiles, not tears.
Count your blessings, not your troubles.
Count your age by friends, not years.

Thank You, Lord, for flowers, stars, friends, smiles, and golden hours. You have blessed!
DEBORAH SANDERS

A Place Prepared

In my Father's house are many rooms; if it were not so, I would have told you. I am going there to prepare a place for you. John 14:2, NIV.

Since we would be driving from Sydney to Melbourne for a wedding, we decided to take the coastal route along the Princess Highway and do some sightseeing. It seemed that we should head for Eden and find a motel for the first night. We negotiated the heavy traffic of south Sydney and passed through many miles of charred eucalyptus forest already sprouting filigree garlands of tender foliage after fierce fires. Then there were delightful beaches and lakes and beautiful vistas. As the hours passed, we looked forward to resting in a quiet room in Eden. We noticed as we drove into the small town that it seemed full of tourists, so we were delighted to find a vacancy at a motel. Because of the holiday season the price had risen considerably, however.

We looked at the town and beautiful Twofold Bay, then returned to the motel for a hot, humid night in an uncomfortable bed, while the neighbors listened to loud television programs. Eden in name was no paradise that night!

Early the next morning we packed the car and journeyed to Melbourne, where we hoped our motel would provide us rest for the next four nights. We were not disappointed. The room was delightfully appointed, the service was excellent, the air-conditioning worked, and we could not hear the neighbors. It was bliss! Ironically, it even cost less than the hotel at Eden.

It is comforting to know that after the heat and exhaustion of the journey of this life Jesus will provide us the perfect, peaceful place to stay. There will be rest in beautiful surroundings with every need supplied. In fact, Jesus, who knows us intimately, is tailoring the accommodation to suit us individually. He knows what it is like to long for a place to lay your head, to escape conflicts, to live in beauty and harmony, for He has lived in this sinful, unpleasant environment. That qualifies Him to be the ideal host for this more than five-star accommodation He is preparing in heaven. And just think, it will cost us nothing. I can't wait!   URSULA M. HEDGES

Yes, Jesus Loves Me

How great is the love the Father has lavished on us. 1 John 3:1, NIV.

I was feeling depleted. I had worked three 12-hour shifts the previous three days. I wandered around the house, still clad in my robe and slippers even though it was midmorning. Finally I decided I could be somewhat productive if I balanced my checkbook.

Whenever I feel sad, lonely, or depleted, I find comfort in saying "Jesus loves me!" So I said, "Jesus loves me!" and then sat down at the table and began to balance my checks with my check register.

My check register said I had written a check for $33.39 to a major discount store. But when I compared it to my check, I was amazed to see $333.39 printed on my returned check. It was true that the last time I had made a purchase at the discount store, the clerk had shown me the amount automatically printed on my check. However, if I don't have my glasses on, I can misread the amount.

At first I panicked. I had no receipt to prove I had made a purchase of only $33.39. In spite of this, I went to the phone and called the store office. I explained my predicament to the lady who answered. She asked for some numbers and the date on the back of the check. She promised to call me back within an hour.

Within 15 minutes the manager called back. "On the day you wrote your check, one of the registers was over $300," he said. "We will be happy to refund the difference. In fact, we'll deliver the money to your home."

"That won't be necessary," I replied. "I have to come to town anyway."

He inquired if I had incurred any extra expenses because of the error. I explained to him that my overdraft protection had covered this.

At the store I gave my returned check to the man I'd been instructed to see. Within a few minutes he returned, smiling, and handed me three crisp $100 bills and a sizable gift certificate.

As I left the store, tears came to my eyes. I again said out loud, "Yes, Jesus loves me!" and smiled as I walked to my car.   ROSE NEFF SIKORA

The Angry Driver

Sincerity and truth are what you require;
fill my mind with your wisdom. Ps. 51:6, TEV.

It was 10:25 a.m., and I was lost! My singing group was scheduled to sing at 11:00 at a small church in Virginia. I had followed the directions, stopped at three gas stations for help, and called the church. Still, I couldn't find the place. Frustrated, I retraced my route.

I approached an intersection. Thinking it was the street I was looking for, I quickly cut over into the left lane without signaling. The brakes of the car behind me screeched loudly. I looked in my rearview mirror and saw the angry driver gesturing at me. I turned left and into a parking lot. She followed me. I stopped my car. She stopped hers, jumped out, and headed toward me. My heart skipped a few beats.

O God, help me, I prayed quickly as I rolled down my window.

"What did you think you were doing?" she exploded, waving her hands about six inches from my face. Her female passenger glared at me from the car.

"I—I'm really sorry. Really sorry," I stammered. "That was a stupid thing to do."

"You're right; that was stupid," she agreed.

"I'm lost," I said. "I've been driving almost two hours. The gas stations can't even help. I'm sorry." My words flowed out in a desperate attempt to justify myself.

"Oh," the woman responded, a little calmer now. "I'm sorry too."

She's sorry? I thought. I was surprised, but relieved at her change of attitude.

She asked where I was going, thought a minute, then realized she didn't know where it was either. Wishing me well, she headed back to her car and drove off. *Thank You, Lord,* I whispered. Still trembling, I drove on, knowing that God had given me the right words to say to someone I had obviously wronged.

IRIS L. STOVALL

The Encyclopedia Incident

A true friend is closer than your own family. Prov. 18:24, CEV.

It was my first day of work at my new summer job. During orientation we were put into teams. I was paired with a lady named Ethel. She was nice, but since this was only a summer job, I had no plans to develop any long-term friendships. I just wanted to do my job and go home. However, each day Ethel inquired more and more about my personal life. After a few conversations, we realized that we both lived in the same nearby city, a few blocks away from each other.

One day after work Ethel asked if she could borrow several volumes of my encyclopedia set.

"Yes," I agreed, "but I've promised to go swimming with my husband and nephew at the local pool this evening."

"We have a pool in the complex where I live. Why don't you come there to swim?" she suggested.

We arrived at her place with all of our swimming gear and the encyclopedias. Before I could get comfortable, I heard laughter as she flipped through the pages of one of the encyclopedias. I was a bit puzzled and somewhat insulted by her reaction to my generosity. After she calmed down she shared the source of her unseemly reaction—she did not think my 1951 edition would contain up-to-date information. I realized that in my haste I had picked up my husband's grandmother's encyclopedia volumes, which are a family heirloom! I too found the humor in this "mistake." Or was it a mistake? Was it God's plan to help break the ice so that a deep, rich, lasting relationship could develop?

After that incident, Ethel and I and our families spent much time together. We studied the Bible together; she attended church with me, and eventually was baptized into the family of God.

A summer job, or a summer opportunity to reach out and witness? I realized then that God can use every situation for us to be a witness to someone, if we are willing. Never close the door on an opportunity to reach out in friendship. You never know what God has in store!   ELLA TOLLIVER

Please Show Me a Real Christian

*Likewise the Spirit also helpeth our infirmities: for we know
not what we should pray for as we ought: but the
Spirit itself maketh intercession. Rom. 8:26.*

Church had been an integral part of my early life. However, during my
adult years I had stopped going to church regularly. I felt justified because I did not agree with the behavior of practicing Christians I knew. I
thought I was more Christian than they who were always "warming a pew."

However, as I found myself becoming more and more disenchanted
with my lifestyle, my friends, my everything, I remember asking God to
show me a better way. I wasn't sure church was it, but I knew that there
had to be something better than what I was experiencing.

I was a single parent trying to enter the teaching profession. I was
struggling to study, work full-time, take care of my child, and do, and do,
and do.

I found a job as an employment readiness counselor. Four of us had
been hired for the summer. We were paired off, and I partnered with Ella.
She was so different from what I had expected. She was actually different
from anyone I had met lately. I didn't know what it was. I found her easy to
talk to. She was a good listener too. I guess what I was most impressed with
was that she did not seem to judge me. She accepted me. The more we
worked together, the more I wanted whatever it was that she had; she
seemed almost to "glow." It was a long time before I made the connection.
She was a real Christian.

I was working on a research project for one of the credentialing classes,
and I needed to borrow some encyclopedias. I asked Ella whether she had
some that I could borrow, and she did. Well—you know that story. (See the
June 9 devotional.) But Ella didn't know that I had been struggling spiritually and emotionally and was really searching for a new direction for my life.

*I am so thankful, God, that Ella and I were put in each other's paths. I
needed to see a real Christian—living Your word—so I could come back to
Your fold, someone who let the Light shine through her to lead me to a life that
has been so much more fulfilling than it was before.* ETHEL WILSON

Totally Trustworthy

Behold, God is my salvation, I will trust and not be afraid;
for the Lord God is my strength and song. Isa. 12:2, NASB.

That stormy Navajo-land night the pitiful cries of a puppy penetrated our sleep. It had taken refuge under the recreation vehicle that was our home while we held evangelistic meetings on the reservation. Morning light revealed a pathetic little bundle of white fur, huddled beyond our reach. My heart went out to this mistreated baby who probably had been dumped off on the highway.

For days fear kept her hidden, daring to come out to eat and drink only when we were out of sight. At times she isolated herself among the rocks on the mesa, the picture of vulnerable loneliness. What trauma had caused her to cower from humans? Could we ever gain her trust?

"Come to me, little Puppylove. You think you don't have a friend in the world, but you do! Don't you trust me?" Though hungry for attention and touch, she rejected my gentle advances.

At last she risked taking food from my outstretched hand, then followed my husband and me when we hiked up the mesa. As she rested in the shade I sat near and softly sang, "I love who you are, really love who you are." Puppylove inched closer on her newly fat tummy and barely flinched when I stroked her soft fur. "Oh, Puppylove, I have wanted to touch you for so long. Finally you trust me! You've been hurt, but now you are willing to give people another chance!" Though her heart was racing, she let me pick her up and hold her close.

My relationship with Puppylove reminds me of God's unconditional love, which calls out to us even if we reject His overtures of mercy. He understands that trust comes hard for wounded ones.

"I have loved you with an everlasting love; therefore I have drawn you with loving kindness" (Jer. 31:3, NASB). We can trust such a deep, abiding love. Fear may keep us at a distance, but Jesus' arms are outstretched. He softly calls us into the comfort of His embrace. "I love you more than you know. Come to Me, I will give you rest. Let Me heal your fears, grief, guilt, pain, and problems. I am totally trustworthy." LILA LANE GEORGE

The Job

*Therefore I tell you, whatever you ask for in prayer, believe
that you have received it, and it will be yours. Mark 11:24, NIV.*

I was a stay-at-home mom for nearly 10 years, doing child care. I knew
how to feed, burp, diaper, and bathe babies, play games, sing songs, and
tell children's stories—all the good things that go with having small children in the house. With little exposure to the grown-up world, I was beginning to talk like babies!

Despite my love for children, I began feeling a desire for the grown-up
world again. *But,* I wondered, *how will I adapt? What do I have to offer the
world? Who would want me, anyway?* I doubted my own worth and ability.

One particularly lonely day I poured out my fears, frustrations, and
feelings of inadequacy to God. I shared how much I longed to be able to
carry my end of an adult conversation. I asked God to help me find something to ease me back into adult society.

I decided to wait until the fall, when both of our sons would be in
school, before I would go back to work. Then one Friday the director of the
Christian day-care center called with an immediate opening. I told her I
would discuss it with my husband. After I hung up, my excitement began
to grow. Maybe this was the answer I had been praying for!

I prayed, *Lord, if this is the direction You want me to go, please have my
husband be equally excited about the prospect of this job.* Not five minutes
later my husband arrived home. To my complete surprise, he was also excited about the prospect. I called the day-care center and requested an interview. Two days later I interviewed and was hired.

God doesn't always answer my prayers just the way I would like Him
to, but He always has my best interest at heart. If I am patient and will listen and follow His leading, what wonderful blessings He has in store for
me. I had that job for three months. It was a stepping-stone into another
job that fulfilled all my heart's desires.

MICHELLE ANCEL

The Picture That Came Home!

If you ask anything in My name, I will do it. John 14:14, NKJV.

I had a "curiosity bump" as big as a goose egg on my head this past summer. Did you know that God cares when even such an insignificant thing as this bothers one? Let me tell you about it.

Several years ago we took an old rowboat and put it in the middle of our front yard, painted the name of our business on it, filled it with dirt, and planted flowers in it. It really had been very pretty some years and was the object of much comment. However, this year was the most unusual.

When our son came over from Anchorage this spring, he said, "I saw a picture of your flower-boat on the wall at Borders bookstore, Beverly." When I asked how he knew it was my boat, he said, "Well, it had 'Moody's Marina' painted on the side of it."

Another friend told me he had seen it in the bookstore also, but when he took his wife in to see it, the picture was gone. I wondered, *Who took the picture? Why was it on the wall at Borders? Where is it now?* So I asked God about it. "If You wouldn't mind, God, I surely would like to know where the picture of my flower-boat is."

The last weekend of August, several months after my prayer, a pilot came in who was a frequent customer. Because of an accident, he had not been in since spring. "I have a gift for you," he said. Naturally I was pleased, but my excitement knew no bounds when he uncovered the picture of my flower-boat.

His wife had been in Alaska a couple years before and had taken a picture of the boat soon after it had been planted in early June. She had entered the picture in a photo contest in Anchorage and won first prize! Consequently it had been shown in several places around the state, including Borders. When that show was over, she had taken it home and told her husband she thought it would be nice to give it to me.

I had to wait all summer to find out about it, but God knew all along and allowed my "curiosity bump" to stay active. I am constantly amazed at the humor and love of our God. How great and loving He is!

BEVERLY MOODY

Faith Matters to God

*Bring ye all the tithes into the storehouse, that there may be meat
in mine house, and prove me now herewith, saith the Lord of hosts,
if I will not open you the windows of heaven, and pour you out a
blessing, that there shall not be room enough to receive it. Mal. 3:10.*

Last night I talked with a friend of mine on the telephone. She told me
she was having financial difficulty. Then the talk turned to the subject
of tithe. Our incomes are very similar. She admitted, however, she was not
faithful in paying tithe and didn't think it was important. I told her there
was a time in my life when I didn't think so either, but I would never go
back to that again. I shared some of my experiences and reminded her that
you can't outgive the Lord.

After we hung up I thought of the blessings I have received since I
started tithing. These blessings have proved to me how much the Lord
wants to give us good gifts.

I have four daughters, evenly spaced between the ages of preschool and
college, which makes life busy and expensive. This year we had extra bills,
so I was concerned about buying school clothes. I prayed before going
shopping and trusted the Lord to help me find the things I needed at a
price I could afford.

The very first place I went had several clearance racks of winter clothes
left from the previous year, with sweatpants for $3, marked down from $26.
Another rack contained sweatshirts for $5. I was able to find a couple of
sets for each of the kids.

One pair of pants was an odd purple color. I knew this would be difficult to match but figured my 9-year-old could wear them at home for play,
if not to school. When I returned home, imagine my delight to find a
sweatshirt that she had not outgrown that matched perfectly! They looked
like they were a set. Everything I had purchased that day was marked down.

I never used to find bargains before the way I do now. What's more,
the kids were happy with them.

The Lord tells us that the whole world belongs to Him. He loves to bestow gifts upon His children. Praise God! I'm a child of the King!

SUSAN L. BERRIDGE

The True Vine

I am the vine, and My Father is the vinedresser. Every branch in Me
that does not bear fruit He takes away. . . . Abide in Me, and I in you.
As the branch cannot bear fruit of itself, unless it abides in the vine,
neither can you, unless you abide in Me. I am the vine, you are
the branches. He who abides in Me, and I in him, bears much fruit;
for without Me you can do nothing. John 15:1-5, NKJV.

In my library work in foreign lands I often came across the misunderstood value of old library materials. One such amazing discovery was a large set of outdated periodical indexes that had no periodicals to which to refer. But they had been carefully shelved and preserved! No doubt they were donated long before, but no one seemed to understand their purpose.

As I directed my staff in the task of discarding the old indexes, I thought of the illustration Jesus used in His parable for His disciples about being useful. It is found in John 15. As I read again the familiar words, I decided that I do not want to be just taking up valuable space for no reason, such as those old indexes.

And as Jesus pointed out, no nourishment can come to the branches if they are cut off from the vine, the source of their nourishment. But a grapevine can produce much fruit when it is connected to the root source of strength, the vine. In the same way, I can produce fruit if I abide in the True Vine, Jesus.

I want to produce fruit like the fruit of the Spirit: love, joy, peace, etc. But without the connection to the True Vine, Jesus, I cannot produce fruit any more than those old indexes could do any good. But just as the fruit comes naturally to the branches as a result of the connection to the vine, so will my spiritual fruit appear naturally.

As a favorite Christian writer of mine says: "The Saviour does not bid the disciples labor to bear fruit. He tells them to abide in Him" (*The Desire of Ages*, p. 677). It is a natural outcome. My effort is to abide in Him. And it is He who gives me strength to do that by His righteousness.

BESSIE SIEMENS LOBSIEN

A Little Mouse Tale

*My God shall supply all your needs according
to his riches in glory by Christ Jesus. Phil. 4:19.*

As I opened the flour bin in my little farm kitchen one morning, I discovered that a little mouse—and possibly even a friend or two of his—had been partying in my last bit of flour. They had left their little "calling cards" to let me know how much fun they had had. To say I was distressed as I dumped the flour and scrubbed out the bin was an understatement.

Not that it mattered. There was no sugar, yeast, or salt with which to make bread anyway. I had thought perhaps I might get together enough change to go to the store to get enough of those to enable me to bake that day, but now I had to dump out the little bit of flour I had. Now what would we do?

As I took a basket of wet clothes to the clothesline to hang, I poured out my heart to the Lord. *You know we have been living from one financial crunch to another since trying our hand at farming. We constantly have to fight with mice. Even though we have milk from the cows, eggs from the chickens, and a sack of lentils someone has given us, as well as some garden produce, we really would like some variety in our diet.* Instead of being thankful for what we had, I was complaining about everything we didn't have.

After hanging the clothes, I walked down the lane to get the mail. There in the mail was an envelope from a friend. I opened the letter and found a $10 bill with a note saying, "I felt impressed that you might need a little extra. I hope this will help."

I ran up the lane, waving the letter and yelling for my three children to jump in the car because we were going to the store. I am sure they thought I had taken leave of my senses.

Not only did we get the necessary flour, sugar, salt, and yeast to make the bread, but other staples as well—and even some peanut butter and jelly to go on the bread.

That evening we enjoyed a bountiful feast and thanked God for supplying our needs—and a few extra wants as well.   ANNA MAY RADKE WATERS

I Have Seen Thy Tears

I have heard your prayer, I have seen your tears;
behold, I will heal you. 2 Kings 20:5, RSV.

I had never felt so abandoned. Family relationship problems, long-term unemployment, and multiple, chronic health problems plagued me constantly. Worse yet, God didn't seem to care. Antidepressant medication had not and would not take away the problems. I couldn't stop crying. I began writing suicide notes to everyone, which only made me sadder.

Abandoning weekend camping plans, I didn't even want to go to church. I knew I would be asked about my red and puffy eyes. My husband suggested a walk in the mountains. I reluctantly agreed.

On the way we listened to a Christian radio station. The promise for the day was 2 Kings 20:5. It was followed by a sermon that went on, seemingly unendingly, with examples of how God cares for us.

Still, I had little energy to walk up the trail. *I could just slip away and freeze to death,* I thought. Finally we came to a giant log, where we ate the lunch my husband had thoughtfully prepared. His efforts really touched me. As we sat there he told me again how much he loved me.

During the next week I heard many assurances of God's love that God must have planned especially for me. Other promises I had heard came to mind. Slowly I improved. I learned these lessons from this experience:

No matter how bad things are, they are never bad enough for us to carry out Satan's plan to destroy ourselves.

Poisons build up in our bodies, affecting our feelings. We may need to sweat them out.

If we fortify ourselves with God's promises daily, He will bring them to our memory when we need them most.

We need to reach out to safe people.

We must keep praying about our needs and know that God answers, although not as quickly as we might like.

We need to focus on the positive things in life.

JOYCE WILLES BROWN-CARPER

Double Rainbow — Double Promise?

For I will see the rainbow in the cloud and
remember my eternal promise. Gen. 9:16, TLB.

The year had been particularly stressful and anxiety-filled. Our high school daughter had married her boyfriend after a basketball game one evening in January. They began a family in March and expected our first granddaughter in December. But the baby came early. Our adult son had just ended a long relationship with his girlfriend, and I knew he was hurting.

The attorney I worked for was semiretiring. That meant I had to work with other attorneys in the large office. My husband changed shifts twice that year, which meant lonely nights for me. We were also trying to deal with early empty-nest syndrome. Our lives were in constant turmoil.

I found it difficult to juggle career, legal support meetings, school obligations, church commitments, and home life. I told myself the Lord should see me through—He had promised. I believed Him and claimed the promises. But little nagging doubts would surface. *Would God really pull lowly, overreaching, overextended me through?*

One beautiful autumn day it had been raining. My morning devotional included God's promise of the rainbow. I felt the Lord speaking directly to me, that never again would such circumstances prevail in my life, that these burdens and frustrations would pass.

My husband and I went to breakfast a few miles from home. On our way back we shared our anxieties. My husband thought the children would be all right, but I told him I needed a distinct sign from the Lord before I could believe.

Suddenly a brilliant rainbow appeared! Then another rainbow cut through it! It was the first time we had ever seen a double rainbow. My husband and I gasped. It was truly magnificent.

The Lord had answered my prayer. Did He know how much I needed it? Of course, He did! Does He always answer my prayers so quickly? Of course not, but He is always in control.

Thank You, God. Your promises are always sure. Friends may fail me, family may reject me, but You are always there. I know You work all things for good to those who love You.
VIVI SUBY

The Bread of Life

Then Jesus declared, "I am the bread of life. He who comes to me will never go hungry, and he who believes in me will never be thirsty." John 6:35, NIV.

It wasn't my usual supermarket. I had just popped in for a few items, but I found something on the shelves that made me very excited. I went to the checkout with a big smile on my face. In fact, I felt so excited I wanted to tell everyone in the shop. When I got home, I phoned my brother and my sister, and I couldn't wait to tell the Australians who were staying with us.

What was it that I found in that supermarket? It was a loaf of bread! But this wasn't an ordinary loaf. It was an Irish plain loaf. It was what I had been brought up on.

Northern Ireland has an amazing variety of breads. We have soda, wheaten, treacle, and potato breads. We have barm-brack, fruit loaf, baps, and pancakes—not to mention various tea breads and variations on all of them, from fals to bannocks. But plain bread was what we ate every day. The bread more affluent people ate was called pan bread, but for us it was only for parties and special occasions.

So what is special about plain bread? Well, it has a firmer texture and more body than pan bread. It has more taste and a crust you can get your teeth into, and it tastes marvelous when toasted. Beside plain bread, pan bread tastes like cotton wool!

Having found it, I just could not get enough of this bread. I ate it every meal. At the same time, another part of me was laughing at the idea of getting so much pleasure from a piece of bread.

I thought, *This is how I should feel about the Bible. I have in my home and in my hands the bread of life. How often do I feed on it? Am I excited to have it? Do I want to tell others about it? I should!*

Right there and then I determined I would appreciate the bread of life more. I would feed on its firm texture and savor its wonderful taste. I would no longer be satisfied with soft pan reading, but I would go for the plain with the crust I could get my teeth into!   AUDREY BALDERSTONE

I Could Never Outgive the Lord

For even the Son of Man did not come to be served, but to serve, and to give his life as a ransom for many. Mark 10:45, NIV.

When we arrived at the Vancouver International Airport, it was one of the happiest moments of our lives. After 10 years of serving as missionaries on two continents, my husband and I had returned to Canada to be with our children. Reunions with family and friends were celebrated with potluck dinners that went on well into the night.

Settled down at last, I decided to relax and take life easy. *After all,* I reasoned with the Lord, *haven't I given all my time for You when we were in the mission field?*

I remembered days when not a single hour was spent for my own benefit, days when working 12 hours or more was never enough, or nights waking up at two in the morning to open our door to some unexpected guests.

Then, Lord, I said more convincingly, *I've done my best for You. Now I feel like a vessel emptied of everything. I've got cracks on the edges and am terribly scratched all over.*

So I perched in my comfortable seat in church and listened to every sermon. I attended every meeting at a women's weekend retreat. I even gracefully refused to take part in church services, because I was there to be filled.

Then tragedy struck a very dear friend of ours. She became sick while she and her husband were serving as missionaries in southern Sudan. A complication developed, but they were in a remote village where there was no medical help. She passed away. I was numb with shock. Tears wouldn't even come. Suddenly my own life was replayed like an old movie. I'd given only *some* of my time, spent *some* of my miserly effort, shared *some* of my worldly goods. How insignificant! My friend gave her all—she gave her life.

Lord, please forgive me of my selfishness. You too gave Your all. Don't let me ever forget that You gave Your life because You love me. Help me to untiringly share my time, my efforts, my goods, my life. MERCY M. FERRER

Shower of Blessings

Fear thou not; for I am with thee: be not dismayed;
for I am thy God: I will strengthen thee; yea, I will help thee. Isa. 41:10.

My husband was pastor at a teacher training college in Ghana when he got the opportunity to go to the United States to upgrade his education. Because of a lack of finances, we agreed that the girls and I would stay in Ghana.

One particular Friday we had no money at home, not even change to take a taxi to church. That night my baby became terribly sick. After giving her some medicine, we went to bed. At midnight I went to check on her, only to find her condition very serious. I needed to take her to the hospital immediately.

In most countries in the world there is no 911 to call. I ran to wake up my landlord's wife for help. She rushed over, picked up my child, and asked me to get ready to go to the hospital. I knelt by my bed and prayed for my daughter's life.

After my prayer I realized I would need money to get to the hospital, to pay hospital fees, and to buy medicine. I frantically searched for something, anything, besides the darkness underneath my bed.

Just then the landlord's daughter came in and said, "I'll take care of the taxi fare and the hospital bill. You can pay me back."

We went to four privately owned hospitals in the area, only to find them closed. My last option was to take her to the government hospital, but I didn't know anyone to get us to the emergency unit. How would I get past the congested waiting room? I could do nothing but pray.

We followed a nurse through the hospital gate. As usual, there were many patients waiting their turn. As we sat down, I recognized the nurse. She was a newly baptized church member and a family friend. She recognized me at the same moment. She rushed to prepare a record card, which she slipped in to the doctor. My daughter's name was called next. This nurse also helped us by collecting the medicine from the pharmacy.

We should not fear, for the Lord is with us. My Lord knew what I needed and what I did not have, and He sent an angel to care for all our needs. Yes, we serve a living and loving God.   ELIZABETH BEDIAKO

Sisters

Delight thyself also in the Lord; and he shall
give thee the desires of thine heart. Ps. 37:4.

Old tattered blue jeans, faded flannel shirts, second-time-around-worn-out sneakers—that was me. I was a typical tomboy. Seen at a distance, clothed in their hand-me-downs, I resembled one of the boys. However, to my parents I was the rose among the thorns. You see, I was the only girl in a family of eight boys.

I relished the homage my brothers paid me when I accomplished a feat they thought only boys could do. But a time came when they said, "You just can't come with us, that's all!"

Then how I longed for and prayed for a sister. I daydreamed of what it would be like to have one. I wanted her to look just like me so everyone would know that we were sisters! I wanted someone to play with, to share secrets with, to dress like, and to even share a bubble bath with.

I never did get a sister. After marriage I still had hopes of a female in my life, but my first child was a boy. As I lay on the gurney, ready to deliver my second child, I thought, *It isn't possible that I will have a girl.* After all, there were eight boys in my family and only one girl. And to make it worse, my husband's family consisted of four boys and one girl. Imagine my delight when my husband announced, "You had a girl!" What music to my ears.

Many, many years have passed since then. Not only did God give me a wonderful daughter, but more than that, He blessed me threefold by allowing her to be my friend and sister. We share our secrets, our sadness, our dreams, our fears, our hopes, and our joys! She is wise beyond her years. She is a gift from God, I am certain. Only a loving Father could understand such a need. The Bible says, "Delight thyself in the Lord; and he shall give thee the desires of thine heart." He did that for me!

Often I lift my heart to God in praise for His blessing. How grateful I am for His supplying my need for a sister and a friend.

Thank You, Father, for my sister—my daughter. SONIA E. PAUL

Learning Patience

They that wait upon the Lord shall renew their strength;
they shall mount up with wings as eagles; they shall run,
and not be weary; and they shall walk, and not faint. Isa. 40:31.

As a physician I had visited the coronary-care unit of our local hospital on numerous occasions. Then one evening, quite unexpectedly, I found myself there as a patient, with my heart beating irregularly. This was not in my plan for myself. Although I was released from the hospital the next day and the problem was not too serious, I was surprised at how weak I felt. I had hoped to return to work in a few days, but a week later I was still unable to do anything.

Then one day, when I was feeling quite discouraged, I found a special Bible promise in my promise box. Isaiah 40:31: "They that wait upon the Lord shall renew their strength." That day two of my church family also sent me cards with the very same text.

This is just what I need, I thought, and so I claimed that promise in prayer. *Lord, I'm not interested in flying like eagles, nor even in running just now. But it would be good to be able to walk without feeling faint.*

The next day I felt much better and went into the garden and did some gardening. I felt that God had answered my prayer.

The following morning I had to be taken to the coronary-care unit, as my heart was again irregular. "Whatever happened to Your promise, Lord?" I moaned. "Didn't You promise me strength? What am I doing back here?"

Again my stay in the hospital was brief, but the weakness persisted. Two weeks later, when I was still not back to work, I read again that verse in Isaiah. "They that wait upon the Lord"—somehow the word *wait* sprang out at me, and I got the message. God was trying to tell me to "be patient."

I learned a lot during those four weeks of enforced rest. While lying down, I was looking up. I did much thinking about the purpose of my life and my need for a closer walk with God. Looking back, I'm grateful for the experience and for those of my church family who sent cards that day to remind me, "Those who wait on the Lord shall renew their strength."

RUTH LENNOX

Rolling Crowns

Look, I am coming soon! Hold tightly to the little strength you have — so that no one will take away your crown. Rev. 3:11, TLB.

I did not loiter after church, nor did I accept the thoughtful invitation to lunch. The previous night I had made visual aids to demonstrate Bible stories and songs we planned to teach the local children in a nearby village that afternoon.

A quick glance at the sky revealed no rain was imminent. God had once again answered our prayers for a fine afternoon, as He had done for the previous many months. The only suitable location to conduct our program was under a spreading tree, and in our area where the two seasons seemed to be wet and very wet, it was unusual to have every Saturday afternoon free from rain.

As my VW, laden with flannelgraph board, visual aids, musical instruments, mats, and helpers pulled up beside the tree, the children were waiting to help us unload. They spread the mats out in the shade, and it was surprising how many small bodies could fit on each one.

One of the children's favorite songs was "I Will Wear a Crown in My Father's House." They were very poor in this world's goods and loved to wear the crowns and robes while they sang. At the conclusion of the singing, the cardboard crowns were placed by the side of the mats and the program continued.

A sudden gust of wind caught us unaware. The visual aids were scattered, and we caught sight of the cardboard crowns rolling across the grassy open field. With one accord the children gave chase and with some difficulty retrieved the crowns and secured them from any future gusts.

We have laid up for us a crown of righteousness, not an imitation one. Through carelessness the children lost their cardboard crowns for a time, and it was only with difficulty that they were regained. What a tragedy if Satan succeeds in using the cares and attractions of this world to suddenly snatch away our crowns of righteousness.

Lord, help me to hold fast to my faith so that no one will take my crown!

JOY DUSTOW

God's Kind of Love

*This is My commandment, that you love
one another as I have loved you. John 15:12, NKJV.*

I just couldn't believe what I had done. I felt awful. I felt worse than awful—I felt physically ill. Unintentionally I had dented someone's car in a parking lot with my car door. But very intentionally, when I finished shopping and no one had come out to the scarred car, I left. I knew it was wrong, but I couldn't afford another bill. And I was afraid of what my husband would say. I knew how important his car was to him, how he'd feel if someone dented it, and I didn't tell him. I hated to disappoint him. So fear caused me to run. I regretted it the moment I left the parking lot but seemed incapable of going back.

In tears I finally told my husband what had happened. He was silent, not saying a word. I knew he was disappointed in me. I couldn't eat dinner, I felt so bad.

I dried my tears and took the boys to their piano lesson. I took along my Bible, too. As the boys practiced their lessons with their teacher, I searched the Scriptures for what they said about guilt. What I found thrilled my heart. God's Word assured me that He hadn't abandoned me. He would continue to love me and transform me. His peace filled me.

Tim was working on the computer when I got home. The bed was turned down, the teapot whistling on the stove. Without saying a word, he ushered me to the bed, tucked me in, and brought me a cup of tea. After putting the boys to bed, he came and just held me. His snuggling presence said it all. *He still loved me. He cared about how I felt.*

He showed me in a tangible way how God feels toward me. So many times when I've blown it again, I'm almost afraid to go to God. I don't like disappointing Him. Yet God is a God of compassion. He too sheds a tear and holds us close. Sometimes He does it through a loved one or friend.

Lord, help me to feel Your unconditional love and acceptance in my life, especially when I feel the most unworthy of it. And help me to be the instrument of Your love and acceptance to another who is hurting.

TAMYRA HORST

Swimming Lessons

But as for you, be strong and do not give up. Chron. 15:7, NIV.

Some time ago after a serious operation I felt I would never be able to exercise again. I could barely make it to the mailbox at the end of the driveway and back again. Clearly something had to be done to help me regain my strength and vitality. For the present, even walking seemed to be out of the question, so I decided to take up swimming, an activity I had always enjoyed. We lived near a large community pool that I decided to visit as soon as possible.

When I tottered in the door, I explained my plan to the lifeguard. "I would like to swim, but only in the first lane so I can get out quickly if I don't feel able to continue," I told her. "Also, could you please walk beside me as I swim?"

"I'll watch you constantly," she promised.

Thus assured, I began to swim. More important, I knew the lifeguard's eyes were always on the water and that if I got into difficulties she was there to help.

At first I managed only one length, but as my confidence grew I lengthened the distance until in a surprisingly short time I was swimming half a mile a day. The gentle exercise in the water helped rebuild weak muscles and hastened my recovery. My husband and I still swim regularly and can testify to its healing powers, especially to those whose bones or muscles are no longer as supple as they used to be.

The Christian walk has been likened to a race, but to me it's more like swimming laps. We can be secure in the knowledge that our Lifeguard is always there, watching us, encouraging us, and sometimes correcting us, giving us an enormous confidence. There were times at first that I felt like giving up, but always the lifeguard challenged me to swim a little farther in the full knowledge that her job was to keep her eye on me at all times and rescue me if I ever got into danger.

Lord, You are my Master Lifeguard, encouraging me to "be strong and not give up." Your eye is on the sparrow and surely on me too, every inch of the way. I trust You; You're always near to rescue in times of danger. I face today with this confidence.

EDNA MAY OLSEN

Lessons From the Past

For everything that was written in the past was written to teach us, so that through endurance and the encouragement of the Scriptures we might have hope. Rom. 15:4, NIV.

Old, abandoned houses fascinate me. Generally my pleas to stop and investigate remain unfulfilled, but on one trip through some of the back roads of British Columbia we stopped to photograph a few. We stepped through open doorways or peered through glassless windows as we imagined where the kitchen had been, the living room, the bedrooms. Then, as we left the old homesites, I wondered why so much mystery surrounded these empty, tumbledown buildings.

I decided the reason for my fascination came from what those houses symbolized. A father, mother, and children represented family. Central heating mandated togetherness. A wood cookstove producing bread, berry pies, and savory soup suggested contentment. Homemade clothes represented resourcefulness. Family worship indicated a belief in God. High days such as Thanksgiving, Christmas, birthdays, weddings, and parties symbolized community.

And just what does this have to do with our lives today? Is heritage God-ordained, or is it the erratic scheme of some long-forgotten personality? What might we lose if heritage is lost? And what might we gain if heritage is preserved?

Heritage lost would mean we would forget the sacrifices of pioneers and the lessons they learned. Heritage preserved gives each of us a focal point from which we remember where we've been and where we now belong.

Much can be gained by looking back and dividing the positive from the negative. We can vow to not repeat the actions of others that influenced us in regrettable ways. We might consider our scars and find ways to help others in the healing process.

God must believe heritage is important, for He provided many ways for remembering—altars, offerings, rainbows, Sabbath, high days, statues, Communion, nature. Are these not all the Lord's enactments for the purpose of reminding His children of His care and love?

Heritage is a topic we must address. Some experiences never, never to repeat. Some to repeat often.   MYRNA TETZ

Surprise! Surprise!

Surely He has borne our griefs (sicknesses, weaknesses, and distresses), and carried our sorrows. Isa. 53:4, Amplified.

The dream was so vivid, so clear, so comforting, that I gave it diary space. I tried to describe the peaceful green scene of my dream in words. Then I forgot about it.

The dream had come during a season of sorrow and heaviness of heart resulting from problems for which I had no solutions. *This could never happen to us!* I had thought, but it had. The mind-numbing shock, plus the responsibilities I carried, was blowing my inner sense of self-worth. Something had to change.

I turned to Isaiah 53, reading until my dulled brain began to comprehend that Jesus Christ had "borne my griefs . . . and carried my sorrows." In those verses I saw a stained-glass picture of Jesus Christ on the cross, and appreciated a little more of what it means when it says He indeed bore my griefs and carried my sorrows. Gradually I learned to leave my burden at the cross and walk with renewed strength.

Then early one morning a phone caller invited us to serve in a totally new environment. We were amazed at this, but delighted to answer yes. We left our home to set up temporary living quarters in our new place of work. I shall always recall, with great pleasure, the next two years. Our troubles fell away as we rediscovered ourselves in serving others. The Lord's plan for us was beyond our expectation.

One day after we had settled into our new location I idly flicked through my diary. I was startled to read about the dream I had forgotten. I looked out of our living room window, up the green, grassy slope that led to the hospital where I was serving as chaplain. It was the comforting scene of my dream. That dream had given me, in affliction, a photographic preview of future blessing.

Thank You, Lord, for Your marvelous love that caused You to go to Calvary, bearing my sorrows, carrying my pain. Help me to leave my burdens at the cross today, knowing You care and You will work things out in Your own time.

LINDA M. DRISCOLL

A Garden of Beginnings

They will be like a well-watered garden,
and they will sorrow no more. Jer. 31:12, NIV.

Although I don't consider gardening as one of my gifts, I thought it
might be fun to experiment anyway. I started my garden by planting
pole beans close to the corn so they could wind around cornstalks as they
grew. Next I added neat little rows of assorted vegetable seeds. Finally I
placed tomato plants in special cages next to where I hoped snow peas
would sprout.

It wasn't long before I saw progress. Then I had to go away for a while.
When I returned, my garden looked like a war zone. The corn had grown to
giant proportions. The pole beans were inching forward on the cornstalks
like snakes winding around a tree branch, ready to overpower it. Earwigs
had attacked the spinach, and the eggplant had completely disintegrated.

The tomato plants blossomed with such profusion that they bent their
cages into a horizontal position. The snow peas, once symmetrically and
carefully placed, managed to extend their vines beyond my most optimistic
expectations. They were so intertwined with the tomatoes that they looked
like one plant.

Needless to say, harvesting was an experience. But at least there was a
harvest! Through it all God put this comforting thought in my heart: *This
garden will last only a little season. If I choose to have another garden, the mistakes and problems of my experimental garden will be buried. The barren
ground will have a new start.*

Sometimes I think of my life as a garden. There's a blend of joys and
disappointments. Some ideas take root and flourish, while other plans die
on the vine. It's then I remember that each day lasts only a little season. I
need to harvest the victories and rake out the defeats. When winter comes,
snow will cover my little garden spot, making it clean and white. Because of
the sacrifice of Jesus, my life is also clean and white. My failures are buried
under His blood.

Each day is His gift of a new beginning. Planted firmly in His love, we
can grow while we wait for the Lord to come and gather His people. It will
be the greatest harvest the universe has ever known.

MARCIA MOLLENKOPF

Growing Up

When I was a child, I spoke like a child, I thought
like a child, I reasoned like a child; when I became
an adult, I put an end to childish ways. 1 Cor. 13:11, NRSV.

As a child my one big dream never quite happened. I came from a large family with very little money, so I'm not sure where my sophisticated idea came from, but I wanted to be an opera singer.

If there was ever an extra quarter to spend my dad would sometimes give it to me, and I'd hurry down to the Lerner Theater to watch and listen to some of the greatest opera singers of the day: Lily Pons, Grace Moore, and Gladys Swarthout.

Several years later the duets of Jeanette MacDonald and Nelson Eddy graced the movie screen, and I was completely captivated by their beautiful voices. It was some years before I had enough money to buy any records of my favorite singers, and I played them again and again.

I always enjoyed singing, mainly for my own enjoyment, but also with friends at church. I remember the first hymn I learned to sing as a duet with my friend Betty. She played the piano and taught me the music so we could sing "Ivory Palaces" together. Whenever I hear that lovely old song the memories come flooding back, and I'm a child again.

A Lily Pons I am not, but I do enjoy music and still like to sing, even though my vocal cords are getting rusty and my voice tends to squeak on the high notes occasionally. A wave of nostalgia sweeps over me whenever I play the old songs. They are a constant reminder of days gone by.

I know my childhood dreams were just that—dreams, nothing more. But I'm not ashamed of my fantasies. We need to have dreams to give us hope, to keep us excited about life, and to motivate us to move forward.

I'm not real sure just when I began to lose my dream of becoming a prima donna. Times changed, and I changed with it. "When I was a child I spake as a child, I understood as a child, I thought as a child: but now I am old and I've put away childish things."

Lord, make this true in all parts of my life today.   CLAREEN COLCLESSER

The Delayed Train

*Call upon me in the day of trouble: I will
deliver thee, and thou shalt glorify me. Ps. 50:15.*

I had been one of the instructors in a training program conducted in
Kottayam, Kerala, south India. After the meetings on Saturday night, I
needed to catch the train that leaves Ernakulam Junction at 9:15. On inquiry
I found that the travel time from Kottayam to Ernakulam is nearly one and
a half hours. Without hesitation I booked my return ticket for that night.

I arranged for a man to drive me to Ernakulam at 6:30. Since I thought
the trip was one and a half hours, I was quite comfortable. I began to panic,
however, when the driver revealed that it takes two and a half hours by
road, and we had to leave at 6:00, at the latest.

Around 5:00 it began to rain torrents, making driving almost impossible. Fortunately, an hour later the rain slackened, and we headed for
Ernakulam. Soon the night set in. Heavy rain had damaged the road, and
the driver lost his way twice.

At 8:50 we were still more than 10 miles away from the city, caught at a
railway crossing. There were nearly 15 vehicles ahead of us. I began to panic
again. *Will I catch the train? What will my husband think when he doesn't
find me on the train? Why didn't I leave earlier? Why was the driver careless?*

Then I remembered that there was no use worrying, because God could
take control of the situation. So I prayed. *God, You know I must catch this
train. My husband will be waiting for me at the other end. He will worry when
he doesn't find me. I cannot contact him, but Lord, You can delay the train for
my sake. It is possible for You to do so.*

God's peace filled my heart. I was sure He would delay the train for me.

We reached the railway station at 9:20 and learned the train was in fact
delayed by 15 minutes.

*Lord, help me today to remember that no matter what happens, You are
in control of the situation. Help me not to worry, but to trust You completely.*

HEPZIBAH G. KORE

Walk Safely

*Whoso walketh uprightly shall be saved: but he that
is perverse in his ways shall fall at once. Prov. 28:18.*

It was a beautiful July day with wispy clouds weaving through the blue sky. It was not too hot, not too humid. I was only a half block from home, and my morning walk had been exhilarating. Oh, how I enjoyed this peaceful time of the day! My three-mile hike took me through our neighborhood park and brought me back down the quiet residential sidewalks. Even though I strode with confidence, I knew from experience that there was good reason to watch for uneven spots in the cement.

I thought, *How lovely it is! How is it possible it will be so barren, icy, and cold in just a few more months?*

I listened to the cardinals talk to each other. I greeted the familiar black kitty sitting lazily on her porch. I noted some new flowers, fragrant and colorful, in one yard. It was fun to watch the squirrels race about, scampering after each other, down a fence and up the next tree. A bunny sat quietly nibbling on some goodies, hoping I wouldn't notice him. There were so many enjoyable sights, sounds, and smells on this route. I was keenly aware of them all.

All of a sudden I was down on all fours. Searing pain shot through my knees, hands, and wrists. I had forgotten for just a few seconds to watch where I was going. Carefully I stood, grateful I could still walk home.

After ice packs, X-rays, medical consultation, splints, and other minor treatment, I was grateful to learn there were no broken bones.

I reflected on my misfortune. I thought about the comparison between my daily spiritual walk and my physical walk. All goes well when I faithfully watch where I am going. I can enjoy the beauty and surroundings around me, but I must not forget to be on guard for the rough spots.

We get into trouble when we are distracted or forget to watch where our path is leading. Sometimes it takes just one misstep, and we experience a painful fall. Every day we need to keep our eyes fixed upon Jesus. He will help us to walk uprightly. He will keep us from falling.

ARLENE E. COMPTON

She Hath Done What She Could

She hath done what she could. Mark 14:8.

Nowadays economy dictates that households are more likely to survive if there is a dual income in every unit. This means that many women, who would have joyfully served as stay-at-home moms, now find themselves in the workforce.

I was one of those moms whose only goal was to be at home raising my two children. Unfortunately, this was virtually impossible, since my husband was a full-time college student. I nevertheless gave my desires to God.

"Give them your best, and I'll take care of the rest" was His response to my prayers. God showed me how to nurture the children spiritually while continuing to work. I was their Bible teacher at church during their nursery years. Our quality time was spent enjoying songs of Jesus, praying, and Bible readings with fun memory drills.

We were blessed to find a Christian caregiver. Her home was spotless. Everything was in place. And there was a noticeable spiritual atmosphere. My son was eager to go to her each morning. Each day he shared with me the stories he had heard. Bible characters came alive to him.

On one particular day when he was 3½, he marched around the house boisterously singing, "'Lift up the trumpet, and loud let it ring; Jesus is coming again!'"

"Where did you learn that song?" I asked.

"Mrs. Osborne," he replied. "Do you like it? Jesus is coming again, you know. Mommy, we have to tell everybody."

Misty-eyed, I thanked God. Not only had He given me a Christian caregiver, but one who spiritually nurtured and molded the minds of my children during their preschool years. Proof of her work is still evident today in those two adult children, whose lives are committed to Christ.

Mrs. Osborne recently died, but I know that in the earth made new she will wear a crown laden with the little jewels of her earthly labor. I praise God for her and pray that my children will reunite with her there. How remarkable that even in the smaller things of life God promises to supply all our needs!

SONIA E. PAUL

Not to Know You Are Lost

There is a way that seems right to a person, but its end is the way to death.
Prov. 14:12, NRSV.

When I was a child, there were four very special days every year I looked forward to. Christmas, of course, was the most important of these. Then came my birthday, Thanksgiving, and the Fourth of July—Independence Day for the United States. Actually, the Fourth of July seemed almost the most special because it came in the good old summertime, and we could do some kind of outdoor activity.

One Fourth of July when I was quite young, we decided we would go to my cousin's sheep camp up on Battlement Mesa. This was quite an outing in those days. We went by auto, and when the road ended, by saddle and packhorses. The packhorses were laden down with all the goodies we needed for a sumptuous picnic.

My cousin Aaron, who was six weeks older than I, told me to follow him; he knew a shortcut into the camp. He had spent every summer in sheep camp and knew the rugged area like the back of his hand. So in a very few minutes we arrived at the camp and began to check out the area. After a wonderful time of exploring and enjoying every second, we decided to shoot off some firecrackers. We were so busy exploring all the wonders of nature that the thought never occurred to me that the rest of the party was long overdue.

Aaron's dad owned the sheep camp and had been coming to it every summer for many years, but for some strange reason he became disoriented and lost. When he heard our firecrackers exploding, he followed the sound, thinking we were lost and calling for help. How utterly dumbfounded he was when he discovered it was he who had been lost!

Even as I think of it many years later, it is baffling to me how a man who had gone up to camp so many times could get so lost. And the worst part was he did not know he was lost. How very sure we need to be that we read the Word of God and follow His instruction sheet so we will not be lost and think we know where we are. Our eternal destiny is the only important thing in this life. Yes, we can think we are so right and be totally lost.

PAT MADSEN

Healing Hands

Jesus saw the woman. . . . He placed his hands on her, and right away she stood up straight and praised God. Luke 13:12, 13, CEV.

"Thank you," I said to my chiropractor. "I feel so much better now. That realignment was just what I needed."

Already the numbness and tingling, the unexplained aches and pains, and the headaches were subsiding. My chiropractor knew my spine. He knew exactly what was needed to get me straight again. This adjustment was part of the treatment to get me back to good health. If only I had listened to my friends years before. Surely I wouldn't have questioned had I known the relief I'd have. My chiropractor, and his wife of the same profession, were loving, compassionate, and knowledgeable practitioners. I trusted them completely.

I hopped off the table, feeling a bit straighter, and headed toward the receptionist's billing station. *Boy,* I told myself, *I feel great already. This is definitely worth the cost.* As I waited to pay my fee, I saw other patients entering the office with their customary aches and pains and complaints. I saw others looking refreshed following their treatment.

Years ago Jesus, our Master Physician, offered to lay His gentle and healing hands on each one of us. He has told us that He can realign our wretched spiritual bodies, laden with the aches and pains of sin, and make us feel better. He understands us better than anyone else, inside and out, and He knows everything that's out of whack. He's ready to give us a gentle nudge, or a firm push, a healing hand, whenever we need it. And in the end our diseased, spiritual bodies will be whole again. We'll be completely healed, made new by the touch of the Master.

Yet how often we ignore the advice of our family and friends who proclaim how much good He can do for us. We even refuse to listen as the Master Himself speaks, sweetly assuring us that He can make us new again. If only we'd accept the loving care He so freely wants to give.

Lord, please place Your hands of love on me today. Set me straight. Do whatever it takes to make me what You want me to be. Make me new again.

IRIS L. STOVALL

The Yellow Dress and God's Love

Yes, I have loved you with an everlasting love;
therefore with lovingkindness I have drawn you. Jer. 31:3, NKJV.

I couldn't help feeling loved every time I passed the yellow dress. I had hung it on the door in my bedroom and passed it often as I cleaned house. I just couldn't believe what God had done for me!

Two weeks earlier my husband had told me to order that yellow dress as his birthday present to me. I had seen it in a catalog and had fallen in love with it. So I called right away, hoping the dress would come in time for an event three weeks away. I was told the dress was on back order and wouldn't be shipped for eight weeks. Disappointed, I ordered the dress anyway. The next week I received a postcard confirming that the dress would be shipped in eight weeks.

The following Friday I was cleaning the house when the thought struck me: *I would sure like to wear that yellow dress to Trent's graduation tonight.* My brother-in-law was graduating from high school that evening. I was going to be gone all afternoon, and it was impossible for the yellow dress to arrive before I left—it had been only two weeks. *Oh, Lord, I know You could send me that yellow dress. Do You think You could have it here before I leave? I'd really love to wear it tonight.*

As I continued to clean, I was convicted of my selfishness. *Lord, how could I pray for You to send the yellow dress? Please forgive my selfishness. I know You love me enough to do miracles for me, but this is unnecessary. I have plenty of clothes to wear.*

I didn't give it another thought until I ran out to the mailbox. Sitting on the ground next to it was a box. Inside the box, hanging on a hanger and ready to wear, was the yellow dress. God had sent it anyway. The dress spoke of a great love, a love of miracles and grace, unconditional love. That's the way God loves us. He loves us no matter how we act or what we do.

Father, thank You for loving me no matter what, no matter how I act. I don't deserve Your love or kindness, yet You delight to lavish me with it. Help me today to see the examples of Your love. TAMYRA HORST

Playing Scrabble

The race is not to the swift, nor the battle to the strong. Eccl. 9:11, NKJV.

It had been a long day, but we were happy because of the superb performance the children rendered during the church service. Later the board
meeting ended with well-thought-out plans and decisions. When we arrived home, it was still early, so I challenged my husband, "How about a
game of Scrabble? We haven't played for a long time."

"Sure, let's have a game," he replied.

I had the first move. I could use only three tiles, so I scored a few
points. My husband's first score wasn't good either, but his second play was
devastating. It wasn't only a triple score, it was a scrabble. One move—98
points! I felt discouraged.

"Can we start all over again?" I asked. "I'm sure I've no chance of winning."

He ignored me, continuing to arrange his tiles. I pretended I didn't
mind continuing, though I knew I was doomed to lose. I told myself, *Ofelia,
you are playing to enjoy the night. Winning is not important.* But believe me, I
wanted to win! As we finished the game, I became concerned that points
would be deducted from my score. He had only two tiles left, and when he
finally laid those two tiles I sighed and said, "I knew you'd win."

He tallied the points and announced, "You won! Congratulations, honey!"

I was flabbergasted. I had no idea I even had a chance.

How often, when trials and difficulties assail us, we're prone to become
discouraged and are ready to quit. Whenever problems at home, work, or
school seem insurmountable, we tend to give up. Trials and hardships over-
whelm us, and we forget how our heavenly Father, who knows our frame,
can sustain us. We focus on our inadequacy instead of looking up to Him.
Hasn't He promised in His Word that victory is ours through His grace?

*Lord, help me not to give up when the going gets tough. Help me to hang
on to the end, for You have promised that victory is mine through Your grace
and Your power. I may not always win in Scrabble, but through You I am always a winner in life.*

OFELIA AQUINO PANGAN

A Precious Burden

And thine ears shall hear a word behind thee, saying,
This is the way, walk ye in it, when ye turn to
the right hand, and when ye turn to the left. Isa. 30:21.

Three days ago I retrieved a child's oak chair from the apartment dumpster. Amazingly, it fit my Emily's little inkwell school desk.

Two days ago I saw the downstairs neighbors moving. I didn't know them except to nod and say hello, as they don't speak English and I know only about five words of Spanish.

Today I suddenly remembered the neighbors' dining room set piled on their son's pickup. It was the same color as the little chair. Maybe it belonged to them and they hadn't thrown it out! I ran down and knocked on their door. The apartment was empty except for the television that their son still had to come for. The lady didn't understand anything I said about the chair. Then I remembered they had moved their dinette directly from the apartment onto the truck pulled right up to the steps, so it couldn't have been their chair.

I changed the subject. "You're moving?"

She opened the door wider. "To New York."

"You have family in New York?"

She said something about her husband being sick. I couldn't understand the details, but the husband was now obviously out of the home and very sick somewhere, which was the cause of her having to now move out of state. Instinctively I put my arms around her. "I'm sorry," I said.

"I cry every day," she sobbed.

I folded my hands together in front of her. "I'll pray to God for you."

After a few more words we said goodbye, and I hugged her a second time. As I walked back upstairs she called out to me, repeating "'Bye." This time there was a lilt to her voice as though if only for a moment the burden had been lifted.

A half hour later I took the garbage out. My neighbors' apartment was dark, the windows empty. They were gone. I stood in the parking lot and shuddered at how quickly I could have lost that golden opportunity, at how quickly darkness comes.

ALEAH IQBAL

A Little Child Shall Lead Them

Let the little children come to me, and do not hinder them,
for the kingdom of heaven belongs to such as these. Matt. 19:14, NIV.

We were in the early stages of building a new home in Victoria, British Columbia, and the workers were preparing the forms so the concrete for the foundation walls could be poured. They had been racing against the clock, as there was a lot of rebar that had to be put into the walls to strengthen the concrete for the two longest walls, which were nine feet high.

On Sunday we were at the site looking at the forms and feeling excited about the walls that would be there by Monday night. Our daughter talked happily about "my new house that's being built."

We went home, had supper, baths, and worship and were kneeling for prayer. "Whom are we going to pray for tonight?" I asked Kelsey. The usual list, including family members, was mentioned, and then, out of the blue, she said, "And the men building my new house." We dutifully prayed, although I was surprised at her special request.

We didn't make it out to the new house until the following evening, when it was nearly dark. We were surprised to see the workers still there. There had been an accident. The concrete had been poured for the walls, but the forms had not been tied off.

When the concrete was poured for the top two feet of one of the high walls, the wall collapsed. The heavy, wet concrete crashed onto the ground below. If any of the workers had been standing near that wall, they would have been seriously hurt, if not killed.

I felt chills in my spine when I saw what had happened. The angels must have protected the workers and kept them away from the dangerous area. How could a 2-year-old child have known that this was the time to pray for the workers? Amazing how the Holy Spirit can speak to the smallest in our midst, and amazing how they respond. It encourages me that God hears and answers the prayers we don't even have the wisdom and understanding to pray without the prompting of the Holy Spirit.

It was another God-affirming instance in my life and an amazing revelation of how He works to achieve His will. LORENA LYN LENNOX

Covering for Our Sins

*You forgave the iniquity of your people
and covered all their sins. Ps. 85:2, NIV.*

Near my home is a narrow gully through an old forest traversed by a small footpath. A stream flows at the bottom of the gully, and the path crosses it by way of a little wooden bridge. This "greenbelt" with a busy road on one side and a housing development on the other was a joy for me to walk through. Its thick undergrowth, tall trees, and babbling stream made it an oasis in the busyness of my life. I felt the serenity of its lovely atmosphere.

Then came winter. The cold nights and daily winds darkened and changed the lovely green of the area. The undergrowth and leaves were gone, exposing an old tire half in the stream and bottles and cans lying about, evidence of human carelessness. Now I even noticed the fallen and rotting ancient trees. The walk was no longer so enjoyable.

In time spring came, and suddenly new green growth was everywhere. The fragrance of freshness and spring showers filled the air. The garbage disappeared under a mantle of green leaves, and even some of the fallen trees sprouted. The older stumps of trees became nesting places for birds, and the birdsongs and squirrel chatter brought joy to my soul. The perfume of new flowers wafted in the air, and all was beautiful again. Once again God, in His love, had covered the ugly and the useless. Walking was again a joy, an opportunity to be refreshed.

I thought of the covering God provides for my sins. I thought about how He covers the effects of my human carelessness with His mantle of righteousness. Over the unpleasant and ugly parts His lovely life of compassion spreads a glorious blanket of fragrance. He can even make good come out of the broken parts of my life, using them for His glory.

My prayer for today, for my life, is that You will continue to cover me, making me a joy to those around me. I want the useless, the old, the broken covered with Your love. May those who come near me today enjoy the fragrance of Your love.   Ruth Lennox

He Leadeth Me? Indeed!

*Trust in the Lord with all thine heart; and lean not
unto thine own understanding. In all thy ways
acknowledge him, and he shall direct thy paths. Prov. 3:5, 6.*

When I graduated from high school, my sister Audray gave me a Bible with today's verse written on the inside page. There were also some flowery words about my being the greatest sister.

At 17 my thoughts centered on fantasies such as pretty clothes, travel to exotic lands, marriage to a Prince Charming, and a possible career in musical theater. After all, hadn't I been offered the chance to cut an all-expense-paid record?

My sister's gift was nice, but certainly not one I coveted. I did respect the Bible, however, and kept it on my nightstand, being careful not to put other items on top of it. I even recorded study texts given in my senior year by a Bible teacher.

Today that same Bible is on my lap. It has become a valued treasure, as I have developed a friendship with its Author. As I think back over my unseasoned youth, I am in awe of how God has directed my paths, including the years I did not acknowledge Him. He has provided a variety of opportunities for spiritual growth, and in His love has blessed me with some of the desires of my heart besides.

My wonderful Prince Charming is also a spiritual mentor and is supportive of my efforts to use my spiritual gifts. Travel to exotic places has been fulfilled via missions that have reinforced my witness for Him. My theatrical aspirations became trivial as the Lord opened doors for me to sing praises to His name, even in Chinese. The pretty clothes? I have some, but I find I really don't like to shop.

I want to say a big "Thanks, sis!" I had no idea when you gave me that graduation gift what a valued treasure it would become, what an encouragement it would be to me.

And Lord, thank You for all those people in my life who have helped me on my journey toward spiritual maturity. Help me today to show my appreciation.

FERYL E. HARRIS

JULY 12

God's Garden

Be ye therefore perfect, even as your Father
which is in heaven is perfect. Matt. 5:48.

This year I planted my garden, as I do every year. I made a mental plan of what I would plant in each row but never wrote it down, because I just knew I would remember where everything is planted. But every year, by the end of the first week, I don't remember what I planted where. Even when the plants come up, I can't tell what vegetable it will be. To a novice gardener like myself the squash, the pumpkins, the cantaloupe, and the cucumbers all look alike.

Well, I didn't remember the plan or the rationale as to why I put them where I did, so I had to wait until they started to produce before I really knew what they were. As the Bible says, "By their fruits you will know them" (Matt. 7:20, NKJV).

In spite of my novice gardening abilities I have learned some valuable lessons about life. What if someone came into my garden to get rid of all the imperfect produce for me? If they came in July and saw pumpkins the size of tennis balls, would they pluck them off the vine because you couldn't yet make any pies from them? If they saw green cantaloupe, would they say, "These aren't worth saving. No one could eat them like this"? And what if they were to see green tomatoes? Would they save them?

All that produce is perfect to me, just not mature yet. Could this be how our heavenly Father sees me? I may be perfect in Christ but may not be as mature as some of my brothers and sisters. It is important to remember that our Father works with each of us in different areas of our lives, helping us to mature. We humans have the tendency to want to pluck out what we feel is imperfection, when in reality it is but a lack of maturity. We are all perfect if we are in Christ.

As Christ's followers we do what we can to help nurture our little garden of God's family. All gardens need proper soil, rain, sunshine, and nutrients or fertilizer. In the garden of God's family we need to remember that the Master Gardener will help us grow to be perfect and mature just as our heavenly Father is perfect. SUSAN L. BERRIDGE

Who's Doing Time?

For we know that our old self was crucified with him so that the body of sin might be done away with, that we should no longer be slaves to sin — because anyone who has died has been freed from sin. Rom. 6:6, 7, NIV.

Former Nixon aide, convicted felon, and converted Christian Chuck Colson tells about a visit to a prison facility near São José dos Compos, Brazil. This prison was no ordinary prison. Years before, it had been turned over to Christians by the Brazilian government to be run according to Christian principles.

Chuck said he found inmates smiling, even the murderer who opened the gates to let him in. He observed clean living areas, people working industriously and living in peace with one another. The walls were decorated with wisdom from Psalms and Proverbs. The guide escorted Chuck to a notorious prison cell once used for heinous torture. Only one inmate now occupied the cell. The guide unlocked the torture cell, paused, and asked solemnly, "Are you sure you want to go in?"

Chuck informed his guide that he had seen the inside of isolation cells all over the world. Slowly the guide swung the massive door open to reveal a prisoner confined within the cell of torture: a beautiful crucifix, hand-carved by the now-converted inmates, portrayed the prisoner, Jesus, hanging on the cross.

Softly and reverently the guide said, "He's doing time for the rest of us."

This is what Jesus has done for us. Through the shame, guilt, humiliation, He paid the penalty. The penalty for sin, regardless of what that sin is, is death. Someone had to die. Either you or a divine substitute. You cannot leave prison until someone dies. Either you or Jesus. Sin put us in prison and behind bars of guilt and shame. Jesus served time for us; He paid the price, and because of it we have been pardoned!

The doors are open. You are free, pardoned. I don't want to remain in an isolation cell once I am free. Do you?

Thank You, Jesus, for doing time for me.

NANCY L. VAN PELT

A Spectacular Show

Behold, he cometh with clouds; and every eye shall see him. Rev. 1:7.

It was an unforgettable July 14 several years ago in Nice, France, on Bastille Day. From start to finish it was a grand celebration that included a big parade with many countries participating. The great array of festive foods and constant fanfare made it a one-of-a-kind day.

As it began to get dark, we assembled in chairs that afforded a good view of the Bay of Angels. The big climax would be the fireworks display, shot from a boat, out a distance from the shore. At the right moment the fireworks started, accompanied by a band that played appropriate music for each display being shown. Gorgeous, vivid colors reflected in the dark waters of the bay. Fireworks roses and cartoon characters and many other things filled the night sky, unbelievably real and huge.

Most exciting was the next to the last display. I gasped as I saw the Star-Spangled Banner appear in the sky, every star and stripe in vivid red, white, and blue, filling the whole sky. So grand! And it seemed to wave for an incredibly long time while the band played "The Star-Spangled Banner." A big lump crowded my throat, and tears welled in my eyes as the symbol of the country where I had lived all my life lit up the night. It would have been touching anywhere, but seemed especially so in a foreign land.

In many ways we are all on foreign soil. Heaven is our real home. Imagine what a big display it will be when Jesus appears in the clouds with a retinue of glorious angels! What a wonder it will be to look upon His dear face, the face that was bruised and spat upon for us. It will be the most wonderful, exhilarating day of our lives. To behold the face of our Redeemer, who loved us so much He gave His very life for us, to see Him coming in the clouds of heaven to take us to our real home, will be the most spectacular show ever seen in the entire universe!   PAT MADSEN

No Good Thing

*The Lord withholds no good thing from
those whose life is blameless. Ps. 84:11, REB.*

As a young college student many years ago, I used to stand in the ice
and snow nearly up to my knees, waiting for the bus. I would think,
*Why does everybody else have a car, but I do not? And neither do I have any
prospects of getting one anytime soon. Why is life so hard for me?*

At that point I was young and hadn't thought about being thankful that
I had bus fare so I could ride, or that I had money for further education. I
hadn't thought about the fact that I had legs and feet that could move without hurting, and winter clothing to keep me warm while waiting. I hadn't
even stopped to be thankful that God was watching over me, protecting me
from all hurt, harm, and danger.

Life reminds me of a little yeast roll, the kind served in some restaurants. The combination of yeast, flour, salt, sugar, oil, and warm water is
mixed together well and kneaded. After much kneading, the dough is
punched down and allowed to rest. In about 30 minutes the dough will rise
to triple its previous height. After the dough is punched down again and
rolled to a desired thickness, it is shaped and will rise nicely again.

Many of us may feel like that yeast roll. We are tossed, turned, and
punched by life. But we rise again, and are better than before. When you
feel like life is punching and rolling you, look around for things for which
to be thankful. God does not withhold any good thing from His children. It
is good to meditate on the Lord and to think of His goodness. He is so
good and merciful, not because we've been keeping His commandments,
but because He loves us.

No matter where you are in life God has a purpose and direction for
you. Things now may seem slow or even boring, but as a follower of Christ,
you have reason to make every day count. It can be a foundation on which
tomorrow will be built.

*Lord, help me today to count my many blessings. Help me to stop feeling
sorry for myself and to start praising You in the midst of the punching and
rolling life may give. Like a lump of bread dough, You can help me rise again
when I'm punched down.*

BETTY G. PERRY

Before I Called

Before they call, I will answer; and while
they are yet speaking, I will hear. Isa. 65:24.

Some friends were moving, and we had decided to give them our garment boxes to help ease the move. For more than a week the boxes sat by the garage door. For more than a week the door had opened and shut with no problem. But tonight the good times were over.

I pushed the button on the remote control, and the door went down to the top box, stopped, and went back up. After several tries I left my 22-month-old son, Eric, in the car while I moved the box.

On my return Eric said, "Mama, 'tuck." I explained that the door was stuck on the box but I had fixed it.

I pushed the door opener again. Once again the door went down to the top box, stopped, and went back up. Once again I left Eric in the car and moved the box—this time five feet from the door—and returned to the car. Once again Eric greeted me with "Mama, 'tuck."

I assured him it was definitely fixed this time, and he clapped. When I pushed the button, the door closed.

A few miles down the road I saw flashing lights. Minutes before, two cars had collided. I was struck with the realization that perhaps the boxes were in the way for a reason. Perhaps those stuck boxes saved Eric and me from being in an accident. Had I not spent those moments trying to close the stuck garage door we might have been part of the accident scene.

Isaiah 65:24 promises, "Before they call, I will answer; and while they are yet speaking, I will hear." As I recalled this text I thanked God for boxes that got in the way. They had delayed me just long enough to avoid a much more serious problem.

Only in eternity will I know, Father, how many times You have delivered me. Thank You! Help me to be patient today when little delays hold up my progress. It just may be Your way of protecting me from danger. What a marvelous God You are! How much You care for me!　　　　MARSHA CLAUS

Killed by Kindness

For the mountains shall depart, and the hills be removed;
but my kindness shall not depart from thee. Isa. 54:10.

When we moved to Hamilton, New Zealand, we were delighted by the fruit that grew in the district. We visited the orchards for boxes of delicious apples, pears, and peaches that we ate raw or preserved. Each autumn we processed boxes of grapes into juice. Although it was hard work, it provided inexpensive food we all enjoyed.

Most of all, we loved the abundance of strawberries that we picked and ate by the bucketful. In fact, that first summer our eldest son developed itchy, red blotches on his skin from eating so many strawberries. Then we discovered a blueberry farm. The fruit was more expensive than other things, but we all became addicted to blueberries.

My husband and children decided we should buy a blueberry bush and grow our own. The best spot was decided upon. With enthusiasm the ground was carefully dug over and all weeds eliminated. It was almost a family ceremony as we carefully planted our little bush with a suitable amount of fertilizer, pressed the soil around it, and watered it.

At first the progress of our green baby was excellent, but soon our precious blueberry plant was struggling to survive. No one could understand it, for we tended it with care. Then one morning it was evident that the promise of blueberries from our bush was a false hope—the poor thing had died.

Secrets came out then. It appeared that both our boys, as well as their father, had all been carefully fertilizing and watering the bush. They had killed it with kindness. It seemed that too much kindness can be a dangerous thing.

Not so with God's kindness. He knows what is good for us. He provides exactly what will help us to grow spiritually. His wisdom, being above human wisdom, directs events so that we can not just survive, but flourish and produce good fruit and produce it abundantly. Besides this, His kindness will never fail; we can count on it every day.   URSULA M. HEDGES

Establish My Feet

Ponder the path of thy feet, and let all thy ways be established. Prov. 4:26.

Sarah, my 3-year-old great-niece, sat mesmerized, watching the graceful glides, spins, jumps, and double and triple axels of figure skaters performing on the TV screen. At the end of the show she announced, "I know what I want to be when I grow up."

"What?" her mother asked.

"A figure skater."

She begged her parents to buy her a pair of skates. Several days later, when her parents hadn't complied with her request, she announced, "My heart already knows how to skate, but someone has to teach my feet."

Performance of any skill requires instruction, practice, and more practice. One doesn't learn to read by sitting in a library. Knowing the tune to a melody doesn't mean one can play it on an instrument. Parallel parking isn't perfected without practice. Having a set of carpenter tools and blueprints doesn't make one a professional builder. Reading a book on gardening doesn't make one a gardener without putting into practice the information given.

Sarah's comment made me think about my Christian experience. *Are my skates sharpened and clad on my feet, pirouetting over the ice to improve my performances? My heart knows right from wrong, the way I should go, but are my feet following the path that leads to eternal life? Do my words and actions show what my heart knows?*

It's not enough to know the benefits of physical exercise and healthful eating habits. I must care for my body as the temple of God. It's not enough to know about the power of prayer. I must make daily communion with God a part of my life.

It's not enough to know Bible doctrines. The story of the rich young ruler illustrates the folly of thinking a knowledge of God's Word is sufficient to make us candidates for heaven. We need to practice its precepts.

Dear Lord, please help me to let my heart direct my feet to serve You and humanity. Help me to practice what I profess. EDITH FITCH

A Bowl of Hot Zosui

He answered . . . "Love your neighbor as yourself." . . . But . . .
he asked Jesus, "And who is my neighbor?" Luke 10:27-29, NIV.

I arose from my bed. Dragging my blanket behind me, I entered the kitchen, turned on the faucet, and poured a glass of water. Shivering, my hand trembled as I reached for my antibiotic. *Ninety degrees outside, and I'm shivering!* I thought as I picked up the thermometer: 103° F.

I tightened the blanket around me, shuffled back to my futon, and lay down to rest. I suppose I could have been uneasy—home alone with a high fever in a foreign country. But I felt secure in knowing that my neighbor up the hill was watching out for me.

I hadn't been resting long when there was a knock at my door. It was my neighbor with a steaming pot. "I heard you were sick, so I brought some zosui," she greeted me.

"Come in," I said. She placed the zosui on the table and pulled a bowl and spoon from her shopping bag.

"Oh, thank you," I said. "I really like zosui."

"Zosui is very good for you when you are sick. I know you will get well soon," she said as she served the thick rice soup.

I savored the combination—rice, eggs, and vegetables in the warm broth. I let the blanket drop to the floor. It was as though I was warmed by the very first bite. I ate the soup, returned to the futon, and fell asleep. When I woke up, I took my temperature again: 101° F. Hey, the zosui was beginning to work! Or was it the antibiotics? Or both? In my childhood my mother's chicken noodle soup could work wonders. Now zosui brought the same comfort.

In Japan, so far from where I called home, a neighbor who could not speak English said clearly by her actions, "I care enough to prepare this for you. I want you to get well." The language of love needed no translation.

To the human eye, we may seem all alone. But God, unseen, is watching us, caring for us like the neighbor on the hill. Though unseen, He stays connected to us. Through one of His agents—like you, like me—He knows how to bring us that bowl of steaming zosui when we need it.

KAREN LINDENSMITH

He's Preparing Me

*"For I know the plans I have for you," declares the Lord,
"plans to prosper you and not to harm you, plans
to give you hope and a future." Jer. 29:11, NIV.*

My brother, Mack, called with the news that his wife's mother had died. It seemed as if it were yesterday that Mack and I had gone through the same grief. The pain was so fresh and real to us all.

My first concern was how he and Kim would hold up, emotionally as well as spiritually. They were new to the Chattanooga area and recently baptized. I prayed that God would comfort and strengthen them.

Kim and I finally talked. She seemed surprisingly calm and in control. As the conversation continued she spoke of God. "Terrie, God doesn't make mistakes. He knows what is best, and I trust Him. He has a plan. I am hurting, but I trust Him."

As I absorbed her words the thought occurred to me, *God has been preparing Mack and Kim for this very moment.* More than a year before, He gently began pulling Mack, then Kim, into a saving relationship so they would have Him as their foundation for this present experience. As we continued talking, it was not with depressed voices, but with hope and joy.

I rejoice in the fact that God has a special purpose for our lives. Kim is right—He doesn't make mistakes; all things work together for good (Rom. 8:28). He slowly and gently prepares us for all the circumstances of our lives.

The funeral is tomorrow, but we are looking beyond tomorrow toward a day of rejoicing when we all get to heaven! He's preparing a place for us (John 14:1-3), and as Mack so eloquently said in preparation for the service, "We as Christians know that those who die in Christ are sleeping. We have hope of the resurrection."

So we wait in anticipation for the fulfillment of God's plan. We trust God's preparation process, in spite of the pain we at times must endure, because with Him the best is yet to come. He's simply preparing us.

TERRIE E. RUFF

Please Listen to Me

*There is a time for everything . . . a time to
be silent and a time to speak. Eccl. 3:1-7, NIV.*

Chad is 19 months old and is destroying his home. He breaks everything he can get his hands on, and his parents have had to board up his window. He has tried to drown the cat, smears feces, and bangs his head. He is emotionally disturbed." The director of the home-based early intervention program was presenting new cases. "Who would like to take this one?"

We teachers all looked at each other. The others were more experienced in the field than I. But after prolonged silence it became obvious no one was going to volunteer for Chad.

"I'll give it a try," I volunteered in an uncharacteristically soft voice. Thus I got involved in the lives of some of these special needs little people.

I prayed all the way to Chad's house that first day. Visions of a wild-eyed, half-crazed child swirled in my mind. Instead, I found a lonely young mother, with an equally young, alcoholic father, who apparently had little success in his own life. Chad was an adorable, if ill-behaved, curly-headed toddler. Slowly his behaviors began to fit. If Mom is so stressed that she spends most of each waking hour compulsively cleaning, what better way to get her attention than to empty your diaper on the wall? It certainly was effective. How quickly this child had learned *If I talk, no one will listen, but if I scream, hit, or bite, someone might hear me.*

We too develop behaviors to get the attention we need. Though they may not be as open as Chad's, they are often as destructive. People—especially people in pain—need someone to listen to them. Job asks for this eloquently: "Bear with me that I may speak" (Job 21:3, NIV). "Oh, that I had someone to hear me!" (Job 31:35, NIV). How many big people are longing for someone to hear them. It is a basic need of the human heart.

In today's world we find ourselves too busy or frightened to speak with each other or with God. If we would live lives that are rich, we must make the time and develop the skills to do both—a time to listen and a time to speak.

VERONICA CROCKETT

A Woman God Can Use

*Render service with enthusiasm, as to the Lord and not to men
and women, knowing that whatever good we do, we will receive the
same again from the Lord, whether we are slaves or free. Eph. 6:7, 8, NRSV.*

Several months ago a woman shared something in a testimony that inspired me. Eleven years previously, when she joined the workforce of a certain office, a friend gave her a heart-shaped magnet with the words "I am a woman that God can use" written on its face. The speaker stated that she placed the magnet on a file cabinet that was visible from her desk. It had remained there all those years, serving as a continuing reminder that God wanted to use her talents for His cause.

That simple, profound statement, "I am a woman that God can use," made a deep impression on me. When I returned home from the meeting, I immediately began scouring craft stores for small wooden hearts, red paint, and magnets. I wanted to make and share this idea with all the ladies in my church and with other friends.

If we all had this constant reminder—and really believed it—what a difference it would make in our own lives, in our homes, in our churches, and in our communities! If we are willing, God can—and will—use us in many ways. Most may actually be such small ways that they will go unnoticed, even by us. Our small Christ-inspired acts and words will become a way of life, as natural as our breathing.

A favorite author of mine has written, "It is not the possession of splendid talents that enables us to render acceptable service, but the conscientious performance of daily duties, the contented spirit, the unaffected, sincere interest in the welfare of others. In the humblest lot true excellence may be found. The commonest tasks, wrought with loving faithfulness, are beautiful in God's sight" (Ellen G. White, *Prophets and Kings*, p. 219).

Lord, I am thankful that I too am a woman You can use. Please help me to be all I can be with Your guidance. Use me today to bless others.

DOROTHY WAINWRIGHT CAREY

When Winter Comes

*There is a time for everything, and a season
for every activity under heaven. Eccl. 3:1, NIV.*

July. What special memories that word conjures up! In our locality we regularly have a spiritual retreat then. Seeing old friends, joining them in worship, hearing God's Word expounded powerfully—all are blessings I wouldn't forgo.

Almost as soon as we return home the black sweet cherries are ready to can. My daughter and I are off to the orchard and come home laden with ripe, juicy fruit. Soon the pantry shelves sparkle with the filled jars. Oh, yes, it's work, but our efforts are far outweighed by satisfaction and anticipation of how good those cherries will taste next winter.

As we're driving through the countryside in July we often see huge piles of wood awaiting the homeowner's saw. He will cut the cumbersome logs into manageable pieces for fireplace or woodstove. In our light summer clothing and with beads of perspiration on our faces, it's hard to imagine that the wood will be needed. But it will—in winter.

Another common sight during this month is immense round bales of hay lining the road at the edge of a field. These bales are dried and then enveloped in white plastic to await the need in midwinter. When snow covers the ground, the livestock on the surrounding farms will be grateful for the hay.

Sometimes it seems that we spend our whole summer getting ready for winter! I prepare for winter because I know it is coming. After all, we've been promised that the seasons will continue until Jesus returns to take us home with Him.

"There is a time," says the wise man of old, "for everything, and a season for every activity."

What season is it for you now? Is it summer? Are you preparing for the winter of life?

Each of us must have a time for study, for prayer, for devotion, for witness. We must have a season for developing and using the spiritual gifts God has given us. The winter will come when it will be difficult or impossible to prepare. Let's take advantage of the glorious freedom of "summer" to glorify God in every way we can.   LEA HARDY

The Wonder of It All

*The heavens declare the glory of God; and
the firmament showeth his handywork. Ps. 19:1.*

I enjoy watching the magnificent sunsets that are so prevalent along the Intracoastal Waterway in South Carolina. I am constantly in awe of that huge red ball, surrounded by imposing clouds of pink and magenta, as it dips into the sea.

Even after the sun has slipped beneath the rim of the water, the glorious array of color lingers until darkness slowly creeps into the western sky, and God's palette is erased for another day. I linger, watching the moving water.

My earliest recollection of any type of flowing water goes back to my grandparents' home in the country many years ago. I remember the narrow, wooden bridge we had to cross to get to their little farm just outside town. The little rickety walkway spanned a small stream that we children loved to play in. There always seemed to be an overabundance of weeds and high rushes growing along the steep bank and down to the water's edge.

Barefoot, we had great fun playing along that stony creekbed, searching for frogs and toads and other tiny wet creatures that might be lurking about. The water was deep enough for splashing yet shallow enough for safe play for the wee ones.

There's something special about moving water that is peaceful and relaxing. I love to sit on the pier and listen to the silence, or walk on the beach where the waves roll in and lap on the shore like some giant fingers grasping for grains of sand.

Water is a necessity. We must have it to drink, to cleanse our bodies, and to wash the earth. We cannot live without it. But God has also used it to provide pleasures for our constant enjoyment on the land, in the sea, and in the sky.

Lord, I thank You for water and the joy it brings to me—ocean sunsets, rippling brooks, waves lapping on the seashore. Thank You for putting beauty into this necessity of life. Thank You for the pleasure water brings.

CLAREEN COLCLESSER

The Heart Garden

But the harvest of the Spirit is love, joy, peace, patience, kindness,
goodness, fidelity, gentleness, and self-control. Gal. 5:22, NEB.

What is my heart garden like? Does it attract the hummingbirds and butterflies? Do people come to my garden to wander leisurely and enjoy the colorful flowers and sweet perfumes that permeate the air? Or do visitors simply walk through the garden and, because of the weeds, not even notice the flowers I have planted? Do others feel free to litter it?

The Holy Spirit wants to be the head gardener in our hearts and is eager to help each of us achieve a high-quality and abundant harvest of the special fruit He promised to us. I am free to decide what kind of plants I want to put in my garden—big or little ones; red, blue, or yellow ones; with or without thorns.

As in every garden, if I do not take care of it continuously weeds will overrun the plants and flowers and stifle their normal growth. I know it is always easier to remove weeds when they are small, because once they have reached maturity it is impossible to extract them with the hands only. I need special tools for the job. And it requires more strength and work on my part.

If I allow the Holy Spirit to work in my heart garden, the perfumed and colorful flowers of love, joy, peace, patience, kindness, goodness, fidelity, gentleness, and self-control will be abundant and visible in my life and will bring happiness to me and others.

I want to take care of my garden to make it bloom. I want it to become a place of love, joy, and peace to those who are around me. Certainly people will feel free to visit and enjoy the beauty and scent of these flowers, but I need the help of the head gardener to do it. I am sure He is ready to come and help me cultivate it and get rid of the weeds.

Thank You, Lord, for helping my spiritual garden grow. Please weed out what is unnecessary in my life so that the flowers of grace may appear to bless others. Cultivate and water me so that my life will be a garden that attracts others to You.

ELLEN E. MAYR

God's Party

Let us celebrate with a feast! Luke 15:23, TEV.

Although most people celebrate a child's accomplishments, we certainly do not celebrate our failures as parents! Should a child go away and end up in a jam, loving parents will help—and even restore—their child. But celebrate with a party?

That's what God does. This astonishing God is not afraid His reputation may be questioned while recovering a failure to Himself. He does not follow His wayward child but gives all that she asks and lets her go. He does not give up hoping, longing, looking for His child's return. Then one glorious day as the Father looks over the universe, He sees her coming home!

This child left home because she thought her Father was too strict. She believed in her own twisted concept that she was not loved. Then she reached the lowest point of her life, and there flickered a small, dim hope that maybe she could go home.

Now the Father did not seem so strict and stern. In fact, Father's home seemed like a good place to be. She thought that if she went home and asked for a job as a servant, maybe, just maybe, Father would accept her back. So she headed home.

Father, who waited daily at the gate, watching for His child's return as if there were nothing else to do in the great universe, finally saw a speck in the distance. It was His child! Running to meet her, Father threw His own robe over the garbage bedecked rags that barely covered her.

Then came the party! Nothing was too good. The only sour note in the happy occasion was the older sister. She who had stayed home, faithfully doing her work, could not understand why all this fuss over a wayward sibling. This ungrateful little sister was receiving all the benefits of being a faithful member of the household after she had wasted it all and now finally dragged herself home.

Celebrate? Never! So thought the older sister. *It's not fair! It's unreasonable! It's downright degrading to flaunt this failure of a kid to the whole neighborhood, let alone the whole universe!*

Yes, there is a difference in the way God celebrates the return of one lost child. Thank You, God!

PEGGY HARRIS

Pain-free

The prayer of faith will save the sick, and the Lord will raise them up.
James 5:15, NRSV.

D ear God, please give the persons who are ill today a pain-free Sabbath."
I had never heard a prayer like that before. Because a woman in the church was dying from cancer, this prayer was repeated many times. It opened my eyes to something that had happened a long time before.

I had broken five vertebrae and was lying in my hospital bed. The first night the doctors came every hour to tickle my toes to check for paralysis. The nurse gave me a strong painkiller and sleeping potion so I could get some rest.

My accident had happened on a Sunday. All through that first week I could sleep only when I was given my painkilling potion concocted by the night nurse. In the morning the pain was back, and I needed more medicine.

On Sabbath morning, however, around 10:00, I suddenly realized I had no pain. In the evening, when the night nurse wanted to give me the medicine, I told her I didn't need it. I told everyone who came to see me how amazed I was that my pain had suddenly stopped. All the time I spent in the hospital, 10 weeks in all, I had no more pain in my back.

Sometimes it takes us a long time to understand what has happened. In my case it took 18 years. Only when I heard the prayer about pain-free Sabbaths did I realize they must have prayed for me in church that Sabbath morning and that my pain stopped just at that moment. How good God is! He didn't just give me a pain-free Sabbath, He stopped the pain completely. I still had to wait for my back to heal the natural way, but God did finally raise me up.

Maybe God is waiting for us to pray for somebody today who needs His healing power. He wants to help.

Thank You, Lord, for being a God who hears and answers the prayers of Your children for those in pain. Help me to be more diligent in prayer for those I know who need Your healing touch. HANNELE OTTSCHOFSKI

Heaven's Bonus

Eye hath not seen, nor ear heard, neither have entered into the heart of man, the things which God hath prepared for them that love him. 1 Cor. 2:9.

Betty and I became good friends through my weekly visits to her bachelor son's home, where she had come to live the last months of her life. I helped with household chores and was her primary source of socialization.

I arrived one morning to find her quite annoyed. When I asked what was bothering her, she puffed through her oxygen tube, "Oh, Bruce's pastor is coming to visit me today."

"And you aren't happy about that?" I questioned.

"No," she huffed. "I suppose he's going to want me to go to heaven!"

Not quite sure what to make of her statement, I cautiously asked, "And you don't want to?"

"No!" she retorted. "Why should I? None of my friends will be there!"

"Well, I'm your friend, and I certainly plan to be!" I said, trying to offset her mood.

Betty spoke in breathy sentences, explaining that her husband had been president of a large textile mill in the East. Her affluent life was a whirl of parties, high-class living, and frivolities of every kind. She said that none of her circle of friends would be in heaven because of the way they had lived. Their only mention of God was in a derogatory way.

I have thought of Betty's comments many times since her death. I've thought of all kinds of things I should, and could, have said to her and didn't. Her comments have made me rethink for myself my purpose for wanting to go to heaven. Would I want to go if I did not know anyone else there?

Of course, meeting Jesus is going to be the greatest joy of heaven. Since Betty did not know or have a relationship with Him, she did not consider it a privilege to be in His company. As wonderful as it will be to have loved ones and friends there, our greatest joy will be in appreciating the One who made heaven possible in the first place.　　　MARYBETH GESSELE

Removals

Come unto me, all ye that labour and are
heavy laden, and I will give you rest. Matt. 11:28.

Just the sight of the place gave me a headache. It was a mess, a real mess. Boxes and junk ready to be thrown away were all over the place. I could hardly move around without hitting something. I wanted to get a glass of water, but I slipped and spilled the water on my cluttered kitchen floor.

We were leaving Cyprus for America. Daniel, my husband, had been on business travels since I had started sorting and packing our things; our two teenage daughters were in boarding school. It was pretty tough working during the day and doing the sorting and packing in the evenings. Many times I was too tired even to go to sleep. My muscles ached. I wished for the day when the movers would come and take everything away.

Finally the day came. The movers, a team of six men, came to load our stuff in a 20-foot container. Although they had brought equipment to make the job easier and faster, it took them almost a day to load and get the container ready to seal.

Danny arrived from his trip in time to assist in the signing of the shipping documents and the sealing of the container. It was after 5:00 p.m. when they left our now empty house. In no time at all we cleaned up the empty rooms. What a relief! It seemed that a heavy load had been lifted off my shoulders.

While relaxing that night, I thought of the load of cares, guilt, and sins we carry in our lives. Many times our lives are in confusion. We are tired, but we can't rest. We don't have peace. Why do we choose to carry these loads? It would be much easier to simply call the heavenly Mover. He is always there and right on time. Didn't He say "Come unto me, all ye that labour and are heavy laden, and I will give you rest"?

Lord, help me today to sort out the confusion of my life. Come and take away all the load I've been trying to lift and move on my own. Clean out the trash and give me peace and rest, as You have promised.

JEMIMA D. ORILLOSA

Before We Call

*And it shall come to pass, that before they call, I will
answer; and while they are yet speaking, I will hear. Isa. 65:24.*

Eleven to 14 firefighters have been killed in Colorado!" the television re-
porter said early that July morning in 1994. I normally don't even have
the television on in the morning, but for some reason I had tuned in just in
time to hear this awful announcement.

Three days earlier our youngest son, Linden, had flown to Colorado to
fight forest fires there. My husband, Dennis, and I were both terribly
shaken. As I silently went about my duties that morning a prayer was never
far from my lips. *Please, God, don't let our son be one of the casualties.*

Linden had had firefighting training in northern Minnesota. At the age
of 30 he had decided to go back to college and take forestry. We were so
proud of him. He loves the outdoors and wanted to find something he
could do to earn a living while being in nature. God had protected him and
kept him from harm while he was "finding himself." Was his life snuffed
out now at such an early age?

I called others to pray for Linden's safety. Many concerned petitions
went up that morning on his behalf.

Later that morning I was delivering auto parts for our business. I had
the radio on, hoping for a positive news flash. Before I made my first stop,
the announcer reported, "All Minnesota firefighters are safe."

"Thank You, Lord!" I cried. While putting on a good front, my heart
had been at a standstill for several hours, so it took me a few minutes to regain my composure.

I rushed to call Dennis with the wonderful news. He was so overcome
with emotion he couldn't speak. How thankful we were that Linden was safe.

*I thank You, God, for answering the many prayers of those who petitioned
You for Linden and our family. What a wonderful God You are! You know
what we need even before we ask.*   Marge Lyberg McNeilus

Tight in the Arms of My Heavenly Father

Fear thou not; for I am with thee: be not dismayed; for I am thy God:
I will strengthen thee; yea, I will help thee; yea, I will uphold
thee with the right hand of my righteousness. Isa. 41:10.

M y husband was about to fly halfway around the world for a week, and I would be left behind with the two children. I was upset and not sure how I was going to manage.

I was used to my husband being away for a few nights in the week, but an entire week was a different thing. He worked for a large multinational company, and if we wanted to have financial gain, I had to accept that this was the way things were going to be.

It always amazed me how many of the moms of my children's friends coped with their husbands being away in the English navy for months at a time. Here I was with only one week to get through, and I was going to pieces.

One night a few days before my husband was due to leave, I had difficulty sleeping. I got really cross with myself, for I knew that if I did not get some sleep soon the problems of the next day would seem insurmountable.

Jesus, please give me the strength I need to get through next week, I prayed. Eventually I drifted into a peaceful sleep.

While asleep I dreamed that I was standing next to Jesus, and He had His arms wrapped tightly around me. What else happened in the dream I cannot recall except for the vivid image of Jesus standing in front of me with His arms tightly about me. This picture remained with me over the next few days and gave me a great deal of strength and much needed encouragement.

I cannot pretend that I enjoyed the week of my husband's absence—I did not. I managed to keep myself busy, however, catching up on many of the jobs that had been put on hold. And the girls and I had several unexpected telephone calls from their daddy during his time away, which helped the time pass quickly.

There have been many times since when have I felt discouraged, but the image of Jesus with His arms about me has remained with me and helped me through.

JUDITH REDMAN

Given Personalized Attention

Yea, I have loved thee with an everlasting love. Jer. 31:3.

It sounds unbelievable, but it is true. It is true, true, true! God cares about me individually. Me, insignificant me. I don't understand why He should love me—there is no visible reason. I am wrinkled and gray. I am sick. I am ugly, inside and out. But He loves me. I have disappointed Him many times, but He forgives me and keeps on loving me.

I don't do anything to make Him love me. I can't carry a tune, so I don't sing beautiful songs to praise Him.

I can't play any musical instrument, so I don't compose majestic music to glorify His name.

I can't preach stirring sermons, exhorting people to serve Him. I don't write poems extolling His goodness and mercy.

I don't even love Him as much as I should. Then why am I so sure that God loves me personally?

It's not because of the glorious sunshine and the life-giving rain that He sends, nor the singing birds and colorful flowers. They are free for all to enjoy.

No; it is because of His individual care for me. Not only in the big things—the daily necessities of shelter, food, and apparel—but in the tiny, insignificant-to-anyone-but-me little things.

An example springs to mind. An old friend sent me a Christmas card but did not include her address. I knew she would appreciate a message from me, but how could I? I had no idea of her address. I knew no one in the overseas country where she lived. I worried about it, but there was nothing I could do.

The next day I decided to clean out a desk drawer. I found several old envelopes I'd been saving to give the stamps to grandchildren. Turning one over, I saw my friend's address in her own spidery, old-fashioned writing.

Luke 12:17 says that God loves me so much He even numbers the hairs on my head. Best of all, He never grows tired of loving me. "Yea, I have loved thee with an everlasting love" (Jer. 31:3). What a wonderful God!

GOLDIE DOWN

The Roaring Nineties

*For my thoughts are not your thoughts, neither are
your ways my ways, saith the Lord. Isa. 55:8.*

My husband, Bill, learned that he was in the midst of downsizing on his job after 30 years of dedicated service. Devastation was an understatement, for in no way was he ready to retire. "What will I do with my time?" he asked.

"You'll adjust," I replied, reminding him that God had always kept His promise to never leave nor forsake us.

Bill was given an ultimatum: bump an employee with less seniority and take a substantial decrease in his salary, or take an early retirement. Early retirement would mean less pension.

Discouragement and depression almost overcame us. We frequently prayed together and applied Proverbs 3:5, 6: "Trust in the Lord with all thine heart; and lean not unto thine own understanding. In all thy ways acknowledge him, and he shall direct thy paths."

We began to do some of the travel we had looked forward to and reaffirmed our marriage vows. Life seemed good. We invested our life's savings in our dream house, but the contractor filed for bankruptcy shortly afterward. We tried to recapture our losses, but to no avail. Then Bill passed away, leaving the rest of us in pain, grief, and sadness.

Flo, my best friend, sat quietly as I bitterly reminisced and complained. "Remember Romans 8:28," she said. The verse raced through my mind as she spoke softly. I prayed for insight. God slowly opened my eyes. Would Bill have lived to enjoy our trips had he not retired early? Would we have been able to express our love by reaffirming our wedding vows after 33 years of marriage? I would have had to relocate had we built our dream house. Things could have been so much worse.

I have learned to thank God for everything. I now understood. "For my thoughts are not your thoughts, neither are your ways my ways, saith the Lord. For as the heavens are higher than the earth, so are my ways higher than your ways, and my thoughts than your thoughts." I sincerely believe that "all things work together for good to them that love God."

CORA A. WALKER

A Daughter Teaches Her Mother

You will not fear the terror of night, nor
the arrow that flies by day. Ps. 91:5, NIV.

"I f ever you are afraid or troubled, turn to Psalm 91 and read it carefully," advised my 17-year-old Moira Rose.

Moira was a student at Helderberg College, a Christian boarding school in South Africa. One of the girls' favorite pastimes was to tell ghost stories at night in the dormitory. Apparently this area of the Cape is noted for its weird stories. One particularly blustery night, with all the correct sound effects present—rattling windows and creaking doors—they huddled together to engage in their favorite amusement.

When Moira eventually went to her own room at the end of the session, she was terrified and couldn't sleep. She knelt down and prayed, "Dear Lord, please give me something to read that will take away my fear and give me peace of mind." She crawled back into bed with her Bible. It fell open at Psalm 91. She had hardly read halfway through the psalm when she was sound asleep.

She couldn't wait to call me the next morning and share her excitement at how the Lord had answered her prayer. I was pleased to hear of her experience and eager to study Psalm 91 for myself.

A few months after this incident Moira was killed in a car crash. I was devastated. One of my coping strategies was to read her Bible from cover to cover, taking note of what she had underlined and the annotations she had written in. Some of the texts seemed to stand out more than others, as if my child were again teaching and leading me to the only way to survive.

I would like to share two of these texts from Moira with you. First Peter 5:7: "Cast all your anxiety on him because he cares for you" (NIV). Psalm 34:18: "The Lord is close to the brokenhearted and saves those who are crushed in spirit" (NIV).

These helped me through the dark tunnel of grief. Moira seemed to be saying to me, "You are not alone; just hold on to Jesus, and He will see you through."

I am looking forward to the day when I can see Him face-to-face and thank Him for His love and comfort, and also thank Moira for helping me.

FRANCES CHARLES

Spiritual Housekeeping

*She watches over the affairs of her household
and does not eat the bread of idleness. Prov. 31:27, NIV.*

I love homemaking. It can seem mundane, yet cleanness and shine provide pleasantness. Soft colors and potpourri fragrance add to the atmosphere. Of course, cleaning and decorating are only a minute part of housekeeping. The aroma of God's love magnifies happy homemaking. Perhaps my pleasure with homemaking is an outcropping of my commitment to God to keep my spiritual house in order.

Remember Joshua? He boldly declared before the assembled Israelites at Shechem, "Now fear the Lord and serve him with all faithfulness. Throw away the gods your forefathers worshiped beyond the River and in Egypt, and serve the Lord. But if serving the Lord seems undesirable to you, then choose for yourselves this day whom you will serve. . . . But as for me and my household, we will serve the Lord" (Joshua 24:14, 15, NIV).

Did Joshua mean that his entire extended family and servants would serve God on Joshua's coattails? Hardly. Joshua's soul burden illumined his responsibility for spiritual housekeeping.

Joshua's declaration motivated a response, "We will serve the Lord our God and obey him" (verse 24, NIV).

So I can't let my husband's—or anyone else's—spirituality be mine. I must live out the same covenant as did Joshua. My clean house must be my experience. No one else can decorate my spiritual house for me.

Thus I call on the housekeeping services of the Helper whom Jesus promised in Romans 8:26: "In the same way, the Spirit helps us in our weakness. We do not know what we ought to pray for, but the Spirit himself intercedes for us with groans that words cannot express" (NIV). He has thus promised to put my spiritual house in order.

Listen! Is that someone knocking at my heart's door? Yes, it's Jesus.

Do You enjoy my potpourri, Lord?   BETTY KOSSICK

A Perfect Day

*To those who use well what they are given, even more will
be given, and they will have an abundance. Matt. 25:29, NLT.*

My friend Mercy called me last week. "Someone stole the angels from the rose bowl you gave the chaplain," she reported. I had given him the rose bowl and angels as a personal gift when his mother passed away several months before. I didn't know that he had placed it next to the guest book in the hospital chapel.

My heart was filled with humble gratitude that he would place my gift in such a special place. From personal experience I know why people enter hospital chapels. As a family we had entered a hospital chapel immediately after the surgeon told us my daddy was terminally ill with perhaps five months to live.

I told Mercy, "Let's pray that whoever took the angels received a blessing from them."

Later, I took the chaplain another angel vase. We sat a few minutes and fellowshipped together. I told him about some of my ideas to encourage others, and about the little gifts I planned to make to give to patients who requested pastoral visits. He liked my idea. He placed his new angel vase next to the guest book.

I've known the chaplain since becoming a hospital volunteer in 1991. During the interview, before I was accepted as a volunteer, he asked why I wanted to be a volunteer. I told him, "I feel that the Lord has asked me to please feed His sheep."

I've shared much personal pain through the years with the chaplain, and he has fed me spiritually. His hugs have given me more encouragement than he could possibly know. I've learned a lot about feeding the Lord's sheep.

*Today I want to be available to feed the sheep You make known to me.
Help me as I introduce myself to those who may be in need. Send Your Holy
Spirit to guide me as You have led others to bless me.*

DEBORAH SANDERS

Pure Springwater

*Those who drink the water that I will give them will never
be thirsty again. The water that I will give them will
become in them a spring which will provide them
with life-giving water and give them eternal life. John 4:14, TEV.*

Thirty years ago I left a Ukrainian village for Moscow to get an education. Years later my husband, Victor, and I returned to the Ukraine. I cannot forget the taste of the water out of a well I used to drink from in my childhood and youth.

Why did the water in the well taste so good? Was it only because the well was good? What was the secret of that unforgettable, fresh, satisfying taste of water?

I remember the cleaning of the wells during my childhood. The water level in the wells was reduced in the summer because of rubbish. That worried the users of water. The people enjoyed the cool, sparkling water after the cleaning.

"Those who drink the water that I will give them will never be thirsty again. The water that I will give them will become in them a spring which will provide them with life-giving water and give them eternal life." In that way Jesus introduced Himself to a Samaritan woman at the well. I see two springs of water in Christ's illustration. The first symbolizes Jesus Christ; the second, you, me, and everybody who comes to quench her thirst for communion with God, to find rest, peace, and consolation. In His presence we become humble, our hearts become clean, our minds and feelings become new.

Springwater, pure water, clean water—it's good that we hear these words a lot and try to save water from pollution. We live among the sins and depravity of this world, and we need again and again to come to Christ through His living Word, to be washed from all rubbish—worldliness, pride, anger, jealousy, irritation, suspiciousness, and envy—that enters our hearts from the polluted environment. Only when Christ makes us clean and gives us living water do we become springs of water that satisfy the poor and comfort those who mourn, awakening to new life.

Praise God, for the living streams of His Word satisfy and give new life!

LUDMILA M. KRUSHENITSKAYA

What Does God See in Me?

The Lord looked down from heaven upon the children of men,
to see if there were any that did understand, and seek God. Ps. 14:2.

As the plane circled over Calgary before directing its course toward Salt Lake City, I looked out the window for landmarks. The 626-foot Calgary Tower lost its impressive height when viewed from the sky. The Saddledome, a uniquely constructed arena for the Stampede City, was about the right size for a Shetland pony. My eyes followed the ant-sized cars crawling along the grids of streets and avenues. The winding Bow River divided the city.

Although the plane continued to gain altitude as it headed south, a cloudless sky provided good visibility of the rural countryside below. I studied the geometric shapes of fields in various shades of green, interspersed with patches of black summer fallow and bright-yellow canola. Dark-green clusters of trees surrounded miniature farm buildings with a few metal silos glistening in the sunshine. I recognized muddy-colored sloughs fringed with white alkaline ash.

As I admired the artistry of the landscape below, I imagined the thrill astronaut John Glenn experienced in 1962 as he circled the earth three times in less than five hours. When he returned to earth he remarked it was quite a thing for a man to be able to see four sunsets in one day—three in flight and one after landing. He was awed by the vivid colors of the sunsets and the brightness of Orion and the Pleiades.

Reflecting beyond what the human eye can see, my thoughts turned to our text for today. What does God in His heaven see when He looks upon earth? Certainly much more than astronauts, pilots, airline passengers, and I do! Scripture tells us He sees the sparrows fall, He knows the number of hairs on our heads, and He sees our hearts.

I paraphrased the text to read "The Lord looked down from heaven upon Edith [substitute your name here], to see if she understands and seeks God."

Lord, I pray that when You look down from heaven upon me that You will see beauty in me. I want You to see me as one with a clean heart who is preparing to meet You, face-to-face. EDITH FITCH

Hats Off, You're With Me

A friend loves at all times. Prov. 17:17, NIV.

I recently read the following Arabian proverb: "A friend is one to whom one can pour out all the contents of one's heart, chaff and grain together, knowing that the gentlest of hands will take and sift it, keep what is worth keeping, and with the breath of kindness, blow the rest away."

There have been times I have dared to trust enough to become vulnerable. I have shared deep parts of myself, only to be hurt and disappointed. There have been times when the source of my pain came from my own spiritual brothers and sisters.

Often we think these experiences are easily forgotten, but they leave an indelible impression on our minds and hearts, and we are changed as a result. Because of these emotional scars, we find ourselves overly cautious and suspicious of those who reach out to us.

Recently, while having a conversation with a friend, he told me I could take off my "hat" with him. He wanted me to trust him. I must admit the memories of my past flashed before me, and then I thought of a French proverb: "A faithful friend is the image of God."

God accepts us and loves us as we are. His love is unconditional, but I must reach out in acceptance of His offer of friendship. I must by faith hope in what is not seen. I must be willing to take off my hat with God. I must trust His unconditional love.

What a wonderful gift my earthly friend gave me, the gift of unconditional acceptance. He wanted me to simply be me. Through his actions he reflected the ideal model of a friend, the One who takes us as we are, our heavenly Saviour and Friend.

What a privilege to come before You and to know I am totally safe, that You already know all about me.

Today, help me to be safe for others too. May we all, with Your love, reach out to others, allowing them to feel safe and secure enough with us, to take off their hats, simply because they are with us, and we with You.

TERRIE E. RUFF

The Last Move

For in him we live, and move, and have our being. Acts 17:28.

Well, I did it again—I made another move after being so sure that my previous move had been my last. My patient, loving son has moved me four times in the past 10 years. Of course, I had good reasons for making each move. After all, a woman can change her mind, can't she?

And through it all, not once did my son say, "Now, Mom, this is the last time," or "Enough is enough."

Actually, I had been trying to fill a void by looking for a community that would give me a feeling of belonging. My son understood this and willingly made one more move.

His patience with me reminds me of my heavenly Father. I have made many spiritual moves to fill a void in my life, looking for the place I belonged. Some of these moves, I am now sure, disappointed my Father. My intentions may have been good, but I had been looking in the wrong places. As soon as I realized this and decided to move back toward my Father, with patience and love He came to me to help make that move as easy as possible. Not once has He said, "Not again." Not once has He said, "Now, Ann, this is your last time."

He truly understands. And in my seeking Him, He so willingly forgives and accepts, "not willing that any should perish, but that all should come to repentance." It was acceptance by Him that I was seeking. He is what I needed all along.

In my present contentment, I know that there is one more move to make, Lord, the one I'm looking forward to the most. You have taken care of all the details. All I have to do is to be ready. No more seeking to fill a void, for You are moving me to that place You have prepared for me.

Help me in my packing and sorting to keep those things that will be useful for my last move. Help me rid my life of those things that could prevent the move. Most of all, help me this day to be ready to be ever with You.

ANN VANARSDELL HAYWARD

Love Your Neighbor

Love the Lord your God with all your heart, with all your soul,
with all your strength, and with all your mind;
and your neighbour as yourself. Luke 10:27, NEB.

Last August I attended a women's ministries congress in Takoradi, Ghana, where more than 2,000 women assembled for a week. It was a big event, and I left very impressed with the activities and programs they presented.

A lady from Ghana, Victoria Daaka, led us in a study of the Bible. The theme of the lesson focused on the story of the good Samaritan. Victoria presented the idea that for the priest and the Levite to assist the injured man was simply a matter of inconvenience. Then she asked, "Which do you think you are—the priest, the Levite, or the Samaritan?"

I could not get this thought out of my mind. I could think of a number of times when helping others was just too inconvenient. Oh, I had good excuses. "I will arrive late to work." "I am too tired." "It's someone else's responsibility." And the excuses go on and on. If I excuse myself, I am acting exactly as the priest or the Levite acted in Jesus' parable.

Just last Christmas God decided to test me in this matter. A friend called. As soon as I met her I knew exactly what I had to do. She was no longer safe in her home, and she could not continue to stay there. So I said to her, "Come to my home and stay with me."

Although I have spent countless hours listening to her problems, I feel so happy that I had the opportunity to act as the good Samaritan did. God has sustained me and given me wisdom. I have learned a lot from this experience and thank the Lord for that. I have had many opportunities to share experiences, pray with her, and guide her in making right decisions.

But the opportunity God gave me was, in a sense, an easy one, because this person was my friend. Now I ask myself: How will I react next time somebody who is not my friend asks for help?

God, help me to react positively so I can help my neighbor, even if she comes at the most inconvenient time.   ELLEN E. MAYR

Disappointment in Prayer

*In bitterness of soul Hannah wept much
and prayed to the Lord. 1 Sam. 1:10, NIV.*

Prayer can be the place of our greatest joy or our most devastating disappointment. There is nothing to equal the confusion, anger, and sorrow we experience when our prayers are not "answered."

Some time ago I experienced disappointment in prayer. My husband and I had planned to work on a particular evangelistic project in one of the churches. We set aside time each day to pray ardently, believing God was able to bring visitors to the program.

We abandoned the program after the second night because there were no visitors—and we felt abandoned by God. I especially felt bewildered, helpless, and astounded. I really believed God would answer our prayers in the way we wanted. After all, we only desired to share God.

Disappointment in prayer is something each of us has to face. What do we do when God apparently lets us down, and when He seems to be powerless, silent, or indifferent to our requests? The story of Hannah shows us.

Hannah came to God, month after month, year after year, with empty arms and an aching heart, knowing that God had the power to bring a baby into her life. But He did not. Her very purpose in life—to be a mother— was denied her. God was in the position to do something about it, yet He did nothing. Whom did she turn to in the disappointment? God. The very One she could have blamed as the cause of the pain!

Hannah did so because she had a relationship with God. He was not an instant prayer-answering machine, but a friend. He was a father with whom she could share her heart. In that relationship He was able to assure her that He knew what He was doing.

Hannah challenged me to not give up on prayer when God seems silent, but to remember prayer is also about being open and honest with God. Hannah challenged me to not give up on God. Her confidence in Him never wavered, and in time God gave her the baby for whom she yearned.

Dear Father God, teach me to be like Hannah in my prayer life.

MARY BARRETT

More Than a Number

I am the good shepherd, and know my sheep,
and am known of mine. John 10:14.

As I entered the checkout line at the grocery store the other day and began to write a check for my items, the checker asked for my store card, my identification. A year earlier when that store had first opened, we had applied for the check cashing card. Among other items on the short application, we had to fill in our driver's license number and our Social Security number. From that, they gave us the card that had still another number identifying us in the store's computer.

Have you ever thought that you were just another number? Think about it. Just about everywhere we go to transact any kind of business, we must identify ourselves with a number—phone number, address, Social Security number, driver's license number, medical card number, store card number, checking and savings account number. The numbers seem to never end.

But there is One who needs not identify Himself to anyone with any number. His touch is found on every flower and tree. He is seen in the majesty of the mountains and bodies of water. The birds echo His voice. Even the animals know His name.

And yet this Great One, who is known of all, is least acknowledged and respected by His most intelligent and valued creation. Even so, to Him we are much more than a number. We are the apple of His eye, His pride and joy, for whom He came to earth as a babe and suffered and died a criminal death as a man.

We must identify ourselves with numbers to transact business here, but to Christ we need merely say, "I'm Your child, a sinner saved by grace. Please forgive me and give me another chance." And what loving parent requires identification numbers of their children? Whether wayward or upright, they are recognized by their face or the mere sound of their voice.

Neither is a number required for our entry into heaven, for He knows us by name and face and works. He knows us by our relationship to Him as obedient children who have done His will here on earth and have maintained a connection with Him. Indeed, to Him we are much more than a number.

GLORIA J. STELLA-FELDER

Lost in the Night

*As a shepherd looks after his scattered flock when he is with them,
so will I look after my sheep. I will rescue them from all the places
where they were scattered on a day of clouds and darkness. Eze. 34:12, NIV.*

My husband and I arrived at the campground in plenty of time to find a good spot to pitch our tent that Friday afternoon. One of my first priorities was to locate the women's restroom and clearly fix the route to it in my mind. This time I was pleased to discover that a large, bright light that could be seen from all over the campground adorned the front of the building. No way could I get lost. I went to sleep that night with confidence.

Around 3:00 I awoke and knew that a short trip to the restroom was in order. I put on my robe, slipped on my shoes, picked up my flashlight, and followed the bright beams of the light on the building to the correct place.

It was only as I began my trip back to my tent that I realized my dilemma. There was no light that marked my tent! I hadn't even checked how many rows over I had come. And in the darkness all the tents looked alike!

I walked down row after row, fearful of waking up the occupants of the tents with my probing flashlight. Nowhere did I see a familiar-looking tent. Finally I realized I was no longer on asphalt but on a dirt trail that headed out into the rocky desert surrounding the camp. Alarmed, I turned around and started back, fearing I would have to keep walking until daylight. I was frightened, crying, tired, and cold. I began to pray as I realized that on my own I was never going to locate my tent!

Lord, wake up my husband and send him to look for me, I cried.

As my feet touched asphalt again, I saw a moving light coming toward me. I quickened my pace. Yes, it was my husband! He had checked the time I had left the tent and, waking later, realized I had been gone much too long and had come looking for me.

As the shepherd found his sheep, as the housewife found her coin, as the wandering son was found by his father, my husband found me. I thank God He cares about sheep, coins, sons, and wives.

CARROL JOHNSON SHEWMAKE

Going Home

*I go to prepare a place for you. And if I go and prepare a
place for you, I will come again, and receive you
unto myself; that where I am, there ye may be also. John 14:2, 3.*

How excited I am about going home! For the past several months I
have been doing a countdown. Now I'm 31,000 feet above sea level
flying south, flying to the warm Caribbean—heading home. My adrenaline
flows. I just can't wait to get there!

A number of thoughts skip through my mind, thoughts of swimming
in the blue Caribbean Sea, of being able to meditate uninterrupted by man-
made sounds, of taking evening strolls in the moonlight. However, I am
most excited about seeing my family and my only niece. Going home is a
great idea. What I am leaving behind doesn't seem important after all.

As I peep through the window and look at the miniature structures
below, my thoughts turn heavenward. Wouldn't it be great to be up and
away, never to return to this planet called earth? I am excited about going
home to heaven. What a glorious idea to be away from sickness, death, sorrow, and crying! No more cholesterol checks, no more worrying about fat
content. No more bills, stress, or worry.

The very thought of seeing Jesus makes me want to leave immediately. I
do not worry about the mansion He's preparing for me. I can trust His ar-
chitectural ability. The thought that makes me want to shout, however, is
that I won't have to leave home! I won't have to be separated from family
or friends ever again.

While I was reveling in my dream, a solemn and sobering thought
came to my mind. *What about my friends and relatives who do not share this
excitement? There is a job for me to do! I must get busy and let them know. It's
time to go home, and I want them to be there with me. I will be much happier
knowing that they are there.*

I want to go home. Don't you?

*Help me keep heaven as my goal today. Help me to take advantage of oppor-
tunities to share my faith and my joy. I'm looking forward to coming home, Lord!*

ANDREA A. BUSSUE

AUGUST 15

The Lump

*Come, all you who are thirsty, come to the waters; and you who
have no money, come, buy and eat! . . . Listen, listen to me, and eat
what is good, and your soul will delight in the richest of fare. Give ear
and come to me; hear me, that your soul may live. Isa. 55:1-3, NIV.*

I had ignored the lump, not wanting to acknowledge its existence. Maybe
if I didn't think about it, it would disappear. When I finally had my annual checkup the doctor said, "There's a lump in your breast. You must
have noticed it yourself." I could no longer ignore it. "We'll have to take a
mammogram to find out more about it," he said.

We did. Then came the phone call. "We don't know exactly what it is,
but it would be better to do a biopsy."

I scheduled the appointment. How long a week can be! And how short.
There were so many things to be done, as if I wanted to have everything in
perfect order before I left. *It'll probably be a harmless lump—but what if it isn't?*

Then in the middle of the night, when I could not find rest, all those
thoughts came back. It was like a big pot on the stove. I kept the lid on
tightly during the day, but in the night it would boil over, and all those terrible thoughts would force their way out from under the lid and run down
the sides of the pot, making a ghastly mess of everything.

I picked up my Bible and opened it at random to Isaiah 55. "Come, all
you who are thirsty." I could not concentrate; I read the verses again and
again, often not understanding a word of what I was reading. And yet they
consoled me. "Listen to me," God said, "that your soul may live."

Every night when sleep eluded me I would turn to these verses. And
every morning when I had to face a new day I did the same. With apparent
composure I went to the hospital after a last night spent in tears.

What a relief when the doctor finally said it was a harmless lump and
that everything was OK. Thank God! I now appreciate life more and understand others in a similar situation. The scar reminds me daily of the message God gave me through these verses.

HANNELE OTTSCHOFSKI

The Upper Room

Jesus then came with his disciples to a place called Gethsemane. He said to them, "Sit here while I go over there to pray." Matt. 26:36, NEB.

Little by little we traced the whole story of that last evening we spent together as His disciples. The table had been prepared with bread and wine. One by one we reclined around the table and greeted each other quietly. We wondered what Jesus was going to tell us. He looked so sad we knew at once it would be something of great importance. He stood up and told us that one of us was going to betray Him. We were shocked and looked at each other questioningly.

We had come from the dusty road, and our feet were not attended to as was the usual custom. Jesus started washing our feet one by one. When He reached Peter, it was too much for him. He jumped up and said, "No, Lord, no!"

Later we spoke of the Garden of Gethsemane. There must have been dismay in His eyes as we fell asleep when He had asked us to watch with Him. His heart was so heavy. He needed our support. At the time we did not realize how much.

Each of us offered some word of retelling the tragic story of those few days. Most of us had tears in our eyes as we retraced the events that had taken place. After another hymn we stood around the table and held hands and each offered a short prayer. Everyone felt uplifted and strengthened as we praised the Lord. We thanked Him for His great sacrifice for us. We asked the Holy Spirit to be with us on that special day and in the days to come.

Not long ago we had the opportunity to relive this scene once again. As we stepped into our church a young lady greeted us. "Welcome to the Upper Room." A program of remembrance had been prepared by a small group of young people. I felt a real breath of fresh air as they told of their love, and we all had the opportunity to dedicate ourselves to His service.

Jesus, as we think again of what You went through to die for us, help us be prepared to live for You today. PHILIPPA MARSHALL

Now, What Shall I Do First?

But seek first his kingdom and his righteousness,
and all these things will be given to you as well. Matt. 6:33, NIV.

W hen the grass turns green in spring and the tulips bloom around the
light pole in the front yard, my eagerness for colorful flower beds re-
vives. Last spring I took a tour around the outside of the house and mentally chose the types and colors of annuals I wanted to try this year.

With my list in hand, I went first to a discount store that always has a
large variety of bedding plants. There were geraniums, marigolds, salvia,
petunias—many choices for a reasonable price. But as I went from aisle to
aisle, I became more and more distressed—everything looked wilted,
droopy, or dead. Another shopper and I commented to each other about
how pathetic the poor little flowers looked.

The plants had been shipped in large trays that held 10 or 12 of the little six-packs. Nearby, an employee diligently removed the empty trays and
quickly arranged the six-packs to fill up the partially full trays. He seemed
to be working efficiently, making good use of his motions.

Because I was dismayed over the poor condition of the plants, I blurted
out to the man, "If someone doesn't water these plants you won't have anything to sell!"

"Yes, ma'am, we're trying to find someone to water the plants," he answered in all earnestness.

I stood there aghast, hardly believing my ears. He (or perhaps his boss)
wasn't dealing with the important part first.

Then I considered my own priorities and was caught up short. Every
spring and summer I lose some plants because they go too long between
drinks. But much more important than the bedding plants is my attention
to the spiritual seed that's been planted in my heart. How easy it is to bustle
around at home or work in an effort to be tidy and organized, and to forget
the number one priority: to "seek first the kingdom of God and his righteousness." If I can't remember what's most important and what I should
do first, my spiritual growth will be like the poor little flowers—wilted,
droopy, or dead.

ROXY HOEHN

Am I Flexible?

*Because I knew that thou art obstinate, and thy
neck is an iron sinew, and thy brow brass. Isa. 48:4.*

Webster defines the word *obstinate* as "unyielding, adhering firmly to
one's opinion, purpose, etc.—sometimes perversely." Let's face it,
the word has a negative connotation. I must admit that being flexible does
not come naturally. One has to work on it.

While attending a Christian seminar, I heard an interesting definition
of the word *flexibility*. The speaker said it means "not setting one's affection
on ideas or plans that could be changed by God or others." I like that. Since
that time I have often thought about this definition that puts an entirely
different slant on everything.

Over the years this human tendency to be inflexible has caused a great
deal of stress—to ourselves, our families, our neighbors, our coworkers,
and our fellow church members. You no doubt know what I mean. All of
us have experienced dealing with people whose mind is made up—"No, I
don't want to discuss it," or "I can't budge on this."

How important is the issue? Sometimes conscience won't let us reverse
our thinking, but many occasions occur when stubbornness prevails. Is
there a Christlike approach to getting rid of a rigid mind-set? Matters are
settled so much easier when we learn to yield when and where we can.

With a willing spirit and prayerful heart, carefully examine the issues.
Where are they on a priority scale? Do they have a high-ranking importance? What will be the consequences if I give in? Or if I don't? Is there an
ethical problem to resolve? Frequently we find that what we think is really
important is really not after all. After exploring our conscience for the appropriate action, move on it. The more we give, the more we receive.

Being flexible is not only a great human characteristic, it is a God-
driven quality that will make for better living in this fragile life. Experts
continue to identify effective methods for getting along with people.
Cultivating appropriate flexibility is one of the best ways!

ARLENE E. COMPTON

At the Appointed Time

*Is anything too marvelous for the Lord to do? At the
appointed time, about this time next year, I will
return to you, and Sarah will have a son. Gen. 18:14, NAB.*

When I read the story of Sarah in Genesis 18, I imagine that she must
have prayed many times for a child. But when she overheard the Lord's
prediction to Abraham, she laughed at the thought that an old woman like
herself could become pregnant and have a child. The birth of Isaac the following year served as proof to Sarah that nothing is impossible for the Lord.

Not long ago my family was in a transition period. My husband had
taken a paid study leave, and we'd been getting by on his study-leave pay
while I stayed at home with our small children. However, the study leave
was coming to a close, and his salary and medical benefits were soon to
end. So I began searching for a job that would support our family while he
continued to study. Jobs in my field were scarce, so I tried to be realistic.

*Any job that has enough income for a family of four to live modestly will
be OK, Lord. I'm not looking for a perfect or high-paying position,* I prayed. I
continued my job search for several months and, to be honest, I did a certain amount of worrying as I tried to trust that the Lord would provide
something—anything!

Then a phone call came saying that a position was opening with an
agency where I had applied previously. The first job I'd applied for was already filled, but they wanted to interview me for an unexpected second
opening. After the interview process, the job was offered to me—with a better salary than I had even hoped for, and with medical benefits, too.

Unfortunately, I would not receive a vacation until I had worked at the
job for six months. I found it no coincidence that the first day I was eligible
for a vacation fell on the first day of the Christian women's retreat I had
planned to attend. God's answer was ideal. And His timing was perfect!
Like Sarah, I've seen firsthand that nothing is too hard for my God.

Do you worry about a problem or a difficult situation? Give God a
chance to work out His answer in your life, and you won't be disappointed.
Perhaps the answer you receive won't be exactly what you expected—
maybe it will be even better!   SANDRA SIMANTON

God's Loving Care

For He shall give His angels charge over you,
to keep you in all your ways. Ps. 91:11, NKJV.

In my younger years I was afraid of all sorts of things. I imagined terrible calamities that could happen. It took years for me to learn to trust God and believe in His promises. I read about the angels and wondered if my angel was really always with me even when I was not always as careful as I should be. And then one day God showed me His care in a personal way.

On a pleasant summer day I was shopping for a maternity dress. The door to the shop had been left open to the sidewalk, and beyond it was a two-lane street. I was momentarily distracted from watching my 2½-year-old son. Busy with my shopping, I was unaware that he had wandered out that open door.

I suddenly felt a touch on my shoulders, turning me around to face the open doorway. As I turned I saw my son as he stepped out the door onto the sidewalk by the street. Quickly I ran to catch him and bring him back inside. I don't remember buying a dress, but I will never forget the touch that turned me around. I believe it was my guardian angel, or my son's angel.

More than 50 years later I still remember vividly those precious moments of God's special care for my son. I want to have faith in God's care always, no matter what happens.

I found a wonderful quote I would like to share: "Every believer who constantly realizes [her] dependence on God has [her] appointed angel, sent from heaven to minister to [her]. The ministry of these angels is especially essential now, for Satan is making his last desperate effort to secure the world" (Ellen G. White, *In Heavenly Places,* p. 101).

Lord, thank You for the ministry of angels. Help me to constantly realize my dependence on You. Thank You for the angel You have appointed to minister to me today. And thank You for the angels that accompany my loved ones today as well. What a wonderful God You are! BESSIE SIEMENS LOBSIEN

Joy

Always be full of joy in the Lord. Phil. 4:4, TLB.

Sad and empty faces stare out from dirty blankets and cardboard beds each morning at sunrise as the homeless scurry about, gathering their meager belongings. All hope for a bright tomorrow is gone—survival is the only game. The streets hold those enslaved by drugs, alcohol, and crime so tightly there is no freedom. The children scamper about trying to stay warm, trying to find food. There is never a day when their stomachs are full. Every shred of dignity is gone.

Sometimes our soul feels this kind of desperation. Sad and lonely, we don't feel the warmth of belonging. Our minds scream with questions unanswered. Emptiness is our daily cuisine. We grab and take and race through life, hoping for joy and a brighter tomorrow. We keep reaching, but the answers seem to slip beyond our grasp.

Thank God, there are some answers! Are you sure about God's love for you? Read Jeremiah 31:3: "I have loved you with an everlasting love" (NKJV).

When you are tired and weak, remember: "They that wait upon the Lord shall renew their strength" (Isa. 40:31).

If your life is lacking joy, read Isaiah 51:11: "Everlasting joy shall be upon their head: they [you] shall obtain gladness and joy; and sorrow and mourning shall flee away."

Hold on to the peace that is promised. Don't worry about anything; if you do this you will experience God's peace, which is far more wonderful than the human mind can understand. His peace will keep your thoughts and your heart quiet and at rest.

Our Lord has His arms out and is calling us to come to Him, to be His child, to rest in His presence. "Come unto Me, all ye that labour and are heavy laden, and I will give you rest."

Lord, it is only in Your presence that I feel secure. My strength comes from You. Joy is my reward as I learn to trust in You. And thank You for providing the answers to my questions and rest and comfort for my soul.

PEGGY CLARK

To Love and Be Loved

A word fitly spoken is like apples of gold in pictures of silver. Prov. 25:11.

S is," he said. "Sis."
It seemed more of a plaintive cry than an urgent one, but I rose from my seat by the window and went to his bedside.

I bent down low over his raised side rails until our eyes met.

"What is it, Dad?" I asked.

There was no answer.

My father had been admitted to the hospital because of numerous health problems, the most serious of which were complications resulting from years of alcohol abuse. For most of my childhood and adult life I'd watched as my dad struggled with this debilitating disease.

It wasn't as if there were enough money to spend on liquor. He had deprived his family of food and milk we so desperately needed during our growing-up years. Now the habit was beginning to take its toll, and all we could do was watch his life ebb away.

His constant anxiety and restlessness made him feel the need for medication more frequently than was allowed, so all that the nurses could do was repeatedly explain, "It isn't time yet." It was during one of the rare quiet times that I had heard him call out to me.

As I waited I noticed his eyes fill with tears. I'd never seen him cry before. For whatever reason, he was not able to tell me what he had on his mind that day. In the years since I've wondered what my father wanted to say to me. My biggest regret is that I failed to press him for an answer right then. I wonder if he wanted to tell me he was sorry for all the unhappiness he had caused our family through the years. Or perhaps he wanted to tell me he loved me, something I'd never heard him say, not once. But he said neither of those things. He died shortly after that and carried his secret to his grave.

I've thought about it many times. How is it possible to go through life and have no real communication with those you love? I decided my children would know we loved them and that their heavenly Father loved them even infinitely more.

How I wish I would have spoken those words to my dad!

CLAREEN COLCLESSER

God's Other Book

The earth is the Lord's, and the fulness thereof;
the world, and they that dwell therein. Ps. 24:1.

When we lived in West Virginia, it usually fell my lot to drive our younger son some 30 miles each way to church school. Part of the year it was dark in the afternoon. The road was winding and narrow, taking all my attention to drive safely, leaving little time to talk.

One afternoon on my way to pick up our son, I had to stop because of roadwork and one-way traffic. For a welcome change, I had a chance to look around. To my right, on the hillside, stood one lone, lovely flower. In a pasture to the left, a wee colt nuzzled its mother. "An in-between-meal snack, little one?" I chuckled.

What was that? Ah! A bird's happy song. And then came the whistle of one of the many long freight trains that made their way up the valley and through the mountains. High above, I heard the drone of an airplane. "H'mmmm," I wondered, "where might it be going? Are the passengers on business, or maybe going to visit loved ones? Bless and keep them safe, Lord."

All too soon it was my turn to become part of the one-way traffic. I prayed that I might always be aware of the beauty around me. I had passed this same spot almost daily but had never enjoyed the sights and sounds as I did this day.

Sometimes we become so involved with the busyness of life that we fail to notice God's other book, His creation. Let's stop, look, listen, smell, touch, and enjoy what God has made for us.

Thank You, Lord, for eyes to see the beautiful world You have created. Thank You for ears to hear the songs of birds. Thank You for the ability to smell roses, honeysuckle, and new-mown hay. Thank You for hands that can feel the softness of a rabbit's fur.

Help me to take time today in my busyness to praise and enjoy the world You have made.

PATSY MURDOCH MEEKER

The Truth or Love?

Woman, where are those thine accusers?
hath no man condemned thee? John 8:10.

Kitty was opinionated. She couldn't resist expressing her opinion on every subject. She intimidated the less bold. One day in a committee, someone told her off in plain English. Kitty was wounded. How could she be so misunderstood?

She called me the same day and invited me to meet her the next morning for breakfast at a quaint inn. She said, "I have something I'd like to talk about with you."

After the waitress had taken our orders, Kitty launched into her subject. "Mary, I need an honest evaluation."

She told her story of the woman's scathing put-down and how shocked and hurt she had been. "Now, am I really such a despicable person?"

I was speechless. I actually had been put off by her at times myself. What should I say? By my silence she immediately picked up the message that I must agree with this opinion.

"Mary, please, tell me the truth!"

I sensed Kitty was in pain. I wanted to help her change so others would like her better. "Kitty, I have learned a great deal from you. I don't resent you; however, many people you deal with are as talented as you, but are less apt to demand that others see things their way. They feel overpowered by you. Maybe if you would let them have their say and get a consensus from the group in a quiet way your opinions wouldn't be resented, and at least part of the time you would win."

You would have thought I had stabbed her in the heart. She turned and looked out the window, and the conversation abruptly changed to comments on the weather. Neither of us finished our food. I moved out of town shortly after that and never saw Kitty again.

I have thought about this conversation many times. Did I say the right thing? Wasn't Christ always soothing and forgiving to sinners? But He also said, "Go and sin no more."

Lord, help me to be receptive and open to advice. Help me to see myself as others see me, but especially as You see me. May I mold my life after Yours this day.

MARY C. EDMISTER

The Letter

But we have this treasure in earthen vessels, that the excellency of the power may be of God, and not of us. 2 Cor. 4:7.

As I opened the side pocket of my purse my eyes couldn't miss the irregular wad of white paper with enough tape to wrap a dozen presents. As I held this priceless treasure in my hand, I recalled its presentation to me a few nights before.

Solana had wanted to join me in my schoolteacher tasks, so I gave her paper, scissors, and tape so she could keep busy as I worked. I was somewhat conscious of her preschooler joy at using my things without too much restriction. After about a half hour, as I was clearing away my things, she presented to me my letter with all the love only a 4-year-old's eyes can dispense. I dutifully received my gift, as I had so many times before, laid it on my desk, and quite honestly promptly forgot it.

Once more, however, Solana would teach me a spiritual lesson. The next day I opened my purse and discovered this treasure had carefully and slyly been placed where I would have it. My initial reaction was a smile and a quick toss to the wastebasket. But then I realized that in my possession was a special gift, created and delivered just for me. It was from one who only wanted to let me know how much I was loved. She was not put off by my indifference to her gift. Her goal was that I was going to have that gift!

When I got home from work that night, I picked her up and told her how much it meant to me to find her gift. Her response was one of shining eyes and delight; yet her words spoke the honesty that only a child has. "You kept my letter, Grandma?" I assured her that it was still in my purse and that I would cherish it.

You give me treasure without number. I take them lightly. Today I want to value each and every one of them, cherishing the letter of love that it represents. And may You always know how much I love You, in spite of the poor, childish gifts I present to You.

VALARIE YOUNG

Your Kingdom Come

*Our Father in heaven: May your holy name be
honored: may your Kingdom come. Matt. 6:9, 10, TEV.*

I was driving through Takoma Park, Maryland, one spring and observed
that this city really looks beautiful. All the dogwood trees and azaleas
make the town sparkle. This suburb of Washington, D.C., began as a summertime getaway for District residents. Over the years it has aged, sometimes not so gracefully. Parts of the city have been refurbished and
redesigned to meet the needs of the community.

This observation started me thinking about us. We are here on this
small blue planet called Earth. God has blessed Christians with the attrac-
tiveness of the gospel of Jesus to share with everyone. We are near centers
of influence in this world, whether it is a big city or a rural community.

As we allow God to work in our lives, we become redesigned. Whether
or not this change in us is only superficial or is a deep-seated allegiance to
God's re-creation in us will show through in our dealings with others. By
this allegiance His holy name will be honored.

How do we look? Do others see a cosmetic cover-up of the scars of life?
Do they see a resemblance to Jesus shining through us that makes them
want to know more about Him? Many people are searching for the peace
that comes from the Prince of Peace. Since we are the ambassadors of the
King of heaven, what kind of message do we deliver to these seekers?

We need to take time today to commune with the Owner of the universe. We need to pause to enjoy the beauties of springtime. We will find
true beauty, restoration, and healing for our souls. Then we can have something truly wonderful to share with others we will meet in days to come.
Soon His kingdom is coming here!

My prayer is that God will shine on you with heaven's love today, dear
sister, precious child of God. May we each be a springtime of delight for
someone else.   PEGGY HARRIS

African Journey

For he will command his angels concerning
you to guard you in all your ways. Ps. 91:11, NIV.

Many years ago my husband, our 2-year-old daughter, and I drove from our mission hospital in central Nigeria into northern Nigeria. With us was a nurse from our hospital and a Christian doctor friend, Martha, from the University Hospital in Ibadan. Martha, who was driving at the time, rounded a bend on a lonely stretch of dirt road. The car skidded on the loose red gravel and veered toward the hillside. It then went out of control, back across the road, and over the edge of a steep embankment. Martha thought, *Oh no, I've killed five people.* However, the car remained upright and bumped its way down the rocky embankment, coming to rest against a tree stump.

We all got out unharmed, but how were we to get the car back up onto the road? We needed help, but we had not seen another vehicle in hours. Amazingly, a few minutes later we were able to wave down a passing car. When the two men looked down at our little car, they asked, "How many dead?" When we assured them no one was hurt, they helped push the car back up the bank and almost back to the road. The last six feet were almost vertical, and there seemed to be no way we could get that car up those last few feet.

Just then another vehicle came around the bend, a van with seven strong African men on board. They literally lifted that car up and placed it on the road. We straightened the front bumper to allow the wheels to turn and climbed in. The car started, and we continued our journey.

The next day we reached Ibadan and Martha's home. Her neighbor greeted us and asked, "What were you doing about 3:00 yesterday afternoon? I felt impressed to pray for your safety then." That was the exact time we had skidded off the road!

As Martha remarked, it felt as if angels had surrounded our car as we went over and down that embankment, and had steered us over the rocks. How grateful we were for the two vehicles that appeared just when we needed them. (And for her neighbor's prayers.)

RUTH LENNOX

The Wilted Azalea

The Lord will deal with us according to all his wondrous works. Jer. 21:2.

In any system we all depend upon each other. Success in life is give and take, depending on one another. The plants around us, animals, our pets—all depend on us. We must care for them.

One Wednesday Casey, a Navajo student, met me as I was walking from church carrying a potted azalea.

"It is dead," Casey commented.

Yes, it was dry. Some of the petals and leaves were brittle and were falling off the stems. I was getting upset about it myself. I should have picked the pot up on Saturday and watered it. I should have watered it after I brought it, but I didn't. Now I was worried it would die.

I had bought the plant as a token of gratitude for a favor done for me. I took the plant, loaded with flowers, to church on Friday to help decorate the church in celebration of Mother's Day. I had intended to give it to the lady next door, who had just turned 90. But I had forgotten to pick it up.

So now I took it home, mixed some plant food in a gallon of water, and soaked it overnight. I left it on the kitchen table and prayed that God would revive it. The next morning I checked on the plant and could not believe what I was seeing. What had looked totally hopeless was now alive and perky because of some prayers and a little bit of work.

Four high school girls took the potted plant to the neighbor, Ila, and sang for her. Ila was in bed at the time because of severe pain caused by osteoporosis and a fall, but she stood up and, with eyes wide open, exclaimed, "This is the biggest bouquet I have ever received in my life!"

God indeed does wonders. Jeremiah 21:2 says, "The Lord will deal with us according to all his wondrous works." And David praises God in Psalm 116:1, 2 by saying, "I love the Lord, because he hath heard my voice and my supplications. Because he hath inclined his ear unto me, therefore will I call upon him as long as I live."

As dependents we can always depend upon God because He is dependable.

ESPERANZA AQUINO MOPERA

What Are You Doing Here?

But the Lord said to him, "What are
you doing here, Elijah?" 1 Kings 19:9, TLB.

It was holiday time, and my friend and I, both expatriate teachers, wanted to do something different. My friend's fiancé was a policeman, so we decided to visit the law court building and see firsthand how the judges and magistrates conducted the cases.

We wandered down to the court buildings, asked for directions, and found a notice board listing the various cases being heard. When we came to the first courtroom, the door was shut, and it was difficult to see through the glass window. Before we had a chance to see inside, a magistrate yelled, "No peeping!" A police officer rushed to the window and pulled the blind down while another one swung open the door and accosted us.

"It is all your fault!" my dark-skinned friend said. "You are very conspicuous with your red hair and very pale complexion."

It was true.

We decided to sit in the gallery to watch proceedings. Her policeman fiancé had brought a fellow in from a distant village to be tried for the crime he had committed. We found a seat and stayed there until the court adjourned for lunch. We decided to return after lunch to hear the verdict.

We were sitting in the gallery, trying to appear inconspicuous, when suddenly a court official appeared in front of me and asked, "What are you doing here?"

I responded with a blank look.

"The magistrate sent me to find out. Do you have an interest in the case?"

I thought of Elijah when he ran away because he did not blend in with those around him and was asked the same question. What was I doing in this land that was not my birth country? Was I here to enjoy living in a tropical paradise, or was I here to be helpful? Was I here to benefit myself, or others?

What am I doing here? I don't always know my motives, Lord, but You made me, and You put me here. Please use me according to Your plan.

JOY DUSTOW

The Crime of Caste

*God . . . hath made of one blood all nations of men
for to dwell on all the face of the earth. Acts 17:24-26.*

I picked up the newspaper lying in the doorway of our house in Hosur,
India. My attention focused on a news item on the front page. A 6-year-
old girl, a student in one of the government schools in the local area, was
drinking water from the common pot that was kept on the school premises.
A teacher had grabbed the steel tumbler from the child's hands and used it
to hit the child hard on her face, breaking her nose and damaging both eyes
beyond repair. Why? The girl belonged to a low caste, and her touch had
defiled the water pot. I was overwhelmed with pity. I thought of my granddaughter—same age, same innocence.

One of the most rigid social forms in India is the caste system. After 50
years of independence, strong caste feelings, though banned by law, still
persist among the Indians, on the whole. Unfortunately, it is even practiced
by many Christians.

One of the most beautiful things about Jesus was that He treated all
people with grace and dignity. He associated with all people—men or
women, rich or poor, tax collector or Pharisee, prostitute or priest. If we
are like Him, we can do no less.

Let's purify our hearts of castes and colors and all forms of prejudice
and discrimination. Let's believe and live in the unity and equality of all
people. Let's not forget there is no distinction of high and low among the
children of God. Nobody should tolerate ill treatment, given to our little
children or anyone else.

When we accept Jesus as our Lord and Saviour, we enter into a relationship in which our sins are forgiven and we are accepted as children of
God. We all belong to God's family, where there is no feeling of caste, gen-
der, or color difference. We are all one in Christ in God our Father.

PREMILA M. CHERIAN

England's Rose

Then the angel showed me the river of the water of life, as clear as crystal, flowing from the throne of God and of the Lamb. Rev. 22:1, NIV.

The sun glinted on a million pieces of cellophane as they shimmered and undulated like waves in the breeze. Nothing I had seen in the newspapers or on television had prepared me for this river of flowers, shaped like a cross, flowing down the drive from Kensington Palace to the place where I stood. Photographs could not convey the life in the flowers nor the smell nor the depth of the river. I was amazed to find that it reached almost to my waist.

It was the week after the funeral of Diana, princess of Wales, and I was in London on business. I had resisted the urge the week before to join the hundreds of thousands who flocked to London to pay their last respects. Now that I was in the area, I was drawn by my love of flowers to see the phenomenon of so many floral tributes. Every railing and tree in Kensington Gardens was covered with flowers. I was intensely moved by what I saw.

It was evident by the outpouring of grief from all sections of our nation—and, indeed, the world—that there is a great void in people's lives. Many grieved for Diana because they identified with her. Single mothers, divorced parents, the ill, sad, depressed, or suicidal, felt that if she could overcome her difficulties, then there was hope for them. She reached out to people. She showed them she cared.

Her death, however, demonstrated to me that people are longing for something or someone to believe in. I longed to tell the grieving thousands in Kensington Gardens that there is Someone who can identify with them more than Diana ever could. Someone alive who can share their joys and sorrows, and who can lift their burdens and give them the promise of eternal life with Him.

I can't speak to the nation as the queen did, but I can speak to my neighbor. I can reach out a helping hand to those who need it. I can show people by my actions that Jesus loves them, that He cares. I can tell them that the river that flows from His palace is made up not of flowers, but of the Water of Life.

AUDREY BALDERSTONE

Peanuts in the Mayonnaise

That ye might walk worthy of the Lord . . .
being fruitful . . . strengthened. Col. 1:10, 11.

Breakfast dishes and school lunch fixings littered the kitchen counter. The phone rang repeatedly and not only was I behind, I was sleep deprived.

"When is the pastor going to be coming home?" "Will he be at prayer meeting Wednesday night?" "Tell him when you go to the hospital today that we need . . ."

My pastor-husband was in the hospital, barely coherent after yesterday's sinus surgery. He would be out of commission for at least a week. It seemed as though I was command central for the church.

The phone rang again. I heard a familiar, troubled voice. Could I listen and help? I reached deep and tried to share hope and courage. The despairing voice didn't change. Somewhere in that tense hour, as I leaned on my elbows and sagged against the cupboard, I was aware of my youngest son beside me. Quietly, he had found a way to climb up, his fat little legs now sprawled around the clutter, as close to me as he could get. He clutched a jar of mayonnaise solemnly and, as if this were the most important thing he had to do, poked unshelled peanuts one at a time into the creamy contents.

It took a minute, but suddenly I had a paradigm shift, if you please. The unimportance I had felt in what I had been doing dropped away. Right here in front, beside, and around me was my work, my pulpit, my chapel. It was a pretty messy pulpit. My unpotty-trained disciple smelled bad at the moment, and the voice on the phone needed more grace and wisdom than I had that day. But I needed to do only what was at hand with what I had. With God's grace, as I turned to Him in my insufficiency, I would be able to give a whole lot more.

Commending my caller to the Great Physician, I brought the phone conversation to a close. I kissed the small mayonnaised face (he'd been tasting as he worked) and scooped him up.

Father, there is no neat desk or serious book-lined shelves in my career world. Yet in spite of chaos, You have given me legitimate work. Help me face whatever today brings.   MARILYN J. APPLEGATE

If There Is Anything
I Can Do, Let Me Know

For if they fall, one will lift up the other; but woe to one who is alone and falls and does not have another to help. Eccl. 4:10, NRSV.

I had become an authority on a subject I wish I knew absolutely nothing about—the sudden loss of a husband. My lover, my soul mate, my husband was dead from a massive heart attack. Within minutes the news spread. The community families were shocked, grieving the loss of Jackie's enthusiasm, dedication, and compassion. The most alive person I had ever known was gone.

The comforters gathered, the plants arrived, the cards came. Dozens offered, "If there is anything I can do, let me know." Many just acted, performing unnumbered kindnesses, demonstrating loving ways to help the bereaved.

How does one do this for someone facing this terrible loss? First, do the obviously necessary. Make calls to relatives, the funeral home, the place of employment. Cut the lawn. Wash the car. Vacuum the house. Do the laundry. Bring food—hot and cold; desserts; entrées; fruits and vegetables; casseroles to be frozen for later use; cans of juice. Bring paperware items, such as plates, cups, garbage bags.

Second, share a special skill. Help write thank-you notes. Fix hair. Offer business skills. Get the car repaired. Fix what needs fixing. A plant-knowledgeable friend sorted my arrangements and gave instructions on how to keep them thriving.

Third, help in creative, nontraditional ways. Give food several weeks later. Bring up a fresh plant after the other plants have started to die. Share books on the grieving process. Go to the grave and get some petals from the flowers and put them in an elegant vase.

As has been wisely observed, "In times of grief, to say or do something meaningful is impossible, but to say or do nothing is inexcusable." Solomon says, "For if they fall, one will lift up the other; but woe to one who is alone and falls and does not have another to help."

Lord, bring to my mind someone whom I can encourage today by a small act of kindness. Help no one in my circle of influence to be alone when she falls. Give me the courage to do something to lift her up.　　WILMA MCCLARTY

My Special Friend

You need to be like your heavenly Father who is selfless and kind
to everyone, even those who don't deserve it. Matt. 5:48, Clear Word.

I guess it was these words from the Sermon on the Mount that impressed me
to befriend her. She was of foreign origin and not like the majority of
women in our church. It seemed that nobody wanted to be her friend; in fact,
they shunned her. So I felt sorry for her, especially when she became a widow.

Being a widow myself, I understood her grief. I became her friend and listened as she shared her heartaches. Her accent was pronounced and she talked
too much, but I continued to listen because I knew it would help her to heal.
We went places together, shared meals, shopped, and ran errands. Whenever
I did special favors for her she always repaid me with some nice treat.

She was overbearing at times, but I hung in there. Then one day I said
something she took the wrong way. She cried, and after that she began to
talk down to me, especially around my other friends. She said things that
hurt my feelings and made me look stupid. I thought, *Now I understand*
why everyone else shuns her. She doesn't deserve my friendship.

Then I read Matthew 5 again: "Now if you do kind deeds only for those
you care about or who care about you, what makes you different from anyone else? Even those who don't believe in God do that. And if you greet
cheerfully only those who cheerfully greet you, what have you done differently from other people?" (verses 46, 47, Clear Word).

I saw that Jesus meant for me to be kind, even to those who didn't deserve it. So though I didn't feel like it, I decided to be kind to her in spite of
how she had behaved toward me.

I think of a favorite quotation about Jesus: "During His life on earth He
was ever kind and gentle. His influence was ever fragrant, for in Him dwelt
perfect love. He was never sour and unapproachable, and He never compro-
mised with wrong to obtain favor" (Ellen G. White, *In Heavenly Places*, p. 31).

Lord, I want Your gentleness, Your forbearance, Your unselfish love. Make
me to be like You before all people. BESSIE SIEMENS LOBSIEN

The Reluctant Missionary

*Restore to me the joy of your salvation and
grant me a willing spirit, to sustain me. Ps. 51:12, NIV.*

When she heard that I was a missionary in Russia, she came searching for me in the Florida medical clinic where I was a patient and where she worked. "My daughter and family have just gone to Russia as missionaries!" Nancy bubbled.

We bonded immediately. Because both of us were grandmothers of toddlers, it took only moments for me to learn about her 2½-year-old Jana. It seems that Jana had a horrible time adjusting to her new culture. I imagined her jabbering in Russian as easily as in English, but her grandmother said it was not so. In fact, Jana resented it when her nanny, Valentina, tried to teach her Russian names for various objects. "No, no," Jana would scream, vengefully saying the word in English. She was frightened when she went outside, frightened when she heard people speaking Russian.

Then one day a tiny, helpless little kitten appeared at their door. Jana squealed with delight as she cuddled the little orphan and played with it. Grandma Nancy said that it was the first time since Jana had been in Russia that she seemed content.

Then the cat disappeared. Jana's parents searched the apartment complex in vain. When they returned to the devastated little missionary, they wondered how this could be part of God's plan. Dad said, "We'll have to ask Jesus to find kitty."

Jana prayed, "Dear Jesus, kitty lost. We cannot find it. Bring kitty back to me." The child hurried to bed, eager for her prayer to be answered. But the next morning when Jana awoke, there was no kitty to play with. Her daddy donned hat and coat and walked around the neighborhood.

"God," he demanded, "why won't You answer the prayer of this little girl?" Tears rolled down his face as he searched and petitioned. Then, there it was—tiny, helpless, hungry. Totally unaware that it was an instrument to be used in reconciliation. The cat was scooped up and delivered into Jana's arms.

Totally docile, this miracle kitty was receptive to the cuddling and tugging of a toddler. When Valentina left that day Jana gave her a big hug and said in perfect Russian, "Goodbye." The corner was turned. Jana was restored.

BARBARA HUFF

Blessings From the House of Pain

Better to go to the house of mourning than to go to the
house of feasting. . . . Sorrow is better than laughter, for by
a sad countenance the heart is made better. Eccl. 7:2, 3, NKJV.

Just a simple knee replacement—about 90 minutes in the operating room, and you'll find yourself in recovery. In three days you'll be going home for Christmas." So said my orthopedic surgeon.

The surgery was far more complicated than anticipated, and the agony began before I gained consciousness. The anesthesiologist did a femoral block, and the pain disappeared. But on my third post-op day, after the three-hour ride home, the femoral block wore off. As fast as the pain had disappeared, it now returned with a vengeance. *Oh, it must be time for my medication,* I thought. So I popped a pill and anticipated relief in 20 minutes. But it did not come. For five weeks I endured incredible torture. Each night I cried myself to sleep, and each morning I awakened after a frightening dream with the same intense pain.

Then one morning the promise of an old hymn rang in my ears. "There Is a Balm in Gilead" played again and again in my mind. I hobbled to my recliner and grabbed my Bible. *Where are those words located? And what do they mean?* I wondered. My search led me to the weeping prophet, Jeremiah, when he asked concerning the wounds of God's people, "Is there no balm in Gilead?" I thought, *Is there no help in Phoenix? Is there no healing? Is there no mending of broken knees? Is there no relief?*

As I continued reading, God's answer was "I will restore health to you and heal you of your wounds" (Jer. 30:17). That promise became my balm in Gilead, my help in Phoenix.

Five weeks of pain became five weeks of blessing as each day God reassured me of His love and gave me tolerance for the pain. He also gave me many gems from His Word to use in my ministry.

This experience demonstrated to me the truth of Ecclesiastes, "The heart of the wise is in the house of mourning." "For by a sad countenance the heart [mind] is made better" (Eccl. 7:4, 3, NKJV).

NANCY A. ROCKEY

Clear Vision

*How excellent is thy lovingkindness, O God! therefore the children
of men put their trust under the shadow of thy wings. . . . For with
thee is the fountain of life: in thy light shall we see light. Ps. 36:7-9.*

Mother loved yellow pea soup and always served it with johnnycake (corn bread). One day Mother put a big pot of peas on to cook. They cooked and cooked, yet the peas were still very hard, and Mother couldn't see what the problem was.

Calling me to the kitchen, she requested, "Check those peas, Dellas, and see what's wrong, would you?"

I began to laugh. "Well, Mother, perhaps you should have used peas instead of popcorn."

She hated glasses and wore them only when absolutely necessary. Had she put on her glasses all would have been clear but, as usual, she couldn't find them. For lunch one day, while on a diet, she packed cottage cheese and grabbed an orange from the table to take with her to work. When lunchtime arrived, Mother was quite hungry. When she tried to peel the orange, however, she discovered that she had mistakenly grabbed a fake orange from the centerpiece, leaving the real oranges still adorning the table. Her missing glasses caused other mirthful mishaps. Mother once washed her hair in hand lotion and brushed her dentures with hair dressing.

Even people with 20/20 vision sometimes find that their eyes can play tricks on them, that things aren't always as they seem. Fortunately, we don't have to rely on our own sight to reveal the things we need most to see. The Lord's vision is truly perfect. Nothing obstructs His view. Nothing escapes His notice. There is no darkness so thick that His light cannot penetrate it and banish it. He has a clear vision for my life, and I can trust Him. I must trust His vision, especially when I question my own.

My life is under Your wings. I trust You to be my light and my sight for this day. Truly, "How excellent is thy lovingkindness, O God!"

DELLAS McCAN

Not Quite Ready

You also must be ready, because the Son of Man will come at an hour when you do not expect him. Luke 12:40, NIV.

Since most of you have less than two months until your expected delivery date, there are some things you need to get ready now. First, pack your bag for the hospital. Some of the things you will need are slippers, a house robe, hard candy, a hairbrush, phone numbers, clothes for the baby to wear home, and a blanket for the baby. Also, it is very important to keep your car at least half full of gas at all times. You never know when your contractions may start."

Jennifer, our Lamaze teacher, gave these instructions to 15 very pregnant women and their husbands, who appeared as ready for the pregnancies to end as were their wives. My husband, Rick, and I decided to follow her directions. But when it came down to it, we didn't.

We just knew our baby would be born a week or so late. The gas level in both cars was allowed to reach near empty before we would stop to fill up. As for preparing the bag, Rick had a trip out of town a month before the baby was due. Since he would be taking the nicest bag, we decided to wait until he returned to pack the bag for my hospital trip.

Then what we knew wouldn't happen happened. While Rick was on his business trip, I had a visit to the doctor, who told me, "We are inducing your labor today. Prepare for a long night." I explained that my bag wasn't packed, and since Rick was out of town, I would have to go home and pack it myself.

The doctor gave me two hours.

When I reached the car I looked at the gas gauge. Empty. (There's a receipt in my son's scrapbook showing I purchased $5 worth of gas so I could go home, pack my bag, and return to the hospital.)

Jesus says in Luke 12:40, "You also must be ready, because the Son of Man will come . . . when you do not expect him." We didn't know when our son would arrive. Nor do we know when Jesus will return. When Jesus returns, He won't give us two hours to get ready or to fill our lives with the character traits necessary for the journey. We must be prepared at all times. Are you ready?

MARSHA CLAUS

Darkness Is a Time to Grow

*If I say, "Surely the darkness will hide me and the light become
night around me," even the darkness will not be dark to you; the night
will shine like the day, for darkness is as light to you. Ps. 139:11, 12, NIV.*

Most of us have days when it seems that God has deserted us. Everything seems dark around us. It's hard for us to smile, and we don't even like the way we look. In the past I have always just endured such times, trusting that tomorrow would be better. *God, why do You leave me like this?* I've wondered.

Then one day I was reading *Screwtape Letters,* by C. S. Lewis. In his allegory Lewis portrays a mentor counseling his under-devil something like this: "Above all, don't let the human being you are tempting know that the dry or dark times when he cannot feel God's presence are the times when he can grow spiritually. When he trusts God, although he cannot see Him or feel Him, the human matures quickly."

I was impressed that God is in the dark times, that they may even be planned by Him. I began to get excited and scarcely could wait to be depressed so I could grow!

One morning I awoke to a dreary day. Problems abounded in my life, and I felt I could not face my responsibilities. As I combed my hair in front of the mirror before leaving for work, I looked at my glum face and realized I was definitely depressed. Then I remembered Lewis's allegory. *Oh, good!* I thought. *Now is my time to grow!* Immediately I glowed with expectancy— and realized with dismay that I was no longer depressed. I was eager to face the day.

Oh, Lord, I complained, *I just missed my time to grow!*

But then the Lord impressed upon me a vital truth. God is not limited by human time. What He needs is complete trust. By trusting His presence in my depression I had grown.

He is in the dark as well as in the light. Although my depression doesn't always lift immediately as it did that morning, I remind myself that God has a purpose for even the days when problems and worries close in around me. After all, the light of hope glows brightest in the night.

CARROL JOHNSON SHEWMAKE

Assurance of Love

You fathers, again, must not goad your children to resentment,
but give them the instruction, and the correction, which
belong to a Christian upbringing. Eph. 6:4, NEB.

I know by experience the pain of having my children leave home, especially the firstborn. It takes time to adapt to and accept the emptiness of the child's room and the lack of daily contact. When my oldest son left for boarding school, I was consoled by the fact that he would go to a Christian school and that I still had another son with me at home.

At departure time I realized the only thing I could do for my son was to pray for him and write him letters. So I decided I would do both. I promised myself I'd write him twice a week, short but informative letters. As soon as he left I started to write the first letter because I wanted him to receive it as soon as possible.

While he was visiting for the holidays I said to him, "Maybe my letters aren't very interesting, since I just tell you about the daily activities."

"No, Mom," he replied. "I want you to continue to write that kind of letter because it makes me feel like I'm still at home."

One day I was surprised to receive a letter from the principal of the school asking parents to write to their children. He said some parents sent letters only when sending money to their children, and the children didn't write to their parents either, except when they needed money.

Everyone needs more than food, shelter, and money to live a normal life. People require continued assurance that they are cared about and valued. When we care and communicate, we are helping others feel secure. Security is an important element that can help young people face problems and difficulties, even as they get older.

Thank You, Lord, for the opportunity this day gives me to reach out to give someone dear to me the assurance of my love. Help me to find a way to touch the life of someone through a letter, a phone call, or a visit. ELLEN E. MAYR

My Rock, My Strength

*My soul, wait in silence for God only, for my hope is from Him.
He only is my rock and my salvation, my stronghold; I shall not
be shaken. On God my salvation and my glory rest;
the rock of my strength, my refuge is in God. Ps. 62:5-7, NASB.*

For many years Yosemite has been the location of our family vacations. With great anticipation I plan each trip, and have never been disappointed.

A few years ago, after some very difficult trials, I was once again considering our annual Yosemite trip. My friends advised that maybe it would be too difficult to go that year because of my family breakup.

I thought about their advice. After considering their suggestion, however, my mental focus turned to the strength of that magnificent rock, Half Dome, which is the symbol of Yosemite. As one drives into the valley, suddenly, looming ahead, is this huge rock that makes up Half Dome. It literally takes one's breath away. I knew I had to go back.

That summer as I sat by the river or hiked the trails, my thoughts kept coming back to Half Dome. This mountain was a symbol of God's stability. He is always there for me, looming above me with strength and power and love. "He only is my rock and my salvation, my stronghold; . . . the rock of my strength, my refuge is in God."

Each year as I once again visit Yosemite, I know when I drive around the last bend that Half Dome will be there, constant and reliable and stable.

Just so my Lord is there for me—always! When I can depend on no one else, my Lord is there. When I feel weak, my Lord will be my strength.

When my life is unstable, my Lord will give me the stability I need. When I feel abandoned, my Lord tells me that His love is enough.

I feel secure, Lord, because You will never leave me nor forsake me. You are my stronghold, my rock, and I need no other. PEGGY CLARK

The Walls Came Tumbling Down

*Therefore encourage one another
and build each other up. 1 Thess. 5:11, NIV.*

Many years ago, on my way to visit my mother, I passed a place where a man was just beginning to demolish a house. On my return a few hours later, there was nothing but rubble. I thought of the story of the walls of Jericho tumbling down.

Several years later I witnessed a similar sight. An attractive building that had taken several months to build had been a place of business, bustling with workers and customers. Then it was suddenly abandoned, perhaps because of unwise decisions, angry words, financial problems, or even bankruptcy. The building stood empty and forlorn for some time. Then one day two big machines arrived. They shoved and pushed, and in a short while the walls came tumbling down. Soon there was nothing left where the building had stood.

As I watched part of the demolition, I compared it to a human life. It takes years to build the walls of one's reputation—belief in God, faith, prayer, lovingly helping others are all part of the walls. Yet someone can reduce a life to rubble in a moment, demolishing what has taken years to build.

Sometimes we make mistakes or fall for Satan's schemes and tarnish our own reputations. Perhaps someone gossips about us, telling lies that are believed, and our walls begin to crumble. But with our Lord's help, we can pick ourselves up and continue to build the walls of our reputation even stronger.

However, it could be the other way around. While we wouldn't dream of going into someone's house and stealing their belongings, our thoughtless words can make the walls of their reputation crumble and fall.

Lord, help me to be a member of the construction crew in other people's lives, never a part of the demolition crew. Help me to encourage, never discourage. Help me to build up rather than tear down another's reputation.

PATSY MURDOCH MEEKER

Designer's Original

*God created man in his own image, in the image of God he
created him; male and female he created them. Gen. 1:27, NIV.*

W e sat in a circle, each ready to disclose. As the group facilitator, I felt
excited about the opportunity to interact with high school students.
Our topic of discussion was self-esteem. I decided to use an icebreaker activity to get started.

"Share with the group something you like about yourself," I suggested.

The responses were varied, including everything from a pretty smile to
nice feet.

We were about to change the pace of the discussion when I noticed one
girl who had not spoken. I thought of her as the lost child of our group. She
seemed so isolated and detached from the rest of us. I tried to draw out a
response.

"I don't like anything about myself," she finally said.

"Let me tell you what I appreciate about you," I responded, looking directly into her eyes. As if on cue, the others began to share things they liked
about her as well. Soon she was engulfed with affirmation. Slowly she lifted
her head and looked at us. Then her face broke into a beautiful smile.

"Thank you," she whispered as her eyes filled with tears. Her joy filled
the room, warming all of our hearts.

As our time together came to an end, we joined hands and prayed. We
all felt a sense of renewed identity and purpose. Through reaching out in
love to someone else, we had received a special gift. We had allowed God's
love to shine through us.

We are God's hands and feet. We are His representatives to a hurting
and dying world. Dare to look around your sphere of influence, allowing
your words or actions to be the saving agents in the life of someone today.
You can let someone know they are a designer's original. In doing so, you
may be the only Jesus someone will ever see.

*Lord, help me to allow Your love to shine through me today to warm an-
other's life, bringing joy and peace to someone who hurts. Help my words of affirmation to put a smile on someone's face today.* TERRIE E. RUFF

Mountain Viewpoints

*I will make my mountains into level paths for them;
the highways shall be raised above the valleys. Isa. 49:11, TLB.*

Well do I remember the first time I traveled through the Rocky Mountains from Alberta to Lamming Mills, British Columbia, to attend my brother's wedding. I felt trapped. How could we get to the other side of those giant boulders? The road ahead appeared to reach a dead end at the base of solid rock. There seemed no way through, around, or over them. To my amazement, as Dad followed the highway and rounded a curve, a way of escape opened for a short distance. Then another dead end confronted us—only to give way to a tunnel.

As a child, to me the Rocky Mountains appeared insurmountable. Life's experiences may seem to us as mountain barriers. The housewife may be reminded of the mountains of laundry and ironing she has to do. A student regrets the mountains of homework she neglected before exam time. To a lover, separation from her sweetheart is like a mountain to cross. To the worrywart, a heap of fears and burdens looms like mountains if she doesn't get a grip on her thoughts and attitudes.

We can approach life's mountains one step at a time, accepting the uncertainty that lies ahead. We can enjoy the diversions along the way, knowing that God has a way around or through every obstacle that looms before us. A giant leap to the other side of the mountain would take away memorable experiences that build strength of character.

Meet your mountain from an artist's viewpoint. See a beautiful feature to paint. Attack your mountain like a mountaineer. Climb it; scale it.

Descend your mountain like a graceful skier. Enjoy a panoramic view of home base. Think of the surefooted mountain goats. Mountains are their haven. Have the vision of a miner who digs for a wealth of hidden minerals in mountains. Speak like the patriarch Caleb, who said, "Give me this mountain" (Joshua 14:12).

Fear not the mountains in your life. Enjoy mountaintop experiences and keep your eye on the Mountain Mover, for He will provide a way through every obstacle. EDITH FITCH

Picking Up Tangerine Peelings

Whatsoever thy hand findeth to do, do it with thy might. Eccl. 9:10.

As a child I heard much about missionaries. Stories, pictures, and songs all urged me to be a missionary when I grew up. This worried me considerably. I was very shy and was petrified at the thought of going to a faraway country and talking about Jesus to groups of people. Although I felt guilty about it, I did not want to be a missionary.

"I'm going to work in an office when I grow up," I announced to my mother when I was in third grade. (I was much older before I realized that missionaries work as administrators, pilots, doctors, mechanics, housewives, nurses, or teachers.)

Although I didn't become a foreign missionary, my daughter did. I remember one day when, with the usual eagerness, I tore open a letter from her. The letter commented on her husband's current projects. She reported on her children's progress in school. She revealed her surprise and dismay when 16 young people signed up for piano lessons. Practice pianos were so few, and she already had six students. Besides, she was a homemaker, secretary, accountant, and hostess for visitors passing through.

"We had a Christmas Eve get-together in the fellowship room," she wrote. "I helped to plan, to get things ready, and to execute that. We had garbage cans placed around in the room, but some people threw their tangerine peelings on the floor! I could hardly believe it. I went around picking them up. When the party was over and the room finally put back to order I went to bed, exhausted."

I was disgusted. Common courtesy would have made that job of picking up tangerine peelings unnecessary. *No, I'm not the missionary type,* I thought. In my mind's eye I watched my daughter stooping to pick up tangerine peelings that thoughtless and ungrateful people threw on the floor. *God bless you, dear daughter, for doing with your might what your hand finds to do.*

Lord, I don't have to be a foreign missionary to work for You. I can serve You by doing my best at whatever my hand finds to do today. Make me a missionary, serving others wherever I am.　　　　　EDNA BARRETT CANADAY

A Talk With God

Be still, and know that I am God. . . .
The Lord Almighty is with us. Ps. 46:10, 11, NIV.

I was driving my daughter, Christyl, to Paul Revere Middle School in Brentwood, California, by way of Sunset Boulevard. It's a thoroughfare with many narrow curves and twists. I was driving in the left lane, next to the yellow divider lines.

Suddenly I noticed a car heading straight toward us from the opposite direction—in our lane! Because of the bright sunlight in his eyes, the driver had failed to see that he had driven out of his lane and into ours.

The right lane was normally full of other cars at this time of day, and it was very difficult to change lanes. There was no time for me to think of what to do to prevent a head-on collision. But at that instant my guardian angel took charge and provided an opening and moved us out of harm's way. The other driver raised his hands up over his head in expectation of a collision. I believe the angel put his car back into the correct lane, avoiding a certain catastrophe.

It's a daily custom for us to have morning devotions before leaving the house, but this special morning Christyl had whined, "Oh, Mom, do we have to pray this morning? We're running late."

I replied, "Yes, sweetheart, we should always start our day with God and receive His Holy Spirit for guidance and protection."

God is there when we need encouragement to stand our ground when it's time to be strong. God is there when we're afraid and need the strength to do what's right instead of what's wrong. And God is there in the late hours of the night and the early break of dawn. He was there on Sunset Boulevard that morning as I drove Christyl to school.

Thank You, Lord, for being always with me, helping me when I'm in trouble. After incidents like this I realize that You are indeed in control. Help me to never forget what a mighty, wonderful God You are.

MARTHA "GENIE" McKINNEY-TIFFANY

God Won't Turn Anyone Away

*Everything that my Father gives me will come to me and
I will never refuse anyone who comes to me. John 6:37, Phillips.*

I had just had an accident. Two security officers, who roamed around the Sierra Vista Mall grounds, came to my rescue.

"Are you OK? Where were you hurt? Whom shall we call to inform?" they asked me.

I thought of my daughter in Madera. "Oh, please call Joy; she's only 10 minutes away," I responded.

It wasn't Joy who came; it was her husband, Ed. He called the insurance company, talked with the police, and rushed me to our family doctor.

My husband and I have always boasted about our family physician, who is so caring and accommodating. But this particular morning, when I needed him most, the receptionist said that he couldn't attend to me because his schedule was full. Then she directed me to the emergency room at a nearby hospital. I was disappointed. I had really counted on seeing my own doctor. Fortunately, Ed was willing to take me to the hospital.

I'm glad God isn't like my family physician, I mused as I left the doctor's office. *God will never cast out anyone who comes to Him. He never turns anyone away. He's never too busy to care for my needs.*

No matter how busy He is or how full His schedule, my God has time for everyone, even for me. I'm not too small in His sight. In fact, I am assured that even if there were only one person on this planet to be rescued, He would have come. What a God we serve!

I could have been killed in that accident. But God cared enough to send His ministering angels to place a hedge of protection around me.

Lord, I'm so grateful I serve a living God, my ever-present protector. I'm so thankful You are always there for me. You never send me away disappointed.

OFELIA AQUINO PANGAN

The Visits

I was sick and you looked after me. . . . Whatever you did for one of the least of these brothers of mine, you did for me. Matt. 25:36-40, NIV.

Some years ago a young girl was invited to Grandma's house for the whole summer. She thought she was the luckiest girl in the whole world. Grandma lived in a little two-bedroom house, just perfect for the two of them. There were cotton and alfalfa fields across the road and lush vineyards nearby. Grandma also had a peach orchard behind her house. The girl could have all the peaches she wanted when they were ripe. She loved peaches and began to dream of peaches and cream, peach pie, and peach cobbler.

Grandma loved flowers, so almost every morning they worked in the large flower garden. Grandma taught the little girl about roses, pansies, and snapdragons. Sunday nights were the best. Grandma and the little girl would go next door to her uncle's house to play games, such as Chinese checkers and dominoes, and to watch Walt Disney movies.

Every Tuesday Grandma went to visit her old aunt, Rachel, who wasn't feeling well, and she took the little girl along. Grandma sat down in a chair near Aunt Rachel, who was propped up on the couch with pillows and covered with a blanket, and began to visit. The little girl sat very still and quiet so she wouldn't disturb Grandma's visit.

Oh, how the little girl dreaded those long Tuesday afternoons. Then about midsummer she was greatly surprised when Aunt Rachel said, "My cat had kittens this week. If you like, you may go and see the kittens in the kitchen."

After that day the little girl longed for Tuesdays and the visit to see Aunt Rachel. She enjoyed playing with the frisky kittens.

The little girl is grown now, but she will always remember how her grandma faithfully shared her gift of time with Aunt Rachel—and with a little girl.

CINDY SLY

My Guilt Is Gone

*My God will supply all your needs from
His glorious riches. Phil. 4:19, Clear Word.*

A *mother should be home with her children through sickness and health, tantrums and smiles,* I thought. Guilt enveloped me as I realized I might have to stray from my ideal when it came to raising our three.

Memories of my own home a generation earlier clouded reality. When I came home from school, Mother was there providing fresh cinnamon rolls and homemade bread. If I was sick and I dialed home, my mother answered. She had always been there when I needed her. I wanted to be that kind of mother.

Twelve years earlier I had married Gary, my best friend. He never complained about reading stories to the boys while I fixed supper. He helped me make our bed in the morning. I loved my tall, balding husband because he was man enough to share home responsibilities willingly. But hardworking Gary, whom I promised to love "for richer or poorer, in sickness and in health, till death do us part," needed help to pay for rent, food, clothing, gas, and electricity.

I was a teacher and could help, but our daughter was now 2. I believed Christian mothers should stay home with their children. I struggled with the fact that we needed the money I could earn. Reality has a way of intruding itself into dreams—dreams that are sometime impossibilities.

I started teaching in the preschool where our daughter attended. I was able to be home when the boys came from school. No, we did not have homemade bread and cinnamon rolls as I remembered growing up, but I discovered that the supermarket makes delicious whole-wheat bread and rolls. Times were different, and our circumstances necessitated a different growing-up style for our children.

God has provided through the years. Our 2-year-old started college a couple years ago. I'm still teaching. Providing a Christian education for our three children has made my working a necessity, and God has provided the necessary job.

Guilt has disappeared because I realize God has led our family in providing for all our needs.

CONNIE WELLS NOWLAN

A Time to Be Silent

A time to rend, and a time to sew; a time
to keep silence, and a time to speak. Eccl. 3:7.

I am never lost for words. It is a rare occasion when I cannot think of something to say. Unfortunately the *saying* too often precedes the thinking. Knowing my weakness, I daily pray for the Lord to take charge of my tongue and give me words to speak—comforting words, encouraging words, kind words, sympathetic words, words of advice (I'm particularly good at that), any words appropriate for the occasion.

A widowed acquaintance lives alone and because of ill health cannot go out very much. Time passes slowly, and she often becomes despondent. Before telephoning her, I ask God to help me choose words to comfort and cheer.

One day I dialed her number. "Hello, Dolly! It's Goldie here. I just called to ask how you're getting along."

"Oh, Goldie, it's so nice to hear your voice. Um . . ." Then Dolly began a recital of her health problems. She told me how many times she had been to the doctor, what he said, what she said, what pills she swallowed, and how many times she took this medicine and that antibiotic.

When she paused to draw breath, I tried to say something comforting, but she rushed on again. She listed the things she'd like to do and really would do if pains and aches did not prevent her. I made sympathetic noises, but she didn't hear them—she was off and running, telling me what a selfish world it is, how no one cares about you if you're "not useful anymore."

Again I tried to interject a word of cheer, but she was so busy talking about her ungrateful relatives that she didn't hear. I changed the telephone receiver to my other ear.

So the call continued for a half hour, with Dolly's voice becoming more animated by the minute. At length she said brightly, "Well, I'd better let you get on with your work now, Goldie. Thank you so much for phoning. I feel ever so much better after our visit!"

Our visit? I hadn't said a dozen words. Then I thought of wise old Solomon's advice about "a time to keep silence." God had answered my prayer, but not quite in the way that I had expected.

GOLDIE DOWN

Lord, Change Me

Without me ye can do nothing. John 15:5.

Some persons have difficulty accepting the fact that the Lord is willing to give them sanctification. They expect to be justified, but they think they need to do something to reach sanctification.

When I was a child I wanted to improve my character by myself. I woke up in the morning full of hope. *Certainly today I will be like Jesus wants me to be.* I made superhuman efforts without success, and my hope was transformed into sadness and disillusionment. I persevered. But the more I tried, the faster I failed. My sadness became depression. I was grouchy. My character became worse.

One evening when I was about 10 years old, I was in such despair I could not pray. I knelt by my bed, my heart full of sorrow. I began to weep. I don't remember how long I cried, but I remember very well that suddenly my head was buzzing with words. *O Lord, I can't change my character. I've tried, but it's impossible. I can't. O please, Lord, change me.*

My tears stopped. My sorrow was changed into peace, and I slept very well. Each evening I repeated the same prayer. Some bad traits of character disappeared very soon, others took time before disappearing.

Today when I look back, my heart is filled with gratitude to our Lord. He has done so much. Since this experience I have forsaken my efforts. I pray to the Lord, and He is happy to give me presents. I am persuaded that sanctification is a question of the sincere prayer of faith, sometimes with tears.

When I tell this experience to some persons, they are skeptical. It is certainly too simple. We hate to be dependent; we want to do things ourselves. Will we do them better than the Lord? Certainly not! Does the Lord want to see us sad and depressed from trying without success? Of course not! If the Lord can give us justification, isn't He able to give us sanctification, too? Is it too difficult for Him?

Lord, I am not the woman I want to be, and no efforts of mine have made much difference. I'm tired of trying to change my character. Please change me into the woman You want me to be.

CHRISTIANE TUOR

In His Image

But we know that, when he shall appear, we shall
be like him; for we shall see him as he is. 1 John 3:2.

Excitement raced through our veins as we sped down the freeway that spring evening to see our newborn granddaughter. Her mommy and daddy were absolutely delighted with her as she lay in her little crib, a picture of contentment.

As I looked into that little face, something shocked me, but I didn't voice my thoughts to anyone. Cradling her in my arms was a real joy, as was kissing her head with its fine silky hair. Love is amazing; it always seems to grow to encircle a new member of the family.

Then it was time to leave the hospital and that precious little family. As we drove home we recalled the joy of our daughter's birth and hoped that her own little girl would fill her heart with similar delightful memories in the days to come.

The phone rang as we stepped into the house on our return. It was my sister, who had just been to see the new baby. "So you saw your little self," she laughed. Her comment emphasized the baby's likeness to me that I too had noticed.

"What do you mean?" I asked, even though I knew what she meant. The baby definitely looked like her grandma!

I had never expected it. Our other grandchildren looked like their parents or perhaps a bit like their granddad. It was a shock to see a tiny little person who looked like me. And as she has grown, the likeness has only become accentuated. I hope as time goes on she and her mother will find themselves attracted to the same things and that they'll enjoy hundreds of times together in the special relationship shared by the baby's mother and me.

It gives me pause to reflect not only on genetics, but on the fact that we are made in the image of God, and others should see my heavenly Father in me—in my face, in my attitudes, in my actions, and in my lifestyle. When He comes again that image will be well defined, for "when he shall appear, we shall be like him; for we shall see him as he is." What a promise! What a destiny!

URSULA M. HEDGES

Giving Your All

And the peace of God, which passeth all understanding, shall keep your hearts and minds through Christ Jesus. Phil. 4:7.

I sat in the darkened shadows of the bedroom and watched the sleeping form. Memories flooded my mind as I thought of the past several years of teaching, perseverance, and expended energy.

How do you know how to be a good parent? I asked God. *How do you know when to speak, when to be silent, when to compromise, and when to hold firm? How do you know when you're doing it right?*

The girl on the bed stirred, as if in answer to my soul's questionings, then settled again into peaceful sleep. She was a challenge, this impetuous teen who was swiftly approaching young womanhood.

How could a second mom person erase the loneliness, stop the fears, dispel the anger, and remove her pain? *How?* I asked God again. *How do I do it right?*

"Just love her," He seemed to answer. "Love when you're tired. Love when you don't get anything back. Love when you see no results."

I don't know how to love that way, Lord.

"I know," God whispered. "That's why I gave her to you."

Gently touching her still hand, I moved from the shadowed room while the truth of His words pressed upon my heart. There is no sacrifice in loving those who already love you. There is no growth in the easy.

A picture of my Example formed in my mind's eye. Jesus, though misunderstood and mistreated, chose to love. He could have given up on humanity. He could have left us alone to reap the results of our own selfish agendas. We could have remained orphans. No one would have blamed Him.

Instead He gave His all for us—His time, His energy, His knowledge, His resources, His plans, His future, and ultimately, His life.

O God, I don't understand that kind of love, but I desire it. I plead for it. Teach me how to love with Your kind of love. I know a young girl who needs it.

JOAN BOVA

The Missing Warranty

God is our refuge and strength, a very present help in trouble. Ps. 46:1.

In order to get some needed repair work done on our house gutters, I had to have our original warranty agreement. As my late husband had handled this purchase and our business affairs in general, I had no idea where this paper could be found.

I went to the local bank and examined everything in our safety deposit box, but it wasn't there. I looked through all the drawers and files in my husband's desk to no avail. I went to our basement, where I found some boxes labeled receipts and business papers. I carefully went through each paper in each of the boxes with no success.

Very exasperated, I started up the stairs to the kitchen. "Why am I going through this?" I said aloud. "Haven't I had enough problems this year?"

When I reached the kitchen, I sat down on a chair and thought about my situation. What should I do next? Then I realized that the one thing I hadn't done was to pray about the situation. So I prayed.

Immediately a thought came into my mind: *Look in the gray box in your husband's closet.*

I opened the box, and there, right on top of a pile of papers, was the warranty paper, waiting for me!

"Oh, thank You, God!" I whispered. "I'm so sorry I didn't come to You first for guidance."

Now whenever a problem arises in my life, I remember all those wasted hours I spent in my search and go directly to the Source of all help—God!

Lord, today stretches before me. I don't know what problem I may face. Just help me to remember to turn to You for guidance and strength before wasting my energy and my time trying to cope on my own. I look to You as my very present help in all trouble.   ROSEMARY BAKER

The Trustworthy Boat

*Some trust in chariots and some in horses, but we
trust in the name of the Lord our God. Ps. 20:7, NIV.*

Our "most fun" vacation is being together as a family on a houseboat on Lake Powell in Utah. In addition to waterskiing, a favorite activity is climbing the huge sand dune at the end of one of the narrow canyon arms. Running full speed down the sand hill, we dive into the pool of water at the base.

We were ready for a little variety one hot afternoon, so we all piled into our low-cut ski boat and headed for Moki Canyon and the sand dune. About 10 miles up the main channel we found that the mouth of the canyon became more and more narrow until it ended in a mountain of sand.

After the kids were well worn out from climbing, running, and splashing, we rinsed off the last layer of sand and jumped into the boat again. The water was calm as we wound our way back to the main channel. As we headed toward the houseboat we realized the waves seemed unusually high. The steep canyon walls had protected us from the wind that had come up and was now beating the main channel water like egg whites. Everyone checked to see that their life vests were securely fastened.

We knew the rule: in a storm the bow of the boat must always head into the wind. If the engine stopped or if, for any reason, we got turned sideways or away from the wind, the waves would swamp that low boat and leave us bouncing through the storm in our life vests.

Slowly, ever so slowly, we made progress until just before sundown we could see our houseboat securely anchored in the distance. A welcome sight! Once again our little red ski boat had delivered its passengers safely back to shore. We had trusted it many times before, and it hadn't let us down.

A short time later, on a sunny, calm day, this same boat we had trusted to get us through the storm was out in the middle of the lake. Without warning, the ignition system went out, leaving us powerless in the water.

David, the warrior, knew that often his enemies trusted in chariots and horses, but he knew to trust in the name of the Lord. Some trust in ski boats and some trust in life vests, but how much better to trust in the name of the Lord!

ROXY HOEHN

A Good Taste of Blackberries

In every circumstance and in everything, by prayer and petition (definite requests), with thanksgiving, continue to make your wants known to God. Phil. 4:6, Amplified.

Have you ever moved four times in six months? If you have, you'll understand our feelings of dislocation when we learned that we must shift all that stuff *again* three months later!

Because of this experience I have empathized with those church workers who are called to be ever on the move. Thinking of the wives reminded me of a postcard sent to my mother's family in 1915. Its brief message reads:

"We have now moved to Newcastle, where my husband is the minister. At first I thought we would not be able to afford fruit, but so far we have had a good taste of blackberries."

When I first read this card as a child, I understood about the blackberries. They grew wild and free—but so did other fruits and vegetables, in our yard anyway. How strange to not be able to afford such necessities.

However, time and experience bring understanding. Isolated on a mission compound after a destructive hurricane, I prayed for a green vegetable for our meal. For three weeks our fresh food menu had been restricted to pineapples from our garden. We needed a change. I prayed in questioning faith. With so much need around us, why would God answer such a petty prayer? And did it even matter to Him that I couldn't be satisfied a little longer with a limited diet? Was it selfish to ask?

I heard a knock at the door and went to see who was there. A well-known village woman stood before me. She came often with goods to sell, and just as often I bought for the sake of helping her. Here she was today, her wizened arm draped with a large bundle of long, green snake beans.

Thank You, God!

I thought of church workers' wives on the move, in isolation, in needy fields. *Dear God, please give them a good taste of blackberries—and maybe some snake beans thrown in for good measure.*   LINDA M. DRISCOLL

Remember When

But this one thing I do, forgetting those things which are behind, and reaching forth unto those things which are before. Phil. 3:13.

We recently visited the area where my husband and I met, dated, and were married. Our meeting place, the living room of a relative's home, has now been converted into an office from which the family business is run. The place where we were married is now a parking lot—a tragic fire completely destroyed the church several years ago. We drove by the house that was our first home. Large bushes and trees had been cut down, a new fence was up, and a sign on the front lawn announced that the place was for sale.

With a twinge of sadness I noted each place that had played such a special place in our lives. I realize that special as those places were, what matters most is the continuing love relationship we share.

I recall where and when I first gave my heart to Jesus. Special as that place and moment in time were, the more important thing now is the continuing love relationship we share and the daily reaffirmation that we are committed to each other. He expresses His commitment to me through His Word. I can read daily of His promises of continued care and plans for my future, including an eternity of happiness in the earth made new.

Daily I reaffirm my commitment to Him. Each morning I pray, "Take me, O Lord, and make me Yours. I lay all my plans at Your feet. Use me today in Your service. I surrender all my plans to You, to be carried out or given up, as Your providence indicates."

The next time I have occasion to visit those places again that are reminders of the beginning of my relationship with my husband, I'll still feel special about them. Although changes have been made to their physical structure, I can rest assured that we have a solid relationship built on a daily basis, and that we will continue to be committed to each other.

Lord, today I consecrate my life to You anew. As precious as are my memories of our relationship in the past, the relationship we have now is what counts.

SHERYL A. CALHOUN

The Right Way

There is a way which seemeth right unto a man,
but the end thereof are the ways of death. Prov. 14:12.

I recently moved to a new community, from a house to an apartment. It was a big change but, oh, what a lovely view I now have! Brilliant blue sky, trees, a beautiful expanse of green lawn . . . Fall has just begun, and the days are noticeably cooler. It's the twilight of these shortening days I enjoy most. I'm reluctant to turn on a light. Instead I just sit, staring out the window, watching the daylight fade.

One evening I heard a familiar sound, one I hadn't heard for some time. Thrilled, I jumped up to get a better look at the honking geese as they headed to a warmer climate. There they flew in their perfect V formation. Several formations flew over in the few minutes before dark. For five nights this wonderful phenomenon of nature continued.

On that first night it suddenly dawned on me that the geese were not flying south but were actually headed east—formation after formation following in the same direction. I wanted to run outside and yell, "Hey, guys, you're going in the wrong direction! That's not south." Then a small voice seemed to say to me, "Ann, they're not following your road map—they're following God's map." I felt reassured.

I once read in a bird book that ducks and geese don't always fly great distances to the south but may go wherever there is sufficient water and food. Whatever their destination, I knew God had imprinted their way.

As much as I enjoy looking out my window, I also enjoy studying God's Word. It is in studying these precious words that I find what God wants me to do, what map He wants me to follow.

Lord, as I study Your Word, please imprint Your map on my mind and heart. Following my own ways can be dangerous. Lead me in the way I should go.

ANN VANARSDELL HAYWARD

The 20/20 Heart

I pray that the eyes of your heart may be enlightened, so that
you may know what is the hope of His calling, what are the
riches of the glory of His inheritance in the saints. Eph. 1:18, NASB.

I have worn glasses to correct nearsightedness since I was 13 years old. My first clue that I had a problem was when I couldn't read the board in algebra class. So I got glasses.

My driver's license has a restriction clause that says I must wear glasses when I drive.

As a young woman I had often been accused of snobbishness because I didn't speak to someone as we passed on campus at college. I learned to recognize friends by their shape, but had to get close up to recognize faces.

When contact lenses came on the market, I tried to wear them. Everything was so much clearer and brighter. However, if I got a scratch or a small speck of something on the inside of the lens, I would be in agony. A corneal abrasion is one of the most painful experiences I have ever had. So I gave up contacts and went back to conventional lenses.

I love the idea that my heart has eyes. Perhaps my heart's eyes are 20/20, even though the eyes in my face are far from it. One way that I can assure that 20/20 heart sight is to ask the Lord each day to show me the way He would like me to go. I can find out the way through daily prayer and Bible reading. Even if I stumble and fall, He will be there to help me up and continue to lead me in the path He has chosen for me. But I must stay in close contact with Him for this special heart sight.

Thank You, Lord, that Your lovingkindness never fails. Thank You that You are always there for me. May the eyes of my heart be open to Your leading. Help me to see clearly others who may need help or encouragement. Give me 20/20 vision in my heart. SHEILA SANDERS DELANEY

Don't Worry; Be Happy

Cast all your anxiety on him because he cares for you. 1 Peter 5:7, NIV.

One night I had been worrying about a lot of things. Things were not working out as I felt they should. Because of all my cares, I had not slept very well.

The next morning I had to take my daughter to the railway station, so I decided to go shopping on the same trip. The first shop was already open, and I was able to complete my errands earlier than I expected.

While driving past another shop, I realized I needed to get something there too. When I pulled into the parking lot, I was surprised that it looked so deserted. Only when I saw a woman waiting in front of the entrance did I look at my watch. Four minutes to nine. The shop wasn't open yet. I decided to wait, and turned on the radio.

"'Don't worry; be happy. . . . Don't worry; be happy'" someone sang. I had heard the song before, or at least snatches of it. But I had never heard the whole song. I decided to listen to it attentively. The longer I listened, the more I liked it. It was exactly what I needed. It didn't take long for the corners of my mouth to turn up. By the time the shop opened, the song was over, and I didn't have to look in the rearview mirror to determine that I was smiling.

Yes, the singer was right. Why should I worry? I had a roof over my head and food to eat and a lot more. I had been full of cares, and now they were gone. That simple little song was just what the great Doctor had prescribed for me for that day. All through the day the words played in my head: "Don't worry; be happy!"

Lord, I have no need to worry, because You care for me. Some days I just need to be reminded. Help me today to cast all my anxiety on You.

HANNELE OTTSCHOFSKI

Hope: A Welcome Companion

Yet there is one ray of hope; his compassion never ends. It is only the Lord's mercies that have kept us from complete destruction. Lam. 3:21, 22, TLB.

I was devastated. The neurologist said that my 59-year-old husband, who had suffered a massive stroke and was paralyzed on his left side, would probably never recover.

"Just apply for full disability insurance," she said.

"Can't you give me any hope?" I pleaded.

"Well," she replied, "a third get better, but a third stay the same—and a third get worse."

I staggered from ICU into the waiting room, fighting to control my tears. Life as I had known it for 30-some years was over. My bright, capable, lean, healthy (cholesterol 120 and low blood pressure) husband had been reduced to a helpless soul in one awful second.

Alone in that crowded room, my heart so heavy I thought it would break, I screamed silently, *Help us, Lord! What will become of Jan? I'm scared!*

A white-coated physician peeked in the door and called a name. People ran to him with expectations, and then shouted with joy as they received the good news about their loved one. I was happy for them, but my own situation seemed so hopeless. No skilled surgeon could transplant the brain cells that had been destroyed. No medication could restore function and productivity. Physical therapy might help, but even that seemed doubtful.

In the depth of my despair, the phone at the nurses' station rang. "Kay Kuzma?" a voice called. I blew my nose and took the phone.

"Kay, I just heard the news about Jan. Don't listen if they say he can't get better. Jan can recover." And then Hans Diehl began to tell me about people who had suffered from devastating strokes and had recovered.

When I hung up, I noticed the sun was shining. I looked around and smiled. My heart began to sing. Hope is a wonderful companion in the time of trouble.

I want you to know that "God is wonderfully good to those who wait for Him." Jan has almost fully recovered now. So when tragedy strikes and things seem hopeless, please remember "there is one ray of hope; his compassion never ends."

KAY KUZMA

We'll Meet Again

And God shall wipe away all tears from their eyes; and there shall be no more death, . . . neither shall there be any more pain. Rev. 21:4.

I like to sit on my little veranda, facing the fields. No houses block my view, so I can look for miles to the Quantock Hills. Seasons change, but the beauty remains with gentle variations, and I feel at ease. I watch the cows moving about the grass, munching away. When milking time comes they seem to know and start walking single file to the farmhouse. Their distinct black-and-white coats enhance the picture. Occasionally there is the noise of a car or tractor or a person taking a dog for a walk. I listen to the birds in the two large sycamore trees in front of my flat.

At present, leaves are changing color and some are already falling silently to the ground, forming a carpet of autumn hues. I see the contrasts of light and shade between the branches. Shadows over the hills and fields are constantly moving as the clouds drift by. In the distance soft mauves and grays even now are changing to light siennas and the earthy browns of Somerset soil. The ground is being prepared before the winter.

I close my eyes, and the words "a new heaven and a new earth" remind me of the beauty and the promises of "no more pain or tears." My husband enjoyed this view with me. When he was ill, it eased his pain and gave him strength. "Best time of the day," he would say as evening came. Shadows were lengthening, and other birds across the way started singing and, it seemed to me, they were agreeing with him.

Sometimes he stretched out his hand, and our fingers would touch. That was always special, and we smiled. We shared these precious times together . . . so simple . . . so beautiful. As the years go by and I am here on my own, the memory is with me forever.

One day there will be far more beauty and peace than this when we shall meet again, well and strong with no more sadness or sickness, to sit at the feet of our heavenly Father for eternity.   PHILIPPA MARSHALL

A Higher Standard

Let all things be done decently and in order. 1 Cor. 14:40.

Popular author Max Lucado in his book *In the Grip of Grace* confesses he never was a "neat freak." During childhood he embraced a high threshold of sloppiness. His mother tried to reform his sloppiness but never succeeded. As long as Max lived at home, he never stacked his dishes or picked up his clothes.

Max was a closet slob who never understood the logic of neatness. Why make a bed if you are only going to sleep in it again that night? Wasn't it easier to stack dishes and do them all at once when all the day's meals were over? Who cared if clothes were left on the floor? You had to put them on again in the morning. Why replace the lid on the toothpaste, only to remove it again the next time? Max was compulsively messy.

Then he got married. His wife, Denalyn, didn't mind his messy ways—if he didn't mind sleeping outside! He minded, so began changing his ways. Denalyn introduced him to the fragrance of Pine-Sol. A physical therapist helped him rediscover muscles used for hanging up clothes and placing toilet paper on the holder. Soon he became a new man and could go three days without throwing a sock behind the couch.

When Denalyn went out of town for a week, he immediately reverted to his previous sloppy habits. He figured he'd live like a slob for six days and clean on the seventh. But a curious thing happened. He could no longer relax with dirty dishes in the sink. He bent over to pick things up, and actually hung his towel on the rack. What had happened?

He'd been exposed to a higher standard. Once exposed to a higher standard, who would want to go back to the old mess? Some women, much like Max, also have poor housekeeping habits. Habits are acts repeated so frequently they become fixed in character and almost automatic in performance, like an addiction. Once they stop making excuses and become aware of their habits, they'll discover they crave organization because they too have been called to a higher standard.

Lord, on this day help me to achieve the higher standard in housekeeping, and in all that I do to which You have called me. NANCY L. VAN PELT

Rejoice With Me

*And when she finds it, she calls her friends and neighbors together
and says, "Rejoice with me; I have found [the] lost." Luke 15:9, NIV.*

The wedding was over. It was simple, with personal touches highlighting
the groom's Romanian homeland. The couple stood before an arch
built by him and his father. After the vows, the couple gave bouquets of
spring flowers to their mothers. Daffodils brightened each table. Robyn and
Lari served cake to their guests. White tablecloths—gifts from the groom's
mother—covered the two tables. Because my grandmother was born in
Bukovina, Robyn had set up a display of that beautiful part of Romania:
photos and a framed etching of a medieval town she and Lari often visited.

Late that night we parents returned to wash and box the plates, goblets,
and cutlery. We finished past midnight. I returned the next day to pack up
the displays. We made several trips to return rented items. I crashed the
next morning. There's no such thing as a "simple" wedding.

A week later I discovered that one of the Romanian tablecloths was
missing. Carefully, systematically, I sorted through everything used in the
reception. I called the rental company. I called the caterer and the friend
who'd made the wedding cakes. I searched everything. No luck. Lari's parents were returning home, and I asked Adela if she could find another just
like it. Not possible. I was sick. Mentally, I retraced every move I'd made.
Nothing helped.

Weeks passed. I searched closets and boxes. Months slipped by. Lari
discovered an original etching was missing too. I lay awake at night, mentally searching for two lost treasures. Sometimes I dreamed I'd found one;
awakening, I would rush to search the box or the closet.

Cleaning the house one September morning, I opened a flat box stored in
the dining room and gasped! There were the tablecloth *and* the etching.
Suddenly I remembered. Packing up, I'd placed both items with the large tray
in its box. I sank to the floor and cried. Then I jumped up and yelled. I called
Robyn and Lari. I told people at work. I almost told strangers on the street.

*"In the same way, I tell you, there is rejoicing in the presence of the angels
of God over one sinner who repents."*   PENNY ESTES WHEELER

Weeds or Flowers?

Your beauty and love chase after me every day of my life. Ps. 23:6, Message.

Once upon a time a king wanted to take inventory of his kingdom. He summoned his two most observant ministers and commissioned them by royal decree. To the first he gave the task of surveying the entire kingdom, documenting the varieties of flowers in that land. To the second he gave the job of cataloging all the types of weeds.

The ministers traveled by coach and by horseback; where horses couldn't go, they hiked. They carried notebooks and wrote at every pause. Through the spring court season and the summer frolics they toiled; they even missed the fall festival.

As the second snow was thickening, they returned to court to make their report. A hush fell on the court as they approached the king. The second minister looked pale and ill. The king called on him first.

He reported, "Your Majesty, my heart is heavy with the report I must bring. Your kingdom is filled with the coarsest weeds and sharpest briers. The farmers can scarcely till the ground for the pests growing in their fields. The forests are overcome with choking thickets. Even your own royal lawn is infested with dandelions. Truly, Your Highness, the best course would be to burn the entire country and start over."

The king was distraught. In despair he looked to the other minister.

With enthusiasm he declared, "Your Majesty, my friend must have visited another country, for your kingdom is filled with the reddest roses and sweetest violets and the most abundant cherry blossoms. Why, the wildflowers alone would fill the royal greenhouses. The water lilies would overflow the royal lakes, and the fruit blossoms would take the royal courtyard to display. The rare and perfumed orchids should be in a horticulture museum for all to enjoy! Truly, Your Highness, this is a magnificent kingdom, and we should declare a national holiday in celebration."

God, You are so good. Help me count the flowers today. I want to celebrate Your goodness and the beauties You have placed here for me to enjoy.

HELENE HUBBARD

The Proverbs Woman and Me

"Many women do noble things, but you surpass them all."
Charm is deceptive, and beauty is fleeting; but a woman
who fears the Lord is to be praised. Prov. 31:29, 30, NIV.

I wonder why Scripture describes the woman of Proverbs 31 as ideal. I am already bombarded by images of the perfect woman: perfect figure, perfect home, perfect husband, and perfect children. Was it to fill me with a sense of despair? I have a comfortable but imperfect home, a loving but imperfect husband, blessed but imperfect children, and a definitely less-than-perfect figure. I know I am not perfect.

God helped me realize that the Proverbs woman is not like the women on the cover of *Woman's Day*. She is not an ancient portrait of some perfect creature who once lived on earth and blessed all with whom she came in contact. Her purpose was not to leave me feeling inept and insignificant. The Proverbs woman is the antithesis of what the world holds out for me to achieve. God's plan is to mold me into the woman He wants me to be. She is the woman I can become with divine help. This passage describes goals for which God desires me to strive. This passage inspires me to keep reaching and stretching to become all that I can become.

How can I obtain these goals? How can I become that incredible pillar of strength, when I'm overwhelmed, out of time and energy? How can I be a Proverbs woman on those days?

I explored the life of Jesus, our example in all things, and began to understand that He did not preach sermons, feed multitudes, or heal the sick every day. He often took time to refresh Himself in prayer and meditation. It was not by His strength that He accomplished these tasks, but by daily reliance on His Father.

God wants me to accomplish what He has placed before me and to trust the rest to Him. He does ask that I do it well and that I do it through and for Him. When I work with Him in this manner, it puts meaning into the simplest tasks.

Lord, I set before me today the beautiful goal of the Proverbs woman. Help me to be the woman You want me to be. CARLENE R. WILL

"If" Is Good

If we love one another, God lives in us. 1 John 4:12, NIV.

The word "if" has never been a favorite of mine. There seems to be so much inconsistency about what it represents, if not downright negativity.

In childhood I heard phrases such as "If you don't stop crying right now I'll give you something to cry about." I never handled those situations very well. I mean, what type of choice is that, especially if you have a frontal right-brain lead as I do and tend to express all manner of emotion through tears? Why, even the thought of something usually prompted me to cry even harder, which would bring on the very consequences I was trying to avoid.

Or how about this one: "If you don't stop laughing immediately you're going to be in big trouble." When one can usually identify something amusing in every situation without even trying to do so, being told to stop chuckling is like asking a mosquito to stop singing (or vibrating) when it's hungry.

Recently, however, I caught a new perspective on the word "if." It happened while I was watching the new Disney cartoon *Hercules*. In this adaptation from Greek mythology, two little imps were plotting ruin against Hercules. At one point the no-good pair were discussing the desired outcome of their diabolic machinations. Their conversational sequence went something like this: "If we do this, and if such and such happens, and then if that happens, then Hercules will be history." They looked at each other for a moment and then cracked up. The first little imp said with feeling, "*If* is good!"

I laughed aloud. For the first time in my life I began to think of *if* in a new way. The more I thought about it, the harder I laughed. The more I laughed, the better I liked the word and the new concept it could portray.

For example, if we are on a journey of personal growth, "if" is good. If we are identifying our innate giftedness and matching the bulk of our activities to that ease of functioning, "if" is good. If we are moving from a position of barely surviving toward one of wholistic thriving, "if" is good. And if we are developing a rewarding spiritual relationship with God, "if" is more than good; it's fantastic!

ARLENE TAYLOR

Golden Moments

Surely the Lord is in this place, and I was not aware of it. Gen. 28:16, NIV.

Our flight from Thousand Oaks, California, had a one-hour stopover in Denver before we resumed our flight to Dulles Airport in Washington, D.C. As we boarded the plane in Denver, we caught a brief glimpse of our friend, Jim, the former pastor of a Maryland church we had attended while living there.

Once on the ground in Washington, D.C., we boarded the shuttle bus that would take us to the terminal where our children were waiting for us. I looked down the long row of passengers who sat facing each other and spotted Jim, sitting opposite us far down toward the other end. He was looking my way, and because it was too far to communicate by voice, he tested my lipreading ability. He tried mouthing his message, but I couldn't understand. Again and again he repeated it, but I just could not tune in to the words he was saying.

Finally the shuttle stopped at the terminal, and passengers began filing out. Jim caught up with us and said, "I was trying to tell you that you were sitting right beside Peggy Fleming!"

Quickly we tried to spot her, but she had vanished. My golden moment had come and gone, and I had missed seeing my figure-skating hero. How different that ride might have been. Maybe we would have exchanged a few words. Perhaps I could even have secured the autograph of this world-famous woman. But I had missed a chance that would never return.

I have wondered since how often I miss the presence of One infinitely more important than any earthly celebrity. Sadly, He is often overlooked when I need Him most, because I am absorbed with earthly trivia. He invites me to give my burdens and perplexities to Him in exchange for His lighter yoke of trusting. He is right beside me, reaching out to me, but my earth-blind eyes often fail to recognize Him.

Lord, I'm so thankful You do not give up. You're always there to bear my burdens and share my concerns. Help me to seek You today and then to listen to Your voice. When I do, I know You'll be there to respond! Every single time!

LORRAINE HUDGINS

Receiving the Gift of Love

For now we see through a glass, darkly; but then face to face: now I know in part; but then shall I know even as also I am known. 1 Cor. 13:12.

Our daughter Morgan was 4 years old. Up until she was 2 she seemed like your typical, overactive toddler. Then we began to notice something wasn't quite right. She would rarely answer our questions. We couldn't get her to hold still while reading her a story. She seemed to be in her own little world. At first we thought it was her hearing. When this tested normal, we began checking out other reasons for her behavior. We were then told that Morgan has Aspergers syndrome, a mild form of autism.

I'm not sure how much she is aware of. She has no fear of consequences, and it is almost impossible to keep her safe. The most painful thing for me to deal with is not knowing how to reach her and tell her of God's love and mine. I am told it is like living in a foreign country for her.

From dealing with Morgan, I think I've come to understand just a little of the hurt God must feel when we are unable or unwilling to receive all the love and protection He has to offer us. My distance from Him must hurt God even more than Morgan's distance hurts me. We have heard of older children with Aspergers who do quite well, and we are hopeful Morgan's situation will improve with maturity.

It is only when we mature as Christians that we begin to understand the fullness of God's love for us. I look forward, as I'm sure our Father does, to the day when we all will walk together with Him and be given a complete understanding of that immeasurable love.

I need to hear Your voice, speaking to me of Your love. Help me to slow down, to listen, and to accept Your love, assurance, and protection offered for this day. And Father, I ask that the day will come soon when we may walk and talk together.   TAMMY B. VICE

Follow the Recipe

*There is a way which seemeth right unto a man,
but the end thereof are the ways of death. Prov. 14:12.*

My husband enjoys home-baked bread, and I've been making it for him for nearly 45 years. However, last year I broke my wrist, so our daughter got us a bread-making machine. "I've tried it and it works well, Mum, but you must use the recipes they supply."

Gratefully, I accepted the machine and studied the recipe book that came with it until I found one that closely resembled my old tested-and-tried recipe. "Be sure to measure ingredients carefully and add them in the order given," advised the book. "These recipes have been devised for this machine."

No problem. I brought out my measuring cups and spoons and meticulously checked each ingredient: flour, yeast, oil, water, sugar (except that I used molasses, as I had always done). Mmmm, it smelled delicious during the baking. But when I turned the loaf out to cool, it had not risen nearly as high as I expected it would.

Three days later I tried again with the same result. I complained to my daughter.

"Are you sure that you are following the recipe?" she asked.

"Of course," I said indignantly. "Perhaps it's not a good brand of wheat meal flour."

After six months of trying everything I could think of, I told our daughter she could have the machine back; there was no way it would make decent bread.

"Are you sure that you are following the directions?"

"Of course," I said impatiently. "I measure the flour and everything else exactly. I have to heat the water to melt the molasses, but I make certain that it is cool again before I—"

"Does the recipe call for molasses? Try once more, Mum, and use sugar."

I did. The resulting loaf rose twice as high as any of my previous efforts. It looked paler, but as nearly perfect as any loaf of bread can be. Dumbfounded, I asked myself how such a little thing could make such a big difference. I'd used molasses for nearly half a century, but that didn't make it right in this instance.

I wonder whether my life is turning out as it should. Am I following the Bible's recipe, or am I substituting something that I've always done for a divine directive?

GOLDIE DOWN

Wise as a 3-Year-Old

So foolish was I, and ignorant. Ps. 73:22.

I entered the kitchen to find my 3-year-old granddaughter, Bethany, standing on her tiptoes on a kitchen chair, moving cans on one of the cupboard shelves. "What are you doing, Bethany?" I asked.

"I'm looking for the popcorn," she replied.

"Here it is," I said. "I'll make the popcorn for you."

"No!" she screamed in alarm. "Don't, Grandma! That is not popcorn. That is seeds."

"Yes, it is popcorn," I insisted. "I know it is popcorn."

"No, it is not popcorn!" Bethany began to cry. "You don't know, Grandma. I know."

"Honey, it is popcorn."

"Bethany, I think maybe Grandma knows something we don't know," spoke up 5-year-old Rachel. "Grandma knows."

I ignored Bethany's continued protests and got out a pan, poured some oil in the bottom, and emptied in some of the yellow kernels. Bethany jumped down from her chair and ran screaming to her father. "Daddy, come quick. Grandma is cooking the seeds!"

He scooped her up in his arms and held her so she could see the popcorn begin to pop.

It was priceless to see her expression of wonderment that those seeds actually were popping and turning into popcorn. She had been looking for the box of microwave packets. Until that moment her knowledge didn't encompass the idea of seeds that popped. She had only seen it come ready to eat out of the hot microwave packet.

How often I have been like Bethany. In my limited view of things I have stood my ground and thought I could tell even God Himself how things ought to be. I could see no other way. My limited experience made the solution very plain to me. Why was God doing things differently? *God, don't You know that won't work! That's not the way it is supposed to be! God, listen to me—You don't know. I know!*

Lord, today help me to be more like Rachel when I face a situation that pits Your wisdom against mine. Help me to be wise enough to admit that just maybe You know something I don't know.　　　　DOROTHY EATON WATTS

Warm Your Feet!

Thy word is a lamp unto my feet, and a light unto my path. Ps. 119:105.

Tucked neatly inside each of our daughters' baby books is an original imprint of their unique footprints taken at birth. There's something cute about a baby's feet. One photo in our older daughter's book is a sonogram picture of her foot, complete with heel and five tiny toes, the whole of which is about the size of the fingernail on my little finger. Amazing!

The world recognizes something special about feet as the shoe industry tries to keep them in style with the latest fashion. The Bible also gives a lot of attention to the subject of feet. Mary recognized them as special when she anointed Jesus' feet, kissed them, and wiped them with her hair (Luke 7:38). Even Jesus humbled Himself as a servant and washed the feet of the disciples (John 13:5).

I have noticed that a person's feet can be a kind of barometer, indicating the body's hot or cold temperature status. I've observed a sleeping child, snuggled under the covers, with one foot stuck out to cool off. I admit that on occasion I have done the same myself. You probably know that if your feet are cold, your whole body seems to be cold as well. And if your body is cold, keeping the feet warm seems to help to warm the whole person.

So with our Christian experience. If our feet are planted on solid ground through prayer, faith, and Bible study, the world around us can be very cold, but our hearts are warm inside.

As we study and learn we must walk in the light we have. Job 23:11 states: "My foot hath held his steps, his way have I kept, and not declined." Having our spiritual feet warm or cold is a daily decision. Where my feet are right now determines my status for this moment. Wearing warm socks today won't help me in tomorrow's weather.

Jesus longs to "guide our feet into the way of peace" (Luke 1:79). It is my desire to order my steps today so that I, as did Enoch, can "walk with God." How is it with you? If your spiritual life is cold, warm your feet!

SHERYL A. CALHOUN

Well Again

I will make you well again; I will heal your wounds. Jer. 30:17, TEV.

Junior camp at Victory Lake was always fun. Crafts. Swimming. Hiking. Softball. There were always lots of activities to choose from, and lots of friends to enjoy them with. One day I decided to play softball. I showed up at the playing field and, after being chosen for a team, got in line to bat. The counselor (who was also the softball coach) warned the team not to stand behind the batter. We'd heard that many times before and knew the reason for the warning: to avoid being hit by a flying bat. We also knew that the batter wasn't supposed to throw the bat or let it fly out of her hands, but was to lay it down before running. But accidents do happen.

We played several innings, and in the usual excitement of the game players started inching up closer and closer toward the perimeters of the infield. Numerous players were standing very close to the danger zone, the area between third base and home plate.

Slam! The batter hit a fantastic fly ball and then, despite the repeated warnings to be careful about throwing the bat, threw the bat wildly. It went whizzing through the air. Kids scrambled in all directions, trying to dodge the bat. *Wham!* The bat smacked a girl in the face. She fell to the ground, screaming in agony, her two front teeth lost in the dirt in which she lay. Shocked beyond belief, the rest of us standing nearby froze. We did nothing even when she stood up and limped, disoriented and in need of assistance.

To this day I wonder if she was able to get her teeth fixed or if she is still having problems with her mouth because of the severe impact. I wonder if she suffers from terrible headaches as a result of the blow to her face.

And I think how, despite warnings from our spiritual counselors and coaches, we stand too close to the danger zone and are injured every day by flying bats from Satan and his wicked host. And it's no accident. They aim to permanently maim or kill! But God, in His lovingkindness, can restore us to perfect health.

Lord, help me avoid the danger zone, and let me not stand idly by, watching the wounded suffer, but gladly proclaim Your promise to make us well again and heal our wounds.

IRIS L. STOVALL

Lavender

*Be imitators of God, therefore, as dearly loved children and live
a life of love, just as Christ loved us and gave himself up for us
as a fragrant offering and sacrifice to God. Eph. 5:1, 2, NIV.*

During a summer vacation in southern France I had a severe case of "lavender mania." The small, remote village we were staying in was in the middle of the lavender region, and we arrived just as the lavender harvest began. In fact, we came just in time for the *fête de la avande,* a festival in honor of lavender.

The whole town was decorated with lavender and market stands all along the streets offered various products of the region, but mainly lavender in its different forms: bouquets, little cotton bags filled with lavender flowers, essence, fragrant pillows, and lavender honey.

Looking down the valley, one could see a breathtaking patchwork of fields of lavender-blue. As we drove through the fields I took deep breaths of the scented air, enjoying each sniff. Our apartment was surrounded by lavender fields, and there was even a distillery working day and night behind the house. I could tell when they opened their machines by the intense fragrance in the air. My family thought I was going crazy, because I would wander around, sniffing the wonderful perfumed air.

Even now I have little cotton bags filled with lavender in my cupboards and in the car. I have lavender essence in a little ceramic dispenser and lavender flowers in vases and bowls all over the place. The odor slowly fades, and it seems the flowers have lost their fragrance until I touch them again, exposing another part, and I can smell the perfume again.

Paul seems to have had a passion for good odors too, considering how often he mentions fragrant offerings in his writings. Like the scented air that surrounds me, I am surrounded by God's love. He let Christ give His life as a fragrant offering for me and for you. And He wants us to live a life of love, spreading a wonderful fragrance to those around us.

Lord, touch me today so that my fragrance will never fade. I want my life to be a sweet-smelling offering of love to everyone in my world.

HANNELE OTTSCHOFSKI

OCTOBER 14

Cheerful Chalet

And the king will answer, "Truly I tell you: anything you did for one of my brothers here, however insignificant, you did for me." Matt. 25:40, REB.

Have you ever played the Ungame? I've enjoyed the Ungame with family members, friends, and lately with teens and their families in therapy groups. A noncompetitive board game, it asks the players to answer questions about life experiences, family traditions, feelings, and ideas. This gives players the opportunity to communicate about topics that might not come up during everyday conversation. One of the rules of the game is that there is to be no talking or interrupting during someone else's turn. Teenagers love this because they have their parents' full attention and feel truly listened to.

One space on the board allows the player a trip to Cheerful Chalet. If you land on this space, you must tell what you did to cheer someone up during the week. This space causes players to stop and scratch their heads as they try to think of someone they've cheered up in the past week. Sometimes it's difficult to think of anything.

Recently I received a big dose of cheer from a friend. I'd been having a frustrating week at work and had been struggling with a difficult personal problem. I was discouraged! I got home from work one evening and discovered a card from a friend I hadn't seen in two years. She wrote that she'd been thinking about me and wanted me to know what a special friend I was to her. What a wonderful boost at just the right time! God answered my need for encouragement through a thoughtful friend before I'd even asked.

Cheering up someone might take only a few minutes. It might be as easy as sending a postcard, delivering a loaf of bread, picking some flowers, or just listening.

Today, Lord, I vow to smile and bring cheer to at least one person. I will make a visit to the Cheerful Chalet—and maybe even bring along a friend or a neighbor. I know that whatever I have done for one of the least of these, I have done for You.   SANDRA SIMANTON

The Test of Love

You have my Father's blessing; come, enter and possess the kingdom that has been ready for you since the world was made. For when I was hungry, you gave me food; when thirsty, you gave me drink; when I was a stranger you took me into your home, when naked you clothed me; when I was ill you came to my help, when in prison you visited me. Matt. 25:34-36, NEB.

Reading a magazine, I found a definition of love that I confess had never occurred to me before. It helped me clarify the concept I had of this magnificent and useful feeling. The author said, "Love is giving." I was very surprised, because every time I wanted to define what love was, only examples of people showing love would come to my mind.

The verse for today confirms this definition. God gave away the most precious possession He had. It was not easy to decide to send Jesus to accomplish the mission of saving the human race. God knew it was a risky undertaking. His Son would have to suffer persecution, jealousy, betrayal, desertion, mockery, beating, and crucifixion. But God loved us so much that He overlooked all these.

The best definition of love is found in 1 Corinthians 13, the "love" chapter. It is the ideal love, the love of God. This is the kind of love we should long for in our lives. How am I loving others? How am I giving to others? I realized I was very selfish indeed. I was giving very little. And I do not mean giving of money, but rather giving of myself—volunteering, sharing interest in and care for others; giving a listening ear.

When Jesus was on earth, He mingled with the people. He taught, healed, and cared for them. He walked long distances to answer the prayer of a mourning heart. Jesus visited people in their homes, even if they had been labeled as sinners. For Jesus the most important thing was to give.

If Jesus came today, would He find me a loving, giving woman, a woman who really knows Him and shares His feelings, values, and priorities for others?

Lord, teach me to love—to give—as You have loved. ELLEN E. MAYR

A Real Disaster Drill

The Lord of hosts is with us; the God of Jacob is our refuge. Ps. 46:11.

It was very late in the evening. I had just hung up the phone when there was a loud, urgent knocking on my door. When I opened the door, I was surprised to see the sheriff.

"Are you by yourself?" the sheriff asked.

"Yes, sir!"

"Did you know we are evacuating everyone within a one-and-a-half mile area?"

"We are? What for?" I inquired.

"An hour ago 48 runaway train cars derailed, and some of the burning ones were transporting toxic chemicals."

The boarding school where I teach was a half mile from the crash site. I quickly called the deans to be sure they had been notified. The school administrators had already gone to check the disaster site. The Holbrook police officers and the sheriffs had quickly spread out to notify all the school residents and community.

The bus was almost full by the time I arrived, and the bus and faculty cars formed quite a parade as we followed the flashing lights of the police cars on the road toward the desert. The boys and girls sang in thanksgiving and praise to God for safety in the experience. We were then transported to an elementary school, where we found shelter.

The next day we were shuttled to two other shelters before returning to the school, safe and thankful that nobody had inhaled the fumes. Subsequent days brought more information about the hydrogen peroxide and toxic sodium that had spilled and caught fire. Authorities told us, "If the derailment had happened just another half mile within the more populated area, a large portion of the city's population could have been wiped out."

Thank You, Lord, for being a refuge in that time of danger. What a comfort this is as I go about my work today to know that the Lord of hosts is with me!

ESPERANZA AQUINO MOPERA

Garage Sales

Let your conduct be without covetousness;
be content with such things as you have. Heb. 13:5, NKJV.

We've all had some equivalent of a garage sale or yard sale. Have you noticed how some people just come to look, with no particular item in mind? They just want to see what someone else has. We all do it because we are, by nature, curious about other people's collections.

It's true that one woman's trash is another woman's treasure. We like to trade stuff. Granted, there are times when we find a bargain that we really need, but that's beside the point here. Most of us collect stuff, one way or another, until there is no place for the treasures. Then some of us need to have sales to thin out the clutter, to let it become someone else's treasure—and problem.

The Spanish have an old saying: "There is no pocket in the shroud." When we leave this earth to ascend to heaven, there is nothing we can take along besides our characters. "A character formed according to the divine likeness is the only treasure that we can take from this world to the next" (*Reflecting Christ*, p. 298).

But even on this earth we can simplify our lives if we follow the advice given in Matthew 6:33: "Seek first the kingdom of God and His righteousness, and all these things shall be added to you" (NKJV). When we walk by faith, "it is the only way to travel to a place called Simplicity. The simpler, more balanced and serene life we're longing for is waiting for us at the end of a road paved with simplifying choices" (Claire Cloninger, *A Place Called Simplicity* [Eugene, Oreg.: Harvest House Publishers, © 1993], p. 60).

The next time you sing the hymn "O Worship the Lord," notice the third verse: "Fear not to enter His courts in the slenderness of the poor wealth thou wouldst reckon as thine. Truth in its beauty and love in its tenderness, these are the offerings to lay on His shrine."

When our life is more simple, we can really enjoy the more important treasures.

I want to be content, Lord, with what I have. Help me to simplify my life so that I can truly put You first. BESSIE SIEMENS LOBSIEN

Parting, Such Sweet Sorrow

Weeping may endure for a night, but joy cometh in the morning. Ps. 30:5.

My youngest daughter, Lora, had long dreamed of spending a year at a church-sponsored college in England. We had lived in Europe with the military for three years and visited England a few times. I wanted her happiness, so I helped her get ready for her journey. I would be accompanying her on the trip so I would be able to envision her days as my thoughts of her flooded my mind in the months ahead. I dreaded the loneliness. It would be the first time in my life I would be living all alone, as my husband had died a few years earlier.

We enjoyed our trip, spending a few days together in London en route. She was so eager to see her college that I realized there was no fear of parting on her mind.

At last I could no longer put off the moment. We toured the campus together, and I helped her when she asked. Too soon I knew I should leave. Lora went to the train station with me, and we clung together as the moment of parting drew near.

With a heavy heart I climbed aboard the London-bound train. I sank into a seat by a window and looked out on the incomparable English countryside. Tears, coming slowly at first, slid down my cheeks. Suddenly I was sobbing with abandon.

In the seat facing me, a prim older woman watched me without comment until at last, as the train slowed for her stop, she stood up, reached over, patted my hand, and said in her captivating English accent, "My dear, it will be better in the morning."

Surprised and unable to speak, I tried to smile a thank-you. She must have seen our mother and daughter goodbye on the platform.

Since that day long ago I have thought many times of the pain and longing I felt. I have thought that perhaps I know just a little of what God must have felt when He had to let His Son Jesus depart heaven to sacrifice Himself on an earth that would not want Him, killing Him before He could return home to His Father.

But gloriously, everything will be wonderful in that golden morning!

MARY C. EDMISTER

A Day in Bed

*Beloved, I wish above all things that thou mayest prosper
and be in health, even as thy soul prospereth. 3 John 2.*

It was one of those sick bay days, when the most important thing was a
fresh piece of tissue and a warm, comfortable bed. It didn't matter one
bit that the sun was shining brightly through my bedroom window, lighting
the room with its irresistible charm, nudging me to get out of bed, nor that
the birds were serenading me in my backyard. The fact that the ornamental
pear trees had put on their most gorgeous dress of blossoms and were unusually spectacular totally escaped me.

I would imagine that almost every woman has had a day or two in her
life when the things she enjoys were eclipsed by illness. It's like living in a
very unreal world. When the flu or cold germs have taken their toll and left
us miserable, we feel we must not take that precious recuperating time, that
we must forge ahead, regardless of how miserable we feel.

The mother with small children needing supervision seldom knows the
luxury of a day in bed. Many people have a job that offers no sick leave, so
a day off means no pay. Being sick is always a hardship.

Fortunately, there are many things we can do to keep sick days at a
minimum. The rules of health carefully obeyed are well worth following.
Actually, the most beneficial cures are preventative medicine. The benefits
are not like a miracle cure, but they can help to keep us in our best health.
The best God-given remedies are virtually free: sunshine, water, rest, air,
exercise, and diet. To some this seems too simple; they think they have no
value. But health professionals are advocating these cures in almost every
magazine, newspaper, or health feature on radio and television. Recently
there have even been features in the media that show that people who have
a deep faith in God and attend church regularly are more healthy and may
even live longer.

*Lord, help me to be healthy today in both body and soul. You have said
You wish us to be healthy and prosper. I trust You.*   PAT MADSEN

OCTOBER 20

Sing a New Song

I will sing a new song unto thee, O God. Ps. 144:9.

H ow are you?" I greeted Donna Jackson, our pastor's wife, one Sabbath morning.

"I'm happy today!" she exclaimed with a radiant smile and gracious hug.

Instantly I felt happy too. Not that I was down in the dumps, but her vivaciousness was contagious. My usual response when asked "How are you?" is "Fine." But that doesn't reveal anything about me, bring cheer to others, or initiate conversation. I liked Donna's cheerful response.

How often we begin conversation with grumbling about the weather, complaining about the neighbor's cat, the high cost of groceries, the increase in taxes, pollution, the environment, violence on the streets, or cutbacks in health care and education. We criticize the young people, the government, the church administration.

If we can't be a solution to the problem, then let us "sing a new song" that promotes a positive attitude. I have determined to give more upbeat answers to "How are you?" I've begun to reply, "I'm feeling great." "Fine! I've had a good week. How about you?" or "Happy! It's good to be here."

A weary mother overheard her two young sons talking about their invalid father, who had a cantankerous disposition. One boy said to the other, "We can be thankful we don't have two daddies to deal with."

Find something to be happy about! If someone gives you an organ recital about her arthritis, her bad day, or her ailing dog, listen attentively but end on a brighter note. Without demeaning her miseries, give her a new song to sing. Have prayer with her, invite her to your home, take her for a drive, give her some baked food, teach her a craft, play a game, or whatever it takes to bring sunshine into her life.

When we sing a new song, those around us are affected. Let's follow the admonition we used to sing in kindergarten: "brighten the corner where you are." Sing songs of praise, hope, and encouragement. Don't harp about the problems in your life.

Lord, I realize I have the choice of singing a sweet melody or sounding a discordant note. Help me to sing a new tune of cheer today. EDITH FITCH

Removal, Rest, and Recovery

Come to me, all you who are weary and burdened, and I will give you rest. Take my yoke upon you and learn from me, for I am gentle and humble in heart, and you will find rest for your souls. Matt. 11:28, 29, NIV.

I finally decided to make the dreaded visit to the podiatrist. He advised surgery to remove my inherited bunions, the source of much pain and discomfort. Dr. Miller told me the progress of my recovery depended on what I did after surgery. With firmness he laid down the law. There was to be no driving or extreme pressure on my feet. I was to pamper them.

Although I had full confidence in his expertise, I had plans of my own. I had no time for pampering and slowing down. I had people to see, things to do, and places to go! As far as my agenda was concerned, I would be driving and walking in no time.

As I write, it has been two weeks since surgery, and I am still in my blue surgical shoes, very dependent on others for mobility. Although challenging, this time of removal from all my activity has been quite refreshing. Stillness and rest seem strangers to this independent woman of the nineties. Yet I know in my heart that I need both if I am to experience recovery, both physically and spiritually. No longer quite as restless, I realize that my body craves this calm.

The words of my mother ring true: "Terrie, you're so tired that you don't even know it." These days of inactivity have cleared my vision. I have paused to ponder God's creation, and I have done so with a new appreciation and enjoyment.

To feel the sun warm my ebony skin or the wind whisper its power against my cheeks, to hear the birds serenade me as I write—all reminders of the joys ignored in my rushed and hurried life.

Lord, help me to not become so busy today that I lose myself and the purpose for which I was created. Help me to take time to feel Your gentle love. Remove me from the cares of this world, rest my weary soul, and restore me physically and spiritually.

TERRIE E. RUFF

Learning to Take

It is more blessed to give than to receive. Acts 20:35.

Memory One.
It was 1948, and our first Christmas together. Warren gave me a pair of dressing table lamps. They were lovely, but . . .

Seeing my disappointed look, Warren hugged me and asked, "What's wrong, honey?"

"I—I thought you'd give me something personal."

I had a lesson to learn.

Memory Two
Time passed, and I was doing a lot of writing for my church's papers. As I dip into my mental memory file, I recall an incident. A friend told me, "Your story helped my child learn to be truthful."

Memory Three
The dress I was wearing had a bright print—well, flashy, maybe, or how about a bit wild? I had gone to a friend's office, and a man I had never met said, "I like your dress!"

I said a simple "Thank you!"

What is so special about the three memories? We often hear the words "It is more blessed to give than to receive." I had finally learned to receive!

When our third son was a baby I seldom got to hear a sermon, since he started fussing about that time of day. Once I read a short article written by our pastor. Later I thanked him for it.

"Oh!" he exclaimed. "That was just one of my old sermons. I guess you weren't there to hear it."

I wished he had learned the lesson I had and simply said, "Thank you."

As children we are taught to give, to share, to be unselfish. But as we grow older, we need to learn to receive a favor, a compliment, a gift.

When God gave us His Son, we didn't say "Oh! You shouldn't have" or "You paid too much." No! We accept His gift with gratitude. Should we do less with our fellow humans?

Lord, help me today to accept with gratitude the gifts of love other people give me today.
PATSY MURDOCH MEEKER

Angels in Orange Caps

For he shall give his angels charge over thee,
to keep thee in all thy ways. Ps. 91:11.

On a beautiful autumn day my husband, Harold, and I were driving
north to our summer apartment in our old 1979 Pontiac. We were
looking forward to spending a few days of relaxation in the country. The air
was cool and crisp, and the lengthening shadows among the tall pine trees
hinted that it would soon be dark.

Suddenly the car began to sputter and cough, and within minutes it died
completely. No amount of coaxing seemed to help. We were stranded in
what seemed to be the middle of nowhere, with night approaching. While I
sat in the car and prayed, Harold began to check wires and hoses. Being a
welder by trade and not a mechanic, he was at a loss to know what to do.

Before long a car pulled up in front of us, and three men stepped out.
They appeared to be outdoorsmen, judging by their plaid shirts and bright-
orange caps. They walked back to where Harold was standing by the car,
and I could hear them talking as they checked under the hood. After several
attempts the car finally started. It seemed to be running smoothly, so we
planned to drive on. Then one of the men suggested we exit at the first exit
ramp. That would take us to a small town where we could get help if we
needed it. We decided to do this.

We started off the ramp rather cautiously and had gone only a short
distance when the car stopped, this time for good. To our surprise and joy,
it had stopped right in front of a small garage that was still open. It took
several hours to complete the needed repairs; then we were on our way
again. We arrived at our apartment tired but safe.

Had we proceeded as we'd planned, would we have found the needed
help out on the open highway? Were those three men really angels? I guess
we'll never know all the answers, but I do know that God is only a prayer
away. As for the three men, well, they were angels to us.

CLAREEN COLCLESSER

A Modern Miracle

I have compassion on the multitude,
because they . . . have nothing to eat. Mark 8:2.

Though the weather was still wintry, the first tourists had already made their appearance in Greece, no doubt influenced by colorful advertising of a supposedly never-ending summer.

We had been notified that 150 youth from the countries of former Yugoslavia were touring Greece, and that they would divide into three smaller groups to attend church one weekend in three different cities—Thessaloníki, Berea, and Katerini—as no one church was large enough to seat them all. The four families that comprise the little church in Berea decided unanimously to offer their 50 visitors a potluck meal after the morning services, and preparations were duly made. However, things didn't work out exactly as we had planned.

A phone call informed us that the group would not be arriving before 3:00 p.m., so after the morning services we all gathered in our home to await our guests. Eventually they arrived, 10 . . . 20 . . . 50 . . . 100 . . . 150! The whole group streamed through the gate and into the house!

"Lord," I cried, "we're really going to need a miracle if all these people are to be fed."

Someone asked a blessing on the food. The group's leader asked that the 50 youth who had had nothing to eat since the previous day eat first, after which, if there was anything left, the remaining 100 could have something to eat too. The meal began, and soon everyone was eating hungrily. One hour later they had all had enough, and there was still food for at least 20 more people.

And that is how we had the privilege of witnessing a twentieth-century version of one of Christ's miracles. On a hillside in Galilee Christ fed a group of 5,000 men, plus women and children. He used a small boy's lunch, freely given, and His blessing on the five barley loaves and two small fishes multiplied this humble meal until all were filled, and there was much food left over.

God has not changed. Christ is "the same yesterday and today and forever" (Heb. 13:8, NIV), and as long as there are urgent human needs to be met, our loving God is still ready to use even small gifts, willingly offered, to bless His earthly children. REVEL PAPAIOANNOU

The Perfect Gift

Therefore, if anyone is in Christ, he is a new creation; the old has gone, the new has come! 2 Cor. 5:17, NIV.

A couple months ago my husband brought home a birthday present for me—an old sewing table he had saved from the garbage dump. You may think that that was a very odd present, but I thought it was just perfect! We have chosen to downshift our lifestyle so that we can minister together, and we've agreed to limit our spending on gifts. This gives us plenty of opportunity for creativity and fun! I love making old things look beautiful again, and I love sewing. So I was delighted with the old sewing table.

It was a simple, dark-wood table, with very battered legs. The tabletop lifted up to reveal plenty of storage and a sliding tray, and underneath was a little drawer, perfect for spools of thread. The table was filled with ancient buttons, sewing tools I didn't recognize, perished elastic, and thread on wooden spools.

We had fun sanding the little table down, painting it cream, color-washing it in soft peach, and stenciling it with a design of powder-blue bows and garlands of honeysuckle. I even stenciled a spray of honeysuckle under the lid so it could be seen when the box was open. I stitched a lining of peach chintz, with little pockets, in an attempt to organize the clutter that always seems to snarl up my old sewing box.

The sewing table, once old and unattractive, has come to life. We don't have great skills, and the table isn't perfect, but it has a charm all its own, and we have an affection for the old piece, a love that has grown out of a few hours spent carefully restoring it and making the best of its few features. In fact the old sewing table looks like a new creation, and certainly the old creation has passed away forever.

I'm glad that God takes me just as I am, almost ready for the dump, and saves me through Jesus. He sees my potential. He cares for me, lovingly restores me, and changes me into a new creation, more beautiful and more useful than ever before. I'm not perfect, but I know that one day I will be transformed in the twinkling of an eye by the Master Restorer into something more beautiful than I can even imagine right now. And that is God's perfect gift to me.

KAREN HOLFORD

I Am Your God, You Are My Child

The Lord who created you says, "Do not be afraid—I will save you.
I have called you by name—you are mine." Isa. 43:1, TEV.

I have a big, fluffy, black-and-white kitty whose name is Spunky de Bootsy, whose white hind feet look like high-top boots. As a kitten he really liked to play and would often pick a time and place that didn't always match my time and place. Neither Spunky nor Bootsy was an adequate name, so I called him Spunky with the Boots, or Spunky de Bootsy. That's his name, and he is mine.

This morning when I let him in he headed for his food dish, meowing all the way, thanking me for feeding him. When he finished eating, he came to me purring loudly. I petted him, rubbed his ears, and told him what a good boy kitty he was and that I loved him. He purred loudly all the while, telling me he loved me too.

Jesus is my friend and my God, and I am His child. He loves me and calls me by my name. He chose me to be His child, just as I chose Spunky de Bootsy to be my pet. He says in Isaiah 41:8, 9: "As for you, O [Beverly], you are mine, . . . for you are Abraham's family, and he was my friend. . . . I have chosen you and will not throw you away" (TLB).

I sometimes really get hurt, hurt so bad I cry or get angry and say things I wish I hadn't, or do things that hurt other people. When I accidentally step on Spunky's tail or foot, I often pick him up and rub my face in his fur and tell him, "I'm sorry, Spunky de Bootsy; I'm sorry I hurt you."

Jesus does the same for me when I hurt. His Holy Spirit's presence is like a soft downy comforter, all soft and warm, comforting and healing. I am so grateful that Jesus understands how I feel and knows what I need to get better.

He loves me so much He took away all my hurts, guilt, shame, sins, and pain by allowing Himself to be nailed to a cross. The nail prints, or scars, in His hands will be reminders for all eternity. What a friend! I'm so glad He is my God and that I am His child. Aren't you glad for that assurance today?

BEVERLY MOODY

Too Important to Keep to Myself

In the beginning was the Word, and the Word was with God, and the Word was God. . . . And the Word became flesh and lived among us, and we have seen his glory, the glory as of a father's only son, full of grace and truth. John 1:1-14, NRSV.

I don't get it, Auntie." The little voice at the other end of the phone that Sabbath morning was plaintive. "How could Jesus create the world, and then after that come to the same world as a little baby? I don't get it. Babies can't create huge worlds for big people to live in."

She was right, of course, unless one factored in the marvelous miracle of the Incarnation. But how could I explain that to a 6-year-old? "Do you have some paper right there?" I asked. "Draw a line across the middle of the page," I continued. "What comes first? What happened in the beginning?"

"God created the world. I told you that." Her tone was vaguely indignant.

"Now draw a picture of that at the left end of the line. Then, in the middle, draw a picture of a baby, then of a cross. What do you think comes at the far end of the line?" (So many questions for one little brain!)

The pause was brief. "Jesus is coming in the clouds to take us to heaven. . . . Oh, I get it now. It's a time line. And Jesus, because He is God, can turn time upside down!" Delight, excitement, and understanding were all wrapped up in her voice. My little theologian. She had granted me a kid's eye view of the essence of God. But there was more.

"'Bye, Auntie. I love you. Now, will you hang up so I can call my friend and tell her? It's too important to keep till church!"

Her words reminded me of a sermon in which the minister had asked what we did about important news. That question kept ringing in my mind's ear. Now my niece had answered it for me. Share it! It's too important to keep to myself!

Life-changing God, help me always to remember that Your gospel is for sharing. And that for You, sharing means much more than mere words.

GLENDA-MAE GREENE

On Vacation

Teach your children to love the Lord by obeying Him. Talk to them about Him whether you're at home or traveling with them, in the morning and in the evening. Deut. 6:7, Clear Word.

While working as missionaries in Madagascar, we traveled to our home country, Chile, via South Africa, where we spent an entire weekend. On Sabbath we decided to visit one of the churches. The pastor preached about the importance of taking God with us on our vacation. He insisted that everyone should maintain a consistent family worship and an intimate relationship with God wherever we visited. He added that sometimes we are so neglectful that we even forget to attend church.

The sermon impressed me for two reasons: first, because we were starting our own vacation, and second because I realized it was a common problem among people who are supposed to be faithful Christians even while on vacation.

It is true that before you go on vacation you feel worn out because you have worked so hard for such a long period of time. Going away for several weeks also requires a substantial amount of planning and preparation. So when at last you leave, the mind tells you that with all the work you have done, you can now take a break from everything, including your daily devotions and personal prayers.

Since vacations are so relaxing, interesting, and fun, it is easy to begin to sever the communication with God by ignoring Bible study—and even the practice of prayer. I am saddened to confess that this has happened to me several times. Because of the lack of communion with God, it has even affected the relationship within our family. You can imagine the problems that arose—boredom, uneasiness, and rebelliousness. I complained a lot, and instead of experiencing a restoring vacation, I finished with an empty heart and soul.

I know Your word and commandments were meant for my well-being. Help me to enjoy Your company, Your refreshing love, and the nourishment that You give me so that I may remain faithful in everything I do.

ELLEN E. MAYR

A Window of Time

*There is a time for everything, and a season
for every activity under heaven. Eccl. 3:1, NIV.*

W e always think there's time," wrote Donna M. Cedar-Southworth in
the Washington *Post*. She claimed that changing her lifestyle to
accommodate being a stay-at-home mom came from a relaxing hour on
the Outer Banks on the East Coast of the United States. As she relaxed she
thought about how she would answer if the Lord asked her, come judgment
day, "how I had spent my time and used my gifts." She reasoned that she
wasn't missing any milestones in her life, but "I was missing my daughter's."

"I was missing her first pair of shoes, her peaches and toast for breakfast, her grilled cheese for lunch." Accordingly, she resigned from her high-
profile, high-paying job to stay home with her 15-month-old daughter.

This Outer Banks contemplation came following a conversation with a
cousin at a family member's funeral. "It is important to show your husband
that you love him every single day. You always think there will be time to
make it up—'it' being the missed dinner with him because you had to
work, or the morning goodbye kiss that was too much of an effort to
muster. But," she finished, "there never is time."

Later Donna and her friend Theresa, an interior decorator, talked about
the window treatments in Donna's wall-to-wall-windows home and her decision to stay home with her daughter. With a yardstick Theresa marked
about two and a half inches with her thumb and forefinger. "There is such
a small window of time that your little girl will be small," observed Theresa.
"I'm so glad for you."

I wonder how often I've said "tomorrow," "later," "sure," "sometime."
There are those letters of encouragement, sympathy, and friendship I need
to write; people I've been impressed to visit and others I could help; telephone calls I should make to ask, "How is it going?"

I'm aware of the influence of my life on others who may model my behavior. And although what I do and what I don't do may not affect civiliza-
tion as we know it, it does impact me, my family, those with whom I work,
those I could help, and my friends—and my relationship with God.

MYRNA TETZ

If the Dead Can Hear His Voice

*And when he thus had spoken, he cried with a loud voice,
Lazarus, come forth. And he that was dead came forth. John 11:43, 44.*

Lazarus knew God's voice and came forth from the tomb. We too can know God's voice and hear Him speak to us. John 10:15 says: "They [My sheep] shall hear my voice."

I attended an early-morning prayer meeting that was being held in a college gymnasium. At the end of the meeting I went to a restroom marked "Disabled"—not to use it, but to pray. I needed to hear God's voice.

To my surprise, when I was ready to leave I couldn't get the door open. Being the person that I am, and not wanting to lose my composure, I knocked softly and called, "Hello; Hello." No response. Again, a little louder. "Hello! Hello!" Still, there was no response. Based on the quiet, I knew that only a few people were left—I could hear them leaving the building. Beginning to panic and yet trying to remain calm, I hit the door with the palm of my hand and yelled. There was still no answer.

Panic time! I screamed, beating the door this time with the heel of my shoe. Composure? What was that?

Nearly every other voice was hushed at this crucial time in my life. Wait! I recognized a voice. There was no time to second-guess or question whose voice it was. They must know I'm in here. There was a space of about two inches under the door. I lay on the floor, my face on the cold tile, my mouth pressed as close to the crack as possible. With everything in me I yelled, "Mr. McCoy! Mr. McCoy!"

I heard the faint reply. "Yeah?"

Praise God. He had heard me! But it was nearly two hours before someone could force the door open and I was finally free.

The Bible relates countless stories of Christ calling people, even from that deep sleep we call death. Lazarus knew God's voice and came forth. So did Jairus' daughter. I am so glad He hears and answers our cries, even today.

You heard my cry. I thank You. Help me this day to learn the sound of Your voice so that I will always be prepared to respond when You call to me.

RACHEL HARGROVE MOORE

The Unconditional Love of Jesus

But you, O Lord, are a compassionate . . . God, slow to anger, abounding in love and faithfulness. Ps. 86:15, NIV.

When we are traveling in non-Christian countries, as Christians our words must be carefully chosen so as not to offend our hosts or their religious beliefs. Over lunch one day our guide was discussing the role of women. She said she understood that all American young people live together before they are married. We had to admit this is partially true, but assured her that there also are a large number who choose to get married first.

In her country, she told us, after the wedding ceremony brides are examined for "purity." If the bride is found not to be pure the husband can reject her, and she may be physically abused and shamed forever.

My husband related to her the story of the woman who was caught in adultery and brought to Jesus by her accusers. Jesus said to the accusers, "If any of you is without sin, let him be the first to throw a stone at her." Soon her accusers left, and Jesus said, "Woman, where are they? Has no one condemned you? . . . Then neither do I condemn you. . . . Go now and leave your life of sin" (John 8:7-11, NIV).

What a wonderful opportunity God allowed us to have in sharing His love and forgiveness with this dear woman who was so receptive to hearing about Jesus! We went on to relate how our children also make mistakes. But instead of throwing them out, we continue to love and nurture them, forgiving them, and training them in the right way. Never before had she heard a story about Jesus, and the idea of love and forgiveness was a totally new concept to her. She said she would think about this.

We were thankful for this opportunity to share Jesus' love for all women, and we pray she will remember this seed of truth and will have the desire to search for more truth.

My prayer for her and other non-Christian friends is that they might learn about Jesus, not as the minor prophet, as taught by some faiths, but as their Lord and personal Saviour. "Salvation is found in no one else, for there is no other name under heaven given to men by which we must be saved" (Acts 4:12, NIV).   GINGER SNARR

I Believe in Miracles

For your Father knoweth what things ye
have need of, before ye ask him. Matt. 6:8.

With a slip and a whirl we found our car taking us into the ditch. Fearing the car would roll, we tensed and waited for the impact. Instead, the car slipped into the ditch backward, going between an electric pole and its anchor cable. The right rearview mirror was sheared off by the anchor, and the car traveled on to hit a fence and some trees. When we came to a stop, I looked at Darrell and said, "Are you all right?"

"Yes; are you?"

I assured him I was.

Several cars and trucks stopped to check on us. One of the truckers commented, "We thought for sure you would be killed. The Lord was with you! Angels were guiding your car through that space."

What a way to begin a trip! We had spent time visiting Peggy and Darin in Hutchinson, Minnesota, and were on our way to Ohio to spend some time with Judy. It was a wonderful, mild Minnesota winter day with good road conditions. A pickup truck had pulled onto the highway ahead of us and had driven slowly enough that we had to slow down to about 15 miles per hour and wait until there was an opportunity to pass. After passing, as we reentered our lane, our red Thunderbird must have hit a patch of ice, sending us into a spin and then into the ditch at 40 miles per hour. The car had considerable damage, and we had to rent a car to continue our trip, but we were safe.

"The angels guided your car through that space," the trucker had said. We are living because of a miracle. Angels had watched over us and cared for us.

At times we may wonder why there aren't more miracles performed today. Perhaps the reason we wonder is that we don't recognize the ones the Lord does perform. I believe in miracles. Our prayers of thankfulness continue to ascend to the heavenly throne for our special miracle.

Open my eyes and heart this day that I may see the many miracles of life that You perform each day. Please help me to stay in an attitude of thankfulness.

EVELYN GLASS

He Is Alive

*And we have seen and do testify that the Father sent the Son
to be the Saviour of the world. Whosoever shall confess that Jesus
is the Son of God, God dwelleth in him, and he in God. 1 John 4:14, 15.*

I knew there was a God, but I couldn't detect His direct involvement in my life. I was born into a Christian home in the 1950s and always believed the doctrines I was taught at the church schools I attended and heard at church every week. However, having been born into the church, I wished I could experience the excitement and newness that I noticed new believers felt. This longing for a real experience stayed with me for many years.

One Sabbath afternoon my husband and I and our three sons were taking a bike ride along the vineyards and orchards in Fresno, California. We were enjoying the beautiful weather and time together as a family. Usually my husband would lead, the three boys would follow, and I would bring up the end of the single file of bicycles. But on this day I was leading, and my husband was bringing up the end. Our oldest son, Sean, who was 8, asked if he could lead, and I consented. We came to an intersection that didn't have stoplights or stop signs. Sean asked if he should cross, and after looking both ways, I told him it was safe. Unknown to me, he wanted to cross in a different direction. Suddenly a van that was traveling at a very high speed came out of nowhere and screeched to a halt, missing Sean by inches.

It wasn't until later that evening that the reality hit me. How different our lives could have been in that instant. The only reason Sean was alive was that the Lord had sent His guardian angel to protect our family. Right then and there I knew that the Lord cared enough for me to reveal Himself to me in this way. Since then I have not doubted the Lord and His involvement in my life. This experience has allowed me to tell others about His love.

Lord, thank You for Your love and concern. I want my testimony to help others to know that You are real and present in their lives as well.   KIM OTIS

NOVEMBER 3

Three Strikes Doesn't Mean You're Out

Is your life full of difficulties and temptations? Then be happy, for when the way is rough, your patience has a chance to grow. James 1:2, 3, TLB.

I thought my life was over when I lost my job at the School of Public Health at Loma Linda University. My identity was built around being an assistant professor. Our family budget was built around the salary I received for my work. And my security was built around the health and educational benefits that resulted. Suddenly, in one awful day, it was being taken from me. I don't cry easily, but I admit I cried when the department chair told me there was no longer a budget for my position.

That was in 1981, and since that time I've learned that the only way you lose is to give up or become paralyzed with fear or depression. For God never takes anything away without giving something better—something that will allow us to grow in patience and become more perfect in character. I would have never started the *Family Matters* radio program and ministry if it hadn't been for that loss.

Often I've been spurred on by James M. Barrie's old Scottish ballad, "Fight on, my men, said Sir Andrew Barton, I am somewhat hurt, but am not slaine. I'll lie me down and bleed a while. And then I'll rise and fight againe." This can be your experience. You may have to "bleed a while," but the important thing is that you will yourself to "rise and fight againe." The strength of your God-directed will can accomplish incredible things.

Victor Frankl once said, "Everything can be taken from a man but one thing: the last of the human freedoms—to choose one's attitude in any given set of circumstances, to choose one's own way" (Victor E. Frankl, *Man's Search for Meaning* [New York: Pocket Books, 1963], p. 104).

Do you have a strike against you? Most people do. But one or two—or even three—strikes doesn't have to mean you're out. You have an incredible ability to regenerate or recreate. God designed you that way. You can experience healing, whether your strike is physical, mental, emotional, spiritual, or financial. Through Christ you can find satisfaction and success if you choose to do so.

KAY KUZMA

Closer Than a Sister

There is a friend who sticks closer than a brother. Prov. 18:24, NASB.

She arrived late, slightly frazzled and very nervous. As I greeted her, Linda shared that she was to sing her first solo during the worship service. She was worried she would have difficulty reaching the high note and staying on key. However, her musically talented sister had assured her she could do it.

"My stomach and legs tell me I can't do this," Linda confessed to the congregation as she got up to sing. "But my sister told me I can!"

I noted the shaking of her legs and her firm hold on the podium. Visibly scared, Linda's tenuous, shaky voice began: "His eye is on the sparrow, and I know He's watching me!"

When Linda reached the part of the song where she had difficulty, I noticed her glance to the organ side of the church where her sister, Lisa, was sitting. Lisa caught the cue, picked up a handheld microphone, and sang with her through the rough spot. Because their voices blended so well, the only difference heard was a slight increase in volume. With increased confidence, Linda kept on singing. One other time Linda gave her sister a visual plea for help, and Lisa again sang with her.

When the song was over, Linda passed by her sister on the way to her seat. They embraced, tears streaming down their faces. Although the message of the song was beautiful, witnessing the encouragement and closeness between the sisters more deeply touched me.

How like Jesus toward me! He is a "friend who sticks closer than a brother," or in this case, "sister." When I'm faced with an overwhelming task, He assures me that I can do all things through Christ who strengthens me (Phil. 4:13). When I'm worried and frustrated, He encourages me (1 Peter 5:7). When I've exhausted my resources, He offers to supply all my needs. When I feel like I can't go on, He reminds me that His strength is made perfect in weakness (2 Cor. 12:9).

Thank You, Jesus, for sticking close to me, for sitting on the front row of my life, encouraging me, helping me when I ask, and embracing me in Your love.

LILLY TRYON

A Gift From God

*Two are better than one. . . . But woe to one who is alone
and falls and does not have another to help. Eccl. 4:9, 10, NRSV.*

It had been an awful day at church, following two other days that had been equally busy and demanding. I felt exhausted. We had come home from a hectic day at one church to get ready to go to the other for a social, where I was in charge. We had an hour to get changed, sort out various things, load the car, and stop off at the shops for some last-minute supplies. I could hardly muster the energy to face everything.

As I gulped down a drink, I opened a small package I had received that morning from a friend. In the package were spiritual thoughts, a home-made angel, and craft patterns. It gave me the courage I needed to get through the rest of that day. Someone cared for and supported me.

Friendship is one of the most beautiful gifts that God has given us. Throughout the Bible we see snapshots of friendships that enriched the lives of those involved: Mary and Elisabeth, Elijah and Elisha, and Ruth and Naomi, among others. But friendship is not just there to meet our social or emotional needs but to meet our spiritual ones, too.

I recently asked God to supply my need for spiritual companionship. Within a few weeks one of my friends and I were writing regularly. We share what's happening in our lives, and we share spiritually. We exchange thoughts on the same verse of Scripture and how that passage can help us in our lives. We also share personal goals and prayer requests.

Sometime after my friend and I started to write, I mentioned to God that I would like a touchable person to share spiritually with too. I now meet with a woman in our church once a week to study the Bible, share, and pray.

God has met the deepest need of my life—to share with others the things about God that are tucked away in my heart. God has given me the joy of being part of someone else's friendship with Him. I thank God for His gift to me.

MARY BARRETT

The Return of the Bee-martins

The eyes of all wait upon thee; and thou givest them
their meat in due season. Thou openest thine hand,
and satisfiest the desire of every living thing. Ps. 145:15, 16.

In the remote town on the western slope of the Colorado Rockies where I was born and raised, we had a yearly event to which we always looked forward. The bee-martins arrived at about the same time every year. We knew when they arrived that spring was truly here, and the cold winter weather was over for another year.

We could hear them making a great deal of noise as they happily reclaimed their old nest high up in a big silver-leaf maple tree in our front yard. They took their work very seriously. Their first job was nest building. We would watch them as they busily tore out parts of the old nest and brought in new materials to rebuild it. We would see them going to and fro with bits of suitable nest-building material in their beaks.

The devoted pair of birds warmly greeted each other after they had gone their separate ways to bring back nest materials or food. Then the male lovingly watched over his mate as she sat on the nest waiting for their precious little birds to hatch.

They never earned an engineering degree or took a science course, so it was a big mystery to me how they could find the same spot each year at the same time, or how they knew just how to build a proper nest. How did they teach their brood to fly and fend for themselves? And how did the family know to leave when the weather started getting cooler?

"Nature and revelation alike testify of God's love. Our Father in heaven is the source of life, of wisdom, and of joy. Look at the wonderful and beautiful things of nature. Think of their marvelous adaptation to the needs and happiness, not only of people, but of all living creatures. The sunshine and the rain that gladden and refresh the earth, the hills and seas and plains, all speak to us of the Creator's love. It is God who supplies the daily needs of all His creatures" (E. G. White, *Steps to Christ*, p. 9).

PAT MADSEN

The Lost Sheep

If you owned a hundred sheep, wouldn't you be concerned if one of them was missing? Wouldn't you leave the ninety-nine . . . and go looking for that one lost sheep until you found it? Luke 15:4, Clear Word.

I tried to ignore the fact. Ninety-nine sheep in the fold and one was lost. Could that lost sheep possibly be me? I was a faithful church member who sometimes traveled 90 miles, one way, to go to church. I did what I was asked. I studied my Bible study guide. I rose each morning in time to study my Bible. I wasn't an alcoholic, I was faithful to my husband, and I enjoyed each Sabbath with my family. Even so, could the lost sheep story apply to me?

The shepherd, knowing the truth, kept trying, using different paths, different methods, different books, different sermons, and different people. And He didn't give up! He waited, patiently.

One Monday morning during my worship time I looked up—really up—at the cross for the first time. I knew I couldn't be good enough to make it to heaven on my own. I needed help. The parable about the lost sheep wasn't just a story or a picture of a lamb in Jesus' arms. That sheep was me, lost without the Shepherd who had died for me.

I thought about crevices, storms, the wind, and the wolves. Tears dimmed my eyes as I thought about my Saviour-Shepherd, who walked around the crevices, through the storms, in the driving wind, and protected me from the wolves that I didn't even realize were there.

That morning He found a sheep that was ready to be carried home, eager to be lifted in His arms, finally realizing its own weaknesses. I knew I didn't have the strength to make it home to heaven by myself. I was ready to let Him carry me.

Sometimes I still find myself trying to work my way home again. But my Shepherd doesn't give up, because He loves me. He is never satisfied with ninety and nine; He wants all. What a wonderful Shepherd!

Lord, thank You for searching for me, even when I didn't know I was lost. Thank You for bringing me home again.   CONNIE WELLS NOWLAN

The Gift of Life

In God I trust; I will not be afraid. . . . I am under vows to you, O God;
I will present my thank offerings to you. For you have delivered me from
death . . . that I may walk before God in the light of life. Ps. 56:11-13, NIV.

While spending our summer holidays at the seaside, my friend Estera and I decided we wanted to get closer to God. We prayed every day, asking God to reveal Himself to us. We waited, but nothing happened.

After returning home, we both received an invitation to a friend's wedding some distance away. We decided to travel together in her car. When Estera arrived with three of her friends, I got into the car, and we started off. Everyone was very friendly as we talked and sang. Later, I fell asleep.

When I woke up I was in the hospital. My back hurt, and blood was in my hair and on my face. I was frightened and confused. Then someone told me the story.

While driving, Estera suddenly lost consciousness. The car turned off the road toward a river channel by the road. But the car didn't fall into the channel or crash into the concrete fence of the small bridge over the channel. It went straight over the bridge. Then the car turned over and landed upside down. I had lost consciousness without even waking up and had fallen out of the car, landing a short distance away. Without God's intervention the car could have turned over right on me.

A man who saw the accident drove us to the hospital. My friends were discharged after an examination, but I had to stay in the hospital for eight days because of head injuries. I was told that when the police saw the car, they wondered if anyone could have survived.

While I was lying in the hospital bed, I realized that God had answered my summer prayer. He had delivered me from death and given me a precious gift of life once again. I felt God's love so strongly that I had to tell everyone about it, and I will continue to do that till the end of my life. I will glorify God in my life.

Thank You, Lord, for the precious gift of life today. I know that You have a special purpose for my life. Help me to glorify You today in whatever I do.

TÜNDE TORMA

Chosen

Ye have not chosen me, but I have chosen you. . . .
I have chosen you out of the world. John 15:16-19.

My fifth-grade teacher lined up the whole class on the school play-ground. "We're going to choose up teams now," she said.

My girlfriend and I excelled in baseball, so Miss Slocum would in-evitably choose us as captains of opposing teams. Why couldn't we ever be on the same team? We'd have an awesome team!

The choosing process began, and we knew exactly who we wanted. But after choosing the best players, there was always the unpleasant task of tak-ing the leftovers. Not until I reached junior high and changed to another school did I realize what it was like to have the shoe on the other foot.

The first time the captains began choosing up sides, I naively lined up with all the boys on the playground. It was obvious they were wondering why I was in line instead of in the cheering section with the other girls. With each captain's choice, my eager hope of being chosen was dashed, until finally there were only two of us left—then the other boy was chosen. I had become a "leftover." With one nod of his head, the captain disgust-edly resigned himself to having a girl on his team.

What a humiliating experience to be chosen last! It hurts. But "chosen" wasn't even the word for it. They would have chosen not to take me if they had their choice.

I tried my best to prove myself in this game that I had excelled in throughout grade school. But junior high boys were stiff competition. My self-confidence eroded, and it wasn't fun anymore. I soon grew tired of the humiliating experience of being "unchosen" last and eventually took my place among the spectators.

Perhaps that experience is one of the reasons today's scripture is mean-ingful to me. Jesus chose me. I didn't have to prove anything. I didn't have to be the best athlete or the nicest looking or even the nicest person. He just chose me.

It feels good to be chosen! Really good. Thank You, Jesus, for choosing me and for loving me unconditionally. And because You chose me, I choose You! Together we'll have an awesome team! NANCY CACHERO VASQUEZ

To Catch a Cardinal

Resist the devil, and he will flee from you. James 4:7.

It was a beautiful Sunday morning, crisp and clear after the snow the previous night. Everybody was busy in the kitchen making pancakes, slicing strawberries, squeezing oranges, preparing the table for breakfast.

Our 90-year-old aunt was busy making spring rolls. She loves making spring rolls. She makes them by the hundreds, ready in case someone needs some, or just to have some in the refrigerator.

Out on our porch the bird feeder had attracted a beautiful cardinal. I called Auntie to come and watch.

"Wow! Beautiful bird!" she exclaimed. "I wonder how we can catch it." She immediately began looking around the house. "I wish I had a cage," she mumbled to herself.

"Why do you want to catch the bird?" I asked.

"So I can put it in the cage where I can take care of it. I want to protect it, and feed it. I don't want it to be out of my sight."

My aunt never caught the cardinal because it flew away when anyone came near.

Just as my aunt wanted to catch the beautiful cardinal, Satan wants to catch us, God's beautiful people. He wants to put us in his cage—not to protect us, but to harm us.

The cardinal was wise. The moment it saw my aunt coming, it flew away. We can do that when Satan tries to catch us. When Satan whispers "God is not fair. He does not love you," we can answer, "Get behind me, Satan; I am God's favored child."

We don't have to be caught in Satan's cage. We can run away from him. We can take God's hand and hold it tight, never letting it go.

Help me, Lord, to run away from Satan's temptations. Let me boldly tell him, "Get behind me, Satan." Help me to hold on to Your hand that I may not stumble or be discouraged.   JEMIMA D. ORILLOSA

Sacrifice Equals Salvation

Behold, God is my salvation; I will trust, and not be afraid:
for the Lord Jehovah is my strength and my song;
he also is become my salvation. Isa. 12:2.

Today is Veterans Day in America. We Americans set aside this special day to remember the men and women who have served protecting our nation. I watch the ceremony from Arlington National Cemetery every year on television. I am always touched by the veterans and their families who are in attendance. Sometimes their faces mirror the anguish that is in their hearts. It is a sobering and solemn occasion.

For more than 35 years, I had daily contact with our nation's veterans. Working in seven different veterans' hospitals, I have observed many of them—young, old, all races, male and female. Some had their bodies intact, but not their minds. Others had physical disabilities that made me want to weep. I am proud of our veterans and felt privileged to assist in their care and recovery.

The stories of their sacrifices as they protected our world are often amazing. All our service men and women hoped to come home safely, but thousands did not. They made the ultimate sacrifice. They were, in essence, our salvation. It is fitting that we demonstrate our appreciation each November.

Often in the news we see the white crosses in the cemeteries far across the sea. It's hard to believe that so many of our dead were not even brought home. So as we listen to the speeches and the reverent prayers, we hear recognition given by dignitaries.

The ceremonies of this day make me ponder another sacrifice of the One who gave His life as the supreme sacrifice. God sent His Son to protect us, to die for us, and to redeem us. All we have to do is accept His promises and believe in Him.

Lord, I believe You are coming again soon. I believe You are my salvation, and that You will bring me to my heavenly home for the greatest reunion of all. How many more Veterans Days will I have until that happy day? Please, come soon, Lord. I want to honor You in person for giving Your life for me.

ARLENE E. COMPTON

No More Shame

And David said unto him, Fear not: for I will surely shew thee kindness for Jonathan thy father's sake, and will restore thee all the land of Saul thy father; and thou shalt eat bread at my table continually. 2 Sam. 9:7.

Merib-baal had had a painful experience. When he was just 5 years old, his father, Jonathan, and grandfather, King Saul, were killed in battle. When she heard the news, his nurse, trying to get him to safety, dropped him, and he became lame in both feet. His name was changed to Mephibosheth, which means "shame."

Can you imagine being called Shame? Can you imagine being reminded of your worthlessness each time your name is spoken? Like Mephibosheth, many girls grow up with hurtful names: fat, ugly, stupid, lazy, unwanted, retarded. Many are treated as if they were a shame. Such mistreatment leaves them as emotionally crippled as Mephibosheth.

But the story has a wonderful ending. David, the new king of Israel, remembered his promise made to Jonathan. He called for the young man and restored to him all the inheritance of his father. Furthermore, he would become like a son to David, living with him and always eating at his table.

Amazing grace! This shameful nobody, who referred to himself as a "dead dog," would live like a prince. He would eat at the table with God's beloved David and David's sons: Solomon, the wise; Absalom, the handsome; Amnon, the crown prince. When Mephibosheth sat at the king's table, he would sit as tall as the other princes. His deformity would be covered.

The promise made to spare his loved ones was given by David to Jonathan before Mephibosheth was born. Therefore, his value was not based on his abilities or lack thereof, but on a relationship. Mephibosheth was a child of the king, so the promise was his.

Similarly, we are daughters of the King, His own because of a promise ratified by blood. When we come into relationship with Christ, the promise is ours. Our value to Him is greater than we can imagine, and we are invited to eat at the King's table as His own daughters. We aren't a shame, regardless of what we've done or what others think of us. Pull up to the table and enjoy His bounty!

WANDA GRIMES DAVIS

To Speak or Not to Speak

Death and life are in the power of the tongue. Prov. 18:21.

The Armory Palace is a museum of immense interest and historical value housed within Moscow's Kremlin walls. Of particular interest in this museum is the collection of Easter eggs done by the artist-jeweler Fabergé. Most were commissioned by Russia's last czar, Nicholas II, as gifts for his wife, Alexandra.

One Sunday as I reached the glass display case that houses the Fabergé eggs, I pressed closer to examine the tiny gold train that Fabergé had placed, as his traditional surprise, into a golden egg he had etched as a globe. The train, about 10 inches long, was a replica of the czar's personal train and could actually be wound up with a tiny golden key to travel some distance.

A tour group gathered around me, so I stepped aside to wait. When they moved on, I stepped up again, next to a tall gentleman who evidently had the same interest as I. Then immediately another tour group edged in, very close. The gentleman whirled around, waving his museum entrance ticket in the face of the tour guide. "I paid for a ticket just like you, and I have the right to see this display also."

Behind me someone muttered, "Rude foreigner!"

The gentleman moved on, and another tour group was fast moving in. As I stepped up to the display case, the tour guide moved close to my shoulder. My American sense of cultural propriety told me to move away. Instead, I summoned my head knowledge of Russian culture and stood my ground. She moved closer; I pushed back very slightly. She kept up with her narration, and everyone saw and heard about the Fabergé eggs, including me. Not only did no one call me rude; they didn't even seem to notice I was there.

The European gentleman's outburst placed in graphic relief the fact that culture and past experience color the way everyone sees experiences. I was privileged to see both sides of this story. When we feel we are insulted, it may be a matter of culture or just a different way of acting. Let us be accepting and loving of those around us today.   SUSAN SCOGGINS

Watchful Juncos

Watch ye and pray, lest ye enter into temptation. Mark 14:38.

During the winter months our bird feeder is filled with seeds. At dusky dawn I've observed birds enjoying their early breakfast. These frequent visitors are usually slate-colored juncos, sometimes called snowbirds because their head, back, and breast are a uniform slate gray, contrasted with an ivory-colored beak. Even though they are rather tame they dart away if I get too near, flashing white outer tail feathers.

In winter they search for food in weedy fields and farmyards. Every day I brush snow away from the feeder so they can find the seeds. One day I also swept the snow away from a spot below the feeder and sprinkled seeds on the ground. As snow fell fast, I watched them scratch the snow away with their feet, like a chicken, in order to find the seeds.

The juncos kept me entertained during long snowbound days. I watched them pick up a seed, lift their heads, look all around, then snatch another seedy morsel. They never eat with their heads continually down; they're always on guard. When threatened, their wings provide a ready escape to a nearby bush where they feel secure.

As I pondered the little juncos' watchfulness I remembered our text: "Watch ye and pray, lest ye enter into temptation." *How many temptations could I escape if I were as watchful as my feathered friends? Am I as quick to dart away on the wings of prayer to the place of refuge when I'm confronted with temptation?*

A special promise came to mind: "There hath no temptation taken you but such as is common to man: but God is faithful, who will not suffer you to be tempted above that ye are able; but will with the temptation also make a way of escape, that ye may be able to bear it." 1 Cor. 10:13.

Father in heaven, thank You for this promise of Your faithfulness in always providing a way of escape from temptation. Each moment, help me be as watchful as my junco friends—ready and willing to escape temptation on the wings of prayer.   NATHALIE LADNER-BISCHOFF

I Just Called to Say I Love You

By this all men will know that you are my disciples,
if you have love for one another. John 13:35, RSV.

L ord, I stand at the threshold of another day. Please guide me as I seek to hold up people I know into the radiant light of Your divine presence.

When I look at the whirl of activity in the lives of those around me I am overwhelmed as I sense their intense loneliness. Many of them seek to fill the vacuum with a myriad of external activities, events, and addictions. *What can I do, Lord, to help alleviate their loneliness or push back their tide of despair? Make me an instrument of friendship molded by Your gentle hands.*

God often works in simple ways to answer my prayers. It doesn't cost a lot of money to be a friend; it only takes time. Kind words, a smile (even to a stranger), a phone call, or an encouraging note is a simple and inexpensive deed, yet so precious. How amazing to realize that God's gifts are readily and freely available—if only we can find the time.

This friendship seed, once nurtured, watered, and fed will yield a bountiful harvest of people who understand what it means to be a friend. As a result, each day I am filled with joy as He finds people in my life with whom I can share my tender bud of friendship.

For example, I've found it isn't necessary to write 10 pages to let a friend know I've missed her at church. A note jotted in haste can mean as much. Often a quick telephone call can cheer someone and let them know you are thinking of them. I might drive to the school early to pick up the boys, hoping to meet a friend and catch up on her life. I sometimes call a friend and invite her over for a spontaneous tea party to make her feel special and to bond our friendship.

Everywhere I look, people around me are isolated and lonely. I thank God that He has allowed me to be an instrument of His love through friendship. I also thank God that through His grace and gift of friendship I can make a difference. I can call just to say that I love you.

CARLENE R. WILL

My Computer

Let this mind be in you, which was also in Christ Jesus. Phil. 2:5.

My computer and I had a close relationship. We spent a great deal of time together and, as the years came and went, I was willing to put up with its limited features. Now and then I relieved it of some of its memory load. I even replaced the hard disk with a larger one and upgraded both the modem and CD ROM, so it still worked well under most conditions.

Finally I felt the time had come to replace it, and since my tried-and-true computer friend had a good many more miles left inside, I knew someone would be happy to have it. After all, term paper assignments must come often on the large university campus near where we live.

I was thrilled with my new computer. It talked to me. It responded to my every need. I reveled in its added features and lost no time in transferring all my files to it successfully. I was happy with my purchase, and I had found a good home with friends for my old computer companion.

But long before daylight the next morning a sinking feeling hit me in the pit of my stomach. True, I had copied my files to my new computer, but I had also left them implanted in that old computer. I took mental note of my various directories and files and wondered what my friends would discover when they connected it to their power supply. Would they still think the same of me if they reviewed the past several years of my mind's output?

I began to do some serious thinking. I possess a computer brain that my Creator-Father has generously given me. Through the years it has accumulated mental documents, some of which I have never revealed. If its contents were to be opened to the world, could my Lord be brought into disrepute?

So I have tried to relieve my computer brain of some of its "memory." I have taken all my un-Christlike thoughts and asked my Saviour to replace them with His attributes. He has promised He would, and with the help of the Holy Spirit I will endeavor to keep my thoughts focused on Him as long as He allows this computer brain to function. When our heavenly Father comes to claim His own, only the good will remain for Him to see.

LORRAINE HUDGINS

Saying Goodbye

Finally, brothers, good-by. Aim for perfection, . . . be of one mind, live in peace. And the God of love and peace will be with you. 2 Cor. 13:11, NIV.

The holiday ends, and the door closes. The last of the children and grandchildren say goodbye, and the last voice fades away. One by one they leave, returning to their own homes, to a world altogether separate from mine. As quiet and emptiness surround me, that empty feeling crowds my heart and a lump creeps into my throat.

For some, goodbye means more than just a holiday goodbye. I think of those who leave for foreign service and those who have laid to rest that special person in their lives. How lonely the holiday season must be. There are those who cannot afford to visit family, or those separated by hostility. I think, too, of the fragility of life. Perhaps the next year might bring to me that same loneliness.

I don't know how you deal with these kinds of feelings, but this is what I do. First, I ask the Lord to give me peace in my heart to be content with such things as I have. Next, I get busy putting the house back in order. If it is Christmas, I put away the festive decorations and dream of the new year. Work is such a blessing!

Oh, yes, a few tears drop along the way, but I begin to count my blessings, which are legion. I rejoice with those who have children and grandchildren living within a day's drive, and not thousands of miles away, as mine are. The Lord always sends me someone who needs an adoptive mother or grandmother; I focus on their needs, and in turn I am blessed.

But my best antidote for the sadness of a goodbye is the knowledge of a soon-coming Saviour and an eternity of no goodbyes. I claim the promises in the Word of God. They bring me comfort, peace, and strength to face another year of separation. It is then the love of Christ fills the void, and I can say with John, "Even so, come, Lord Jesus." I long for that day when there will be no more separation, no more loneliness, no more goodbyes.

JUNE LOOR

Neighborhood Networking

A friend nearby is better than relatives far away. Prov. 27:10, CEV.

After more than a dozen relocations, I was determined this time to get to know my neighbors. We shared five acres with four other brand-new houses on a quiet road just outside Centralia, Washington. As each new family settled in, I decided to welcome them. I made cards on my computer, provided a small gift of strawberry jam, and went knocking on doors.

It's amazing how hard it can be to get to know people. It is difficult to cultivate friendships with those with different lifestyles, busy work schedules, or who wish to remain private. It takes courage to initiate friendships because of the fear of rejection. But I knew Jesus would want me to love my neighbors.

As our relationships developed, we shared our joys and sorrows. Each family has its own challenges—health problems, cancer, surgeries, deaths of loved ones, financial stresses, or unemployment. But we were there for one another. We bartered talents and goods. We exchanged recipes and parenting tips. We helped one another with child care, fed each other's pets, and kept watch when someone was away. Brenda gave me massage therapy treatments, and I did computer projects for her. We prayed together and bonded in genuine love.

One day our family pet was struck and killed by a delivery truck. Cassy, a sheltie collie, had been with us for more than 12 years. She had survived many miles of cross-country moves. First, Mindi came to comfort me and helped me cover the dog. Later she brought a dinner casserole for my family. Mike shared prayer and a beautiful card of sympathy in behalf of his family. We had a simple burial. My son made a wooden stick cross with a red ribbon for the blood of Jesus. As we mourned together, we were so thankful for our neighbors who were near. I will always cherish my neighbors' kindness and support.

Even though it was another temporary placement, I am so glad Jesus placed us together on Oregon Trail Road. We are all scattered in different locations now, but I will value those friendships for eternity.

CAROL J. SMITH

The Welcome Sign

The Spirit and the bride say, "Come!" And let him who hears say, "Come!" Whoever is thirsty, let him come; and whoever wishes, let him take the free gift of the water of life. Rev. 22:17, NIV.

My husband and I enjoy spending a Sunday afternoon on a pier in the harbor at Durban, South Africa, watching ships from different parts of the world sailing in. Recently we noticed that an enormous billboard has been erected in a strategic position clearly visible to arriving foreign visitors who use the harbor. It has vivid, diagonal stripes in the colors of the South African flag, and across each stripe the word "Welcome" is written in 14 different languages.

This eye-catching sign set me thinking. *I wonder what effect it will have on weary sailors who have seen nothing but the ocean for weeks on end. Surely they will feel excited at the prospect of being on land once more and of being told in their own language that they are welcome.*

My imagination raced on. *Maybe there will be a similar sign welcoming weary pilgrims as we enter heaven. Only this time the welcome sign will be in all the languages of the world. And Jesus Himself will be there to welcome each one personally.*

The thought of the reunion of loved ones sends a thrill up my spine. There will be tears of joy as we hug them and tell them how much we have missed them and looked forward to this day. Jesus will wipe away those tears, and all memories of past suffering and heartache will be erased from our memories.

I suddenly became impatient and asked, "How long, Lord?" I felt pangs of homesickness. Before that day there will probably be mountains of disappointments to conquer, many tempests to be weathered, and the valley of the shadow to be crossed.

However, I know that with Jesus beside me the future is no longer formidable. The hardships we have to endure on our journey will pale into insignificance when we see the welcome sign and hear Jesus say, "Enter you who are blessed by my Father! Take what's coming to you in this kingdom. It's been ready for you since the world's foundation" (Matt. 25:34, Message).

FRANCES CHARLES

Lessons From a Daffodil

If I were you, I would turn to God and present my case to him. We cannot understand the great things he does, and to his miracles there is no end. He sends rain on the land and he waters the fields. Job 5:8-10, TEV.

We'd had a particularly dry, cold winter that left our south Australian garden looking dreary and drab. Nothing seemed to have its usual color. Then one morning I found a beautiful King Alfred daffodil in all its golden glory completely dominating the scene. I had been so involved noticing the dreariness that I had completely missed the appearance of the daffodil bud.

All day the sun shone brightly, and when I arrived home from work my beautiful daffodil no longer stood erect. It was now drooping, its stem and leaves all withered. The whole plant had been affected by the warmth of the sun. I had forgotten the all-over dryness. I should have given it some water that morning. I wondered if it would survive. I determined to give it a drink before going to work next morning.

During the night there was a light shower of rain—not much, but the effect on the daffodil was magical. No longer was it withered and droopy, but crisp, brilliant, and erect once more. I was delighted with the effect, but taking no chances, I gave it a drink.

Our spiritual lives are sometimes like that daffodil's experience. We are so busy looking at the humdrum details of life that we forget to look for the blessings. While our lives are going along nicely, if we are not careful, the spirituality of our soul dries out without our noticing, just as the soil of the garden had dried out unnoticed. Then when Satan puts the spotlight of trouble on us, we wither spiritually because we have not taken the time to read and study God's Word, to pray, to meditate on His goodness. Then we must turn to God and present our case to Him. He sends His Holy Spirit to water our souls so they will be transformed as visibly as was the daffodil.

Water my soul today, Lord. Help me to spend time every day with You and Your Word so that I may not wither, but flourish as a daffodil after rain.

MAY SANDY

Our Ever-vigilant Heavenly Father!

Are not two sparrows sold for a penny? Yet not one of them will fall to the ground apart from the will of your Father. Matt. 10:29, NIV.

Our family, along with close friends, were enjoying an annual get-to-gether at Virginia's Lake Anna when one after another of the group decided to enjoy a "twilight" swim. Some went in the water in appropriate swimwear, while others, the younger set, began to toss one another off the dock, fully clad, into the warm water. Our two eldest grandchildren were immediately caught up in the fun and leaped off the dock to join the others already in the water. The youngest, Eric, watched with great interest. Walking to the edge of the dock and pointing at the dark water, he asked me a simple question: "Grandma, what's in there?" I assured him there were some fish in the lake but that it was the same water he had spent the better part of the day splashing in. It just looked different because he couldn't see the bottom without the sunshine.

After watching the others running and jumping into the water, letting out hoots of joy when they surfaced, he could stand it no longer. "Grandma, I want to go in too—but I want you to go with me."

"Go ahead," I urged him. "You'll like it! Your brother and sister are in there."

He was not easily convinced. I watched as he walked to the edge of the dock and peered down at those he envied, then stepped back to survey the whole situation. Finally he could stand it no longer. He spotted a ski rope neatly wound into a circle, lying "unattached" on the dock. He walked over and took the end of the rope and carefully wrapped it twice around his waist. Then walking to the edge of the dock, he jumped into the water.

How often have I reached out to grasp false security when I couldn't see the future clearly? I knew Eric was safe because he had a life jacket on and because I was watching him carefully. I also knew that the rope he clung to offered only superficial security. I wonder how often the Lord smiles when I reach out to grasp false security, knowing all along I would be OK because He was watching over me! What peace! An ever-vigilant heavenly Father watching over His children—including you and me.

ROSE OTIS

A Princess Forever

How great is the love the Father has lavished on us,
that we should be called children of God! 1 John 3:1, NIV.

When I was a little girl in England, my friends and I would dream of being princesses. We would dress up in lacy drapes, make tiaras from kitchen foil, walk about sedately, and have elegant tea parties. We imagined that princesses were perfectly happy, having anything and everything they ever wanted. Even when I was older and watched several royal weddings, there was something deep inside me that wished I could dress in all that frothy silk and lace and look so beautiful.

But princesses aren't happy forever. The tragedy of Princess Diana's life and death reminds us all that a royal life is not the happy world imagined by romantic little girls swathed in lace. Soon after Princess Diana's death, I thought about her wedding day, a day when I had wished I could be a part of that lovely world, a wish that now seems so absurd. I thought of the challenges, the misery, and the mistakes in her life, the harassment she received at the hands of the reporters, the gossip in cheap newspapers, problems with the in-laws, and the misery of having an unfaithful husband. I no longer wish to be a princess like Diana.

I compared my life to hers. I thought about the richness of baking chocolate-chip cookies for my children and sharing them together. I thought about the fun of stitching and painting presents for my friends, not merely buying them from Harrods. I thought about the satisfaction of making the housekeeping budget reach to the end of the month. I thought about what it means to have a husband who loves and supports me. I thought about the tiny details in my life that make me feel like the richest person in England. I love the joy of ministering with my husband. It's wonderful to have a happy, healthy family. Peace of mind is priceless. And the greatest richness of all is knowing that God loves me, sent His Son to die for me, and will one day take me to heaven.

I'm mature enough now to know princesses aren't happy ever after. But I also know that I am a princess in God's eyes. He is my Father. That makes me a princess today, and a princess forever. KAREN HOLFORD

Listen

Be still, and know that I am God. Ps. 46:10, NIV.

My preteen "daughter" was her usual, talkative self. We'd read our evening Bible story and talked to God about our day. We were enjoying some snuggle time, but instead of winding down, Cecilia was winding up again.

Her usual line is *"Madre, una pregunta,"* which is Spanish for "Mother, just one question." This time the topic was about having a baby brother. Why not have another child? Or maybe adopt a child close to her age? Wouldn't a playmate be great for her?

I reminded her that a brother could be pesky. She thought about it and decided that a baby would be better. As she got older and would bring her boyfriend home, a pesky brother could be a pain, but a baby could be so darling.

Cecilia, a Colombian orphan, became a part of our family while she was receiving medical treatment here in America. She was aware that my husband and I hadn't been able to have children, but she felt sure that it was possible somehow.

"Why don't you and Dad have a baby?" she insisted.

"Ask God why." I figured that response would take care of her questioning for a little while. Instead, she bowed her head and proceeded to do exactly what I suggested.

There was a long pause. I wondered if I should say something so she wouldn't feel that God didn't answer her, but I decided to wait. Cecilia finally broke the silence and to my surprise began to tell me what God had communicated to her.

Cecilia said she understood why we didn't have a baby. Dad, as a pastor, had more than enough work; I was very busy editing a magazine; Cecilia was in school, so couldn't help much with a baby; and besides, one child was enough for our family now.

I was astonished at what God had told her. It definitely was not what could have come from Cecilia's own mind, especially as much as she wanted a baby brother. My heart thrilled to know that God had spoken to her.

God has often spoken to my mind with encouragement, ideas, or answers. Listening to God is a habit I've been cultivating. I'm so thankful Cecilia's learning to stop and listen too. God does speak. Are you listening?　　HEIDE FORD

Light in the Gloom

Your word is a lamp to my feet and a light for my path. Ps. 119:105, NIV.

The phone rang. "Please, can you come, Mom? I really need you here." It was my married daughter, who lived 700 miles away and was having some medical problems.

I responded as any mother would. "I'll be there as soon as I can."

At 6:00 the next morning my husband and I set out on the 50-mile drive to the airport. We would try to get me a seat on the first plane to our daughter's city. It had begun to snow the day before, and when we left home it was snowing hard. The freeway at that hour on a Sunday morning was not busy. It was still dark, and the swirling snow made visibility poor. The snowplow hadn't cleared the road yet. Worried about our daughter and never comfortable in poor road conditions, I was becoming more and more tense. "Please, God, take care of us all," I prayed.

We saw some lights ahead of us. Although we couldn't make out the taillights of the semi because of the snow swirling around its wheels, we could see two small top rear lights. They gave us direction in the near white-out conditions, and the ruts made by the truck gave our car better traction. We followed that truck for 40 miles to the edge of the city. It was then getting light, the snow had stopped, and the truck took the next exit. The rest of the journey to the airport was much clearer, and I did catch that plane.

As we drove those miles, I thought of a hymn we used to sing years ago: "Lead, kindly Light, amid the encircling gloom, lead Thou me on." I thanked God for sending a truck that wintry Sunday morning to lead us through the gloom.

Sometimes our lives are dark and gloomy, and we can't seem to see our way. We are fearful for the future, and the present is swirling around us, obscuring our view of God. His Word is a light at these times. I'm so glad God gives us that light in difficult times. It's a Book full of the most wonderful promises of His leading.   RUTH LENNOX

The Good Fight!

*I have fought the good fight. . . . Finally, there is laid
up for me the crown of righteousness. 2 Tim. 4:7, 8, NKJV.*

I was having fun in my first Boxaerobics class. Taking a class that combined boxing techniques with aerobics was challenging. I watched the instructor show techniques that would help me get the ultimate workout.

"OK, hands up," she announced. "Get your body stance like so. . . . Make fists, and make the meanest face you can. Think of someone you really dislike."

I stared in the mirror and stifled the urge to laugh. We looked ridiculous! I listened to the instructor explain the dynamics of having a positive mental outlook, of looking self-assured. "It all shows in your workout," she said. I looked at my reflection. My arms were up in fighting mode, my feet were firmly planted, my hands were balled up, and my face had a grimace sure to scare even myself. *Do I look wimpy to others?* I wondered. *Am I really sure of myself?*

My fellow boxers and I jabbed at ourselves in the mirror, darting and dodging, advancing and retreating. I kept myself moving, light on my feet, to outsmart my imaginary opponent. I thought of the real fight we each face with the true enemy, the devil himself. How often in life he shows up at ringside, ready to assail us on all sides and bring us to our knees. How many times he jabs at us, waiting for the knockout blow. Did I have the right mental attitude, a look of self-assurance that told him I meant business? Would I, like others, be just another sparring partner in his brutal attempt to win? Would I allow him to psyche me out? To steal my crown?

"No way," I said as I continued sparring with myself. I put everything I had into my workout. I meant business. "He's not going to win." I realized that meant I needed to commit myself to mastering every technique available to me to fight the good fight. I determined at that very moment to improve my battle techniques, to use God's proven strategies, and no matter how big or small the battle, to allow God to fight for me. I was getting my crown! I would be victorious.

IRIS L. STOVALL

Strangers and Friends

For if you love those who love you, what reward have you?
Do not even the tax collectors do the same? And if you salute
only your brethren, what more are you doing than others?
Do not even the Gentiles do the same? Matt. 5:46, 47, RSV.

Jesus' words suggest that Christians be evaluated on how they treat strangers, people from whom they can expect no returns of favor, no exchange of affection, no financial reciprocity. Within one month two incidents happened to my family that remind me of this teaching.

While my son was in class, someone backed their car into his car and then left, leaving a dent and chipped paint that had to be fixed. Since the bill didn't exceed the deductible, we paid for the repairs ourselves. I assume that whoever hit the car figured that since we were strangers—or at least people who would have no way of tracing the person at fault—then there was no need to accept responsibility. "They will never know." And to this day, we don't.

Three weeks later quite another experience happened. We were trying to load a 10-foot ladder into a four-door Buick. The ladder was sticking out much too far. We tried to minimize the danger by telling ourselves we had only a mile to go and could take side roads to avoid much traffic.

"May I help?" asked a total stranger, who obviously had been observing our struggle to get the ladder into the car. "You folks don't want to drive like that; too risky. Here, I'm in no hurry. Let me take the ladder for you in my truck."

We protested weakly because his offer was just too needed to turn down. He would take no money. When he had offered to transport the ladder, he had absolutely no idea as to how many miles he was offering to go.

The next time you are tempted to do a random act of meanness to a stranger, do a random act of kindness instead. Why? Because if you reserve your gifts, aid, affection, or money only for those you love or who can love you in return, you are behaving no better than do the heathen. The merit of your Christian genuineness might be measured instead by the way you treat strangers.

WILMA McCLARTY

Wealth of Spirit

I will sing to the Lord because he has blessed me so richly. Ps. 13:6, TLB.

The fishing camp of tiny tents amid the scrub brush dotted a sandy bank. An Eskimo woman sat on a crumbling log and stoked at the fire pit under a cauldron. Now and then she flashed a gentle smile at the visitors or said something to one of the fishermen.

It was a scene straight out of *National Geographic*—a wide, winding river in a remote part of Russia, craggy fishermen muscling beat-up rowboats as they drifted lazy wide arcs of netting, stern enough for even the king salmon.

My husband, son, and I were escorted by our host, the minister of health for the region, in thanks for the windfall of medicines we had brought from benefactors in the United States. We were astonished at the size of the magnificent fish being caught in the ancient tradition.

There was much shouting as each net filled to capacity. The men fell to the bloody work of cleaning the catch, hacking out the roe for caviar, scooping the entrails back into the water.

A woman pared gnarled potatoes and tossed them, with an occasional small onion, into the pot. Potato soup sounded welcome to me. But then large hunks of fresh fish began to appear beside the pot, and she threw them in as well.

"Fish soup for you," our host explained. At that a jovial fisherman hoisted a trophy-sized bleeding head and declared, "Best part." To my dismay, he flipped it into the brew. I peered in just as the head floated up and an eyeball followed me reproachfully. The woman smiled and kept stirring.

We ate soup that evening, grateful for the warmth and for the friends we had made that unforgettable afternoon. I rummaged in my pocket for something, anything, to thank this gracious woman. A bag of peanut M & M's was all that was left of lunch. I held it out to her. "For you," I said. "Thank you."

As I laid the lumpy, yellow bag in her cupped hands, her eyes caressed the gift as if it were a handful of jewels. In two languages she spoke. "Spasiba; I am rich woman."

And then in the dark, she turned and meted out her riches to each of the men who made up her village world.   MARILYN J. APPLEGATE

Spending the Day With God

How precious to me are your thoughts, O God! . . .
When I awake, I am still with you. Ps. 139:17, 18, NIV.

Most of us wish we could spend more time with God each day. Our crowded lives often keep our responses to His leading at a minimum, and we long for a minute-by-minute awareness of His presence. May I suggest something you can try?

You're in the shower, and the hot water is flowing over your body as you apply the soap for cleansing. Think of the water of life and the cleansing that Christ promises as you confess your sin. It's a great time to pray, a great time to remember.

It's breakfasttime, and you're pouring cereal into a dish and toasting a piece of bread. Christ threshed grain for nourishment as He walked through a field and reminded us He is the Bread of Life. As you thank Him for your morning meal, thank Him too for His life lived for you.

As you are feeding your baby or sending your children off to school or writing to your grandchildren, remember that even as you love them, God the Father loves you. You give your best to your family, so God gave His Son for you.

You're on your way to work or to pay some bills or to shop for groceries. As you meet or pass cars and drivers, think how God has created each person very differently from you and how He loves each one with an everlasting love just as He loves you.

In the grocery store you'll find reminders of God and Jesus, too. As you pass the cereal shelves and see oatmeal, remember the story in the Bible of the young man who sowed wild oats and thank God for His leading in your life. You see the laundry soap called Bold and are reminded of the experience of Peter and John, who "spoke the word of God boldly" (Acts 4:31, NIV). You purchase grapes and are prompted to recall Christ's blood, given for you. You may choose the shampoo No More Tears and thank God for the promise of heaven that all tears will be wiped away.

Sunshine reminds you of the Son of Righteousness, and darkness that Christ is the light of the world. As you see the stars, think about the star in the east at Christ's birth.

I've mentioned only a few ways to keep God with you all day long. You'll think of many others. MYRNA TETZ

Oh, Magnify the Lord

*Oh, magnify the Lord with me, and let us
exalt His name together. Ps. 34:3, NKJV.*

As I finished cleaning my study I suddenly saw a tiny wisp of smoke curl up through the sunlight streaming from the window. My first thought: *Dust particles.* Then came a faint burning smell.

I traced the wisp to the La-Z-Boy chair. A small black hole, accented by a wisp of curling smoke, was being eaten into the fabric. Then I saw my three-inch magnifying glass standing in a holder parallel with the chair. The sun streaming from the window was passing through and intensifying its power to a concentrated heat, causing the fabric to smolder. Quickly, I moved the magnifying glass.

Closer inspection turned up another spot—larger, deeper, and very black! When had it happened? Why hadn't there been tragic results? The fact is, the sun never stands still, and the window is only so large. The effects were necessarily brief. Providentially, God sent the orbiting sun on its way, averting a tragedy.

I looked up the word "magnify": Increase, enlarge, enhance, expand. I have a new understanding of the word.

"Oh, magnify the Lord," we read. Was God revealing a truth that had escaped me previously? The lesson unfolded as I stood in the warm rays from the window. Magnification had occurred when the glass was in the right spot, at the right time, and was being submissively "used."

I had utilized the magnifying glass many times. The glass was a valuable tool, but in my hands it never even hinted at starting a fire. Only when the sun shone through it could it start a flame. Only when its magnification touched another object did it turn into a burning, living, fire.

"Oh, magnify His name." God longs to light a flame through me. Like the sun's revolution, the Son of Righteousness is moving on in our lives. We cannot be stationary and expect to magnify His name. We must move on with Him. We must keep abreast of that powerful line of focus in order for the magnification to strike a critical mark. We must be in the center of His will. What a challenge!

JODI EULENE DODSON

Letting Love Heal

Let mutual love continue. Heb. 13:1, NRSV.

From across the circle I looked at the attractive woman with pretty red hair but didn't realize the impact of the comment she was about to share. Our group had been talking about friendship and its value in our daily walk as Christians. As the discussion developed, I noticed her forehead wrinkle as she spoke.

"I really can't relate to what you are talking about," our new acquaintance said. "I've never had anyone to call a best friend. I don't see why that is so important."

I thought of the many friends God had given me throughout my life, and my heart went out to our friendless newcomer. *I guess I'll have to be your friend,* I thought as I studied the strained face.

She was not an easy one with whom to develop a friendship. Oh, she was friendly enough and enjoyed being involved in the group's activities, but she always kept a protective wall up so no one had the chance to get too close.

Little by little we began to do things together—having lunch, planning an activity, or sharing a ride in our cars. I always asked the Lord to show me how to reach her, and I prayed for her constantly. How I longed to help her learn how to trust!

A couple years later, with many a crisis behind us, I received a letter in the mail from my friendless friend. "Thank you for everything you have done," she wrote. "You have woven your way into my life. You are truly my dearest friend."

Let us remember today that God offers Himself as our dearest Friend. He is a friend we can trust, who will never let us down. When life's cruelties send hurts and damage to our hearts, a loving God counteracts by sending His healing love to the hurting ones. Are you willing to be a love representative for Him?

Use me today, Lord, however You will, to bring Your healing love to some friendless, hurting heart. I want to be Your love representative to someone today. Please lead me to that special person. JOAN BOVA

DECEMBER 1

His Eye Is on the Sparrow

*Behold the fowls of the air: for they sow not, neither do
they reap, nor gather into barns; yet your heavenly Father
feedeth them. Are ye not much better than they? Matt. 6:26.*

The view from my window was a winter wonderland; it reminded me of
a scene from a Currier and Ives Christmas card. Many of the schools in
our county were closed because of blowing snow and frigid temperatures.
As a teacher in one of those schools, I welcomed the day off to do some
things that had been on hold for a while.

Gazing outside as I planned my tasks for the day, I noticed some birds
eating weed seeds left over from last summer. I wanted to see them better,
so I filled the bird feeder. It didn't take them long to discover the free dinner. Some pecked at the sunflower seeds to open the outer shell, while others snatched what dropped on the ground. I felt warm and cozy in my
house as I watched the birds buffeted about by the swirling snow.

They didn't appear to be a bit cold in their thick feathery coats. When
the wind blew hard, some of the feathers separated, revealing the thick layer
of down that kept them warm. I marveled at how our Creator had provided
for them. They didn't need the seeds I had put out. They had a whole field
of seeds that were theirs for the taking. They had warm down coats, and
they get new ones every year! Who of us has it so good?

The Bible tells us that God's eye is on the sparrow. It also says the Lord
feeds the birds of the air and asks why we have cares about anything. In
1 Peter we are instructed to cast all our cares on Him, for He cares for us.
What a lesson we can learn from the sparrow! If God cares for them, won't
He surely take care of us and all of our needs?

*Lord, today help me to trust in You no matter what cold winds buffet me.
Help me to remember that I am of much more value than the sparrows. You,
who cares so well for them, will take care of my needs too. Thank You!*

SUSAN L. BERRIDGE

Speak the Word

Let your speech be always with grace, seasoned with salt. Col. 4:6.

I struggled for words. The class assignment was to write an article using only one-syllable words. I didn't think it was possible, but once I started, it became an interesting challenge to make sense with these little words. It was December, and we were in the midst of our first snowfall of the season. What better topic to use than the one-syllable word "snow"? Snow makes me think of the cleansing God offers and reminds me of His blessings. I thought to myself, *My classmates are professionals and sophisticated people—maybe this would sound foolish to them.* However, I liked the word I chose about God, and it went well with the peace found in our home that I described that evening.

In class others gladly read their articles first. They were very clever in their use of the one-syllable words. Some were intense essays, showing anger about divorce and the rights of women. I pulled my article out of my briefcase and thought, *I can't read this; it's too simple after the deep feelings I've heard others express.* Nevertheless, when Mrs. Cohen asked, "Anyone else ready to read?" I raised my hand, and she nodded for me to begin.

The room was still when I had finished. Mrs. Cohen looked pleased. "What a wonderful portrait of a marriage—and with such ordinary things."

Janet, sitting next to me, whispered, "I liked that piece."

Later, as Janet and I stepped out into the darkness of the night on our way home, she said, "I just loved your article. Why, I could almost see God as you read it." And she lifted her hands toward the starry sky.

Sitting alone on the subway, I thought, *We must not hide our God; others are needing and waiting to hear from us.*

Help me, Lord, to be willing to share with others the blessings You give me so freely. Help those I meet today to see You in my words and actions. Give me courage to witness for You wherever I am. DESSA WEISZ HARDIN

Snowdrifts and Life Changes

And we know that all things work together for good to them that love God, to them who are the called according to his purpose. Rom. 8:28.

I watch the snow fall in gentle flakes and feel lazy and warm inside the protecting walls of my home. The window reveals the outside world without exposing me to its cold, wet elements.

After enjoying the beauty of the world outside and the feeling of snugness inside for a while, I begin to realize what the snow means in terms of tomorrow. There will be ice on the windows of my car. There will be slippery walks and icy roads to navigate. There will be traffic delays and the need for an extra layer of clothing.

Beyond tomorrow there will be drifts of snow, no longer lovely as they become solid heaps of gray debris cleared from walks and driveways. Those heaps will represent effort, cold fingers, wet shoes and gloves, and sacrifice of precious reading time taken from an already busy schedule. The lovely sense of snug laziness fades as the drifts begin to build outside.

I think of the need for change in my life. As I contemplate the potential loveliness or an improved circumstance, I sometimes forget the accompanying effort and inconvenience. The anticipated result seems so pleasant that I am startled by the realization that these changes will not occur without a price.

Unlike the weather, my life choices are under my control. My decisions will determine whether change takes place. The lovely drifts of snow mark enjoyable changes in my environment, but they also demand the expenditure of energy and time to maintain efficiency and safety. Changes in my life demand no less. Health and fitness, interaction with God and others, and personal skills will grow only as I invest my time and effort.

A quirky snowman across the street celebrates an invested energy that would not settle for a solid gray drift of unwanted snow. Seeing that bold little fellow, I straighten my own shoulders and determine to reconsider that discarded challenge to change a thing or two in my lifestyle.

STELLA THOMPSON

Thirst

O God, Thou art my God; I shall seek Thee earnestly; my soul thirsts for Thee, my flesh yearns for Thee, in a dry and weary land where there is no water. Ps. 63:1, NASB.

Long ago in a wonderful land of abundance lived a woman named Najia. It seemed that Najia had everything she could want. But she also had a problem. She shared her concerns with her husband, telling him how she had been dizzy and her mouth was parched.

"Exercise," he said. "The more you exercise, the better your health."

Najia began a running program that afternoon. With great enthusiasm she ran through the village, down the path, and back home. When she got home, she felt worse than before. Her head was throbbing, and her throat hurt so badly she couldn't swallow.

Najia's condition worsened. Her lips were now bleeding, and her skin was dry and scaly. It was time to visit the medicine man. He listened as Najia told of her headaches, dizziness, dry throat, cracked and bleeding lips, and scaly skin. The medicine man jumped up with excitement and exclaimed that he had discovered a cure for these symptoms—a mixture of herbs and spices made into a salve and placed on the affected areas. The medicine man assured her of health within the next few days.

Instead, after a few days Najia was experiencing a high fever. Her family gathered around, fearful that the end was near.

Desperate now, the wise man from the next village was consulted. Najia was carried to his home. The wise man asked her many questions and examined her as her family nervously awaited an answer.

"Have you been experiencing thirst?" asked the wise man.

"Yes," whispered Najia.

The wise man smiled and placed his hand on Najia's feverish head. "The solution is very simple. Drink water every day."

Often we seek the world over for answers to our longings, trying hard to find solutions. But it is not dependent on what we do; it's whom we know. Our Lord is the only one who can satisfy our deepest needs. When we are overwhelmed by the drought in our soul, we must seek the Lord, the Water of Life.

Lord, fill me with Your Spirit. I am thirsty, and only You can satisfy the thirst in my soul.

PEGGY CLARK

The Beautiful Laughter of Friendship

*When God's children are in need, you be the one to help
them out. And get into the habit of inviting guests home for
dinner or, if they need lodging, for the night. Rom. 12:13, TLB.*

An SOS prayer request came from my friend Dianne. The house they had purchased had been sold out from under them. They had already enrolled their daughter in high school, but now had no place to live.

Without even consulting my husband I said, "Move in with us until you can find another place."

As it turned out, we needed them more than they needed us, even though we didn't know it at the time. They may have needed a place to stay, but we needed the laughter, the talk, the fun, and the stimulation of good friends.

My husband, Jan, had just suffered a stroke. The doctor had recently said to him, "Jan, you need to laugh more." But when it's just two people and the daily routine of reading, writing, paying bills, figuring past-due taxes, and exercising reluctant muscles, there isn't much to laugh about.

All that changed when the Kosarins' van pulled into our driveway with a trailer load of boxes, books, a guitar, Legos, and a pet mouse. For three months we laughed, sang, talked far into the night, and laughed some more. Everything was funny.

The house is quiet now. The Kosarins moved into their own home. We miss the telephone calls for Carli—four or five each evening. We had almost forgotten the fun of being the answering service for a popular teenage girl! When Jan and I come home, we miss 10-year-old Oscar running out into the garage to greet us. Even now when I think of those active evening hours with the children, I have to smile.

God knows so much better than we what we need. My prayers had focused on us: "Lord, strengthen Jan's muscles; help him overcome his limp; help him have faster reaction time; help me to be able to pay the bills." Let me assure you, my prayer was not, "Lord, send some children to live with us." But that's what we needed most at that time in our lives. Friendship and laughter have certainly enriched our lives.   KAY KUZMA

A Remedy for Worry

*Therefore I tell you, do not worry about your life . . . Look at
the birds of the air; they do not sow or reap or store away in
barns, and yet your heavenly Father feeds them. Matt. 6:25, 26, NIV.*

When I learned we had to move, I wanted to live in a particular village, just outside of Cheltenham, England.

"It is impossible," cautioned my ever-practical husband. "The area is too expensive, and it's on the wrong side of town for our ministry."

Imagine our surprise when God led us to live in the village I dreamed about.

Bishop's Cleeve is the largest village at the bottom of Cleeve Hill. Driving into the village always causes feelings of peace within me. I love driving past the splendid regency houses of Cheltenham and entering the narrow country lanes, framed by wild blackberry bushes, that lead to the close where we live. We motor past lush green fields that feed lazy sheep and majestic horses.

To see that hill gives me great strength. Early in the morning, as I spend time with God, I pull aside our bedroom curtain to gaze at the hill. Whether it is enveloped in a gentle mist or aglow with faint rays of the sun, its presence gives me great tranquillity. When I feel stressed, snippets of the hill soothe my distressed thoughts.

Viewing the hill always reminds me of Psalm 121. David says, "I lift up my eyes to the hills—where does my help come from? My help comes from the Lord" (verse 1, NIV). The strength and solidness of the hill reminds me that God is strong and powerful enough to deal with my problems. He is dependable enough to take care of my worries. Gazing at the hill urges me to release my concerns to God.

The way in which Cleeve Hill speaks to me has taken me by surprise. Having something tangible to remind me of God's power has deepened my confidence in Him. Perhaps that's why Jesus told us to look at the birds of the air, the lilies of the field, even the hairs on our head, when we are worried.

We all need something visible to help us focus on God. Why don't you see what you can find?

MARY BARRETT

Ready or Not

Therefore be ye also ready: for in such an hour as
ye think not the Son of man cometh. Matt. 24:44.

Having a real estate agent's sign in the window is like perpetually having that unexpected relative drop in on you. There is never a day when you can relax your grip on the vacuum cleaner or scrub brush. Our house was up for sale, and for an entire week realtor activity was scheduled. On Monday the house sparkled for the video crew. On Tuesday and Wednesday the house shone for possible realtors with their clients. Friday was scheduled for realtor caravans to parade through.

But Thursday belonged to us. Painters were coming, so bright and early I removed everything from the mantel and cleared the hearth, moved furniture, took down pictures, and stacked them in the middle of the floor. I stripped the bed and loaded the washer with sheets, piling clean laundry on the kitchen counter while I helped my husband replace the drapery hardware on our sliding patio doors. Rods and hardware covered the dining room table, and billows of curtains were strewn over the floor—when the doorbell rang. It was not the painters. It was the realtors.

"We weren't expecting you today," I apologized. I stood meekly at the door, receiving calling cards. Twenty of them.

The realtors milled through our cluttered house like ants over an anthill, and finally left. Thankful that the ordeal was over, I looked at the clock. It was almost lunchtime. We had just begun to eat when some unscheduled prospective buyers arrived. Now the kitchen clutter added to the mayhem.

My friendly, outgoing husband delightedly showed them through the house. I fled to the shelter of the patio and reflected on the morning.

I recalled the text in Matthew 24:44. We had been acting out a parable that entire morning. "For in such an hour as ye think not . . ." I realize now that I cannot be unprepared for a single moment. My Saviour's coming will be a joyous occasion, but preparation for it is no laughing matter. I'm determined to keep this heart temple that God has given me pure and clean every moment of every day. He has purchased it, and He will be pleased to take up residence within it when I am ready. My destiny depends on it.

LORRAINE HUDGINS

Hidden Pictures

*Praying always with all prayer and supplication
in the Spirit, and watching thereunto with all
perseverance and supplication for all saints. Eph. 6:18.*

I was the only woman attending a leadership training seminar. The presenter fixed several 3-D pictures on the wall and challenged us to find the hidden pictures. I could see only the surface. Those who saw the hidden pictures were excited and exclaimed, "Oh, how fascinating! This is real beauty!" Eventually, more and more people saw them, but I could not. Noticing my disappointment, a friend explained the technique.

My husband followed the directions and succeeded. "Haven't you seen them yet, Hepzi?" he asked.

Tears filled my eyes. Was I a dummy? Well, I decided to prove I was not. Therefore, instead of listening to the lectures, I stared at the pictures and prayed earnestly. I did not want to give up. During the break I stood in front of a picture and prayed, "God, please help me see it. I must see what is hidden. Don't let me be disappointed."

As I fixed my eyes on the picture, a cross practically leaped out of the frame toward me. It was the cross on which my Saviour died to save me from sin! I was overwhelmed. As I continued to gaze at the cross it appeared to multiply. The depth of the actual picture was fascinating. "Thank You, God, for helping me see it," I whispered.

Within a short time I saw all the hidden pictures. I was thrilled. A few days later, as I was boasting about my accomplishment, my mind drifted to the Holy Bible, which contains hundreds of live pictures.

How often have I read it on the surface, not really seeing or comprehending the hidden beauty of it all! How often have I been discouraged because I did not claim the promises and the words of comfort.

Thank You, God, for helping me see new pictures of You. The more time I spend with You and Your Word, the more power and strength I receive. Thank You for showing me what is hidden in Your Word. HEPZIBAH G. KORE

Staying Close

*No one who has left home . . . or sisters . . . or father or children
. . . for me and the gospel will fail to receive a hundred times as much in
this present age . . . and in the age to come, eternal life. Mark 10:29, 30, NIV.*

Following God's lead isn't always easy. You want to be in His will, but
that doesn't mean there won't be some pain and loneliness involved.

Recently I left my sons, sister, father, numerous friends, and familiar
surroundings in the West to live in the East. I felt convinced that God
wanted me here, but it was painful to leave them all behind. The people
here welcomed me warmly; however, feeling that I belong takes time.

It was hard to get settled into our rental. I put pictures around the
house where I thought I might like them, only to have them sit there for
weeks because I couldn't make a decision. I finally got tired of seeing them
on the floor and stumbling over them, so I gathered them up and placed
them in a spare bedroom. Then the bare walls bothered me. I prayed,
"Lord, help me feel settled here. Help me accept this as being where You
want me to be and make this my home."

When it came to putting my granddaughters' pictures up, I couldn't do
that, either. It was too painful to see their photos. They only made me miss
them all the more. I talked with them by phone. It tore my heart to hear the
4-year-old ask again, "Where are you, Grandma?"

"I live far away now," I reminded her.

"Why?" she asked. "Why did you move so far away? I like it better
when you live close. . . . I want you close."

"So do I, honey. So do I."

That conversation has stayed with me. Staying close to God is what sus-
tains me here, feeling comfort from His love, knowing He loves my granddaughters even more than I and will stay close to them too while we are
apart. I long for that day when there will be no more separation by miles,
and we will all feel at home with God, family, and friends.   LOUISE DRIVER

That $20 Bill

Test all things; hold fast what is good. 1 Thess. 5:21, NKJV.

I could not believe my eyes. There on the grass by the sidewalk, about six feet away, was a $20 bill. How did it get there? I was thousands of miles away from the United States, serving temporarily in an Asian country. This particular day I had decided to go for a walk to get some exercise. And there before me was a $20 bill that I suspected someone had lost.

I leaned over to pick up the money. Yes, it did look like a $20 bill at first glance, but then I noticed something terribly wrong with this money. Instead of the picture of Andrew Jackson, there was a picture of a scantily dressed female.

Something else was wrong with this money. Someone had stamped a miniature map and some phone numbers across the bill, as well as some writing. It was an advertisement inviting everyone to go to a certain address to see some porno on the Internet.

My anger began to rise. I felt it was an insult to my country to deface a $20 bill like this. Someone had done a beautiful job; it was done on good quality paper. It was a good advertising gimmick—it had caught my attention immediately. But it was not genuine.

Since the Garden of Eden Satan has been trying to remove the face of God from everything good. Can you imagine how outraged God becomes as He sees Satan's counterfeit work? Sadly, Satan is often successful in deceiving us. I believe that's why we have so many theological disagreements, so many missing members in church pews week by week, and so little intentional witness for the Lord.

We need to look closely at everything that's thrown in our pathway and ask God to help us sort out the genuine from the counterfeit—especially where doctrine, music, and entertainment are concerned. Let's look for the image of God on everything. If it's not there, avoid it like the plague!

ROWENA R. RICK

The Gift

I tell you, now is the time of God's favor,
now is the day of salvation. 2 Cor. 6:2, NIV.

My mother and I slipped quietly into the crowded auditorium and began to look for a place to sit. I don't recall the event, but even at the age of 7 I felt embarrassed because we were late. The man on the platform was already talking, and I wanted only to melt quickly into a seat.

Suddenly the speaker raised his voice and shouted, "You! Little girl with the brown hair!"

Startled, I looked up. So did everyone else. To my horror, I saw his finger pointing directly at me.

"Look what I have for you," he said, holding up a beautiful doll. "Just come here and take it. It's yours."

The doll's blond hair tumbled down over her shoulders. She wore a long gown with colors that seemed to sparkle in the stage lights. Instead of racing up to claim my prize, I froze.

The man waited patiently. Reading the frightened look on my face, he said, "It's OK—I'm giving it to you. It's free."

I pulled on my mother's coat sleeve as a strong hint for her to go with me. Taking a step forward, she gently urged me to go alone. By now, however, my arm was firmly attached to hers, and my feet were almost embedded in the carpet.

"This pretty doll is really yours," the man continued. "All you need to do is come and take it. But hurry! Time is running out."

Still I hesitated.

"Come right now," the man urged. When he saw I wasn't going to move, he said, with a sad tone in his voice, "I'm sorry. I can't wait any longer. We're out of time."

My window of opportunity vanished, and so did the lovely doll.

Some years later I heard another Man speak. He offered me a better gift, the gift of eternal life. I felt drawn to Him. He seemed so wise and kind. I only had to come to Him and the priceless treasure would be mine. Yet I hesitated. But Jesus waited patiently, His arms reaching out to me. "Come," He said, "while there's time." I remembered the lesson of the doll and began my walk toward eternity with Him. MARCIA MOLLENKOPF

Judge Not

Do not judge, or you too will be judged. Matt. 7:1, NIV.

The church pews were filled with nicely dressed worshipers that cool December morning. A young couple entered, and although their clothes were clean, they were dressed in T-shirts and jeans. What's more, their two small boys were in their sleeper pajamas.

Why would they come dressed like this? I wondered.

I soon learned why when the pastor shared the news of a fire the day before. This family had lost everything when their home burned.

Instantly my slightly critical thoughts changed to condemnation for myself and admiration for them. Under similar circumstances, would I have come to church, or would I have used the lack of proper clothes as an excuse to stay home? It's so easy for critical thoughts to spring unbidden into the mind and so hard to learn the important lessons such as don't judge, or you too will be judged.

Recently I drove into a crowded parking lot at a small shopping area. Looking about for an empty space I noticed a van parked in such a way that it was taking up two spaces. I mentally began to criticize the driver for his sloppy parking. After some time I finally found what seemed to be the last available parking spot.

When I had completed my errands, I returned to my car and saw that the driver of the van was also getting into his vehicle. The reason for his sloppy parking was now very obvious. With great effort and the help of a friend he was able to get from his wheelchair into the driver's seat. Since the only parking space for those with disabilities was already occupied, he had no choice but to park as he had.

Lord, today help me to be less critical and judgmental of people. Help me to have unconditional acceptance of others, remembering that "The Lord does not look at the things man looks at. Man looks at the outward appearance, but the Lord looks at the heart" (1 Sam. 16:7, NIV).　　　　BETTY J. ADAMS

Shelter Me

He brought me to the banqueting house, and his
banner over me was love. S. of Sol. 2:4, Amplified.

Had we remembered more accurately the ups and downs of the way, we may not have ventured out on the Blue Mountains walk to celebrate our fifty-fifth wedding anniversary. But we didn't.

Having done these same walks with our children, it was a special treat to look out over the valleys and waterfalls. However, one thing was different. Our world had become environmentally alert. The new signs read "Please, keep to the walking tracks; this is a fragile environment."

Now, the general Australian bushland appears anything but fragile. Tough, wiry grasses vie with prickly shrubbery and gnarled trees for the little nourishment provided by a sandy, rocky soil. We discovered old friends in the pink boronia-curtains, and tall, flamboyant, red waratahs, framed by green-gray gum trees, as well as a kaleidoscope of daintier blooms. Where was all this fragility?

Closer observation revealed that each plant chose its friends well, for all fitted into their own ecosystems. Shadowy, mysterious cliffs and rock faces were softened by mosses and ferns growing no other place, while on the sunny side, daisies delighted us. We realized that the fragility lay in the relationship of plant to plant, plant to soil, and warmth and water. Each was indispensable to the other.

My thoughts naturally meandered to that unique relationship called marriage. Its toughness, its tenacity, its fragility, as well as its individuality are reflected in this vast, wild bush garden. After 55 years of togetherness, our marriage environment, like the Australian bushland, may appear tough and indestructible. Yet life has given us an awareness of the constant need to actively preserve the priceless relationship fabric of our love. No matter how threadbare it may appear at times, this protective shelter remains secure, shielded under the banner of the One altogether lovely.

LINDA M. DRISCOLL

Caring With a Cast

Casting all your care upon him; for he careth for you. 1 Peter 5:7.

I looked at my arms, both encased in plaster casts because of a fall. I laid them on my desk at the retirement facility I managed and agonized over what I should tell my friend. She was the social director of a nearby convalescent hospital. I had agreed to give her facility a piano and organ musical program. Should I go ahead with our plans? I could pick out the melody with the right hand and fumble around with some bass notes, but my music was definitely not up to par. After a talk with my heavenly Friend I decided to do the program in spite of the obstacles.

The week before the program brought incredible stress. Problems seemed to leap at me from every quarter. Friday night came, and I had not a clue as to what I would do. In the quiet of my apartment that evening I begged the Lord to help me. He seemed to say, "Pick music that will feed your own soul tonight."

Gradually, as the hymns and gospel songs I chose ministered to my own troubled mind, I let go of my anxiety. With plaster from my fingers to elbow, left-hand octaves would be impossible. Fancy chording was out, but I knew One who could use my simple music.

After the program one of the nursing assistants came to me in tears. She threw her arms around me. My program had blessed and strengthened her, but my greatest joy was yet to come.

Sometime later I moved away but was invited back by a friend. On Friday evening we attended an agape feast in the foyer of the sanctuary. As we ate the simple food by candlelight and recounted the first Communion service with Christ, I noticed a woman smiling as though she knew me. When we broke for the foot-washing service, she rushed over and asked if I remembered her. I had to admit her name escaped me. However, my joy knew no bounds as she recounted our experience together at the convalescent hospital and the part it played in her subsequent return to the Lord and to church.

Oh, how close I came to canceling that appointment.

Thank You, Jesus, for taking my anxious care and using it to Your honor and glory.

DONNA LEE SHARP

The Faith of a Child

Ask, and it shall be given you; seek, and ye shall
find; knock, and it shall be opened unto you. Matt. 7:7.

We had just spent Christmas at our home in Southampton, England. We were now going to celebrate the new year with my parents in Birmingham, some 120 miles away. During our visit we had planned to see a school friend, who lived with her family about an hour's drive from my parents' home.

During the Christmas season the weather had been particularly mild, but the climate could be fickle. We set out late one afternoon to begin our journey to visit our friends. Strong winds and heavy rain had been forecast. We didn't see these particular friends very often, so nothing was going to stand in our way now that we had the rare opportunity to visit them.

All went well until we had been traveling for about a half hour. The sky began to darken and the wind got a little gusty, and it began to rain. The children slept in the back seat, unaware of the bad weather. Or so we thought. The wind got stronger, the rain got heavier and soon turned to hail. The sky was very black, making it quite difficult to see, but we continued on our journey.

As the hail beat louder and louder on the roof of the car, we were suddenly aware of a little voice: "Dear Jesus, please make the hail stop because I don't like the noise. In Your name, amen."

At that moment we passed underneath a motorway bridge. As we emerged out the other side there was no hail. Nor was there any rain—it was completely dry. The little voice from the back of the car was then heard to say: "There, Mommy, I asked Jesus to make the hail stop, and He has, just like I asked Him to."

What a big lesson in faith we can learn from a 6-year-old child. It is the simplest things in life that can teach us the most and remain in our minds the longest.

Lord, when the storms of life beat around me, help me to come to You
with the faith of a small child, knowing You are able to make the storm stop.
But if it doesn't stop, please remind me that You are with me in the storm.

JUDITH REDMAN

The Joy of the Lord

Rejoice evermore. Pray without ceasing. In every thing give thanks;
for this is the will of God in Christ Jesus concerning you. 1 Thess. 5:16-18.

For a long time I thought joy was something I would experience when I was satisfied and circumstances were peaceful and happy around me. I was going through a particularly trying time when a dear friend said to me, "Anne, have you ever thought of praising God in your trouble?"

I did think about it. I also studied my Bible and prayed. The Lord reached my heart through His Word in Thessalonians. I was convicted that God wanted me to practice joy as a way of life.

Not too long after that my decision to practice joy was sorely tested. It was Christmas, and my husband and I had made plans to visit our son and his family for the holidays. I had pictured in my mind how my 5-year-old grandson and I would play together. I'd bought a little carpet with roads and a town printed on it and an endless variety of little cars, trucks, fire engines, and taxis to drive on the roads. I was going to have a great time playing with my grandson.

Things didn't turn out the way I had planned. Our son is divorced, and our grandson's mother would not allow us to see him. It was a terrible disappointment. As I agonized over the situation, I thought, *Lord, I have chosen to practice joy in my life. Now how can I find joy in this situation? Lord, thank You for giving me joy.*

My son also has a daughter (different mom) with whom I was having a bit of trouble bonding. I was very guarded, wondering how much of my life to invest in her, protecting myself from more pain. But do you know what God did for me? He gave me joy! Because of the absence of my grandson that Christmas season, God gave me the uninterrupted time to interact and bond with my granddaughter. That was a wonderful gift! God knew what I really needed.

It is through these times of pain mixed with joy that I have come to realize that joy doesn't spring up in my emotions. It is a gift from God, triggered by my will. It is something I choose to practice in my life. Praise the Lord!

ANNE L. WHAM

Actions Speak Louder Than Words

But be ye doers . . . , and not hearers only. James 1:22.

For the first time in his life my husband was in the hospital. For several months he had been plagued with unexplained dizzy spells, and on that last day of November, while teaching a class he had blacked out and fallen to the floor in front of his astonished students. The emergency room doctor decided to keep him overnight for observation. However, his stay was extended for more than three weeks when a CAT scan revealed a fractured skull and a concussion. A week later he underwent surgery for a ruptured duodenal ulcer. Concerned friends and coworkers prayed for his recovery and taught his classes.

Not wanting to spend a lot of time selecting a Christmas tree, I unwisely picked out a very large one. The back seat of our Honda was folded down to make room for the tree, but instead of tying the branches down, the young man who put it in the car thrust it in, trunk first. Big mistake! It was only after much pulling, pushing, and struggling that I got that monster out of the car. Then with great effort I heaved it into a bucket of water in the garage, and there it sat for days. There was no way I could lug it into the house.

Friends and acquaintances offered a cheery "Let me know if there's anything I can do to help." My answer was always "All I need is somebody to help me get that tree into the house," but to no avail. Until . . .

On Saturday night I joined the group decorating our church for Christmas. After we finished, one young man said, "Let's go!"

Bewildered, I said, "Go where?"

"To put your tree up!"

He and his wife got the tree into the house, trimmed the trunk so it would fit the stand, put the tree in place, and put all the lights on.

How grateful I was that they had not only heard my spoken need but had responded. They were doers and not hearers only. I want to be a doer too.

MARY JANE GRAVES

The Missing Guest

*For unto you is born this day in the city of
David a Saviour, which is Christ the Lord. Luke 2:11.*

The family got together to celebrate a friend's birthday. They spent weeks preparing, buying presents, and decorating the house. They even fixed special food. The birthday party was a huge success, and everybody agreed it was the best birthday ever and that they should all get together and celebrate it again the next year. The only person who didn't have a good time at the party was the birthday boy himself. You see, in the rush to get everything ready for the special day, nobody remembered to invite him.

It sounds ridiculous, doesn't it? A birthday party without the guest of honor? It happens—during Christmas. We get so busy trying to find the perfect gifts for family and friends that most of our preparations take place at the shopping mall rather than at church. It is ironic that the idea of giving gifts to loved ones has become so distorted that many people equate money with love. Instead of generosity, greed flourishes as children brag about the gifts they get rather than concentrating on those they give. Some children grow up with only a fuzzy notion of the Christmas story, but they can describe Santa in great detail and name all his reindeer.

This Christmas why not make Christ a part of the celebration? If gift-giving has gotten out of hand in your family, set a limit on money spent on gifts and stick to it. Instead of merely exchanging presents with people you know, why not share your bounty with less-fortunate folk? Contact local charities and buy gifts for a family in need. This is a very special way of remembering Jesus on His birthday.

Rather than trying to fit time for a religious celebration into a crowded holiday schedule, mark this time on your calendar before your social commitments. There's no rule that says you have to attend every party you're invited to. Being physically exhausted and emotionally drained is a poor way to commemorate the birth of Jesus. Put the Birthday Baby first on your list instead of last. He is the reason for the season! GINA LEE

The Best Gift

It is more blessed to give than to receive. Acts 20:35.

There was little to get excited about that Christmas of 1934. Money was scarce, and my chances of taking part in the gift exchange at school seemed pretty remote until I explained to Mother that the teacher had set a limit of 10 cents per gift. Then she consented.

After the names were drawn I went shopping. I scanned the five-and-dime stores, walking up and down the aisles, looking for just the right gift. Finally, there it was—a handsome harmonica. And it cost only a dime; so I bought it.

After wrapping it, I took it to school and placed it under the Christmas tree with the other gifts. Every day I would look to see if there was a gift with my name on it. There was none. Time was running out—it was the day before our party and still no package for me.

The day of the exchange I ran to school and looked under the tree again. There it was: a very small, round package wrapped in dirty, wrinkled tissue paper.

After recess the teacher began to distribute the gifts. She called several names, and then I heard my name. I walked to the tree, and the teacher handed me the funny-looking little round package in the dirty, wrinkled tissue paper.

I unwrapped it rather cautiously and was horrified to see a dirty old tennis ball. To top it off, there was no name tag on it. Who would do this to me? I was so embarrassed and disappointed, but I tried to hide it till I got outside. When I got close to Miller's field, I threw that tennis ball as far as I could into the empty lot.

When I arrived home I told my mother what had happened. She sat me down, and we had a talk. "Perhaps that dirty tennis ball was all he had to give," she said.

Although that wasn't much consolation right then, she tried her best to smooth things over. But my heart was hurting.

It took some time, but I did come to understand. I really had received the ultimate gift—that of giving rather than receiving.

CLAREEN COLCLESSER

The Blessing of Praise

Now the God of hope fill you with all joy and peace in believing, that
ye may abound in hope, through the power of the Holy Ghost. Rom. 15:13.

The north wind blowing through the Ozark Mountains seemed to go right through me as I worked outside cleaning screens and feeding the rainbow trout we raise. Instead of mumbling and complaining, as was my custom before Jesus called me, I thanked Him and praised Him for the bright, sunny day and whatever blessing came to mind. Joy unspeakable filled my heart.

As I fed the trout in our fishing area, the fine dust from the feed blew into my face and eyes. And I thought to myself, *Joyce, you need to move so you can see.*

Even as I was thinking this, the wind calmed. I believe that the Holy Spirit was there with me as I praised God, and that God changed the wind to further my joy and praise. I fed the trout, laughing and praising God, thanking Him for blessing me. After I finished feeding those fish, the wind slowly picked up again. It was too good to be just a coincidence.

What a wonderful heavenly Father! You calm the fierce winds that batter us and give us joy unspeakable and peace that passeth all understanding. You know what we need even before we ask it!

Sometimes we go to God only when there is a crisis, or we have given up on what we can do to solve a problem. But this experience reminds me that God wants to have a continuous relationship with me. He wants to give us daily joy and peace, not just get me out of trouble.

Lord, whatever winds batter my soul today, whatever trials come to distract me, help me to be filled with hope, joy, and peace that only You can give. Put a song in my heart and words of praise on my lips.   JOYCE BREEDLOVE

Part of the Family

*For his Holy Spirit speaks to us deep in our hearts, and
tells us that we really are God's children. Rom. 8:16, TLB.*

A friend was invited to share Christmas dinner with our family. After we had finished our meal, the telephone rang. It was my younger sister, who lived in another state and was spending Christmas with her husband's family. Rather than take turns talking to my sister and brother-in-law, and thereby missing parts of the conversation, we preferred to use every available telephone extension and make it a six-way party call. Our dinner guest thought it such a funny sight to see us clustered eagerly around each of the two or three telephone receivers that she found her camera and took a photo. She didn't realize that at our house what she saw was not at all unusual. For her, calls from family members were infrequent and seldom pleasurable. It helped me appreciate the blessings of a loving family.

On another occasion a friend visiting our home picked up the little notebook we use for writing messages to one another. I was surprised at how touched she was as she read the notes, because the messages they contained reflected the practicalities of running a household and were not at all personal. They were such things as, "The cat is in [or out]"; "The cat has [or hasn't] been fed"; "Gone to get milk—won't be long"; "So-and-so called—please phone him." I suppose to our friend, who had not had the benefit of a stable home life, these very ordinary examples of family communication were somehow symbolic of the affection and stability that she yearned for but never had.

Incidents like these not only make me realize afresh how wonderfully God has blessed me, they also make me realize the importance of sharing "family feeling" with others.

Offering hospitality is one way of sharing, but an equally successful approach is to help make one's local church as much like a loving family as possible, a place where anyone can feel at home and find love and acceptance as a child of God.

*Jesus, You were born in a manger because there was no room in the inn.
At this special season, help us open our hearts, homes, and churches to those
who need the blessing of family.*   JENNIFER M. BALDWIN

Mini Miracles for Christmas

If you have faith as a mustard seed, you will say to this mountain, "Move from here to there," and it will move. . . . Nothing will be impossible for you. Matt. 17:20, NKJV.

Early one morning I told God about my problems and needs for the day, asking yet again for a sign of His unfailing love to me. My prayer went something like this: *It's two days until Christmas, Lord, and we have now been told that the secondhand bike we had lined up for our son is the wrong size, and the birdcage we were going to get for our daughter is unavailable. Lord, we have two children, a limited amount of money, and some faith. If You can pull this one off, Lord, I will try never to doubt You again. Amen.*

An hour later, while driving home, I felt I should buy a newspaper. Perhaps there would be something in the classifieds. *Two days before Christmas?* I skipped the urge and drove on. As I neared the last paper shop before I reached home the impression continued, so I purchased the paper and drove home. Among the classifieds I read, "Birdcage with stand, black, $30." *Sounds interesting,* I thought. *I'll wait until 8:00 a.m. before I ring.*

"Come on over" was the reply when I called, and by 9:00 my daughter had a beautifully decorated round birdcage on a wrought-iron stand. It was worth far more than we would have been prepared to purchase new; we were delighted. *So far so good,* I thought as I told my children of my prayer, and we all marveled at the quick answer.

Young David said, "What about my gift?"

"Just wait and see," I replied, and we did.

At 7:00 that evening a distant neighbor phoned. "I've got two bikes here for sale. You can have them both for $30." An hour later our son had a bike for Christmas, and we all had a large gift of love from a faithful God.

Sometimes I am in wonder at the grass-roots care my Lord has for me. Two little kids in need of Christmas gifts, one Mom in need of a faith gift, and all granted for a Christmas I will long remember.

Christmases are always special times, and I pray that this year your Christmas will be touched by a mini miracle from above.   RUTH RAWSON

It Can't Be Stopped

For whatever is born of God conquers the world. 1 John 5:4, NRSV.

While living in Texas I encountered many strange creatures who tried to share my house at different times. At the time it didn't bother me to stomp, swat, exterminate, eliminate, or kill such nuisances so they wouldn't infest the house with their presence and families.

On one occasion I was just about to step onto the back porch, a concrete slab, when a very large spider scurried from under the baseboard. I had never seen such a huge spider. It looked very much like an innocent and beneficial daddy longlegs except its stomach was 10 times as large as any I had ever seen. Not wanting to make a mess all over the porch, I gingerly stepped down on it, and lo! About a thousand (or so it seemed) little spiders scattered all over the porch.

I immediately wondered about the reproduction capabilities of that mother spider I had just annihilated. Of course, I tried to stamp out the little ones on the spot, but many of them escaped. I began to feel badly about what I had done and wondered all day what kind of spider that mother was. I've since read about female spiders who carry their young in a brood sac on their back. When released, the babies scatter in all directions.

As I reflected on how the spider left so many progeny to carry on her line, it made me think about the Word of God, and how it has been passed down through the ages, in spite of many efforts to suppress it. The message gets through and flourishes, even when the messenger has been killed. The message of the Bible keeps going to all the world in spite of attempts to stop it. The small band of disciples entrusted by Jesus to carry His message of salvation did a marvelous job of getting it started. Jesus told them to carry it to the ends of the earth, and now nearly the whole world has heard it. Can His second coming be far off?

GWEN LEE

The Homecoming

Let us lay aside every weight, and the sin which so easily ensnares us, and let us run with endurance the race that is set before us. Heb. 12:1, NKJV.

It was our first Christmas since our marriage, and we were determined to go spend it with family. Unfortunately my husband worked until 11:00 Christmas Eve, so we had to leave after he got off work. Our little VW Bug was packed with Christmas gifts, and it had begun to snow lightly. We laughed about having a white Christmas and headed for his home in upstate New York, four hours away.

Unfortunately it began to snow more intensely, and the snow got deeper and deeper as we traveled. Sometimes we had to get out of the car and use my husband's army shovel to get ourselves out of snowdrifts. Other times he got out and pushed the car while I steered us out of the snow. Often we skidded. Nevertheless, we kept on because we were going home. Although we were tired and sometimes cold, we kept on because we had images of Christmas dinner and Christmas fellowship before us.

Then within a few blocks of home we could go no farther. The snow-drifts were too deep. We decided to try from another direction. We had been on the road for more than six hours but we kept going. Never once did we think of turning back. We were almost there when we got stuck. Even after being rescued by a snowplow, we couldn't proceed farther in that direction.

So we went back to the earlier route. The road was still blocked, and once again the car got stuck. So we got out and walked, although neither of us had boots. We didn't worry about the Christmas presents or our luggage. We just took ourselves. We just wanted to get home. We arrived cold. I had one shoe missing, a loss I didn't even notice because my feet were so cold. Our family was waiting for us with open arms and warmth.

Sisters, we are on our way home. We will meet obstacles and disappointments. At times we will slip and slide, but we are going home to celebrate—not for a holiday, but for eternity with our Master. Let's not let anything keep us from our goal. God will be waiting at the door for us.

EDITH C. FRASER

Born in Bethlehem

*For unto you is born this day in the city of David
a Saviour, which is Christ the Lord. Luke 2:11.*

I loved Christmas. My mother always decorated a corner of our living room with poinsettias around a small Nativity scene. The house was adorned with garlands of pine needles and small yellow apples. The aroma greeted us the moment we entered.

My aunt Stella displayed one of the nicest and largest Nativity scenes in the neighborhood. There were little houses with small lights inside, shining stars and clouds hung from the ceiling. The high mountains were in the back. Far away you could see the little sheep grazing and shepherds taking care of them. Men, women, and children could be seen coming down the crooked roads, the large baskets on their heads filled with all kinds of fruits and flowers. Down in the valley was the village, and everyone was coming down to see Baby Jesus.

In the far corner of the scene, also down in the valley, was the manger with the virgin Mary and Joseph, the cow and the donkey, but no Baby Jesus. You see, He was not supposed to be born until midnight on December 24. My cousins and I were intrigued and excited. We didn't want to miss this big event. Many times during the day I sneaked into that room and wondered when He would come. Could it be possible that He would come early and I would miss Him?

On the night of the twenty-fourth every member of the family managed to keep awake until midnight. As the clock struck midnight we all wished each other "Feliz Navidad!" No one ever noticed how Aunt Stella managed to make Baby Jesus appear in the manger, but all of a sudden He was there! I was the happiest. My eyes grew big with wonder when I saw the face of Baby Jesus. I was only 5 years old then, but the birth of Jesus is still real in my life. He was born in a manger, and the angels filled the hills with heavenly music. The shepherds left their flocks and ran to see Baby Jesus. Jesus was born in Bethlehem, but He was also born in my heart many years ago, far away in the mountains and valleys of Guatemala. RAQUEL HAYLOCK

A Childhood Christmas

*Praise the God and Father of our Lord Jesus Christ for
the spiritual blessings that Christ has brought us from heaven! . . .
God was kind and decided that Christ would choose us
to be God's own adopted children. Eph. 1:3-5, CEV.*

As a 4-year-old girl, I adored my mommy and daddy. They were every-thing to me. Busy though she was, Mother rocked me when I was sick or tired. Daddy read to me and taught me to read. Life was good with four brothers and one sister. We didn't have many of the material things in life, but I felt loved and treasured. Although money was in short supply, we didn't realize we were poor.

Christmas was here, and we had our traditional Christmas Eve supper of potatoes and vegetables—and lutefisk. Lutefisk was the star of our meal, a dish of our Norwegian heritage. I don't know if I really liked the taste of it so much as I enjoyed it because I loved my dad and knew it was a favorite of his.

As I came down the stairs on Christmas morning I looked at the most awesome sight my young eyes had ever seen. On Grandma's small round table stood a glorious Christmas tree. Arranged around the base were eight Fifth Avenue candy bars—one for each member of our family. The glitter-ing tinsel and ornaments on the tree were a marvelous wonder. What joy filled my heart!

As I grew up I realized that the little tree was less than three feet tall and its decorations were simple. But it doesn't matter. The excitement and joy I felt over that simple Christmas and the beautiful tree is still vivid in my memory. I don't remember what gifts we received, or if there were any gifts.

Though the years have brought more glorious holiday seasons, filled with gifts and family gatherings, the joyful Christmas of my fourth year will always be special, because I was part of a family who loved me.

I have another family, a family with whom I feel loved and cherished. I have met Jesus, and He adopted me into His loving family. On that long ago Christmas Eve He brought love, joy, and hope to every family on this earth. Knowing Him makes every day as special as that first Christmas morning.

EVELYN GLASS

My Birds

*Look at the birds of the air; they neither sow nor reap nor
gather into barns, and yet your heavenly Father feeds them.
Are you not of more value than they? And can any of you by
worrying add a single hour to your span of life? Matt. 6:26, 27, NRSV.*

It was a cold, winter morning with just enough snow on the ground to
encourage the birds to feed from our feeders in a rather frantic way. I sat
by the window admiring my feathered friends but thought of the past week
when we could not solve the problem of the squirrel eating what seemed
like tons of seed meant for the birds. Finally we found a feeder that was
guaranteed to keep out squirrels.

As I spent some devotional time with my Lord I wondered, *What can I
learn from these creatures?* It was then I saw my own life in focus. Why do I
worry so? I had finally solved the squirrel problem for the birds. Does not
God, who loves me more than I love birds, solve my problems? A roof over
the feeder protected the seed. My angels hover over me to protect me. God has
even protected the seed of His Word so I can claim His beautiful promises.

Why do the birds push each other off the feeder? Is this not like my nature, to be greedy and selfish and push away others, rather than to share?
Why did it take so long for the birds to find the feeders? Am I so involved
with the cares of this life that I don't find the seed meant for my salvation?
Do I take small bits of the seed and accidentally throw away that which
could also provide nourishment? Do I pick up what has fallen to the
ground and thank God for small blessings in my life? Why are we frightened away when something or someone seemingly bigger than we comes
along? Why can we not trust? Why do we not sing as the birds when our
hearts are lonely?

As I looked through the smudged glass windowpane I resolved to take
the Lord's message and make it mine: "Therefore do not worry about tomorrow, for tomorrow will worry about itself. Each day has enough trouble
of its own" (Matt. 6:34, NIV).

*Lord, today starts with a new, clean page in my life—may I be less anxious
and trust You, my heavenly Father, more!*
JUNE LOOR

He Helps in Amazing Ways

When you ask God for help, believe that you will receive it, and He will help you in ways that will amaze you. Matt. 21:22, Clear Word.

Since we would be gone for a few weeks during the Christmas holidays, visiting our children and grandchildren in Michigan, my husband and I decided to have our mail forwarded to our children's address. This was something we had done before, and it had worked perfectly.

When we arrived in Michigan, we learned that no mail had been delivered yet for us. After nine days I called our home post office and was told that all our mail had been forwarded. Several more days slipped by, and still no mail. I called both post offices—no mail. The Michigan post office told me that because of the holidays it might take up to a month to receive our mail. Knowing we would be returning home at the end of the week, I decided to pray. My heavenly Father knew where our mail was and could get it to us before we left our children's home.

It was the day before we would leave. Again I prayed. About 7:00 p.m. the doorbell rang. A deliveryman had a large box labeled "Priority Mail," addressed to us. Inside were two packages, containing more than 70 Christmas cards and some business mail. I thanked the Lord for being so interested in two of His children that even our mail reached us before we left to return to our home in Florida.

"Our heavenly Father waits to bestow upon us the fullness of His blessing. It is our privilege to drink largely at the fountain of boundless love. What a wonder it is that we pray so little! God is ready and willing to hear the sincere prayer of the humblest of His children, and yet there is much manifest reluctance on our part to make known our wants to God. What can the angels of heaven think of poor helpless human beings . . . when God's heart of infinite love yearns toward them, ready to give them more than they can ask or think, and yet they pray so little and have so little faith?" (E. G. White, *Steps to Christ*, p. 94).

PATRICIA MULRANEY KOVALSKI

Smooring Christmas

*But Mary kept all these things and pondered
them in her heart. Luke 2:19, NKJV.*

Dry needles fall from the balsam fir. Ornaments glitter beside tiny
Christmas lights. Gifts now belong and are used. The last crumbs of
cookies melt in soapy dishwater. Today I put Christmas away. I gently wrap
each ornament, each chosen for our family by my daughter, or mother, or
sister, or friend. The tissue wrapping comes from the New Year's basket my
sister sent. Mary wrapped Baby Jesus in swaddling clothes, strips of cloth—
good for wrapping things.

I carefully place the wrapped ornaments in a cardboard box that held
the orange-raisin and date-walnut cookies and tea cakes my mother sent.
Mary laid Jesus in a manger, a box—good for holding things.

Our black-and-white cat seems disappointed as I coil up the strings of
Christmas lights and shiny tinsel rope she has enjoyed these weeks of
Christmas. Now the box is full, lidded, ready to tuck into its closet corner.
The jostling of tree limbs fills our house with balsam fir fragrance. It is time.

I unscrew the fir from its stand and toss the soapy sweet water onto the
flower bed where peonies will grow next May. And I wrap the balsam fir in
its white linen tablecloth skirt and carry it to next year's vegetable garden. I
lay the tree on the ground and shake its needles from the tablecloth.
Tonight snow comes to cover the tree.

Just as Gaelic women smoored the coals of their fires with gentle heap-
ings of ashes, in the name of the Holy Three who are one, in the promise of
a fire kept well and ready to waken with tinder next morn, I smoor the
glow of Christmas with tissue and boxes and snow. I smoor Christmas in
the name of the Holy Three who are one. I smoor Christmas as Mary did
that first Christmas, and keep well the promise that Christ will come.

CAROL JUNE HUTCHINS HOOKER

Sending God an SOS

*He shall call upon me, and I will answer him: I will be
with him in trouble; I will deliver him, and honour him. Ps. 91:15.*

It was the thirty-first day of December. Sunset was rapidly approaching. I had never before experienced an electronic fast, but beginning at sunset there would be no television or radio for 10 days. It was my day off, and I rushed to finish my chores so I could bring the New Year in with worship.

The telephone rang. "Tanya and I waited more than an hour at church, but no one was there," said my sister.

"Oh dear, I told you the wrong time. The service will be starting at 7:30, not sunset. I'm sorry," I apologized. I couldn't bring myself to tell her that I really didn't want to go, especially since I had invited them to our New Year's service.

While searching for something to wear, the phone rang again. This time the voice said, "Have you heard?"

"Heard what?" I asked.

It was one of my coworkers telling me that one of our security guards was currently being held hostage at gunpoint at the hospital where we worked. She said that when the gunman was refused his medical records, he went into a rage and fired several shots in the building. Luckily no one was hurt.

Before I left for church I called one of my friends on the job, and we had prayer. I called my prayer partner and another coworker and prayed with each of them as well. I also asked them to request the prayers of their congregations after learning that they had both planned to go to their church for New Year's services.

During the service I testified to God's goodness to me and my family throughout the year and proceeded to tell them about our security guard being held hostage on the job. I asked my congregation to pray that the Holy Spirit would take full control, and that the gunman would turn himself in without injury to his hostage or himself.

After the meeting, as I unlocked my door, the phone was ringing. It was my sister telling me that our prayers had been answered. The gunman had handed the gun to the security guard and turned himself in while we were petitioning the Lord at prayer meeting. CORA A. WALKER

A Tale of Two Travelers

But godliness with contentment is great gain. 1 Tim. 6:6.

Once upon a New Year's Eve two women passed through a busy airport. One was wealthy; the other was rich. Which would you rather be? To help you decide, here is the story as I experienced it.

The first woman was returning from a dream vacation. Her tropical attire and the cruise line inscription on her souvenir bag made that apparent. Her jewels, her sculpted hair, and her bearing bespoke an existence in which "once-in-a-lifetime" vacations happen at least once a year.

The second woman was an ordinary traveler, returning home from a holiday with relatives. From the droop of her shoulders as she sat in the waiting area an onlooker would have judged it had been a long day for her. Indeed, it had. And her final flight of the day, it turned out, had been overbooked. She had been bumped to an itinerary that would take three extra hours and two flights instead of one to get her to her destination.

The first traveler's plans had changed too. She had been upgraded to a seat in first class. As she disembarked, she went straight to an airline employee to express her— Well, no, it wasn't appreciation. Her face set in harsh lines, she berated the airline and denounced the flight crew. It seems that although she'd been seated in first class, she had been served a sandwich rather than a first-class meal. Judging from her vehemence, her entire vacation had been ruined as a result.

What of the second traveler then? In spite of her obvious weariness, her eyes glowed as she told a fellow traveler about her changed itinerary. The airline had given her a voucher for supper—10 whole dollars! And best of all, she'd been compensated with a free airline ticket. It put within reach a destination she'd dreamed of. She praised God for this opportunity.

One traveler was wealthy, the other was rich. Put another way, today's verse says, "And religion does make your life rich by making you content with what you have." Which commodity is available to all—wealth or riches? Which secured for its possessor a happy new year? As a traveler through this life, which would you rather be, wealthy or rich?

KATHLEEN STEARMAN PFLUGRAD

Biographical Sketches

Betty J. Adams is a retired schoolteacher who has written for *Guide* and who enjoys going with teenagers on mission trips to other countries. She works with community services and writes for her church newsletter. Hobbies include quilting, traveling, and grandchildren. **Apr. 1, Dec. 12.**

Priscilla Adonis is from Cape Town, South Africa. She is a retired minister's wife, mother of two adult children, and enjoys working with the children in her local church. Her hobbies include crocheting, flower arranging, writing letters, and trying new recipes. **Feb 18, Mar. 18, Apr. 28.**

Michelle Ancel is involved in adult Sabbath school and social events in her local church. She is currently employed by the Michigan Conference of Seventh-day Adventists in the Lake Union and spends her summers with her boys, working at Camp Au Sable. Her hobbies include reading and cooking. **June 12.**

Marilyn J. Applegate is a writer living in Washington. For 30 years she and her husband have been involved in pastoral and hospital administration work. A current project of hers, now that she is living in the Northwest, is researching the missionary influence in the opening up of Old Oregon. **Feb. 3, Sept. 1, Nov. 27.**

Gretchen Armstrong lived in Des Moines, Iowa, at the time of this writing. **Feb. 4.**

Rosemary Baker, a freelance writer living in Iowa, is author of *What Am I?* (a children's book) and has had contributions in *Shining Star, Kids' Stuff,* and other magazines. She is a member of the Iowa Poetry Association, is active in church and volunteer work, enjoys working with children, and lists arts, crafts, poetry, music, and painting among her hobbies. **Sept. 23.**

Audrey Balderstone recently helped operate several businesses while obtaining her Master of Arts degree in English literature. She serves on various committees in her church and community, is president of the Adventist Business and Professionals' Association, runs a home fellowship group, and writes for flower-arranging magazines. **Mar. 27, Apr. 6, June 19, Aug. 31.**

Jennifer M. Baldwin writes from Australia, where she is the clinical risk management coordinator at Sydney Adventist Hospital. She has served in various capacities in her local church, including elder, worship leader, and Bible class teacher. She enjoys writing and traveling. **Dec. 21.**

Mary Barrett works with her husband in pastoral ministry, especially in evangelistic outreach. She is the mother of two girls. Her first book, *When God Comes to Visit,* was published in 1997. She is very interested in devotional and prayer ministry, enjoys being with friends, walking, and having time to turn her newly acquired house into a home. **Mar. 13, Apr. 15, Aug. 11, Nov. 5, Dec. 6.**

Elizabeth Bediako is a native of Ghana. She and her husband, four children, and one grandson live in Maryland. She is an office clerk at the General Conference of Seventh-day Adventists and enjoys traveling, photography, cooking, and sewing. **June 21.**

Appy Niyo Benggon and her husband came to the United States from Sabah, Malaysia, in 1992 and now live in California. Appy worked as a professional secretary for 12 years but now stays home with their 21-month-old daughter. She loves reading, traveling, and searching for additions to her extensive collection of frog pins and figurines. **Apr. 13.**

Denise Hancock Benner is a wife and mother of three preschoolers. Growing up in Indonesia gave her a love for travel, and being born into a pastor's family gave her a love for singing and music. She leads song service in her church, is in charge of the children's stories, and teaches a teen Bible class each week. Her favorite pastimes are reading and sewing. **Mar. 25.**

Susan L. Berridge is a registered nurse and driver's education teacher. She has a master's degree in education and teaches health occupations at a vocational school. She and her husband enjoy living in a rural setting with their four daughters, ranging in age from preschool to college. Her hobbies include painting, gardening, outdoor activities, and, most of all, being a mom. **June 14, July 12, Dec. 1.**

Annie B. Best is a retired public school teacher. She and her husband of 48 years have two grown children. She enjoys being with her three grandchildren, reading, and listening to music. She has worked as leader in the cradle roll and kindergarten departments of her church, which she enjoys and finds rewarding. **Apr. 4.**

Marjory Button Bodi is a nurse and birthing expert who loves babies, knitting, and crocheting. She says she learns spiritual lessons from nature through her log cabin windows in upper Michigan. She has two grown daughters. **Apr. 23.**

Joan Bova directs disabilities ministries for the Southern Union Conference and Florida Conference of Seventh-day Adventists. She is an enthusiastic public speaker and enjoys educating others. She and her husband live in Apopka, Florida, with their two teenage daughters. **Feb. 14, Sept. 22, Nov. 30.**

Joyce Breedlove lived in Highlandville, Missouri, when this devotional was written. **Dec. 20.**

Avis H. W. Brown is the dean of student development at New York Institute of Technology in Manhattan, New York. She has served as Sabbath school superintendent, deaconess, assistant musician, and family life coordinator and is active in community and civic organizations. Dr. Brown is the mother of one young adult and three teenagers. **Mar. 10.**

Joyce Willes Brown-Carper is a professional musician, former elementary school teacher, and freelance writer, who has had children's stories and articles published in the *Review*. She practiced law for several years but is now pursuing her dream to be a full-time writer. She and her husband have two daughters, Elizabeth and Helena. **June 17.**

Darlene Ytredal Burgeson, who works in business management and sales training, was formerly district sales manager of an international company. She has been active in a variety of church activities. Her hobbies are photographs and family albums, gardening, sending cards and notes to those who live alone, and visiting nursing homes. **Apr. 21.**

Nanette Burks is a native Californian. She is a chief petty officer in the U.S. Navy, where she has served for 18 years. She enjoys singing, writing letters, music, and cross-stitch. **Apr. 11.**

Betty R. Burnett, from northern Michigan, recently retired from the United States Department of Agriculture. She is enjoying every new day. Her great loves are her grandchildren, the great outdoors, and reading. Well-turned phrases make her glow. She makes a great loaf of bread, too! **May 17.**

Sarah L. Burt is a home-schooling mother of three, a registered nurse, and Bible study leader in her church. She enjoys reading, gardening, cooking, music, and nature. **Apr. 3.**

Andrea A. Bussue was born on the Caribbean island of Nevis. She holds a master's degree in education and teaches at a special education facility in Washington, D.C. She has been the children's choir director and superintendent at her local church in Hyattsville, Maryland. She loves children and enjoys reading, traveling, sewing, cooking, and meeting people. **Mar. 24, Aug. 14.**

Sheryl A. Calhoun is a homemaker, wife, mother of three daughters, home school teacher, and registered nurse. The family is currently on temporary assignment in England, where she is coordinator of the children's Sabbath school, a member of the youth team, and a deaconess. **Sept. 26, Oct. 11.**

Edna Barrett Canaday, a retired clerk-treasurer for the city of College Place, Washington, has held offices for various clubs and her church. She was editor of the Blue Mountain Gem and Mineral Society's newsletter. She has two daughters and four grandchildren. Currently she is involved in volunteer work. **Sept. 14.**

Dorothy Wainwright Carey is a retired federal government worker who lives in Ocala, Florida, with her husband of 42 years. She has been privileged to be involved in church work at all levels. Her interests include writing for anthologies, reading, all furry creatures, outdoor activities, travel, family, and friends. **July 22.**

Pam Caruso is the mother of 10 grown children and grandmother of 10. Her interests include classical music, fitness, and grandchildren. She is women's ministries leader at her local church. **Feb. 29.**

Terri Casey has been married to Mike for more than 20 years and has been blessed with two children and two grandchildren. She works as a lab supervisor for a dermatology and laser practice and is a safety officer and consultant for several medical practices. She teaches the youth Bible class at church, loves to walk, Rollerblade, quilt, read, camp, and write. **Jan. 2.**

Shari Chamberlain currently serves as a chaplain at Ukiah Valley Medical Center in California. She has also worked as a pastor and health evangelist. Her hobbies include travel, biking, gardening, and visiting with friends. **May 3.**

Frances Charles is a retired school principal. She is the women's ministries coordinator for the Natal-Free State Conference in South Africa. She is a bereavement counselor and a caregiver at a hospice. She has published a book, *My Tears, My Rainbow*. Her hobbies include writing and making pretty things. **May 12, Aug. 3, Nov. 19.**

Premila M. Cherian is a retired teacher who taught at Spicer Memorial College in the Home Science Department for 28 years, during the time her husband was president of the college. She has three children and six grandchildren. **Aug. 30.**

Peggy Clark is an administrative assistant working for the city of San Diego. She has a love for nature and spends as much time outdoors as work permits. She spent more than 15 years in Seventh-day Adventist ministries beside her husband and is a member of the Tierrasanta SDA Church. **Aug. 21, Sept. 10, Dec. 4.**

Jan Clarke is a "relocated" Australian who is the finance director of Stanborough Press, a Christian publishing house in England. She is a church elder and treasurer with interests in history, reading, writing, public speaking, genealogy, and women's ministries. **May 6.**

Marsha Claus is a stay-at-home mom who helps with cradle roll at her church. Her hobbies include traveling, writing, and spending time with her husband and son. She taught grades 5 and 6 for two years before becoming a mother. **July 16, Sept. 7.**

Clareen Colclesser is a retired L.P.N. who enjoys writing letters and short stories, interior decorating, and poring over her large collection of interior decorating books and magazines. **June 30, July 24, Aug. 22, Oct. 23, Dec. 19.**

Kay Collins has had the wonderful privilege of serving her Lord as a Bible worker, singing evangelist, and preventive health educator in team-ministry with her husband for 25 years. She was published in *Energized*, a daily devotional book, and has written more than 400 gospel poems and 50 songs of faith and happiness. **Feb. 24.**

Arlene E. Compton lives in Lincoln, Nebraska, with her husband. Children, grandchildren, travel, reading, writing, table games, and friends occupy her leisure time. A retired nursing administrator, she remains active in church and professional organizations. **July 2, Aug. 18, Nov. 11.**

Judy Coulston has a Ph.D. in nutrition and a private practice in Fresno, California. She has done a speaking tour of Australia and hosted and coproduced a highly rated weekly television program. Her latest venture is teaching pathophysiology. She teaches adult Bible classes, is active in women's and prayer ministries, and is ever longing for Christ's second coming. **Feb. 26, Apr. 2.**

Lena Cressotti has retired but still keeps active in her church in Connecticut. Lena has almost finished writing her life story. Her other interests include swimming, reading, playing the organ, doing crafts, and oil painting. **May 11.**

Veronica Crockett, a family consultant, works with families of children with medical/genetical disabilities and University of Oregon students in early intervention fieldwork. Veronica is active in church, women's ministries, and a Bible study group and has been published in denominational magazines. She enjoys biking, strength training, active sports, reading, and hiking and camping. **July 21.**

Christina Curtis is a reading specialist with a master's in education. At one time she studied to become a Benedictine nun. When she has time, she likes writing, organic gardening, and camping all over the country. **Jan. 27.**

Laura Pascual Dancek, a speech-language pathologist, stays home to be a full-time mother to her 16-month-old daughter. She lives in Port Charlotte, Florida. **Apr. 9, May 14.**

Lynn Marie Davis writes from Georgia. She is a sign-language interpreter for the Cobb County public schools. She enjoys presenting workshops on "Steps to Making Your Dreams Come True." Her hobbies include walking, creative cooking, and learning through participating in workshops. **Jan. 23.**

Wanda Grimes Davis is a staff chaplain at a hospital in Portland, Oregon. She is married, the mother of three, and enjoys preaching, teaching, and facilitating small groups. She is a licensed pastoral counselor. **Nov. 12.**

Ivani Isabel Melo de Ana was residing in Brazil when she submitted this devotional. **Apr. 20.**

Maria de Jesus Vale Menezes lives in São José, Santa Catarina, Brazil. She is retired, a widow, mother of four children, and has two adopted grandchildren. She was an elementary and high school teacher and educational supervisor in state-run schools. She has been a member of the Seventh-day Adventist Church for 26 years and still actively serves Christ. **May 4.**

Sheila Sanders Delaney is currently enjoying retirement and a recent marriage by traveling and being a homemaker. She is actively trying to witness to friends and neighbors to the best of her ability. **Mar. 22, Sept. 28.**

Jodi Eulene Dodson is a composer, musician, and graphic arts designer. Her self-published book, *I Just Can't Do It, God*, reveals her journey from birth to loss of spiritual hope and eventual return to God. Since her reconversion, she is involved in writing and speaking. **Nov. 29.**

Goldie Down teaches college classes in creative writing and has 20 biographical books and a textbook to her credit, as well as numerous stories and articles in Seventh-day Adventist Church papers. **Aug. 1, Sept. 19, Oct. 9.**

Linda M. Driscoll was the first female theology graduate from Avondale College, Australia, and has since worked as a chaplain. She and her husband, Bill, enjoy the outdoors, walking, hiking, camping, swimming, nature study, and good books. **June 28, Sept. 25, Dec. 13.**

Louise Driver lives in Beltsville, Maryland, with her husband. They have three grown sons and three granddaughters. At church she is involved with music, youth, and women's ministries. She also works in women's ministries at the General Conference of Seventh-day Adventists. Her hobbies are singing and music, skiing, reading, crafts, gardening, and traveling to historical places. **Dec. 9.**

Joy Dustow has worked in education in Australia, Fiji, New Guinea, and Thailand. She and her husband live in a retirement village outside Brisbane, Australia, where she is active in the spiritual and social activities of the village. **June 24, Aug. 29.**

Mary C. Edmister retired after seven years in real estate. She is presently the leader of the 50+ Fellowship at the La Sierra University Seventh-day Adventist Church. She has completed two books of biographies with genealogies and pictures that were self-published in 1996 and 1997. **Aug. 24, Oct. 18.**

Sylvia M. Ellis lives with her pastor-husband in Vale, Oregon. She has spent most of her life as a teacher in elementary and secondary schools in the United States, and as a college teacher overseas. She currently works for a local community college and as a substitute teacher. She enjoys gardening and growing and arranging flowers. **June 4.**

Alice Fahrbach and her husband make their home on the shores of Lake Superior in Michigan. Alice is a retired nurse and mother of four grown children. She enjoys the outdoors, bird-watching, skiing, and short-term mission trips. **Mar. 31.**

Jocelyn Fay is a copy editor at the Review and Herald Publishing Association in Hagerstown, Maryland. She enjoys genealogical research and collects Cat's Meow Village special collection pieces and antique blue-and-white china. Her newest pastime is learning more about the Mid-Atlantic states. **Jan. 22, Feb. 25.**

Cristina Fernandez, a secretary, teacher, and counselor, was born in Chile. She has dedicated her life to helping youth, adults, and families through her counseling. **Apr. 12.**

Mercy M. Ferrer, originally from the Philippines, writes from British Columbia, Canada. For 10 years she and her husband have been missionaries to Egypt, Cyprus, and Russia. They have two children, both in college. A previous contributor to the women's devotional, she loves cooking, entertaining, trying new recipes, traveling, photography, reading, and word games. **June 20.**

Lorena Finis serves as languages instructor and intercultural programs coordinator at River Plate University in Argentina. She loves photography, music, sports, dogs, reading, and playing Pictionary with friends. **Mar. 29.**

Edith Fitch is retired after 41 years of teaching, the last 28 years being in the church school at Canadian University College, College Heights, Alberta. She enjoys writing (her computer is her "best friend on earth") and has devoted many hours to research for church and school histories. Her hobbies include needle crafts of hardanger, Brazilian embroidery, and tatting. **July 18, Aug. 7, Sept 13, Oct. 20.**

Heide Ford is the associate editor of *Women of Spirit,* a Christian women's magazine. A registered nurse, she holds a master's degree in counseling. Heide and her pastor-husband, Zell, live in Thurmont, Maryland. She enjoys reading, hiking, and whale watching. **Nov. 23.**

Marla Hinson Fordham submitted this devotional while she lived in Bothan, Alabama. **Apr. 7.**

Linda Franklin is a florist with a greenhouse in British Columbia. She grows and plants the flowers for the city of Chetwynd, and started the Chetwynd Garden Club and Farmer's Market. She holds a Bachelor of Science degree in medical technology and serves her church as deaconess, women's ministries assistant, a flower arranger, and plays her accordion. She especially enjoys prayer ministry. **Mar. 5, Apr. 22.**

Edith C. Fraser is a college professor who is chair of the Social Work Department, adjunct professor at several other colleges, and family director for her church. She is a speaker, family counselor, and consultant in the United States, as well as internationally. **Dec. 24.**

Norma C. Galiza and her husband have two married daughters, a son in college, and another daughter in high school. She works for the Hawaii Conference as the administrative secretary-cashier. Writing has been one of her favorite pastime activities, in addition to music, reading, sewing, and organizing various events. **Mar. 30.**

Edna Maye Gallington is part of the communication team at Southeastern California Conference of Seventh-day Adventists and a graduate of La Sierra University. She is a member of Toastmasters International and the Loma Linda Writing Guild. She enjoys freelance writing, music, gourmet cooking, entertaining, hiking, and racquet ball. **Jan 21.**

Lila Lane George, who works with her husband in Arizona, is involved in evangelism. She is the mother of two ministering sons and enjoys playing with her six grandchildren, hiking, reading, and artwork. **Jan. 20, June 11.**

Marybeth Gessele lives in Oregon, where she enjoys country living and visits from friends and family. She has authored one children's book, *No More Cinnamon Bear Cookies.* **July 28.**

Evelyn Glass lives with her husband on the family farm in Minnesota. Evelyn is involved in her local community and church. She serves as Women's Ministries director for the Mid-America Union Conference of Seventh-day Adventists. She enjoys writing, speaking, sewing, refinishing furniture, and playing with her grandchildren. **May 8, Nov. 1, Dec. 26.**

Mary Jane Graves worked as a secretary, school registrar, and librarian before retiring in North Carolina with her minister-educator husband. She enjoys reading, gardening, church activities, and family, which includes her mother, two sons, a daughter-in-law, two granddaughters, and many others. **Dec. 17.**

Ellie Green is president of E. Green & Associates, a consulting firm. A prolific writer and full-time lecturer who enjoys speaking at Christian women's retreats, she pursues her pastime interests in painting (oil, watercolor, and chalk painting) crocheting, and knitting. **May 7.**

Glenda-mae Greene is assistant vice president for student services at Andrews University in Berrien Springs, Michigan. A third-generation educator and Seventh-day Adventist, she enjoys many phases of church work—speaking, teaching, encouraging. **Jan. 26, June 3, Oct. 27.**

Gloria Gregory is an associate professor of nursing at West Indies College, Mandeville, Jamaica. A graduate of Andrews University's extension program with a master's in education, her hobbies include handicrafts, playing word games, sewing, and gardening. She and her husband have two girls. **Apr. 10.**

Nancy Hadaway lived in Grand Terrace, California, at the time of this writing. **Jan. 18.**

Lynnetta Siagian Hamstra is the associate director of women's ministries for the General Conference of Seventh-day Adventists in Silver Spring, Maryland. Born and raised on the tropical island of Borneo, in the state of Sabah, Malaysia, she inherits her love for music from her mom, and for traveling from her dad. She and her husband live in Columbia, Maryland. **Jan. 10.**

Dessa Weisz Hardin lives with her husband in Kennebunk, Maine. Her passion is overseas travel—to learn and enjoy, but also to visit her two daughters, who live in Europe. Another delight is working with children on reading. She teaches first grade in her town's school and the church school. **Jan. 1, Mar. 6, Mar. 28, Dec. 2.**

Lea Hardy has retired in South Carolina, where she continues to enjoy family, friends, and working for God. Lea writes, performs in a church outreach drama group, presents seminars, and delights in keeping in touch with and encouraging former students. **July 23.**

Joyce Wertz Harrington "retired" from nursing when she started a family. Currently she works part-time in several mental health offices. Joyce began her on-and-off relationship with writing during her high school journalism class and her tenure as school paper editor. More recently she is journaling her way through emotional and spiritual recovery. Her all-time favorite place is the beach. **Jan. 17.**

Beatrice Harris, a retired Bible instructor and church school teacher, lives in Columbus, Ohio, with her husband, where she is a church elder and evangelism committee chair. She's a published author of religious articles and has two adult children and two grandchildren. **Feb. 13.**

Feryl E. Harris is a Bible Instructor who serves the Mountain View Conference of Seventh-day Adventists in West Virginia as director of Sabbath School, Children's Ministries, Women's Ministries, and Trust Services departments. In her not-enough spare time she enjoys writing, singing, music composition, reading, walking, and short-term mission expeditions. **July 11.**

Peggy Harris is a church elder and has her own insurance business. She is the chair for the W.A.S.H. Board (Women and Men Against Sexual Harassment and Other Abuses), producing materials on the subject of abuse and prevention. She does biblical hospitality seminars and writes both poetry and prose. Most important, she is a wife, mom, and grandma. **Feb. 6, July 26, Aug. 26.**

Raquel Haylock spent many years with her husband and three children as missionaries in the Inter-American Division. A retired secretary, she has written articles about children for religious publications and has worked in children's Sabbath school departments. Her hobbies include reading, flowers, and helping people. **Dec. 25.**

Ann VanArsdell Hayward has recently moved to a small town in Tennessee after serving 30 years in the health-care industry. She is an active worker in her church and enjoys reading and sightseeing. **Aug. 9, Sept. 27.**

Helen Lingscheit Heavirland lives in Oregon, where she enjoys bird-watching, reading, and writing. She has authored many short pieces and the book *Falling for a Lie.* **Jan. 31.**

Ursula M. Hedges is a secondary teacher/administrator. Born in India, she and her husband spent many years in mission service in the Pacific, Australia, and New Zealand. Ursula is a church elder and has published books, stories, and articles. She is an interior designer, enjoys reading, producing dramas, sewing, cooking, and writing. **June 6, July 17, Sept. 21.**

Alethea Hendrieth lives in Pensacola, Florida, with her husband and their children. She has been an elementary teacher for 23 years and is active in the Music Department and the youth ministry of her church. Some of her favorite things to do include reading, playing the piano, writing, sewing, and attending women's retreats. **Mar. 20.**

Carolyn T. Hinson resides in Atlanta, Georgia, with her husband of 44 years. She teaches the learning-disabled and has served as director of women's ministries in the South Atlantic Conference of Seventh-day Adventists. She loves Bible study, reading, writing, public speaking, walking, jogging, caring for houseplants and tropical fish—and people. **Feb. 22, Apr. 14.**

C. Khamliani Hmingliana writes from India, where she is the women's ministries director for the Mizo Conference in Mizoram. **Feb. 21.**

Roxy Hoehn gets real pleasure from riding in the boat while watching her family water-ski. This often happens in Kansas (she lives in Topeka), where she is the women's ministries director for the Kansas-Nebraska Conference of Seventh-day Adventists. **Aug. 17, Sept. 24.**

Karen Holford has authored *Please God, Make My Mummy Nice!* and several other books, as well as numerous articles for a variety of journals specializing in family themes. She and her husband have three children and enjoy working in family life education. **Jan. 14, Mar. 19, Apr. 18, May 23, Oct. 25, Nov. 22.**

Carol June Hutchins Hooker is a community health nurse in Maryland, who is married to a math teacher. They have two teenagers. She enjoys sewing, singing in the church choir, and seeing how God leads people. **Dec. 29.**

Tamyra Horst has authored *Strengthen Your Church Through Women's Ministries, How to Hug a Heart, A Woman of Worth, The Gift of Friendship,* and several articles. She is the women's ministries director for the Columbia Union and the Pennsylvania Conference and is active in her local church. She is also Tim's wife and Joshua and Zachary's mom. She loves to read to her boys, walk, talk with friends, and collect teapots and snowmen. **June 25, July 6.**

Helene Hubbard is a developmental and behavioral pediatrician living in

Bradenton, Florida. She and her husband revel in their adult children and their grandchildren. **Oct. 4.**

Lorraine Hudgins, a retired administrative secretary, lives with her husband in Loma Linda, California. She is the author of two books and scores of published articles. Her hobbies include writing, oil painting, and memorizing Bible texts. She is the mother of five grown children and has 11 grandchildren. Her greatest joy is her morning quiet time with her heavenly Friend. **Jan. 13, Oct. 7, Nov. 16, Dec. 7.**

Barbara Huff works at the Euro-Asia Division office in Moscow, Russia, as an administrative assistant in development. She and her husband have two adult children and three grandchildren. Barbara enjoys reading, shell collecting, birding, walking, swimming, knitting, and crocheting. She is also a freelance writer and a serious amateur photographer. **Jan. 12, Mar. 3, Sept. 4.**

Aleah Iqbal is a home-schooling mother in Willimantic, Connecticut. Her publishing credits include a book of poetry, original recipes for community cookbooks, and health store newsletters. Currently she's writing a children's book. **July 8.**

Charlotte Ishkanian is the editor of a series of denominational mission story magazines for adults, teens, and children. She lives in the Washington, D.C., metropolitan area and is the mother of three young adults. Charlotte is actively involved in children's ministries in her home church. **Jan. 11.**

Julia James has been the associate director of women's ministries and the assistant director in the Ministerial Department of the Southern Asia Division of Seventh-day Adventists in Hosur, India. She's provided a special ministry to the pastors' wives and as staff nurse and teacher. Her interests include reading and church work with her husband. She has four adult children. **Feb. 12.**

Lois E. Johannes retired from mission service in Pakistan, India, Singapore, Okinawa, and the Caribbean, as well as several institutions in the United States. She has two daughters, four grandchildren, and two great-grandchildren. Now living in Loma Linda, California, she is a treasurer at her church and is involved in volunteer work. **Feb. 7, Feb. 28, Mar. 15, May 2.**

Heidi Lillian Kamal is a Norwegian writing from Pakistan, where she lives with her husband, Raafat, and their two daughters, ages 7 and 5. She teaches secretarial courses at a college and studies theology. Heidi enjoys music, swimming, aerobics, reading, handicrafts, and baking. **Jan. 15.**

Catherine F. Kambo is a registered nurse and certified midwife living in Sierra Leone. She teaches in the children's department at her home church and loves reading and caring for plants, animals, and people. She has three daughters. **Feb. 27.**

Carol Brackett Kassinger is the director of education at a hospital in Kentucky. Recently married, she's a registered nurse and has two adult sons. She enjoys reading, scuba diving, traveling, shopping, meeting new people, and learning. **Apr. 30.**

Faith Keeney has flown many missions into Mexico during the past 26 years to bring physicians, dentists, and other health-care workers to isolated villages. She loves reading, poetry, painting, and hiking. **May 24.**

Marjorie Kincaid has worked in the Personal Ministries Department of her local church. She has had several devotionals published and likes family time, walking, reading, and pursuing a pressed-flower hobby. She has three adult children and six grandchildren. **Mar. 2.**

Marilyn King writes from Oregon, where she and her husband live in happy retirement. This great-grandmother enjoys family and homemaking, music, nature, her church, Bible teaching, and health evangelism work. **Jan. 9.**

Hepzibah G. Kore is the women's ministries director of the Southern Asia Division of Seventh-day Adventists. Two favorite pastimes are reading and gardening. **July 1, Dec. 8.**

Betty Kossick enjoys her work as a freelance writer, writing teacher, and public speaker. Active in the Seventh-day Adventist Church since her baptism in 1950, she serves with the Ministry of Love, Inc., under the auspices of World Vision. She's a spokesperson for United Way, a Toastmaster, and participates with other community groups to round out her "ministry of encouragement." **June 1, Aug. 4.**

Patricia Mulraney Kovalski retired after 38 years of teaching. She now spends her time doing crafts, giving teas, teaching reading as a volunteer, and traveling with her husband—especially to visit their children and grandchildren. **Apr. 24, Dec. 28.**

Ludmila M. Krushenitskaya is the director of women's ministries for the Euro-Asia Division of Seventh-day Adventists. Born in the Ukraine, she has taught mathematics in academy and worked as an economist. She rounds out her busy life with reading, gardening, enjoying nature, walking, and traveling. **Aug. 6.**

Kay Kuzma is the president of Family Matters, a media ministry providing services to families through a syndicated radio feature, a television broadcast, and a free quarterly newspaper, *Family Times.* She has written more than a dozen books, including *A Hug and a Kiss and a Kick in the Pants,* and *When You're Serious About Love: Straight Talk to Single Adults.* **Sept. 30, Nov. 3, Dec. 5.**

Bienvisa Ladion-Nebres, born in the Philippines, presently lives and works with her husband in Lubumbashi, Congo. She uses her talents in the personal ministries and music departments of her church. **Apr. 17.**

Nathalie Ladner-Bischoff writes from Walla Walla, Washington. She retired from nursing to pursue interests in homemaking, reading, writing, skiing, and gardening. She's published several magazine stories and a book, *An Angel's Touch.* **Nov. 14.**

Margaret B. Lawrence, a nationally recognized educator and the first female elder at the Berean church in Baton Rouge, Louisiana, writes a column for the local newspaper. Sewing and public speaking bring her particular joy. **Mar. 26.**

Gina Lee enjoys teaching a class for beginning writers and working at the library. More than 500 stories, articles, and poems carry her byline. She shares her home with four cats. **Dec. 18.**

Gwen Lee serves as head deaconess in her church and works with its community services and prayer chain ministries. She lists traveling, photography, quilting, genealogy, and corresponding with friends and relatives on the computer as happy ways to spend free time. **Dec. 23.**

Lorena Lyn Lennox lives in Victoria, British Columbia, with her husband and their young daughter. She's a full-time mother and former editor of a weekly newspaper. She relaxes with cross-stitch, sewing, cooking, running, and gardening. **May 31, July 9.**

Ruth Lennox is a trying-to-retire physician, who is head elder of her church and women's ministries director for the British Columbia Conference of Seventh-day Adventists. She enjoys having fun with her three adult children and two delightful granddaughters. Writing and producing monologues of Bible women intrigue her. She and her husband, John, also a physician, spent nine years in West Africa. **June 23, July 10, Aug 27, Nov. 24.**

Karen Lindensmith writes from North Dakota, where she is a pastor's wife and the mother of two school-age children, John and Emily, both of whom were born in Japan during their parents' ministry there. She has had several articles and devotional readings published. **July 19.**

Bessie Siemens Lobsien is a retired librarian who served in several colleges. For years her poems, essays, and stories have been appreciated by readers of church papers. She is a volunteer at the local library and serves her church as communication secretary. **Jan. 24, June 15, Aug. 20, Sept. 3, Oct. 17.**

June Loor lives in her mountain home in western North Carolina, where camping at the ocean and playing with her five grandchildren claim top priority. She is involved in her local church and does volunteer work at the hospital. **Nov. 17, Dec. 27.**

Siegrid Odette Lütz wrote this devotional while living in Brazil. **May 27**

Phyllis Thompson MacLafferty has been in all 50 states and spent 18 years as a missionary in Hawaii and Brazil. This 90-year-old retired schoolteacher gives weekly devotional talks, helps in the children's Sabbath school department at church, and is active in outreach to others. She has a son and a daughter, five grandchildren, and four great-grandchildren. **May 21.**

Pat Madsen lives in California, but often travels elsewhere. She likes gardening, painting in water color, music, arts, and crafts. A former editor in chief of her high school paper, Pat is a Sabbath school superintendent and teaches a class after church. **July 4, July 14, Oct. 19, Nov. 6.**

Philippa Marshall writes from England, where she is women's ministries coordinator and communications secretary. She is a retired nurse and massage therapist and enjoys attending and helping out at women's ministries retreats. A writer of articles and poems for Christian publications, her hobbies include reading and art. **Aug. 16, Oct. 1.**

Ellen E. Mayr is a department director for women's ministries, child ministries, and family life. She can be heard singing along with her piano in Africa, where she and her husband have been missionaries for more than 13 years. **Mar. 23, July 25, Aug. 10, Sept. 9, Oct. 15, Oct. 28.**

Dellas McCan is a New England transplant, who's thriving in Oregon with her husband of 40 years. They enjoy country living with their next-door neighbors—their three daughters and five grandchildren. For many years Dellas was the librarian of her church. After discovering the joy of writing, she's entered into a postretirement career in freelance writing. **Sept. 6.**

Wilma McClarty is the chair of the English Department at Southern Adventist University. She's a public speaker and a writer who has received many honors and awards, including the Sears, Roebuck Teaching Excellence and Campus Leadership Award for 1991. She was widowed in 1997, when her husband, Dr. Jackie Lee McClarty, passed away. She is the mother of two adult children. **Sept. 2, Nov 26.**

Maria G. McClean, originally from Barbados, lives with her husband and daughter, Kamila, in Toronto, Ontario, Canada. She enjoys Bible trivia, music, writing, and taking long rides in the country. **Apr. 26.**

Martha "Genie" McKinney-Tiffany is head deaconess, church clerk, Sabbath school teacher, greeter, usher, and singer in various choirs at the Van Nuys, California, Seventh-day Adventist Church. She spends the rest of her time homemaking, visiting the sick and elderly in convalescent centers, and serving as an active PTA member. **Sept. 15.**

Lorna Jones McKinnon retired from a major insurance company after 36 years. She is active in her church as communications director, social planner, and Adventist Youth sponsor. Her hobbies include reading, computers, crossword puzzles, and writing. **Mar. 11.**

Marge Lyberg McNeilus comes from Dodge Center, Minnesota. She has been church clerk for many years and is women's ministries leader in her church. Helping in the family business, four adult children, seven grandchildren, traveling, writing, photography, crafts, and music keep her busy. **July 30.**

Patsy Murdoch Meeker enjoys writing, especially for church papers. A great-grandmother 12 times over, she enjoys reading, photography, and volunteering at the nursing home owned by her son and his wife. **Aug. 23, Sept. 11, Oct. 22.**

Marcia Mollenkopf, a retired public school teacher who lives in Klamath Falls, Oregon, is involved in local church activities. She has served as a church school board member and enjoys reading, bird watching, hiking, sewing, and crafts. **June 29, Dec. 11.**

Beverly Moody is a bookkeeper and cashier for a retail fuel business for float planes and boats she and her husband operate in rural Alaska. Her hobbies are music, people, and getting involved in church activities and with former mission school students. **May 1, June 13, Oct. 26.**

Rachel Hargrove Moore is the sixth of 13 children. She has two children of her own and is a licensed day-care provider. She plays in the church handbell choir and is an assistant teacher in the kindergarten Sabbath school department. **Oct. 30.**

Esperanza Aquino Mopera lives in Virginia Beach, Virginia. She watches birds and dolphins, walks on the beach, gardens, and writes. She has four adult children and four grandchildren to enjoy. **May 18, Aug. 28, Oct. 16.**

Barbara Smith Morris is executive director of a nonprofit retirement center and has served as a Tennessee delegate, representing housing and service needs of the low-income elderly. She has four adult children and six grandsons. **Feb. 23, Apr. 27.**

Bonnie Moyers lives with her husband and two cats in Staunton, Virginia. She is a certified nursing assistant, musician for a Methodist church, and does painting and papering, and freelance writing, whenever she can fit it in. Her writings have been published in many magazines and books. **Feb. 17, Mar. 14, May 5.**

Valda A. Nembhard is a native of Jamaica, West Indies, but now lives in Loma Linda, California. She served with her husband in pastoral ministry in Jamaica, Grenada, Trinidad, and the U.S. for 44 years and has taught elementary school. **May 30.**

Mabel Rollins Norman lived in Avon Park, Florida, until she passed away February 6, 1998. Her work was published in magazines, newspapers, and women's devotional books. She was known for her encouraging cards and letters. **Jan. 5.**

Connie Wells Nowlan has been an English teacher, a girls' dean, a preschool teacher, wife, mother—and always a writer. Her devotionals reflect her experiences. **Jan. 8, June 2, Sept. 18, Nov. 7.**

Erika Olfert, born in Slovenia, now lives in Washington state. She and her minister-husband have been missionaries in India. She is a registered nurse, working as consultant and teacher. Her interests are youth and women's ministries, oil painting, knitting, reading, swimming, bike riding, singing, and practical writing. **Feb. 9.**

Edna May Olsen lives in England, but visits her daughters and granddaughters regularly. She is actively involved in her small church and is a published writer. Her hobbies include reading, writing, and hiking with the local Ramblers. **May 29, June 26.**

Jemima D. Orillosa and her husband and two teenage daughters live in Silver Spring, Maryland. She works as a secretary in the Secretariat Department of the General Conference of Seventh-day Adventists and enjoys making friends and telling them about God's love. **Mar. 9, Apr. 8, May 15, July 29, Nov. 10.**

Kim Otis is secretary to the superintendent of education for the Southern New England Conference of Seventh-day Adventists in Lancaster, Massachusetts. She and her husband, Don, have three sons: Sean, Brandon, and Eric. **Nov. 2.**

Rose Otis, formerly the director of women's ministries for the General Conference of Seventh-day Adventists, is now vice president of the Texas Conference of Seventh-day Adventists. She began the women's devotional book project and edited the first six volumes. She enjoys water sports with her family, writing, and being home. **Apr. 25, Nov. 21.**

Hannele Ottschofski is a pastor's wife in Germany. Born in Finland, she has lived in several European countries, as well as in Africa. She has four daughters and likes to read, write, and sew. She directs a choir in her local church and is the editor of the local Shepherdess chapter newsletter. **July 27, Aug. 15, Sept. 29, Oct. 13.**

Ofelia Aquino Pangan reads, travels, crochets, gardens, and plays Scrabble in central California—but only when she isn't playing with her grandchildren. **Jan. 6, Feb. 2, July 7, Sept. 16.**

Revel Papaioannou, who lives in the biblical town of Berea, teaches Revelation seminars and English. Her hobbies include hill walking, gymnastics, collecting stamps, coins, and telephone cards. Two elderly aunts live with her, the older of whom is more than 100. **Oct. 24.**

Gwen Pascoe uses her imagination to create stories and word puzzles for children. Even though she's had 15 titles published, she admits she's not very good with a word processor. **May 9.**

Sonia E. Paul is the assessment counselor for the adult-degree completion program at Oakwood College in Huntsville, Alabama. She enjoys literature, writing, cooking, and entertaining. **June 22, July 3.**

Julia L. Pearce is chair of the Nursing Department at Pacific Union College. She enjoys reading, sewing, writing, and traveling, but also has interests in church and health education. Julia is a consultant for women's health and gives presentations on women's history. **May 28.**

Betty G. Perry has been a practicing clinical anesthetist for 27 years. She and her husband have three adult children and two grandchildren. **July 15.**

Ivadel Peterson received the 1998 Zapara Award in recognition for excellence in teaching—for 32 years. This grandmother of 14 lives with her two cats in Washington. She pursues her interest in music by playing the piano and organ for several churches and retirement homes. Her husband of 44 years died in 1994. **Jan. 7.**

Kathleen Stearman Pflugrad lives in northern Michigan with her husband, David. She enjoys reading, listening, volunteering, camping, canoeing, and traveling, and has written for books and magazines. **Dec. 31.**

Barbara H. Phipps, a retired reference librarian, taught library science at Andrews University in Michigan and Pacific Union College in California. She has been published in *Adventist Review,* The *Youth's Instructor, Insight,* and professional journals. She wrote *Test Tubes and Chalk Dust,* a biography of her father, B. H. Phipps. **Feb. 10.**

Birdie Poddar is from northeastern India. She worked as an elementary teacher, cashier, cashier-accountant, and statistician before retiring in 1991. Sewing, gardening, and composing poems are some of her hobbies. **Feb. 1, Mar. 12.**

Myrtle A. Pohle worked with her physician-husband in the mission field and Arizona, establishing a hospital and building churches. They raised three children, assisted foster children, and helped prepare hospitals for accreditation. She has one published book and has had numerous poems printed in the *Adventist Review*. Now more than 95 years old, she reads, writes letters, and chats on the telephone with friends. **Feb. 19.**

Alice Heath Prive recently moved to Los Angeles to work on a Ph.D. in ethics and religion at the University of Southern California. Good times are being with friends—old and new—and sneaking some time to read "just for fun." **Apr. 16.**

Ruth Rawson and her husband live in the country town of Albury on the Murray River in New South Wales, Australia. She teaches at a Christian college and is actively involved in community work. She finds pleasure in crafts, writing, reading, camping, bush walking, and cross-country skiing. **Dec. 22.**

Judith Redman works from her home as a child minder and is family life leader for her local church. Her interests include crafts, caravaning, and playing squash. **July 31, Dec. 15.**

Lynda Mae Richardson is a single mother of an autistic child. She has been involved in the music and women's ministries departments at her church. She also writes, produces, and directs special church programs. A published writer, Lynda enjoys singing, computers, writing, hiking, friends, and nature. **Jan. 4.**

Rowena R. Rick is retired and living in Pennsylvania after 41 years of church service, about half of which was spent overseas. At the time of her retirement she was serving as an associate treasurer of the General Conference of Seventh-day Adventists. **Dec. 10.**

Barbara Roberts is a homemaker who enjoys her grandchildren. She serves her church as elder and Sabbath school superintendent. Her interests include writing (poetry and devotional articles), growing orchids, reading, and sewing. **May 13.**

Nancy A. Rockey is a counseling psychologist who with her husband, Ron, codirects the Family Health Ministry of Faith for Today. With a background in nursing and family therapy, Nancy speaks at women's retreats and camp meetings. The Rockeys live in Sun City, Arizona, and have two daughters and four grandchildren. **Sept. 5.**

Terrie E. Ruff, assistant professor of social work and family studies and associate director of the social work program at Southern Adventist University, describes herself as a "people person." She likes to travel, make music, write, and do public speaking. **July 20, Aug. 8, Sept. 12, Oct. 21.**

Deborah Sanders shares from her personal journal, *Dimensions of Love,* and goes by the pen name "Sonny's Mommy." She's been married for 30 years, has a married daughter, and a mentally disabled son. She makes and sells crafts to fund her personal ministries outreach and is an active witness in her community and in her church. **June 5, Aug. 5.**

May Sandy is a teacher-librarian in a school/community library at Tailem Bend, South Australia. She is the church clerk and serves in the Women's Ministries Department of the local church and conference and is active in community affairs. Her interests include gardening, knitting, and being grandma to five grandchildren. **Nov. 20.**

Susan Scoggins moved to Russia in 1995 with her husband, who is the publishing director for the Euro-Asia Division of Seventh-day Adventists. She likes to do lots of artsy and musical things, but finds that travel is higher on the agenda these days, since the country spans many time zones. **Nov. 13.**

Marie H. Seard is thankful for good health. Traveling during the fall months to see the changing colors of the leaves is a treat for her. She hopes one day to visit Capistrano, California, when the swallows come back. She and her husband live in Washington, D.C. **May 26.**

Donna Lee Sharp thoroughly enjoys playing the piano and organ for three community organizations and two churches. Birding and traveling to visit six children and seven grandchildren in various parts of the globe round out her busy schedule. **Dec. 14.**

Donna Sherrill was living in Jefferson, Texas, when this devotional was submitted. **Mar. 16.**

Carrol Johnson Shewmake is a freelance writer who has had many articles, stories, poems, and books published. She and her husband, John, served 43 years in pastoral ministry, and in their retirement are actively involved with the prayer ministry in the churches in their area. **Aug. 13, Sept 8.**

Judy Musgrave Shewmake lives in northern California with her husband and their four children, whom she teaches at home. She is the editor of *The Adventist Home Educator,* a monthly newsletter for SDA home schoolers. Her favorite hobby is writing, but in any spare time she enjoys reading, genealogy, and making memory scrapbooks. **May 20.**

Rose Neff Sikora and her husband live in the beautiful mountains of western North Carolina. She is a nurse whose interests include camping in the travel trailer, writing, spending time with her three grandchildren, and helping others. She has had articles and stories published in the local newspaper, *The Times News; He's Alive,* and *Women of Spirit.* **June 7.**

Sandra Simanton is a family therapist in North Dakota. She lives with her husband and two children in Grand Forks, where they are involved with the children's program at their church. Sandra enjoys sewing and reading. **Aug. 19, Oct. 14.**

Brenda Simnett-Pratt has taught languages in England and been a social worker. She immigrated to the United States in 1975. A nursing home administrator and college professor, she left education to take up body therapy and natural healing. She is a member of MENSA. **Mar. 8.**

Cindy Sly is a registered nurse who works in the neonatal intensive care unit of

Hennepin County Medical Center in Minneapolis, Minnesota. She directs women's ministries in her church and home-schools her 11- and 9-year-old daughters. Her hobbies include sewing, photo albums, and cross-stitch. **Sept. 17.**

Carol J. Smith lives in Ferndale, Washington, with her husband and two sons. She is a human resource specialist and works with vocational rehabilitation clients. Carol has been active in women's ministries for 18 years. Her hobbies include reading, freelance writing, camping, canoeing, hiking, and snow and water skiing with her family. **Nov. 18.**

Ginger Snarr, a 1960 Walla Walla College School of Nursing graduate, currently is a homemaker in Vancouver, Washington. She and her husband, Dudley, have done humanitarian work in the former Soviet Union and have made several trips there. **Oct. 31.**

Gloria J. Stella-Felder works in communications for the Northeastern Conference in Queens, New York, where her husband pastors a congregation. They have a merged family of four grown children and four grandchildren. Gloria enjoys singing, listening to music, writing poetry, public speaking, and practicing the guitar. She has published a book of poetry, *My Inspiration.* **Aug. 12.**

Ardis Dick Stenbakken is director of women's ministries for the General Conference of Seventh-day Adventists. She and her husband have two adult children. Ardis delights in helping women grow in their love and service for the Lord. Someday she hopes to quilt, paint, and cross-stitch again. **Jan. 29, Mar. 4, Mar. 17, Apr. 5.**

Chelcie Sterling-Anim, a secretary at the Trans-European Division of Seventh-day Adventists, is a Bible instructor and lay preacher. She enjoys working with young people and is actively involved in Pathfinders. Her hobbies include badminton, music, reading, and needlework. **Feb. 11.**

Elizabeth Sterndale is in retirement—but not retired. Currently, she is the volunteer administrator for Women in Renewal in Michigan, a center and residential facility to help families who have suffered from domestic violence. After being a nurse, Liz was director of Women's Ministries for the North American Division of Seventh-day Adventists, and is currently president of ASDAN/NAD, the nursing association. She enjoys camping, reading, and volunteering. **Feb. 5.**

Helen Stiles is editorial secretary of *Signs of the Times* magazine in Nampa, Idaho. She's written numerous short articles. Her love of travel recently took her to Tibet. **Jan. 3.**

Iris L. Stovall enjoys singing, videography, creative writing, working with computer graphics, working out at the gym, and listening to soul-stirring music. She's an administrative secretary and assistant editor of the monthly newsletter in the department of women's ministries at the General Conference of Seventh-day Adventists. Iris is married and has three adult children. **May 10, June 8, July 5, Oct. 12, Nov. 25.**

Vivi Suby (aka Ginny Suby) is the mother of two grown children, wife of an airplane enthusiast, a paralegal by profession. She enjoys her granddaughters, reading, journaling, prayer meetings, and classical music. **June 18.**

Loraine Sweetland is a retired librarian and teacher in Tennessee who enjoys reading, computing, medical journal indexing, and antiques. **Jan. 16.**

Arlene Taylor is the risk manager at St. Helena Hospital in northern California. She is also founder and president of her own nonprofit corporation, pledged to promoting brain-function research and providing related educational resources. An internationally known speaker, she enjoys traveling around the world presenting seminars about the brain and personal/spiritual growth. **Oct. 6.**

Audre B. Taylor is an administrative assistant for ADRA International and a practicing psychotherapist in the Washington metropolitan area. An elder in her church, she is a published writer and the recipient of the NBC (channel 4 in Washington, D.C.) Angel Award in national competition for one of her choral performances. **Jan. 19.**

Myrna Tetz is managing editor of the *Adventist Review*. Born in Nebraska, she graduated from Walla Walla College. Most recently she was vice president for advancement at Canadian University College, managed an Adventist Awareness program in Vancouver, British Columbia, and produced *Lifestyle Line*, a weekly two-hour radio talk show. **June 27, Oct. 29, Nov. 28.**

Stella Thompson, wife, mother, and teacher of literature and composition, is currently completing a graduate degree in rhetoric and linguistics. Her favorite church roles have included coordinating a women's ministries group and teaching a young adult class. **Dec. 3.**

Tabitha Mershell Thompson graduated from Oakwood College with a Bachelor of Science in business management. She works as a computer support technician and as a real estate agent with her family-owned business. Her interests include listening to music, reading, playing with kids and computers. **May 19.**

Ella Tolliver is on the staff at Solano Community College in northern California, where she serves as a counselor and instructor. She is active in her church and is a sought-after speaker and workshop facilitator. She and her husband, John, have three adult children and six grandchildren. Reading and sharing her faith are favorite activities. **June 9.**

Tünde Torma is studying theology at Marusevec Seminary in Croatia. She is active in missions programs at her church and works with children during summer camps, leads a choir, and plays guitar and piano. Tünde likes music, basketball, and poetry. **Nov. 8.**

Dotti Tremont is a single parent who works as a secretary for the purchasing and contracting office at the Department of Veterans Affairs in Anchorage, Alaska. She teaches in the primary division at church and has had several short stories published in *Insight* and *Primary Treasure*. **Mar. 21.**

Lilly Tryon writes from Pennsylvania, where she is a registered nurse, pastor's wife, and home-schooling mother of two boys. Her interests include doing things with her family, flower gardening, scrapbooks, reading, writing, playing the piano, and singing. **Nov. 4.**

Christiane Tuor left France when she was 25 and now lives in Switzerland. At age 12 (and not yet baptized), she summed up the adult Bible lessons, and at 14 she had a Sabbath school class of 6- to 10-year-olds. Now, at church, she reads the missionary report. She likes reading, hiking, swimming, doing exercises, and, above all, speaking with our Lord. **Sept. 20.**

H. Elizabeth Tynes enjoys her work as secretary-treasurer of the South Florida Community Services Federation. Writing short stories, poetry, vocal music, and homemaking are a few of her hobbies. She once received a $1,000 savings bond for a poem she submitted in a contest. **May 25.**

Nancy L. Van Pelt is a certified family life educator, best-selling author, and internationally known speaker. She has written more than 20 books and traversed the globe, teaching families how to really love each other. Her hobbies are getting organized, entertaining, having fun, and quilting. Nancy and her husband live in California and are the parents of three adult children. **July 13, Oct. 2.**

Junell Vance, musician and a retired nurse, now spends her time nursing souls, and has served as women's ministries director in her union conference. She has two children, one foster son, and 10 grandchildren. Junell enjoys people, singing, and talking to birds. **Feb. 16.**

Nancy Cachero Vasquez is volunteer coordinator for the North American Division of Seventh-day Adventists. She is coauthor of *God's 800-Number: P-R-A-Y-E-R,* and a former missionary who enjoys reading, writing, shopping, and spending time with her husband. **Nov. 9.**

Tammy B. Vice is a singer/songwriter who feels that the Lord has given her music to heal the spirit and enjoys sharing it with others. She sings and tells children's stories at local schools and says her work with special needs children has brought real joy. **Oct. 8.**

Donna Meyer Voth lives in Michigan, where she is a church school teacher, a Reach to Recovery volunteer for the American Cancer Society, wife, and mother of one daughter. She is involved in Bible studies and likes to bicycle, camp, and especially to travel every chance she gets. **Feb. 15.**

Nancy Jean Vyhmeister edits a scholarly journal, teaches mission classes, and helps students write dissertations at the Seventh-day Adventist Theological Seminary in Michigan. For fun she writes for church publications, teaches a Sabbath school class, and helps women understand that God really does love them. She enjoys homemaking and her family, which includes two adult children and two grandsons. **Apr. 19.**

Cindy Walikonis, a registered dietitian, is a clinical dietitian at the Veterans Hospital and a nutrition consultant for a local health agency serving AIDS/HIV-positive clients. Supporting those dying of AIDS has been one of her most rewarding experiences. She has taught college and done freelance writing for *Insight* and

Primary Treasure. **May 22.**

Cora A. Walker lives in Queens, New York. She is a nurse and an active member in a local SDA church in Queens. Reading, writing, sewing, classical music, singing, and traveling fill her leisure time. She has one son. **May 16, Aug. 2, Dec. 30.**

Mae E. Wallenkampf is a homemaker and former music teacher. She likes to sing in a group, play the clarinet, cook, bake, entertain, and write. For more than 15 years she typed and word-processed the manuscripts for all her minister-teacher-author husband's books, Bible study lessons, articles, and correspondence. She enjoys her three children, five grandchildren, and two great-grandchildren. **Jan 28.**

Anna May Radke Waters dearly loves God and helping people to know of His love for them. Playing Scrabble, traveling with her husband of 46 years, doing counted cross-stitch, knitting, and crocheting are favorite pastimes, when she finds time to relax. **June 16.**

Ruth Watson had her first story published in the *Youth's Instructor* in 1960. Other writing has included stories, articles, a cookbook, and a songbook for children and a children's monthly magazine in the Thai language. Retired in 1997 as office manager for her husband's medical clinic, she can now read to her grandchildren. **Feb. 20.**

Dorothy Eaton Watts was the director of women's ministries for the General Conference of Seventh-day Adventists when this women's devotional book was being put together. She is now associate secretary of the Southern Asia Division, a freelance writer, editor, and speaker. A missionary in India for 16 years, she founded an orphanage, taught elementary school, and wrote more than 20 books. Her hobbies include gardening, hiking, and birding (with more than 1,000 in her world total). **Jan. 30, Mar. 1, Apr. 29, Oct. 10.**

Terri Webb was 14 years old and a sophomore at Rio Lindo Adventist Academy in California at the time of this writing. She is now a sophomore music major at Pacific Union College in Angwin, California. She enjoys writing and singing. **Jan 25.**

Anne L. Wham is director of women's ministries, children's ministries, and Sabbath school ministries for the Dakota Conference of Seventh-day Adventists in Pierre, South Dakota. Her favorite hobby is bird-watching. **Dec. 16.**

Penny Estes Wheeler is a writer, speaker, and editor of *Women of Spirit.* When Penny was a child, Bukovina seemed a mystical place to her, and visiting it and its friendly people was a dream come true. She longs for heaven, eager to be with her grandmother again, and to introduce her to the rest of the family. **Oct. 3.**

Connie Hodson White now lives in Nebraska with her husband, Ralph. A former software engineer, specializing in the design of databases, she now works on her home computer. She also plays piano and organ for community church services, works with animals, and promotes healthful living and vegetarian cooking. Her main interest is mending broken people. **Mar. 7.**

Carlene R. Will is a homemaker whose special spiritual gifts include ministry to women. Her specialty is sharing her love of God with others through frequent tea parties. Carlene and her family make their home in the Pacific Northwest. **Oct. 5, Nov. 15.**

Mildred C. Williams, a physical therapist, lives with her husband in California. She is a published writer and enjoys teaching a Bible class, public speaking, gardening, and sewing for her two adult daughters and little granddaughter. **Feb. 8.**

Ethel Wilson is a language development specialist, presently on the staff as an instructor with the Center Unified School District in Sacramento, California. She is fluent in Spanish, French, and Japanese. She has one adult daughter. Ethel's hobbies include writing, crafts, and interior decorating. **June 10.**

Valarie Young has served as the Nevada-Utah women's ministries director since 1994. A public high school teacher in Las Vegas, Nevada, she lives with her husband, Lyn, father-in-law, Chuck, and her granddaughter, Solana. Her hobbies are reading, cooking, and, most recently, gardening. Her devotional in this book first appeared in a conference women's newsletter, *A Woman's View*. **Aug. 25.**